NEW DIRECTIONS IN ARCHAEOLOGY

Editors

Richard Bradley
Professor of Archaeology, University of Reading

Timothy Earle
Professor of Anthropology, University of California,
Los Angeles

Ian Hodder
Lecturer in Archaeology, University of Cambridge

Colin Renfrew
Disney Professor of Archaeology, University of Cambridge,
and Master of Jesus College

Jeremy Sabloff
Professor of Anthropology and the History and Philosophy of
Science, University of Pittsburgh

Andrew Sherratt
Department of Antiquities, Ashmolean Museum,
Oxford

DOCUMENTARY ARCHAEOLOGY
IN THE NEW WORLD

DOCUMENTARY ARCHAEOLOGY IN THE NEW WORLD

EDITED BY MARY C. BEAUDRY

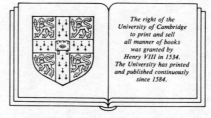

The right of the
University of Cambridge
to print and sell
all manner of books
was granted by
Henry VIII in 1534.
The University has printed
and published continuously
since 1584.

CAMBRIDGE UNIVERSITY PRESS

CAMBRIDGE

NEW YORK   NEW ROCHELLE

MELBOURNE   SYDNEY

Published by the Press Syndicate of the University of Cambridge
The Pitt Building, Trumpington Street, Cambridge CB2 1RP
32 East 57th Street, New York, NY 10022, USA
10 Stamford Road, Oakleigh, Melbourne 3166, Australia

First published 1988

Printed in Great Britain at the University Press, Cambridge

British Library cataloguing in publication data

Documentary archaeology in the New World. –
(New directions in archaeology)
1. Ethnology – America – Methodology
2. America – social life and customs – Sources
I. Beaudry, Mary C.   II. Series
306'.097   E20

Library of Congress cataloguing in publication data

Documentary archaeology in the New World.
(New directions in archaeology)
1. Archaeology and history – United States.
2. United States – Antiquities.
3. Material culture – United States.
4. United States – Industries.
I. Beaudry, Mary Carolyn, 1950–   .   II. Series.
E159.5.D63 1987   973.1   86-31755

ISBN 0 521 30343 5

CE

CONTENTS

CONTRIBUTORS

L. E. Babits, Center for Low Country Studies, Armstrong State
     College, Savannah, Georgia
M. C. Beaudry, Department of Archaeology, Boston University
J. V. Bowen, Office of Excavation and Conservation, Colonial
     Williamsburg Foundation, Williamsburg, Virginia
K. J. Bragdon, National Museum of Natural History, Smithsonian
     Institution, Washington, D.C.
M. R. Brown III, Office of Excavation and Conservation, Colonial
     Williamsburg Foundation, Williamsburg, Virginia
J. B. Curtis, Box KP, Williamsburg, Virginia
H. Langhorne, 2929 Calhoun Street, New Orleans, Louisiana
J. E. Long, Department of Anthropology DH-05, University of
     Washington, Seattle
G. L. Miller, Office of Excavation and Conservation, Colonial
     Williamsburg Foundation, Williamsburg, Virginia
H. M. Miller, Historic St Mary's City, St Mary's City, Maryland
S. A. Mrozowski, Department of Anthropology, University of
     Massachusetts, Boston
F. D. Neiman, Department of Anthropology, Yale University, New
     Haven, Connecticut
A. Praetzellis, Department of Anthropology, University of California,
     Berkeley
M. Praetzellis, Anthropology Research Facility, Sonoma State
     University, Rohnert Park, California
P. R. Schmidt, Foundation for African Prehistory and Archaeology,
     Brown University, Providence, Rhode Island
N. S. Seasholes, Department of Archaeology, Boston University
G. W. Stone, Historic St Mary's City, St Mary's City, Maryland
A. E. Yentsch, Historic Annapolis Inc., Annapolis, Maryland

Introduction

Mary C. Beaudry

Historical archaeologists readily acknowledge the advantage that documentary evidence gives them over prehistorians. Yet often, in many ways they seem puzzled over how to handle the historical record. Many view archival material as a control lacking in prehistory. They tend to follow one of two paths in their research: they may use historical sites as test cases for models developed in prehistory; or they set out to discover whether archaeological evidence properly reflects the documentary record or *vice versa*. Neither of these approaches can be viewed as highly productive, for the questions answered through such studies bear little interest for serious students of the New World past. Perhaps the tautological nature of much research in historical archaeology is part of the reason that historians often find little merit in the field.

Historical archaeologists clearly do not have a *direct* link in their own research to the questions posed of the documentary record by historians, primarily because archaeologists necessarily tend to focus upon material culture – in the ground as well as in the documents. Most historians would still view such material as merely illustrative to what they consider the major issues in historical inquiry.

Likewise prehistorians probably care very little whether their theories are proved or not by historical archaeologists, despite the latter groups' purported edge through the use of documentary controls. Most prehistorians deal with totally different categories of phenomena than do historical archaeologists; the historical period in the New World presents the researcher with an elaborate array of complex pre-industrial and industrial cultures whose transportation, communication, and exchange networks were global in scope. Even the most large and complex prehistoric societies could not be described in such terms. Although many ideas can profitably be adapted from prehistory to historical archaeology, the two disciplines require, for the most part, different research strategies. In other words, historical archaeologists must devise research problems of their own and decide for themselves the issues and questions that require their attention, if they are to contribute anything of worth through their efforts. To do so, historical archaeologists must develop an approach towards documentary analysis that is uniquely their own.

Such an approach is presented in this reader through a series of essays that go from documents to archaeology or from archaeology to documents in order to provide data relevant to research problems that were developed by scholars trained in the field of historical archaeology. It is unlikely that researchers trained in other fields would pursue the same topics in quite the same manner. Historians are quick to point out that history is not 'what happened in the past'; rather, it is *the act of selecting, analyzing, and writing about the past*' (Davidson and Lytle 1986, xix). The historical archaeologists who authored these essays came to the documents with new notions of what could be gleaned from them, notions arising from a materialist perspective on the past dictated by the nature of archaeological evidence. These essays aim to demonstrate to historical archaeologists that the historical record, far from being a finite body of specialized information, is rather a bountiful trove of fresh insight into the past.

These readings are in part case studies and in part 'how-to' essays. That is, a few are in themselves historical, as they were, within the field of historical archaeology, groundbreaking early examples of how an historical archaeologist might formulate a proposal for incorporating probate inventories or account books into archaeological analysis. Other essays are specific case studies that illustrate innovative uses of documentary evidence in solving archaeological problems.

The essays are grouped into four broadly defined sections. The five chapters included in Part I are vivid examples of the role of documentary analysis in archaeological interpretation. Chapter 1, 'Legends, houses, families, and myths: relationships between material culture and American ideology', by Anne Yentsch, reveals that in early America, when women inherited land or houses, their property was less likely to be accorded the same significance in local history and legend as were land or homes that passed through the male line. Anne Yentsch illustrates how filiopietistic local histories produced in the nineteenth and twentieth centuries consistently ignored females and other minorities. Such histories have become reified in local oral tradition about historic houses, resulting in a highly selective process of remembrance that memorializes houses that were built or owned by prominent male citizens and 'forgets' houses owned by women. This selective memory creates difficulties for the archaeologist in terms of locating and identifying historical homesites as well as in interpreting the remains of those they excavate, for their conclusions are often at variance with the lore to which local inhabitants cling tenaciously. Yentsch points out common elements in house histories and shows that when viewed as origin myths, stories about old houses become not so much inaccurate histories as reflections of Americans' beliefs about their past.

Julia Curtis, in Chapter 2, 'Perceptions of an artifact: Chinese porcelain in colonial Tidewater Virginia', examines a single artifact type – Chinese export porcelain – found in abundance on seventeenth-century sites in the Chesapeake. She uses artifactual analysis, documentary evidence from shipping records and shipwrecks, probate inventories, and dated historical collections of porcelain in order to delineate the significance of Chinese export porcelain in international trade. Curtis argues that the rigorous use of documents to disclose these relationships can be applied to other artifact groups as well.

In Chapter 3, Peter Schmidt and Stephen Mrozowski examine Revolutionary War-era tactics developed by colonial merchants for smuggling contraband goods into the colonies; shipping records and secret account books are used to illustrate the prevalence of smuggling as well as its acceptance as a deliberate strategy of resistance against British authority. This study sheds new light on the significance of smuggled goods found on eighteenth-century colonial sites and provides intriguing suggestions of the ways in which the archaeology of eighteenth-century shipwrecks can contribute to our knowledge of how smuggling was accomplished.

Chapter 4, 'Words for things: linguistic analysis of probate inventories', by Mary C. Beaudry, shows how a linguistically based analysis of documentary sources, in this case probate inventories, can provide a means of interpreting the cultural significance of specific items of material culture in colonial America. This method provided the impetus for the typology developed in Chapter 5, 'A vessel typology for early Chesapeake ceramics: the Potomac Typological System'. Here the authors use documentary data as a means of developing a functional archaeological typology that, so far as possible, reflects the folk classifications of the people who used the objects found on historical sites.

The second section of the book contains seven essays that are more strictly methodological in nature, and introduces the reader to a variety of document classes that are useful to archaeologists. Chapter 6, Garry Wheeler Stone's 'Artifacts are not enough' is a convincing argument for an approach to documentary analysis that encompasses the entire spectrum of material goods that inventories itemize, not merely those likely to be unearthed from archaeological sites. Stone argues that archaeologists who attempt to excavate from documents only the sorts of data they obtain from the archaeological record limit their ability both to interpret the cultural significance of excavated remains and to make those remains relevant to the interpretation of broad historical questions.

Chapter 7, Marley R. Brown's discussion of the behavioral correlates of seventeenth-century Plymouth Colony probate inventories, was first written in 1975. Although it has not been previously published, it served as a springboard for a number of probate inventory studies, including those presented in Chapters 8 and 13. Brown's essay points out that inventories, because they are detailed lists of household items, should offer seemingly limitless opportunities for archaeologically oriented studies; the fact that inventory studies have been very common in historical archaeology is ample testimony to the accuracy of this statement. Kathleen Bragdon, in Chapter 8, takes an innovative approach to the use of probate inventories; her direct comparison of inventory data with excavated assemblages from different types of sites was the first published study that combined quantified data from both documentary and archaeological sources.

The first three chapters in the second portion of the book focus on the use of probate inventories as aids to archaeological interpretation; the remaining chapters of Part II explore a variety of documentary sources useful for historical archaeologists conducting site-specific or regional studies. Chapter 9, by Nancy Seasholes, provides a comprehensive review of cartographic sources relevant to historical archaeological research. The cases discussed are all from

Massachusetts and were, for the most part, background studies for cultural resource management surveys of portions of downtown Boston and outlying areas; the types of maps employed in these examples are widely available elsewhere, however, and the caveats about their use and interpretation are applicable to any cartographic research.

In Chapter 10, Lawrence Babits discusses the ways in which military records may be employed for interpretation of military sites in addition to their application to regional population makeup and hence to regional surveys. Chapter 11 deals primarily with probate inventory data; in this essay, Bragdon uses an ethnohistorical approach to examine the ways in which the material possessions of the Christian Indians of New England reveal the degree to which the Indians had, by the eighteenth century, become acculturated to Anglo-American culture. Such a study is especially useful to archaeologists attempting to interpret the archaeological evidence for 'Praying Indian' towns as well as for other Contact Period or historical native American sites.

Deed research forms the basis for the study of Rockbridge County, Virginia, population and land transfer practices presented by Langhorne and Babits in Chapter 12; this preliminary case study revealed that information on inheritance patterns also reveals kinship linkages that provided women with landholding opportunities not otherwise available.

Ecological questions are increasingly of interest to historical archaeologists, who realize that the beliefs and technologies of European Americans caused them to adapt to the New World environment very differently than did native Americans. It is this realization that prompts historical archaeologists to question whether models used to study the prehistoric past are useful for understanding historical cultures. Anne Yentsch, in her analysis of the relationship between subsistence strategies and local environment on colonial Cape Cod, Massachusetts (Chapter 13), addresses the broad issue of how inventory entries reflect the ways in which individuals perceive and organize their world. She examines at length the close relationship early Cape Codders had with the environment and the ways in which a seasonal round of activities shaped daily life. Yentsch is able to demonstrate that the classification of goods and animals in probate inventories is a direct reflection of their cultural significance in terms of traditional subsistence patterns and the organization of labor.

Accounts books as well as probate data provide the basis for Joanne Bowen's discussion, in Chapter 14, of the application of the concept of seasonality to faunal remains on historical sites. In 'Seasonality: an agricultural construct', Bowen stresses the importance of interpreting early American subsistence patterns in their proper context through developing models based upon historical agricultural practices and points out the pitfalls of an unquestioned use of prehistoric subsistence models that are based upon exploitation of wild food sources.

The final section of the book contains three chapters that address issues of consumerism, status, gender, and ethnicity, all topics of recent interest to historical archaeologists working in the New World. Each indicates how rigorous use of documentary data can provide a sound footing for archaeological analysis and interpretation. Chapter 15, by George Miller, uses information drawn from nineteenth-century price lists and catalogs to develop a scale that measures the degree to which individuals invested in ceramics as opposed to other goods. This landmark study provides an index for other archaeologists to use in interpreting their own materials and paves the way for further research into marketing and consumer practices as important factors in the formation of the nineteenth-century archaeological record.

Stephen Mrozowski, in Chapter 16, considers two types of sources available in historical newspapers: letters from readers and advertisements. Newspaper ads provide information on pricing and availability of ceramics and other goods; such information helps the archaeologist to refine dating techniques as well as to account for local variations in product availability. Both ads and anecdotal letters in local papers reveal a great deal about the role of women as consumers in the post-Revolutionary era as well as changing attitudes about the role of women in general. Mrozowski points out that many of the deposits excavated from early nineteenth-century sites may be in part a result of the development of marketing strategies aimed at women, who assumed a prominent role as consumers in the years leading up to the Industrial Revolution in America.

Praetzellis, Praetzellis, and Brown recommend the use of sources such as exhibition catalogs and newspaper ads to establish a baseline of nineteenth-century middle-class consumerism as the foundation for delineation of ethnicity in the archaeological record. Their study promotes the novel yet utterly sensible concept that historical archaeologists must understand what comprised the norm for consumer behavior in nineteenth-century America before they can properly interpret anomalies that may reflect choices based on class and ethnic distinctions.

This book reflects the increased sophistication that historical archaeologists have, over time, brought to the study of the documentary past in the interpretation of historical sites in the New World. What is more, the essays reflect the development of research interest in topics such as women's roles, consumer behavior, ethnicity, and urbanization. Although the theoretical perspectives are drawn primarily from anthropology, these essays reveal that historical archaeologists must use historical sources critically in order to offer insight into the recent past. It is the innovative combination of archaeological and historical analysis that makes these essays contributions to documentary archaeology.

Part I

Archaeology is not enough

Chapter 1

Legends, houses, families, and myths: relationships between material culture and American ideology

Anne Yentsch

Peter Schmidt describes landscape 'as a series of images in which history is held' and notes how physical objects situated in the landscape call to mind the oral traditions of a people (Schmidt, personal communication). This paper explores these images through a discussion of legends about old American houses. The internal structure of these legends, or house histories, is considered first in terms of historical evidence about family and property and second as embodying myths of kinship and social structure, reflecting a world view in microcosm. What appears in a structural analysis of these tales is a common theme. It matters little whether a house was forgotten or remembered; the content of the message is similar. The content conveys information about relationships among individuals in American society and is a form of ideology that utilizes the medium of physical objects as the mechanism for its conveyance. Material culture, the core of archaeology, is thus an active agent through which a people's mytho-history is held and told to succeeding generations.[1]

1.1 Introduction

Myths and legends serve to express certain ways of thinking and feeling about the society and its relation to the world of nature, and thereby to maintain these ways of thought and feeling and pass them on to succeeding generations.

(Radcliffe-Brown 1933, 405)

Condensed with the passage of time, local lore and legends are inextricably interwoven with the material fabric of old houses. Seemingly riddled with inaccuracies, the genre appears inconsistent. Analytical problems affect its use by scholars as an information source. Earlier in this century, some prehistorians considered the relationship between oral tradition and archaeology, but with the exception of a few individuals such as Henry Glassie (1975, 1982), Peter Schmidt (1978), and Dell Upton (n.d.), historical archaeologists and architectural historians have been reluctant to confront oral tradition about old houses; they have rarely examined thoroughly the legends incorporated into written local or family history of the sites they excavated or the dwellings they record. The situation is thus: on the one hand, oral tradition often seems inaccurate when viewed in the light of the precise time measurements by archaeologists. Yet, on the other hand, oral tradition indisputably embodies folk history.[2]

With respect to this issue, one question is whether stories about old houses might be a form of American mythology? If legends about old houses are an expression of American mythology, then encoded within them is ethnographic information on social values and folk ideas about kinship, community identity, society, history, culture, and nature. For myths, as discussed by Firth (1967, 284), 'form a moral system and a cosmology as well as a history,' embodying a set of folk beliefs expressing social ideas and values and situating people within society.

Most people are familiar with legends about old houses. Enter almost any town along the Atlantic seaboard and still standing will be an old house identified as the home of an original settler. Folk dates of such historic houses usually fall between 1670 and 1740. The actual date varies from one community to another, corresponding to the approximate date of actual settlement. Those on the seacoast are earliest and those in the interior lands settled later are more recent. At the same time it is not uncommon for archaeological evidence to confirm later eighteenth- and nineteenth-century occupations for the historic house.

In part this occurs because of the sparse representation in the archaeological record of deposits associated with earlier periods on continuously occupied sites (cf. Starbuck 1980). When present the frequencies of earlier artifact types are far lower than those of artifact types common in the later eighteenth century (cf. Deetz 1973, 36–7). The effect of the late eighteenth- and nineteenth-century landscaping activity also destroys evidence of earlier occupations. Sometimes archaeologists conclude the folk dates assigned to houses in legend are at best questionable or false and unusable. Architectural features sometimes resolve the contradiction, and analysis by architectural historians often plays a crucial role in establishing the construction date and hence the dwelling's actual age. If no other data are available, a prudent archaeologist must take the archaeological evidence as primary. Yet this does not explain the contradiction posed by the seeming inaccuracies in the stories told about the house. Nor does it necessarily help the archaeologist work out the details of the site's occupation vis-à-vis town or local histories where the folk date may be presented as established fact.

My experience suggests that dates assigned houses in oral tradition are rarely accurate. This alone may not mean that they should be disregarded. An initial consideration of the issue discloses that there are houses remembered and houses forgotten. Three questions become focal and are discussed within this chapter:

1. Is there a pattern to house histories or are houses randomly remembered or forgotten?
2. Are there ethnographic clues contained within these bits of false information about old homes?
3. Can one explain the existence of legends about houses and, with anthropological techniques, use these to learn about American historiography as a process at the community, or folk, level? In doing so, what era is highlighted?

With these three questions in mind, information is provided on examples of houses and house histories in rural communities of New England and in Maryland. Initially these examples are viewed from a historical frame of reference, that is to say, they are considered to embody information about individuals and, specifically, about family men who built houses. I will consider what family reconstitution, deed research, probate records, and other historical documents reveal about these individuals, paying attention to their kinship ties to other occupants of the house. This is in accord with customary archaeological procedures for investigating the history of a given site; but I will also consider the form of legends to see if perhaps the individual who built the house is

transformed in the stories that are told. It is the consideration of transformation that introduces a structural frame of reference to this study.

At the same time, there is also an implicit concern in this paper with function, and specifically with the ways in which kinship relationships were related to property ownership. The actual configuration of events (conveyed in the documentary record) that regulated the passage of ownership of a dwelling from one individual to another reflects normative social values of seventeenth- and eighteenth-century individuals. How ownership was transferred is reflective of the real world and is of direct relevance to historical archaeology.

In the seventeenth and eighteenth centuries, people also held beliefs about what should happen to houses (i.e., 'ideal' sets of values about property), not of concern here. In the nineteenth-century legends told about houses, ideal values were at the fore and are highlighted. In particular, these values related to social structure, displaying hierarchical relationships between men and women, and between Anglo-Americans and people with differing ethnic identities such as Afro-Americans or European immigrants. These legends conveyed social boundaries, told of categories of people, and situated family members within these. They transmuted certain men into founding personages, certain women into phantasmagorical creatures, and black Americans into non-entities. The legends also provided a cultural map of the natural world and situated a legendary person and his family within it. An example of this is the local lore that created a map placing Elizabeth Blachford, a reputed witch, and her home, at the fringe of the community. This is but one example of how, in their role as a social ordering mechanism, house histories provided cultural boundaries for persons and events together with a frame of reference for daily life. In a Durkheimian sense, they were a mechanism promoting social cohesion situated within the home.

It should be emphasized that the oral traditions discussed here, while linking houses to the seventeenth and early eighteenth centuries in terms of their purported age, are traditions whose origins probably lie in late eighteenth- and early nineteenth-century family knowledge. While the traditions appear to be a product of a later time period imposed on an earlier one, their cultural importance is indicated by the fact that although the content itself differs, the traditions are structurally similar over a wide geographic area. The same transformation occurs, the same values are emphasized (i.e., continuity of family, the ability to overcome hardship, participation in the first wave of settlement in a town, service to the community, military leadership and valor, courage, a Christian world view), and time and time again, they are linked to a mnemonic entity or extant building located in the community.

This occurs because, like tombstones, houses serve as historical records set in the landscape. The history of a house is the history of a family or sequence of families. No matter that the culture itself differed, and that if the inhabitants of the house during a later period were to suddenly find themselves encountering the harsh reality of seventeenth- or early eighteenth-century life, they would experience culture shock: the existence of an old house gave the illusion of continuity and an alignment between past and present, between the nineteenth-century inhabitants and their antecedents. Created as mythology, the legends wrapped around houses operated according to principles of mythological thought, obeying a logic (encountered cross-culturally) wherein normal boundaries of time and space, the real and the non-real, were differently manipulated than in the rational thought guiding day-to-day activity (cf. Godelier 1977).

In the examples presented below, folk history sometimes collapses time and space to link a house with an earlier era, negates or dissolves the existence of individuals, well remembers others, particularly those associated with sacred space, but also those men who serve as folk heroes. In doing so, it conveys the values of the community and the belief system of the culture. It is able to do this because it is not only local history, but mytho-history.

Myths are illusory representations of man and the world, inexact explanations of the order of things, culturally construed, a way of speaking and a way of thinking about the world in which things are transmuted. To be specific, in folk history, houses undergo a transmutation and substitute for human experience; they stand for family members and kinship ties. When one speaks of houses, in folk history, one is also, despite the fact that an inexact analogy is used, making explicit relationships between family, society, and history through the medium of a house by associating the behavior of the person who built it or controlled it with the physical fabric of the house. House-linked myths exist in our society and will do so as long as they are functional in terms of contemporary ideology.

1.2 Houses remembered
1.2.1 The Vincent House, Edgartown, Massachusetts
Faced with archaeological evidence that the site of the Vincent House was first occupied c. 1720–40, with architectural evidence that the Vincent House was built later than 1656, and with documentary evidence of an earlier Vincent residence inside the nucleated portion of the town itself, family members affirmed their version of the house's past. Thus, in the summer of 1977, while doing deed research on Martha's Vineyard in conjunction with the removal of the Vincent House from its rural location to Edgartown, where it could serve more easily as a local museum, the strength of legends about houses was brought home to me with remarkable clarity. Reprinted in the *Dukes County Intelligencer* in 1978, Mabel Keniston Baker's earlier narrative reiterated the oral tradition: 'the William Vincent house, built about 1656, is one of the oldest in Edgartown' (Baker 1978, 61). An editor's footnote on the same page explained that 'there is now doubt about precisely when the house we think of as the Vincent House enters the tale she tells; she was a Vincent through her father.' Elsewhere, the director of the Vincent House Project, C. Stuart Avery, acknowledged the 'age' problem created by the deed research

and the archaeological investigation of the property done under the direction of Myron Stachiw, while also accurately recognizing that these in no way diminished the value of the house as a historic property or the feasibility of using it as an architectural resource center on the island (Avery 1978).

Albeit disappointing to some family members, the discovery of deeds to a house situated elsewhere in the town pointed out the inaccuracy of the belief that William Vincent moved to his home on Long Pond in 1656 when he married Susanna Browning. William had only one son, Thomas, whom he disinherited in his will of 1697 because of Thomas' unacceptable demeanor towards his parents (Baker 1978, 62). Thomas lived off the island away from his family for a while, married a Connecticut woman, but returned to Martha's Vineyard and lived on Long Pond, where he died in 1740. The family belief is that Thomas inherited the family homestead from his mother, with whom he was reconciled after his father's death. Deeds reveal that Thomas Vincent *purchased* the family homestead from his mother in 1710–12 and did not receive it as a family legacy. The archaeological evidence indicated that the purported William Vincent site was occupied at the earliest during the 1720s or 1730s. The preliminary documentary research suggested that the house was probably the residence of Thomas Jr, dating to 1723/4 (summarized in Stachiw 1978, 25–6).

As mythology, what does the family tradition accomplish? First, it transforms the actual individual, Thomas Jr, who built the house, into an ancestral person, William Vincent. Next it links the Vincent House to the first male Vincent to live on the island and to the origin of Edgartown. Then it gives William Vincent, in his role as the Vincent progenitor, a well-built, durable home demonstrated by its survival over three centuries. Finally it implies that the prodigal son, Thomas, repented his earlier demeanor and was forgiven by his mother for this behavior, receiving in turn a house as his Biblical share of the family estate. To do this, the tradition collapses time and violates spatial boundaries. It also ignores the role of Thomas Jr, namesake of the prodigal son, thus visiting the sins of his father on a subsequent generation. In essence, the tradition sets out a series of ideal relationships that mask the real-world experiences of the Vincent family.

The house in question was built by Vincent men during the era in our past when communities were tightly knit networks of individuals consisting of multiple, often large, kin-based household units within which economic activity occurred. Each person and family group fitted into a niche of the hierarchically based social order. The social order within the family served as metaphor for social order within the community. Focused on farming, fields, and cultivated soil, members of society required land; the most valuable land was tamed and plowable, i.e., cultural land, not natural land. In addition to inheritance, a judicious marriage offered one alternative for procuring land, but the primary means for achieving upward social mobility was through migration westward to the frontier with its promise of abundant, available

Fig. 1.1. Hancock's Resolution showing house, wing, and stone outbuilding

land. In any given community, among those who remained at home, not all inhabitants were prosperous, not all individual family units would survive unbroken until the children reached maturity, nor would all patronymic kin networks persist through time in a given locale. Death was ever present, dissolving basic family units (primarily nuclear), reducing the larger kin networks, altering the structure of a household, and creating social situations that gave rise to serial monogamy. The family rather than the community had the primary obligation to serve as caretakers of the young, the old, widowed men and women. Within this social context houses functioned as signs for family units; clusters of houses signified community. The Vincent House conveyed both the identity of the family and their placement in the community as enduring and successful farmers. A similar situation existed at Hancock's Resolution.

1.2.2 Hancock's Resolution, Anne Arundel County, Maryland

In Maryland, members of the Hancock family looked back in time and established a link with the early settlers of the province in the stories they told of their home. They sustained a link to the seventeenth century by claiming that the Susquehannocks labored to move the stone that Stephen Hancock used to build his house in 1668. The Susquehannocks helped Hancock build the house because of Hancock's military prowess, his ability to protect both English and Indian from Seneca raids extending south to the Magothy River. A

Northumbrian, Hancock received his military training when he fought in the army under Cromwell, a fitting military heritage for someone who signed a pledge of loyalty to King William of England in 1694.

Built of rough-hewn ironstone, the Hancock house is durable and solid in appearance (see fig. 1.1). The native stone building material places the building midway on a continuum between nature and culture and roots the house to its region of the Chesapeake. The site itself hints of seventeenth-century origins, for, like many seventeenth-century domestic sites in the Chesapeake (Smolek and Clark 1982), it stands on a low sandy knoll approximately 800 feet from the head of Old House Cover on Bodkin Creek where the Patapsco River meets the Bay. Within its surrounding fields lies a small family burial ground where many members of the Hancock family are at rest. Visually, the house and its surroundings convey an image of past time, of control imposed on the land, of Indian alliances, of successive generations of Marylanders involved in peaceful, successful settlement in a new world. As the family sees it:

> Life at Hancock's Resolution changed very little in the almost 300 years it sheltered the Hancock family. Each day brought its problems, its hardships, and its satisfactions; the problems were solved, the hardships endured and the satisfactions remembered. The Hancocks and their neighbors were resolute people, working, saving, wasting nothing; by such as these was our America created. (Calvert 1965, 10)

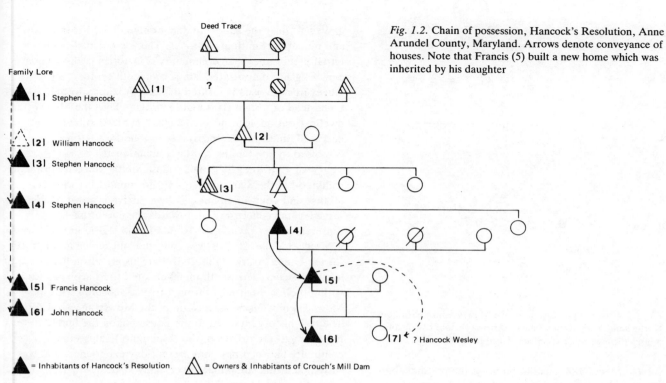

Fig. 1.2. Chain of possession, Hancock's Resolution, Anne Arundel County, Maryland. Arrows denote conveyance of houses. Note that Francis (5) built a new home which was inherited by his daughter

Deed Trace

Family Lore

[1] Stephen Hancock

[2] William Hancock

[3] Stephen Hancock

[4] Stephen Hancock

[5] Francis Hancock

[6] John Hancock

▲ = Inhabitants of Hancock's Resolution   △ = Owners & Inhabitants of Crouch's Mill Dam

[1] [2] [3] [4] [5] [6] [7] ? Hancock Wesley

Despite the oral tradition handed down over the generations in the Hancock family, an analysis of kinship charts and deeds reveals this was not the original Stephen Hancock's dwelling house, while simultaneously disclosing evidence of a frequently practiced land acquisition strategy. Hancock came to Maryland landless if not penniless, and he acquired property through marriage to a sixteen-year-old heiress, Rebecca Crouch. Rebecca's father William died in 1675, leaving her a legacy of land at Crouch's Mill Dam and two other parcels, all located on the Broadneck peninsula, south of the Magothy River, in Anne Arundel County (Wright and Baker 1980). These lands, acquired by marriage, were inherited by Hancock's eldest son, William (see fig. 1.2). His mother remarried.

Later, William leased a right to land near the Patapsco. While retaining the family home at Crouch's Mill Dam, he also became a tenant farmer, renting property on Homewood's Range (a parcel known as Fair Jerusalem), near Bodkin Creek. He probably did so to procure additional lands for his younger son, Stephen, the namesake of the original Hancock. The family established a home of sorts and, by analogy with other Maryland homes of the period, it was probably a wooden structure, possibly of post-hole construction, small, with a dirt floor; it would not have been an elaborate home.[3] If, like many of its Chesapeake counterparts, it left only ephemeral traces on the land and was of log or roughly framed, one might even consider that it lay closer to nature than houses of stone or brick construction.

The stone house known as Hancock's Resolution is now a national landmark. Ownership was transferred to Historic Annapolis, Inc., in 1964; the property is undergoing renovation

to become a county museum with an interpretive program focused on rural farming in the nineteenth-century Chesapeake. As part of the background research on the property, a history of the family and an architectural analysis of the structure was undertaken by Nancy Baker and Russell Wright, A.I.A. (Wright and Baker 1980). Both researchers agree that the building was constructed sometime after 1760. Archaeological testing by Henry T. Wright (1971) produced similar findings. There is no date, no physical evidence that the house dates to the second quarter of the eighteenth century, although a smaller building lying slightly north has not been thoroughly tested and evaluated.[4]

As with the Vincent House, the family history of Hancock's Resolution explicitly contradicts the findings of experts in local history, in architectural history, and in historical archaeology. The Hancock family history also collapses time, thereby associating the original Stephen Hancock with his eighteenth-century descendent, and also dissolves spatial boundaries, thereby substituting the present house site for that of the earlier seventeenth-century farm at Crouch's Mill Dam located approximately twenty miles further south; it 'overlooks' the tenure of tenant farming. A similar situation with another permutation exists with the Mowry-Smith house and its oral tradition.

1.2.3 Mowry-Smith Farm, North Smithfield, Rhode Island

The Mowry-Smith farm in North Smithfield, Rhode Island, is another dwelling that has been mythologized. It is identified in oral tradition, in modern local history, and in nineteenth-century family history (Yentsch 1981; Nebiker 1976;

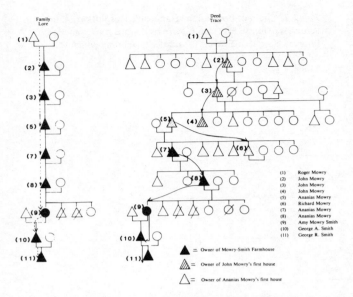

Fig. 1.3. Chain of possession for the Mowry-Smith Farmhouse in North Smithfield, Rhode Island. Arrows denote conveyance of houses through inheritance and Deed of Gift.

Mowry 1909; Steere 1881) as the home of the original John Mowry, who settled in northern Rhode Island in the late seventeenth century when the regions north of Providence were first opened to settlement. As one Mowry descendant wrote:

> Our homestead has been known for nearly two centuries as the Ananias Mowry farm ... We are not positive who built the house or in what year it was built. Tradition has it that John the 2nd built it and that it is not far from 200 years old (i.e., of late seventeenth century origin).
>
> (Mowry 1878)

While architectural analysis suggests that portions of the house were built in the late seventeenth or early eighteenth century, archaeological investigation reveals that the land on which the Mowry-Smith farm stands was not occupied until after the American Revolution. As part of the historical research, family reconstitution charts were made for each occupant of the site. These indicated that John the second and Ananias were father and son and that several intervening sons named Ananias were born before Amy Mowry in 1808 (fig. 1.3).

The farm became linked with the Smith family when Amasa Smith married Amy Mowry in the nineteenth century. Amy was born in the house in 1808 and grew up on its land. She also continued to live in the house, with Amasa, after her marriage. She could trace her lineage through earlier male ancestors directly to John Mowry the second, an Original Proprietor in the town records of Smithfield. The family link was clear, and it was worth preserving because each of the Mowry men held prestigious positions in the community, some were well educated and some were among the wealthiest men in the town. The Mowry family was linked to the house that in turn was linked to the first Smithfield Mowry; the house served as an ancestral shrine. At the same time there was also a

graveyard near the site, containing only a few Mowry graves and numerous Smith gravestones. The use of small family burial plots rather than community cemeteries in this region of New England dates to the late seventeenth century. Such graveyards are usually located in close proximity to the homestead of a significant male kinsman. Thus the Mowry dwelling was adjacent to sacred space controlled by the deceased Smiths and in proximity to a house site once possessed by the Smiths and later abandoned.

Amy Mowry's husband, Amasa Smith, worked during his childhood in the Slater cotton mills to support his widowed mother and younger siblings. He was active in town politics, served as tax collector, and, towards the end of his life, represented the town in the Rhode Island legislature. He was upwardly mobile. His son was educated and served as an officer for the Union Army in the Civil War; his grandson became the local physician. The Smith men validated their achieved rank within the town partially through their association with the Mowry family and by possession of the Mowry ancestral shrine. The folk history attached to the house linked the family to the past (i.e., to the origins of the community), suggested a continuity between past and present-day experience, and was sustained in the community over many years.

1.3 Houses in symbolic space

The Vincent, Hancock, and Mowry-Smith houses were identified with established families in their communities. The houses became mnemonic devices; memories attached to them. These memories constituted a storehouse of family associations that people used in remembering family, community, and their place within each. As successive, related kin resided in the dwelling, information was passed from one generation to the next. The dwellings served as visible bonds, expressive of continuity over time and of the kinship network that bound one generation to the next. The houses substituted for the abstract genealogical bond by serving as signs of kinship.

In any investigation of house histories, one finds that these tend to celebrate those families and individuals who dominated the political system in a community and who also, through a variety of strategies, were able to amass quantities of land. Often these were wealthy individuals, but acquiring land was not solely an economic venture. One had to be astute in other ways as well and particularly with respect to inheritance procedures. In Maryland, an inheritance system based on primogeniture prevented landholdings from fragmentation. In New England, where partible inheritance was the norm, landholdings were held together using different tactics. In both areas, family size and other demographic variables created conditions that required families to use a number of different strategies to care and maintain family members as well as to acquire and maintain land. Still, generation after generation of the fortunate remained on the land. Those with little land or opportunity often left the community. Dwellings of the former were remembered; those of the latter forgotten. The oral traditions surrounding both Hancock's Resolution and the

Mowry-Smith House show this process in operation and are permutations of the same theme visible in the family legend about the history of the Vincent House.

At the same time, the houses and house legends discussed above, from three geographically separate areas of the country, are all illusory representations of local history. Each legend transformed an individual who built a home into an ancestral personage, negating the activities of later generations by allocating responsibility to earlier men. While stressing the importance of family, local history, like family genealogy, is often subversive and serves to mask what actually transpired. The information it preserves is designed for the 'ethnographic present' that, in these cases, was the nineteenth century. Like memory, it is selective. The explanation for the disregard of traditional historical evidence lies in the nature of mythological thought. Mythological thought does not operate according to the same logic as rational thought. Leach writes that it is 'characteristic of traditional mytho-history that the real world of experience is surrounded on all sides by another world of imagination' (1982, 62). It is the world of imagination that alters time and changes space; what is really real remains the house. Information about the house is not the primary message conveyed, but rather a set of ideas and ideals about family and society, and once the real house is transmuted into a symbol of ideal family it inhabits imaginary space just as thoroughly as it does physical space.

Only a glimpse, however, is caught of the imaginative world within these legends, for they exist under a mask of normalcy that sets them apart from more exotic, fantastic origin myths. Yet that is what they are. And, as origin myths, they also touch upon man's relationship to nature. With ancestors who served as town fathers or founders because they were present in the first settlement of a region, families used legends to establish a relationship to England as their country of origin while simultaneously conveying that their ancestors were among those who 'overcame' nature in the New World, bringing it under control through settlement and conversion to agriculture. This makes it understandable that the Hancock legend includes the rather unusual claim that Indians transported the stone for their ancestor's home, for in doing so, they signified that not only did Stephen Hancock tame the land, he also militarily curbed Indian aggression and turned Indian labor to profit for his family. Many cultural values, including ideas about power relationships and social inequality, are expressed within the context of the stories surrounding houses. These use physical attributes of the house and imbue them with imaginary elements, thus strengthening their role in mythological thought.

Houses become icons of superior strength and intellect. This has been nicely described by Dell Upton (n.d.) in an article that tells of fantastic functions of simple architectural features in subduing the Indians. Under the label of 'crazy house stories', he relates folk explanations for narrow staircases, for high windows, for brick-end structures. From New England to the Chesapeake, Indians could be killed one by one as they came up, or went down, narrow staircases; high windows prevented their arrows from entering a house; other tiny openings (facing directly downwards) enabled Englishmen to more easily kill attacking Indians; brick gable ends on buildings protected inhabitants from Indians sneaking out of swamps at the sides of lots. Similarly, in explanations for other architectural features, houses demonstrated the superiority of one group of individuals over another – over pirates, servants, slaves – and, simultaneously, identified the occupants as Christians through the means of cross-and-bible doors or Holy Lord hinges.

If houses were icons, it follows that the disappearance of a house should both disrupt the mnemonic process and shatter the associated mythology. When houses disappear from the landscape, the event that caused their destruction may be remembered well, particularly if it is linked to something of more than familial interest (e.g., an Indian attack, a hurricane or tornado, a wide-spread fire). Oral tradition correctly assigned place to the site of the Eel River Massacre, as Harry Hornblower's excavation of the R.M. Site at Plimoth Plantation demonstrated (Deetz 1968). On the other hand, it seems that if a home is moved or torn down with its parts and pieces utilized elsewhere, then its mnemonic quality dissolves slowly rather than catastrophically destructing. The place where the house once stood may remain mnemonic if no one reclaims the land and builds on the site again. There are some clues that this occurs more frequently with sites linked closely to the sacred domain (e.g., churches and graveyards) or to truly heroic figures (e.g., Miles Standish), or to battlegrounds such as that at Eel River.[5]

Sometimes the link is sustained through a place name that persists over time; Brick Kiln Road, Shipwright's Street, Lambert's Cover. On Naushon Island, off the coast of Cape Cod, oral tradition clearly identified one eighteenth-century cellar foundation as 'the home of the imprudent farmer' (Yentsch 1974a) while oral tradition in Wellfleet, Massachusetts, identified a scatter of visible surface debris as the remains of Samuel Smith's tavern on Great Island, and men remembered the wording of his tavern sign (Reeser 1967). Otis, in his *Genealogical Notes on Barnstable Families* (1888), mentions more such examples.

Why are these places remembered while others are forgotten? Part of the answer emerges when one looks at those whose existence has passed from local knowledge. Family homes remembered and family homes forgotten are, in reality, two closely related elements in local historiography that tell of social structure and hierarchy within the community. They are equivalent acts; the logic behind them is the same. Superficially unrelated, remembering and forgetting factual details of home and land ownership accomplish the same ends.

1.4 Houses forgotten

One might even claim that the more thought-provoking examples revolve around those men whose homes were neglected in oral history or local lore, for these tell of people displaced and removed from the 'ancestral' network of individuals residing in a region. In each instance, the first step seems to be the association of a house with a woman rather than a man. Women did not fall within the same cultural category as men and were perceived as possessing lower status. Thus the first phase in denigrating an ancestral home involved its transference from the male world to the female, either in mythology or in the real world of experience. It is no accident that a very old Annapolis home occupied by free blacks from the 1780s throughout the nineteenth century is still known as Aunt Lacy's Bakeshop rather than by association with its white, male builder's family name.

Homes remembered in legend associated with female ownership (denoted by the feminine possessive, 'her' house) are not common. This is true even though women did live alone, or without male heads of household, as widows or elderly spinsters. One can see their names entered on the census lists, and female heads of household are mentioned occasionally in other documents. The unusual example of Elizabeth Lewis Blachford discussed here is described both in Otis (1888, 99–102) and in Reynard (1934, 172–80), and it involved eighteenth-century witchcraft. It also demonstrates how local lore precisely situated people on a continuum moving from wilderness to settled town lands, each step denoting cultural clues about the character of the individual and his or her place within society.[6]

Fanciful details of the supernatural activities of Liza 'Towerhill', née Elizabeth Lewis, are given in Reynard, while Otis presents the more factual data, pointing out that her father's home was located deep in the Cape Cod woods, two miles from their nearest neighbor. Elizabeth Lewis grew up in a forest clearing on the shores of Crooked Pond in a region of town rarely visited by Englishmen and normally traversed by Indians. When she married in 1728, her husband, William Blachford, built another woodland home half a mile away on Half-way Pond on another isolated plot of land given to the couple by Elizabeth's father. For whatever reason, many local people believed Elizabeth Blachford to be a witch.[7] Her husband died leaving her with seven children, four under the age of sixteen, and she never remarried. Otis tells how her youngest son, William, married and then lived with his wife 'in the house which was *his mother's*' (1888, 103). This seemingly innocuous statement, however, is almost the only mention of a 'feminine' house in his detailed, five-hundred page history of the town, with the other being Aunt Beck's Museum, a house controlled by a decidedly eccentric woman.[8]

In this example, there is a woman who is a witch who controls men, using them as steeds at night, possesses a black cat as a familiar that swims through the sea to attack Cape sailors, while living in the depths of the Cape Cod woods. Extraordinarily powerful, her home in legend is situated at the very border of the wilder Cape Cod lands on the edge of Half-way Pond. Her home, in other words, is located as far from the cultured landscape of the town as possible. Further-more this dwelling, while built by her husband, did not pass

from him at death to his sons as was customary but remained 'hers'. This example suggests that a woman's house was something apart and/or that houses and families ideally were entities normally controlled by men, and that were these to come under female control, their history could be abridged. Otis records evidence of Elizabeth Blachford's religious piety and defends her from the charge of alleged witchcraft (conveyed only in the oral tradition), but the very existence and strength of the stories does suggest something unusual about her life. The question thus becomes whether other house histories are abridged for other homes that passed outside the direct male descent line to female relatives?

1.5 Families forgotten

The two examples presented below illustrate different facets of the process and in each case, the history of the site was abridged. They are the Mathewson Farm House and the Todd Farm located in New England. The Mathewson Farm site was discovered as part of a Phase II study of Rt. 104 in North Smithfield, Rhode Island. The work was done under contract to the Institute for Conservation Archaeology at Harvard University in the spring and summer of 1980. During the investigation of a prehistoric site located by shovel test pits along the proposed highway route, sherds of scratch blue stoneware and English delftware appeared in several test units. The sub-surface testing was then expanded to further delineate both the prehistoric and the historical occupation. Of the latter, there was limited but conclusive evidence that it existed and, while archaeological work ceased, the documentary research was continued until the occupants of the site were identified (Yentsch 1981).

1.5.1 The Mathewsons

The property belonged to the Mathewson family. This was a family almost unmentioned in the town histories. Census data revealed that there were six Mathewson families living in North Smithfield in 1780, but only one was left by 1840. The Mathewson family was never thoroughly integrated into the network of Mowry families that dominated the local village; few inter-marriages between the two families took place.

There was limited evidence of the family in the town histories and in the oral tradition (which formed the basis for these histories), but what was remembered was the fact that Winchester Mathewson was brutally murdered in 1774; no trace of his body was ever found. The presumed perpetrator was a stranger – a vagabond or tramp – who wandered unknown into town and disappeared equally unknown; the only evidence of his existence was the subsequent non-existence of Winchester Mathewson. Yet the fact that a *stranger* was responsible is an important element in this story for it draws an implicit line between unsanctioned behavior, done by strangers, and the behavior of others in the village.

Investigating the first Mathewson[9] to settle in Rhode Island for clues of the family that lived in North Smithfield, we discovered that his name was Daniel, that he lived in the northwest corner of the state, where he was an original proprietor of Burriville, and that he had eight sons and six daughters. His Burriville land was insufficient to provide for all his heirs. Hence a need to acquire more land existed within the Mathewson family. It should be noted here that the system of primogeniture that was prominent in the inheritance system of England, and transferred to the Chesapeake almost intact, was altered in New England. The eldest son received a double portion, according to Biblical law, but others shared equally, and men actively sought land for their younger sons. Hence one might say that land brought Daniel Mathewson out of Burriville, but he was also a member of a kinship network that had nodes in North Smithfield by virtue of a first marriage to Sarah Inman and a third marriage to Sarah's sister, Charity. By these two marriages, his children also possessed a claim to Inman land as their matrilateral legacy.

The Inmans owned land in North Smithfield adjacent to the Mowry land. During the early eighteenth century, two sons of Daniel Mathewson were given portions of this land. The property on which the mid-eighteenth-century artifacts were found belonged to either the murdered Winchester Mathewson or to his brother, Othniel, who died in 1806 and lies buried in a Mathewson family graveyard, adjacent to the property, that is not recognized by the town as signifying the presence of Mathewsons in their midst, for it now bears the name of Sheldon's Corners.

No member of the Mathewson family held prestigious political offices in North Smithfield; while Mowry men served on the town council, the Mathewsons served as hemp viewers. Male members of the family left town and sought land elsewhere. Several of the women married and remained in the community, but none married a Mowry. Without an imposing mnemonic structure (e.g., a gravestone) surviving, without the possession of political and economic power in the community, without kinship links in the town that commanded attention of later generations of local residents, knowledge of the Mathewsons was forgotten in folk history. Perhaps they were never perceived as members of the community because of their strong political, familial, and land links to nearby Burriville, a village that lay at the western edge of Smithfield.

Throughout the nineteenth century, women of the Mathewson family continued to live on the family land in North Smithfield. Martha Mathewson, for example, married a shoemaker named Stephen Sheldon, and they built a house on Mathewson land in a spot that by the third quarter of the nineteenth century became known as Sheldon's Corners (see fig. 1.4). My suspicion is that one cultural factor that affected knowledge of the Mathewson family's continued existence in town was an emphasis on patrilineality that developed in this same era, contrasting with the bilateral system (using patronymic surnames) that existed previously. Since the oral traditions that pertain to houses are primarily family lore, undoubtedly recounted within the house itself in domestic contexts, a stronger emphasis on one component of the kinship system might produce accompanying alterations in the

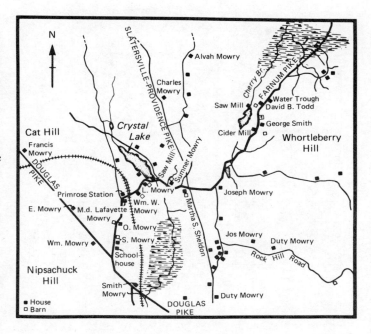

Fig. 1.4. A portion of the 1895 Everts and Richards map showing the project area in North Smithfield, Rhode Island

mythology. The situation is ambiguous and puzzling unless one accepts that what is of critical ideological and social value within the house legends is the male chain of heads of households.

Neglect of this family in the local history, i.e., in the oral tradition, led nineteenth-century historians to overlook them in their written narratives and, as one consequence, twentieth-century cultural resource managers were also unaware of their presence and their abandoned family homelot. The documents that told of this family were relatively clear and easy to locate. It was not a bias in the primary records that led to the omission of Mathewsons from the town histories. Although a full search was precluded by the terms of the archaeological contract, we could trace the family once we knew it existed. Ellen Rosebrock, the project historian, worked back in time using male members of the family (those with Mathewson surnames) as her link to the past.

The linkage in the next case, however, had to be traced through Sarah Callum-Bartlett-Smith-Andrews, a thrice-married woman; the records we needed were difficult to find. Yet what emerges also tells of the relationship between individuals, their kinship ties, and family obligations to women not related by direct descent. Again, the pivotal point at which knowledge was lost or discarded occurred with the transferal of the family property to Sarah using informal and undocumented procedures. Her right was subsequently confirmed through title passed to her and her husband at a later date.

1.5.2 Todd Farm

Todd Farm (see fig. 1.5) was built c.1749 according to the folk history in North Smithfield, Rhode Island. Oral tradition

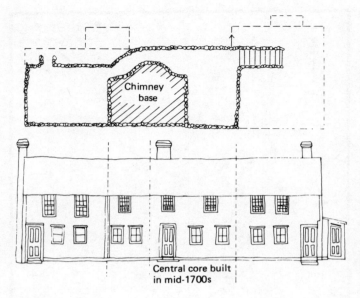

Fig. 1.5. Todd Farm, North Smithfield, Rhode Island

about the history of the house persisted in the community as late as World War II. The fabric of the building was old and the core of the building was a central-chimney dwelling that had been added to over the years. Even a cursory glance revealed that the house dated further back in time than the deed to David Andrews. Both the folk history and the appearance of the building suggested an earlier occupation than the artifacts recovered from the limited testing program. These formed a very small sample, insufficient for reliable statistical analysis, although the presence of creamware sherds pointed to a site that might have been occupied from c.1770 onwards.

The situation was thus: the architectural evidence suggested an early to mid-eighteenth century building; oral tradition gave a construction date of 1749; the artifactual evidence pointed towards c.1770; the deeds told of nothing dating earlier than 1821. The nineteenth-century owner was David Andrews, a man born in Mendon, a Massachusetts town thirty miles to the north, who had no visible ties between his paternal family and the North Smithfield community. Working with the idea that the town was relatively closed to outsiders, there had to be some link between the nineteenth-century Andrews occupation at Todd Farm and the earlier ones if, indeed, the house was as old as the folk history recounted.

When no information that tied David Andrews to the community could be found, the search was extended to see whether there was a relationship that existed via his wife. The link between the Andrews occupation of Todd Farm and its early inhabitants was formed through Andrews' wife, Sarah, who was once the wife of Daniel Smith. The link appeared in family reconstitution charts that contained information on *both* sides of the family (for family reconstitution charts designed to reveal bilateral kinship ties, see Yentsch 1975).

Background information on Sarah revealed that she married a forty-year old Quaker in 1788 and in 1798 married again, wedding Daniel Smith. By 1808, she was wed to a man from her home town of Mendon, David Andrews, and had given birth to Daniel Smith Andrews. These facts linked individuals from Mendon to each other and to the Smith family (see fig. 1.6).

While the legend surrounding the Todd Farm, however, identified the era when the house was built (c.1749), it obliterated the Smith family tenure at the farm and named David Andrews as the mythical person associated with the origins of the dwelling. Ultimately, in an out-of-the-way location, a deed from a Daniel Smith to David Andrews dated 1821 was secured. It was found by researching the Smith rather than the Andrews surname.[10] David and Sarah Andrews were the parents of three daughters and a son, David Smith Andrews, who died young. Mary Ann married Nelson Taft of Mendon and lived in the house; Abigail married Albert Todd and also lived in the house. The Tafts were childless while the Todds had two sons who eventually inherited the farm from their mother and their mother's sister.

The Smiths, who were the family that actually built the house (located within a quarter-mile of the Mowry-Smith home), were the family for which Smithfield was named. Daniel was an important first name in their family; each generation had one or more individuals named Daniel Smith among the different family lines. It was the Smith association that eventually allowed a complete deed trace of the property to be finished. But the kinship relationship of the Smiths to Sarah was not one of direct descent, nor, in all probability, was Sarah the first wife of Daniel Smith. In any event, she had already been married once when she wed him. She possessed a legal dower right to his estate, but this was not how she procured

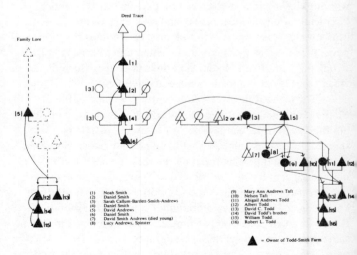

Fig. 1.6. Chain of possession, Todd Farm, North Smithfield, Rhode Island. Arrows denote conveyance of house. Sarah (3) married either Daniel Smith (2) or (4); the records are unclear on this point. Individuals denoted by dotted circles and triangle are ignored in the family tradition

ownership of the Smith farmhouse. The property came into her next husband's possession through a real estate sale made after the family had lived in Smithfield for several years.

1.6 Kinship, social distance, and cultural separations

In the real world of pragmatic social action, the Todd boys secured their family legacy in Smithfield through a matrilineal kinship tie that involved their direct descent from Sarah Callum-Bartlett-Smith-Andrews. This fact is not clearly conveyed in the stories that surround the house. The fictional inference, in the community name for the property, disassociated them from female kin, although it did denote the role played by David Andrews. Such acts masked the procedures by which the bilateral system worked, including the extent and importance of collateral relatives and one's jural obligations to them. It indicates an ideological differentiation made between patrifiliation and matrifiliation, emphasizing the former.

The idea that real estate transactions in a pre-industrial community were based on some kind of personal knowledge and relationships between individuals is common sense. The family as an extended network of kin necessarily was involved in economic activities and performed many tasks now no longer associated with family. Given the changes that have occurred in society, one can view folk histories of buildings both as family history and as history in the process of transformation, reflecting transformation in the family-kin-economic sphere of cultural activity and affected by the removal of many work-related activities from the domestic sphere with the growth of capitalism.

To understand archaeological data and place it within a historical context requires an understanding of the cultural separations that set apart people of one era in the past from those in another. Cultural separations, while discernible archaeologically, can only be understood anthropologically. Furthermore, many occur in domains of culture that are implicit, i.e., in cultural categories that now form part of our taken-for-granted notions of the world. Beliefs about kinship, for example, fall within one set of taken-for-granted notions about social process.

David Schneider in a book entitled *American Kinship* (1968) defines the kinship system that is part of the structure of modern American society. This is a system that, under its guise of seeming inevitability, can be easily assumed to operate in the American past. American kinship during the seventeenth and eighteenth centuries formed a bilateral system equivalent to the antecedent English system described by Leach (1973). Yet the extent and strength of the bilateral systems is obscured by emphasis, arising in the nineteenth century, on its patrilineal segment. This emphasis may have evolved as a mistaken notion suggested by the existence of patronymic naming procedures, as local historians fell prey to the implicit taken-for-granted notions about the nineteenth-century kinship systems. Thus they unwittingly projected onto the past a patrilineal ideology. Nevertheless, deliberately or not, they projected onto the

past a vision of the world that they could relate to and one that validated their position in the ethnographic present. Other social boundaries were also defined and can be seen in a study of the historiographic process. For example, the role of oral tradition about houses and the way in which it validates the social status of the contemporary occupant of a home is well illustrated in the traditions that surround homes of the poor.

The identity, lineage, and social status of a family determine whether a house is remembered or forgotten. The history of a house validates the social position of its occupants, but in doing so, it can also dispossess others. If a house is forgotten or its occupation abridged in folk history, not only is its existence denied, but the existence of those who made it their home is also denied or set aside.[11] They become people who no longer merit further consideration in local history, for they constitute a group perceived as non-members of a community, if not as non-entities. By way of illustration, one can cite the contemporary history of alley housing in Washington, D.C., carefully detailed in Borchelt's 1981 monograph on alley life.

1.7 Alley houses

Alley houses were built in Washington in the late nineteenth century. These formed enclaves within the shelter of a city block; the houses/shacks were reached by alleys running through the block or by a blind alley. The enclaves had their prototypes in European cities of much earlier vintage (Chalklin 1974, 202–6). They also existed in colonial cities like Annapolis, Philadelphia, and Boston, although little is known about them. Alley housing, like alley inhabitants, formed a class apart.

Houses that fronted on the street were part of the wider community. Fenced backyards provided effective boundaries between the alley community and the inhabitants of street dwellings. Buildings in the alleys were poor structures – hovels, cottages, or shanties. The people who lived within them were from the lower ranks of society and, by the late nineteenth century, these were primarily Afro-Americans in southern sectors of the United States and members of other ethnic minorities in northern cities. Those who lived on the street were of higher social rank. They claimed, despite second story windows that overlooked the fences and the alley rooftops, to know nothing of the alley community and, if possible, did not even acknowledge its existence.[12]

The alley communities of Washington, D.C., are gone now; the shanties of Nottingham, England, have also disappeared. There are, in Washington, a few locations where remains of such buildings still stand and today house the elite. The shanties and shacks were converted, labeled 'carriage houses' or even 'slave quarters' by those who now dwell within them and, by inference, are associated with the larger, more prestigious dwellings fronting the streets (John Vlach, personal communication). A few folk historians have conducted studies on these neighborhoods, but their past is largely unrecorded, and we do not often recognize that within the alley community lived people who adapted to city life through the mechanisms of a folk society, thereby keeping their folk identity and its cultural integrity alive for almost one hundred years in an urban setting.

Primarily alley communities were forgotten. The links between them and the present occupants of the renovated dwellings shattered as gentrification of the buildings proceeded. Indeed, for the present residents to be tied to these earlier folk would root Washington's elite to an unknown and unfamiliar space and time. To draw the link between the modern inhabitants, the Afro-American occupation of the nineteenth/twentieth century, and the even earlier Anglo-Americans living at poverty level, would be to link upwardly mobile city dwellers to poverty, instability, discontinuity, family upheaval, and exploitation. In other words, the linkage would be to non-sanctioned rather than culturally valued traits of daily life.

This reality was masked by the mythology that developed in which the shanties were transmuted into carriage houses that then served, in a mythical analogy, as extensions of the mansions of the rich. The shattered linkage created a boundary between past and present. The traditions serve as a mirror image to those created by inhabitants of dwellings associated with cultural heroes (e.g., the first English settlers) where a time–space boundary is dissolved to draw closer patrilineal ancestors. In each case, the house serves as a metaphor for family.

1.8 Legends, houses, and ideology

In summary, different examples of house legends have been presented and discussed. The probability that these accomplish the same task, binding society and promoting solidarity, has been considered. Differences within the genre, revolving around male–female roles and whether ethnic boundaries were mediated, emerged simply as different themes expressing the same cultural values. With the transmutation of the house to family, its locus shifts from physical space to imaginary space, if not sacred space. Masking the experiences of the real world, the house and its associated family stories become a mechanism for social cohesion.

It is argued here that house legends belong to mytho-history and that they conform to a different logic, one that places ideological symbols by the family hearth through a process which enmeshes them with the physical fabric of a building. By analogy, the house itself serves as symbol of the family. It is also suggested that the ideology underwent a transformation in the late eighteenth and early nineteenth centuries, although, because of the nature of the topic studied (oral tradition), there is only limited access to similar information for the earlier period, and this idea cannot be easily verified using equivalent information about earlier houses. In all probability, however, the ideological statements contained within house histories are echoed elsewhere and could be studied as Slotkin studied Indian–white relations in *Regeneration through Violence* (1973).

What can be verified is the manner in which the bilateral kinship system operated; this can be done using family reconstitution charts and other demographic records. The relationship between an individual's status in the family and property ownership can be ascertained. And, when this is done, it becomes clear that ties to one's maternal family (matrifiliation) can have as significant economic and practical consequences as patrifiliation. The patrilineal ideology, however, masks the importance of this relationship.

Readers may ask what use it is for archaeologists to know of the existence of a patrilineal bias in American ideology? Some archaeologists may question whether this is not superfluous anthropological information unrelated to the interpretation of historical sites. There is one very practical reason why archaeologists should be aware of the social structure of the American communities of the past. Knowing it one is able to find documents and to use them in a way that is not possible otherwise. Many of the documents that archaeologists find most useful, such as deeds, wills, probate inventories, church and town records, are artifacts that exist because of kinship obligations or community responsibilities. These obligations and responsibilities were orderly, patterned, and regular. They reflected a cultural classification of people and events. Knowing the system in which they operated gives one knowledge of past social process that, in turn, is useful in locating more elusive documents.

Using anthropological information about the past to locate documents is using it merely as a tool, not as an analytical endeavor. Archaeologists work with objects created in a social context formed by culture until, at some point in their existence, they come to reside within an archaeological context. Their role is not passive for, in Schiffer's words, 'they actively structure social interaction (Hodder 1982), and influence the course of social change (Rathje 1979)' (Schiffer 1983, 676). In doing so, objects fulfill technomic, socio-technic and ideotechnic roles (Binford 1962). It is certainly true that in order to understand how objects participate in a cultural system, one must also understand their limitations. Some of their limitations are imposed by the formation processes and preservational characteristics of the archaeological context that are being thoroughly studied by scholars in a number of stimulating studies (Binford 1979; Hodder 1983; Schiffer 1976, 1983). Yet an artifact's primary limitation is that it is no longer a functioning element of a world-in-action once it enters the traditional (i.e., below-ground) archaeological record.

While the remains of houses below ground consist of archaeological features or artifacts, standing ones are architectural entities that remain functional elements of a world-in-action. And, as pointed out in this essay, it is primarily standing structures that are remembered in family legends. Further, legends are elements of mytho-history and therefore part of a nation's ideology. Provocative studies by Glassie (1975, 1982), Upton (1982, n.d.), and Rapaport (1968, 1982) have paid close attention to the ideological parameters of space within houses and to the role of architectural features in expressing internalized beliefs. In doing so, they have utilized a structural frame of reference and introduced an ideological focus in architectural studies that is infrequently found in archaeology (Leone 1982). Glassie concluded that changes in the structure of dwellings accompanied a political transformation, thus establishing a relationship between the domestic domain and the larger world, between the form of material objects and social order:

> Virginia's period of architectural change – 1760 to 1820 – was indeed a time of massive strangeness, a time for fear and courage. Houses closed and became symmetrical while the American world transformed, shifting from dependent colonial status through violence into independence. (1982, 400)

Houses, in Glassie's belief, became closed and symmetrical with spaces that separated and contained as a new ideology swept through the land. Houses, in other words, were one mechanism that people used to compartmentalize and categorize their world, making new distinctions between themselves as social individuals and others. If Glassie's belief is accurate, the fact that legends about houses begin to mirror these same distinctions is not surprising. One could draw courage from stories linking one's domicile to individuals who bravely and fearlessly fought Indians even as one feared the intrusion of strangers into the community with the arrival of nineteenth-century European immigrants or uneasily faced the flow of change in ways of earning a living. As mythology provided analogies, the ability to survive encounters with hostile Indians provided a frame of reference for facing other Europeans and their unfamiliar languages and lifestyles. As new immigrants entered New England towns in the early nineteenth century to work in the mills, the townsfolk extended the house-related legends held in the private domain into the public sector with parades celebrating the town's founding fathers and other rituals that celebrated the origins of the community itself.[13] Written narratives depicting local history proliferated as people looked to the past to predict the future. People made individual pilgrimages to old houses, incorporating them into town, state, and national mythology.

The use of historic houses, or villages, as ancestral shrines gained further impetus with the growth of the preservation movement (Fitch 1972; Lynch 1972; Hosmer 1978; Schlereth 1980). One result is that archaeologists today are increasingly called upon to verify dates of houses and to provide information about lifestyles of the occupants unavailable through architectural analysis. In this, their work supplements that of social historians and American folklorists. This is not a neutral task. Until one recognizes the mythological element that persists, like a constant thread, throughout these preservation projects, and treats historic properties as representing metaphors for the origin myths customary in other societies, the ideological elements cannot be unmasked. Meanwhile, inseparable and undistinguished, the mythological elements intrude upon archaeological analysis, and scholars are unwitting participants in the creation of newly formulated or revised myths.

Until historical archaeologists confront the fact that historical experience consists of both the world-as-lived and the world-as-thought and find a means to analyze this dialectical process as it affects objects, they will remain imprisoned by the limitations of their data. In the physical layouts of old houses, we can see the world-as-lived only in fragmentary form; we can begin to see the world-as-thought when we conceptualize house plans as incorporating both real space and imaginary space expressing social order. We can trace the world-as-lived in the analysis of the family structure of a household, and we can begin to investigate the inter-relationship between it and the world-as-thought in the analysis of myth and legend encoded in local lore. The relationship between objects and symbolic function, their role in communicating elements of shared beliefs, is thrown into relief. Simultaneously, evidence of change emerges that signals a nineteenth-century modification on the configuration of earlier cultural form.

The first homes in the New World were functional and sparse, dugout houses implanted in fields or sides of hills, semi-subterranean domiciles. Created with materials derived locally, the houses merged into the land and into nature. Carson et al. describe them as simple structures where men and women with their families could stay 'dry and warm' for two, three, or four years until there was time and money to build a slightly better home, one still perceived by folk as 'very mean and little' (Carson et al. 1981, 139–40). Noting their method of construction, Carson concludes that Chesapeake homes 'were not only *not* built to last, they *were* built in ways that termites could not resist' (Carson 1978, 56). Family members lived in these small, unsophisticated homes, more carefully and culturally finished, less natural than the cruder dugouts, yet still unrefined, season after season until the family had sufficient funds to invest in a better home. Men placed financial priority on acquiring land and livestock, perceiving these as a means within Anglo-American society for an improved standard of living, upward social mobility, and higher social ranks (Jones 1980b).

Eventually, after one, two, or three generations, a family could build a substantial home that was fair to behold, created of brick or finely turned clapboard, situated in a tamed landscape containing settled towns. It is these later structures, built by eighteenth-century gentlemen and yeomen farmers, that endure and are conceived of, in folk belief, as the homes of our ancestors. With the mistaken assumption that these later buildings existed from earlier points in time, the structures have become evocative symbols of European power to reform wilderness, turning natural space into cultural space, to take something remote, strange, and convert it into something familiar and close to man. In doing so, new social boundaries were created; some individuals were dispossessed, others were denigrated, and a few were elevated to ancestral status. A new ideology was formed, penetrating the domestic domain to reshape the kinship system, separating individuals once conjoined through family activity, masking the world of experience, hiding social boundaries. Wrapped around homes, enmeshed in their fabric, the message was vocal and unequivocal. Taken for granted, the ideology became as evocative as the buildings in which it resided. Its medium was the core of archaeological inquiry, material culture, and its origins lay in the culturally construed symbolic relationships between objects, ideas, and power.

Notes

1. This research was funded, in part, by the Institute for Conservation Archaeology, Harvard University, and by Historic Annapolis, Inc. The views represented are, however, solely those of the author. The paper itself could not have been written without the support, advice, and encouragement of St Clair Wright, Carol Ballingall, Peter Schmidt, Robert Jay, and Mark P. Leone.

2. I have taken my definition of oral tradition from R. A. Gould's study of the relationship between archaeology and oral tradition at the Pt. St. George Site (Gould 1966, 4) and modified it. Gould's definition is: 'informant testimony that is not based upon the actual experiences of the informant or upon experiences shared within his lifetime but rather upon accounts of experiences or knowledge which have been transmitted orally to the informant across the span of at least one generation.' My modification has been to include not only informant testimony procured directly, but to use nineteenth-century narratives as additional sources where it was relatively obvious that the individual was utilizing historical information gathered in the manner noted by Gould. Town and family histories are replete with such data, often specifying which local informant provided the testimony. In other cases, the omission of specific historical documentation implies the use of oral tradition. In no case was a specific bit of information conceived of as representing oral tradition when a specific reference to a verifiable document such as a deed, town record, will, etc., was made and used as evidence. Gould also notes that the validity of oral tradition has been of more concern to anthropologists and folklorists than to archaeologists, but there was a spurt of interest in this topic by prehistorians and a continuing interest shown by ethnohistorians. Pertinent studies by archaeologists include those by Fewkes (1893), Hodge (1897), McGregor (1943), Pendergast and Meighan (1959), and Meighan (1960). Jan Vansina's seminal work, *Oral Tradition* (1965), using African sources, was a path-breaking study, and his ideas were incorporated into the study of African prehistory by archaeologists including Schmidt (1978).

3. Information on typical eighteenth-century buildings in the Chesapeake was provided by Orlando Rideout VI of the Maryland Historical Trust, who has worked actively in this field for the past ten years. He drew not only on his own experiences as a fieldworker in Queen Anne's County, but also on unpublished reports on file at the Trust's offices in Annapolis. Few of these data are published and much has been derived archaeologically. See the review article by Carson et al. (1981), Garry Wheeler Stone's doctoral dissertation (1982), or Dell Upton's forthcoming article (Upton n.d.).

4. The base of a large, ironstone fireplace was located, but no traces remained of footings, which implies the presence of a post-hole structure. The fill in a small, five-foot square root cellar cribbed with wood and approximately 2.6 feet deep, associated with this building, dated to the first quarter of the nineteenth century. No information was obtained on the construction data; the area was tested and full-scale excavation has been delayed, pending funding, since 1972. Additional work done by Yentsch in 1981 accompanying fence installation produced similar results to those reported by Wright (1971).

5. Three sites excavated by Plimoth Plantation have been located by oral tradition in conjunction with more traditional archaeological procedures (James Deetz, personal communication). These include Wellfleet Tavern, the R.M. Site, and the Standish Site. Of these, the Standish site location was known because a nineteenth-century commemorative monument had been placed on it, purportedly through the use of oral tradition. The R.M. Site was the location of the Eel River Massacre in King Philip's War, and its location had been conveyed in oral tradition since the 1670s. Thus one was associated with a folk hero and the other with a military battle. In the Chesapeake, Old Chapel Field in St Mary's City was found to be the location of the first English Catholic church (c.1640?) in the New World (Michael Smolek, personal communication). In existence for only a short period (c. thirty years), the church was dismantled and its bricks used elsewhere. The source of the bricks and the original location were maintained in local lore and were substantiated by Smolek through both excavation and location of historical, documentary evidence.

6. In a study of linguistic terms defining categories of English animals, Leach points out that the following relationships can be seen as equivalent: (a) Self ... Sister ... Cousin ... Neighbor ... Stranger (b) Self ... House ... Farm ... Field ... Far (Remote) (c) Self ... Pet ... Livestock ... 'Game' ... Wild Animal. What he means by this is that 'we employ the words in set (c) ... to make statements about the human relationships that belong to set (a)' (Leach 1966, 36–7). The words chosen to describe the location of Elizabeth Lewis Blachford's childhood home (Crooked Pond) and her home after marriage (Half-way Pond) as well as the emphasis on their forest location, the presence of Indians, the presence of wild animals, uncannily fit his paradigm. Each word chosen to describe aspects of her life falls at the furthest scale, and denotes her position at the edge of the continuum from culture to nature, from self to stranger, far, and wild.

7. Accusations of witchcraft are specifically discussed by Otis, but more details are provided by Reynard. While embroidered, the core of these tales is maintained in Reynard's 1934 reweaving of the local lore. All of these are standard activities often associated with witches (see Demos 1982; Thomas 1971; or Douglas 1970). They include the use of black cat as a familiar, turning humans into animal forms, and midnight dances. Reynard does not list her sources, and hence this work is not considered a reliable retelling of Cape Cod folklore, but neither is there any indication that her stories are fictional and, in fact, traces of them can be seen in the written nineteenth-century narratives.

8. Aunt Beck kept a local museum, never threw anything away. As one example, she saved bones to make soap for more than thirty years, stuffed all over the house, until in old age, during a hot summer, she was persuaded to throw them away, and neighbors took an ox-cart full to the town dump. Other eccentricities are detailed in Otis, pp. 93–7. She could not, under any circumstances, be considered an average woman leading a normal life.

9. Sources used in research on the Mathewsons and the Smiths, Todds, and Andrews families included town histories (Steere 1881; Arnold 1895, 1859; Austin 1969; Bailey 1975; Bayles 1891 Mowry 1878, 1909; Nebiker 1976; Robinson et al. 1974; Todd 1920) and original town records on file in the town clerks' offices in Lincoln, Rhode Island, Central Falls, Rhode Island, Smithfield, Rhode Island, in the Providence, Rhode Island, Registry of Deeds, and at the Rhode Island Historical Society.

10. The usual procedure in undertaking a deed trace is to begin with the latest owner and work back in time. Knowing kinship ties o

occupants of a dwelling, however, enables one to 'jump' the records and look for other possible sources of information in wills. Essentially, one uses knowledge of the way the kinship system worked, i.e., the jural obligations that families had, as one means of procuring information.

11. Robert Engs' study of Hampton, Virginia, leads to a similar conclusion. In the research on the development of Hampton Institute and a consideration of the 'blacks and Northern whites' who worked to develop this educational establishment, Engs paid close attention to the town of Hampton itself and talked with many individuals in the community. His description of the physical town is vividly phrased, comparing it to a frontier settlement (i.e., the founding phase of a community) located in the West: 'its unlighted streets were impassable mud bogs in winter and spring, changing to choking alleys of dust in the drier months' (1979, 161); 'black landowners in the country got only land no one else wanted and in small plots adequate only for subsistence farming. A similar situation existed among black owners of city lots' (ibid., 177). He notes an informant who described the town as 'a straggling collection of small wooden houses and shanties' (ibid., 161). What is important about this is the selectivity with which these post-bellum years of black property ownership are remembered. Engs writes eloquently of the out-migration of blacks from the community, noting that it was one result of racism. He specifically discusses local history and the way it neglects the role black inhabitants played: 'They [Hampton's nineteenth-century black inhabitants] are the proudest product of "Freedom's First Generation." That their origins, and the special people and events that created them, have been nearly forgotten illustrates how little we yet know or understand about black life in the post-bellum south' (ibid.,

204). This in turn, is linked to local tradition in a discussion of property contained in a footnote that states: 'Most important among the insights gained from those I interviewed was the discovery of the extent of black property acquisition during the post-Reconstruction period. Much of that property has now reverted to white hands and few besides old time residents are aware that it ever belonged to blacks.' Thus the conclusion one reaches from reading Engs' research is that his results parallel the situation discussed in the text vis-à-vis alley housing.

12. While enrolled in a class on ethnohistory at the University of Maryland in 1982, my students gathered data on alley housing including the perceptions noted here.

13. The addition of middle names to the basic first name/last name identification of individuals in the third quarter of the eighteenth century enabled people to name children in honor of more than one deceased relative and, with this, one also begins to see the middle name used to associate individuals with folk heroes. This is an alteration in a view toward the past that is echoed in other domains of life. For example, Mathews notes that the 'Forefathers' Day' was first celebrated in Plymouth in 1769 and in Boston in the late eighteenth century (by 1797) (1914, 295), and the custom of celebrating the founding of towns grew from that era onward. Publications of the Massachusetts Historical Society start in the late eighteenth century with notations and descriptions of towns, prompting a growth in individually printed town histories throughout the nineteenth century, many of which are being reprinted now. Family genealogies also begin to make a strong appearance beginning in the nineteenth century. All of these signal a re-emphasis on the origins of families and towns similar to that conveyed in the oral traditions about houses.

Chapter 2

Perceptions of an artifact: Chinese porcelain in colonial Tidewater Virginia

Julia B. Curtis

The analysis of both primary and secondary documentary sources in combination with dated collections and the cargoes of shipwrecks illustrates the role of Chinese export porcelain in international trade and in the seventeenth-century Chesapeake. The social, economic, and cultural implications of a single artifact type are shown to be related both to the complexity of world-wide trade and to transformations within colonial Tidewater Virginia society. The methodological approach to Chinese ceramics as an artifact type can also be used to analyze other artifact groups found in an historical context.

In 1607, a small band of Englishmen established the first permanent English settlement in North America at Jamestown, a malarial peninsula on the north bank of the James River in the colony of Virginia. Most accounts of the early years of settlement, and indeed of the seventeenth century in Virginia, whether written by historians, archaeologists, or material culture specialists, stress the primitive quality and material deprivation of life in early Virginia. Little mention is made in these accounts of a curious cultural phenomenon, the widespread penetration of a Chinese artifact – export porcelain – into the colonial marketplace.

Among the several million objects unearthed by archaeologists in the James River basin, the Chinese export porcelain sherds comprise one of the largest single groups of artifacts recovered. Until the late 1970s, however, these collections remained largely unexploited. This neglect was probably in part a result of the fact that, despite the vast number of books written on Chinese export porcelain, none of them pertain to the rather ordinary wares found on Tidewater Virginia sites; archaeologists and curators had few sources to which to turn for information on dating the sherds.

The present study of Chinese export porcelain sherds in the four major archaeological collections in and around Williamsburg (see fig. 2.1 for the location of the sites from which the collections were excavated) illustrates the necessity of documentary research and the written word to a study of artifacts. The sherds are susceptible to interpretation on several different levels, all but the simplest of which is informed by the written word.

The Chinese export porcelain sherds and the vessels to which they belonged speak to the archaeologist, ceramicist, and historian on three levels.[1] An early Ching blue and white tea bowl, found and reassembled at Jamestown, could be described even by the most untutored amateur as a small bowl covered with a blue-colored decoration on a white background (fig 2.2). This level of interpretation, which is totally factual and subject to simple classification through practical analysis, might be designated the pre-iconographical description.

A more tutored scholar would recognize that the bowl was made of porcelain, rather than earthenware or stoneware, probably produced early in the reign of the Emperor Kang Hsi (1662–1721) and that it was of a size then used as a tea bowl by

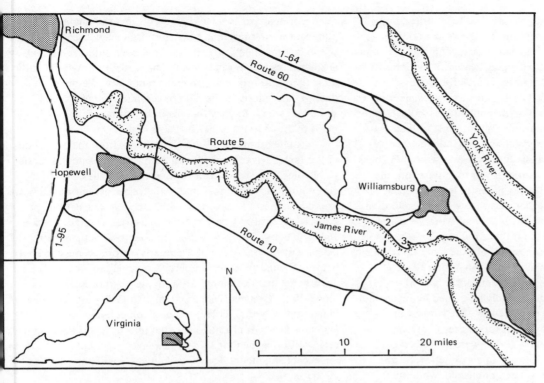

Fig. 2.1. Map of Tidewater Virginia showing study area: 1 = Flowerdew Hundred; 2 = Governor's Land; 3 = Jamestown; 4 = Kingsmill

Fig. 2.2. Tea bowl c. 1665. Jamestown National Historic Site

the Chinese. The scholar would also recognize that the bowl was decorated with a blue glaze, covered by a whitish over-glaze, and that the underglaze blue lotus and scroll pattern decorating it evokes one of the eight Buddhist symbols, the lotus, symbol of faithfulness. This level of analysis could be designated the iconographical level, involving as it does a knowledge of objects and events and symbols attained, not just through practical experience, but through a knowledge of past concepts and practices transmitted through the written and/or spoken word.

To the inquiring student of artifacts, be he or she archaeologist, art historian, or historian, the early Ching tea bowl will speak even more eloquently in the language that Irwin Panofsky designated as iconology. The tea bowl, found as it was on the banks of the James, is Chinese exportware, although this fact did not necessarily preclude its use in China as well, and archaeologists have found such wares in the Far East and on some sites in the mid-East and the coast of Africa (cf. Sassoon 1978, 21, no. 9, 27, no. 16). Such a student would know that the bowl's function in Europe and the colonies would probably have differed from that originally intended by the Chinese; tea was little imported to England or to North America until well after the mid-seventeenth century. The inquiring student might also discover that, while the bowl might be designated as a luxury item in the society to which it was exported, the wide distribution of such wares within early colonial society on the James River precludes its being viewed automatically as a status symbol of the colonial elite.

The iconological interpretation of the early Ching tea bowl goes beyond the iconographic to inquire into what Ernst Cassirer called the cultural symbolism of a work of art or an artifact (Panofsky 1962, 16). What the object meant, even subconsciously, to the civilizations that produced and made use of the artifact, involves the student in a complex series of questions that can only be answered through the use of written sources. The student of Chinese porcelain sherds, whatever his or her scholastic training, is forced to study a wide range of artifacts, the domain of the art historian, a large number of sites, the domain of the archaeologist, and to consult many primary and secondary literary sources, the domain of the historian, in order to fathom the 'intrinsic meaning' of an object to the civilization to which it belonged. And as Irwin Panofsky has so eloquently argued, 'it is in the search for intrinsic meanings . . . that the various humanistic disciplines meet on a common plane instead of serving as handmaidens to each other' (ibid.). Thus, if historical archaeologists are to lend their work a significance beyond the particular and pedantic, beyond vessel typology and the quantitative analysis of food waste, they must use the written word as well as the trowel to inquire into the past, to comprehend the iconology inherent in the artifact.

For the student of material culture, an understanding of the iconography of an artifact involves identifying the material of which it is composed and the form of the object. In the case of ceramics, one sherd may represent the sole material remains of a whole object, so determining its original form requires a knowledge of the possible ceramic forms of the period under investigation. This knowledge can only be gained by recourse to secondary sources as well as to museums. The student of ceramics should study the variety of forms prevalent, for example, in earthenware and tin-glazed ware as well as in Chinese export porcelain; whole examples of delftware, for example, may have survived or been published, while their Chinese counterparts were reduced to sherds. A correct interpretation of the symbolism used to decorate Chinese porcelain in the seventeenth century can only be attained by reference to secondary sources.[2]

Further investigation of the iconographical implications of an artifact involves dating the object or sherd. The question of dating appears to me, an historian, as a critical one for the archaeologist, since the dating of individual artifacts determines to a great extent the interpretation of a site. A close study of Chinese export porcelain can be particularly useful to the archaeologist because many varieties of wares made between c.1600 and 1740 can be dated with great precision, thus providing the archaeologist with the next best thing to a dated coin. The written record is of inestimable value in dating the artifact. By written word I mean not just archival material; I also include the marks on the porcelain.

The Chinese did not mark the great majority of exportware, but they did mark some. A few marked pieces have shown up in the James River basin; some examples will be discussed presently. By studying marked pieces in museums and in illustrated books, the student can gain a good grounding in the stylistic evolution of Chinese export and other ceramics of a particular period. This same technique can be used, for example, in dating many metal objects, using the hallmarks on silver as a source. And design books published in the eighteenth century provide a similar source for furniture, as do the occasional dated pieces. One can hardly overstress the importance of dated artifacts to the construction of a chronology of styles. A lack of attention to dated examples and examples with an established *terminus post quem* has resulted in remarkably sloppy dating in a variety of fields.[3] The study of

the decorative arts is relatively recent, and the quality of publications on the subject varies enormously, a result perhaps of the fact that many writers have not been subjected to any academic discipline whatsoever. The student of material culture must therefore proceed with great caution on the question of dating, particularly in the field of ceramics and glass, and should endeavor to construct his or her own chronology in the fields relevant to his or her investigation.

A few examples of porcelain sherds from the collections in the James River basin illustrate how dated examples, either whole pieces or sherds, can be used to establish such a chronology. The footrings and body fragments of two tea bowls found at Jamestown arouse great interest among ceramicists (fig 2.3). The footrings bear a cyclical mark that could be read as 1606–7, 1666–7, or 1726–7. We are able to date them to 1666–7 because of the discovery of a similarly decorated mustard pot bearing the marks of the emperor Cheng Hua (1465–1487), an apocryphal mark often used during the reign of Kang Hsi (1662–1721) (Jenyns 1965, 36). Colonial Williamsburg's beaker, illustrated in Ivor Noël Hume's book on ceramics at Colonial Williamsburg, bears a hallmark that tells us it was made in the reign of Chongzhen (1628–44). It was found, incidentally, in an impeccable eighteenth-century context (Noël Hume 1976, 43, fig 2).

The Virginia Research Center for Archaeology (VRCA) has rim sherds of a small saucer of a very common pattern bearing a six-character mark of the reign of Cheng Hua in calligraphy characteristic of the period of Kang Hsi. The drawing of the Chinese woman on this saucer is very similar to that on plates made for Johannes Comptoys bearing his coat of arms, granted in 1684 (fig 2.4). Since Comptoys died in 1695, the plate, the Virginia saucer, and other similar wares can be dated between 1685 and 1700 (personal communication, Christian Jorg, Curator, Groninger Museum, Groningen, Netherlands). This early date is reinforced by a group of plates decorated with scenes of the Rotterdam riot of 1690. A

Fig. 2.3. Footrings of two teabowls bearing cyclical dates of 1667–7. Jamestown National Historic Site

Fig. 2.4. Meatplate with arms of Johannes Comptoys c. 1685–1700. Author's collection

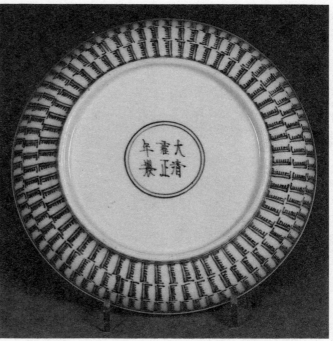

Fig. 2.5. Saucer with debased Sanscrit characters. Yung Cheng mark and period (1723–1735). Author's collection

commemorative medal was struck shortly thereafter and plates, tea bowls, and saucers made in China after the medal. The border decoration of the VRCA's rim sherd is stylistically identical to the border of plates bearing the scene derived by the Chinese from the medal (Howard and Ayers 1978, vol. I, 60). The Comptoys and 'Rotterdam riot' plates are thus useful in affixing a more narrow date to a saucer bearing an apocryphal reign mark.

A marked example found in London and bearing a six-character mark of the reign of Yung Cheng was helpful in dating a tea bowl found at Jamestown decorated with Sanscrit characters (fig 2.5). This ware, found throughout southeast Asia, was made for about three hundred years, and is therefore difficult to date without a marked example. (See Willets and Poh 1981, 6 and 54, for a discussion of nineteenth-century wares like the earlier tea bowls found at Jamestown.) By making an effort to study dated ceramics in museums and books, one can build up a repertoire of key artifacts that will stand one in good stead in the field and in the laboratory.

Two groups of artifacts with established *termini post quem* have proven indispensable to the dating of seventeenth- and early eighteenth-century Chinese export porcelain: artifacts in historic collections with terminal dates, and artifacts recovered from shipwrecks. Three important historic collections have firm *termini* and, like the wrecks, we have the terminal dates because we have the documentation. The first is the collection of export porcelain at Schloss Ambras. Sir Harry Garner studied part of the collection; his findings have been published by the Oriental Ceramic Society (Garner 1975). The

collection belonged to the Archduke Ferdinand II of Austria, who died in 1595. The inventory of the collection, taken a year after his death, survives. Unfortunately, none of the pieces is individually identifiable; no inventory numbers were used. But the general nature of the wares is discernible, particularly the kinrande bowls (decorated with red overglaze enamel and gold on the exterior and underglaze blue on the interior). Garner's study made it possible to date a bowl recovered from the wreck of the *Sea Venture*, which inspired Shakespeare's play *The Tempest*. The ship was sent out to resupply the first settlers at Jamestown and sank off Bermuda in 1609 without reaching Virginia. In Garner's discussion of the Schloss Ambras collection, he often uses dated examples to fix quite a precise date to the individual pieces he discusses.

The Chinese porcelain collection in Dresden is a superb documented collection. Two kinrande bowls remain of the four that we know the Florentine ambassador gave the elector of Saxony in 1585. The majority of the collection was formed by Augustus the Strong, whose lust for Chinese export porcelain induced him to trade six hundred of his dragoons to King Frederick Wilhelm I of Prussia in return for 151 large pieces of porcelain from the Prussian collections. The very large lidded blue and white vases he acquired from Frederick Wilhelm have ever since been known as the 'dragoon vases'. Augustus was also responsible for starting and funding the Meissen factory, which copied many of the Chinese and Japanese wares in his collection. The Dresden collection was inventoried in 1721, with a supplement in 1727; a number was engraved into each piece in the collection (State Art Collections of Dresden,

Fig. 2.6. Kraakware dish, c. 1600. Author's collection

Fig. 2.8. Bowl with Cheng Hua marks on interior and exterior footring. Author's collection

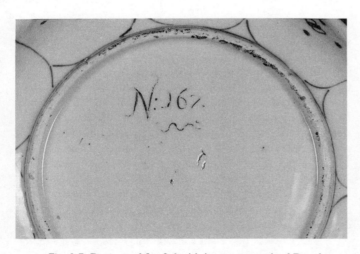

Fig. 2.7. Reverse of fig. 2.6 with inventory mark of Dresden collection

German Democratic Republic, 1978, no. 102, 169–71). The inventories make the collection invaluable to the study of exportwares produced prior to 1730, a date rendered significant because the Chinese practice of marking some exportwares was by then out of favor, and the gap between export porcelain and Chinese domestic wares was widening rapidly.

These collections are not without pitfalls for the unwary. The kraakware plate illustrated (figs. 2.6 and 2.7) belonged in the Dresden collection; the 'Johannem mark' on the back of the dish indicates that it was inventoried in the eighteenth century. Yet the plate dates to about 1600 and is similar in design to

sherds found at Flowerdew Hundred, on the south bank of the James River. As is often the case with documents pertaining to an archaeological site, the inventories themselves do not date the artifacts; they only supply *termini post quem*. Bearing in mind this proviso, however, the student of Chinese export porcelain can put the documented collections to excellent use.

A student of the iconography of seventeenth-century material culture will find the collections of Chinese porcelain from the Ardebil Shrine of value. The porcelains, now housed in Tehran, have been brilliantly studied by John Pope (1956). Despite the fact that much of the collection predates the reign of Wan Li (1573–1619), it has a firm *terminus post quem*. Three manuscript transcriptions survive describing Shah Abbas' establishment of the collection at the Ardebil Shrine in 1611 (Pope 1956, 8).

The collection from the Ardebil Shrine has solved no individual mysteries in Virginia, but material from the collection has shed light on finds from Drake's Bay, in Marin County, California, and on the ceramics from the *Witte Leeuw* (*White Lion*) wreck site.[4] A bowl in the Iranian collection has indirectly facilitated identification and dating of two types of ceramic vessels found off St Helena that may well turn up in future excavations in Virginia. The Ardebil bowl is decorated on the exterior with a band of flying horses above ten groups of floral sprays and a border of overlapping petals above the footring. Around the interior runs a band of landscape typical of the period from about 1590 to 1620, containing mountains, pagodas, banners, phallic rocks, and the odd sailboat. Pope dates the Iranian bowl to the late sixteenth century (1956, 138, plate 105, no. 29.394). Its interior border is directly related stylistically and iconographically to the landscape on the interior rim of a more crudely executed bowl in the author's possession with Cheng Hua marks on both the exterior and interior footrings (fig 2.8). The landscape on the interior of the Cheng Hua bowl resembles in every way the decoration on several of the twenty covered bowls excavated from the site of the *Witte Leeuw* (van der Pijl-Ketel 1982, 159). A similar covered bowl, illustrated in *Porcelain and the Dutch East India Company*, was incorrectly identified by T. Volker as Japanese (1971, plate XVII, no. 32). The exterior of the Cheng Hua bowl is decorated with three large cartouches containing a peach surrounded by leaves painted in a manner identical to the decoration on a whole and a partial bowl found among the load of the *Witte Leeuw* (van der Pijl-Ketel 1982, 175–6). All these vessels can be said, with some assurance, to have been manufactured between 1590 and 1620. Furthermore, the Ardebil Shrine collection has been particularly useful in attempts to establish a stylistic chronology for kraakware, an undertaking of consequence to the archaeology of the James River basin (ibid., 49).

The study of the iconology of Chinese export porcelain is greatly enhanced by the study of the artifacts collected from East Indiamen wrecked on the voyage home. The wrecks create even more problems for the student than the documented collections, however, because they are seldom clean excavations (cf. Von der Porten and Peron 1973, 7; van der Pijl-Ketel 1982, 26). They are of use to scholars, however, primarily because the documents relating to their cargo and disposition survive. Where the documents are incomplete, as they are in the case of Drake's landing in California in 1579, I think one must hypothesize with great caution. But the similarity of the bulk of the artifacts from the wrecks makes them a critical source for dating and otherwise identifying the Chinese export sherds found in the James River basin.

Several wrecks have proved useful for the study of Chinese porcelain in colonial Virginia: the wreck or wrecks at Drake's Bay, possibly in 1579, certainly in 1595; the *Witte Leeuw* in 1613; the *Concepcion* in 1641; and the *Goteborg* in 1745. Neither of the two books published on the *Concepcion* contain photographs of the Chinese porcelain recovered from the wreck, but Polaroid photographs taken shortly after their retrieval showed bowls and dishes stiffly painted in abstracted designs based on kraakware (personal communication, Suzanne Valenstein, Curator, Metropolitan Museum, New York). The *Goteborg*, a Swedish East Indiaman, is well documented but little published (Roth 1965). The ship, laden with porcelain, sank immediately upon obtaining its home port of Gothenburg in 1745. The photographs of its porcelain indicate that the Swedes ate off exportware very similar to that found in Tidewater Virginia in the 1740s (ibid., 12 fig. 7).

The sherds from two wrecks have been of particular importance to the dating and identification of exportware sherds in the James River basin. The material from Drake's Bay has been important in establishing a chronology of late sixteenth- and early seventeenth-century wares. The many whole objects and sherds from the *Witte Leeuw* enable archaeologists and ceramicists to establish with certainty that considerable quantities of Chinese porcelain reached Virginia within a decade of settlement.

The finds at Drake's Bay represent an example of the problems that can arise in assessing a body of artifacts when the documents relating to it are not precise. The artifacts recovered from Drake's Bay have been described and photographs published in various articles, books, and pamphlets (Shangraw and Von der Porten 1981; Von der Porten 1968, 1972). But the lack of concrete documentation for the exact location of Drake's landing in 1579 raises problems about assigning that early a date to some of the Chinese ceramics recovered at Drake's Bay. The earliest accounts extant of Drake's 1579 voyage to the Pacific were written respectively twenty and fifty years after the voyage and do not describe the precise geographical location of the landing (Hanna 1979, 85–8, 96–9). On the basis of these accounts, Drake appears conclusively to have landed somewhere within the thirty-eighth parallel, in an area inhabited by the Miwak Indians, but that area encompasses miles of shoreline that has changed since the sixteenth century.

It is probable that Drake and Sebastian Rodriquez Cermeno were the only western captains who landed in the area of Drake's Bay. The difficulties created by winds and currents made sailing down the California coast a very chancy venture in the sixteenth century, and surviving documentation indicates that no one attempted it unless forced to do so (personal communication, Edward Von der Porten). Such forced landings inevitably loom large in the accounts of the few voyages to the Pacific that took place in the late sixteenth century. Drake and Cermeno, a Portuguese captain on his way from Manila in the *San Augustin*, were the only two captains known to have landed in the vicinity and known through documentation to have carried Chinese porcelain aboard. Furthermore, a very good circumstantial case for Drake's landing at Drake's Bay has been made by Raymond Aker and Edward Von der Porten on the basis of geographical and geological evidence, and Von der Porten and Clarence Shangraw have carefully separated wave-worn sherds from broken wares found at Drake's Bay and related the former to Drake's cargo of 1579 (Aker and Von der Porten 1979; Shangraw and Von der Porten 1981). In the absence, however, of any documentary record of the exact location of Drake's landing and any artifacts specifically connected with Drake, it might be prudent to assign a *terminus post quem* of 1595 to the porcelain found in the Indian middens at Drake's Bay; Cermeno's account of his shipwreck survives and is quite precise about its location, the present-day Drake's Bay (translated in Wagner 1924).

Lacking firm documentary and artifactual evidence of Drake's landing at Drake's Bay, students of the artifacts found there will have to decide the issue for themselves. There is, of course, the possibility of wrecks in the area for which no documentation survives, a possibility that muddies the waters considerably. But many of the sherds from Drake's Bay bear a great resemblance to whole pieces in the Ardebil Shrine collection, so that they can definitely be dated as a group to the late sixteenth century. Some of the cruder wares among the sherds from Drake's Bay resemble a small group of Chinese export porcelains excavated on sites in Tidewater Virginia and thus confirm the early date of the Virginia artifacts (van der Pijl-Ketel 1982, 18–19).

The ceramics from the *Witte Leeuw* have provided the single most useful source for a study of the iconography and iconology of the Chinese porcelain sherds in the James River basin. The study of the documents relating to the *Witte Leeuw* and the ceramics from the ship enables us to date many of the sherds found in the James River basin and also provides strong circumstantial evidence for their means of transport to the Virginia colony. The documentation involving every possible aspect of the ship's activities is superb, and most of it remains in the archives of the Dutch East India Company. The Department of Dutch History at the Rijksmuseum has recently published an exemplary reference book on the finds from the ship, *The Ceramic Load of the Witte Leeuw*, in which these documents are cited, and, in some cases, quoted extensively. The bill of lading survives for the *Witte Leeuw*'s homeward voyage in early 1613, but makes no mention of any Chinese porcelain, which proved to be the preponderance of the finds (ibid., 19–20). There are also numerous accounts of the sinking of the *Witte Leeuw*. The most complete account of the ship's destruction was written by John Tatton, master of the *Pearle*, an English ship that had joined the small Dutch fleet on the journey home from Bantam, on the northwest coast of Java. According to Tatton, the *Witte Leeuw* was blown up by a malfunction of one of its own guns during an engagement with a Portuguese carrack in Jamestown harbor off the island of St Helena. The stern, which probably contained the diamonds the ship was carrying to Holland, was blown to pieces, but the porcelain, packed in pepper, was remarkably well preserved under the circumstances.

The excavation of the *Witte Leeuw* presents some problems, largely because of its location. Jamestown was a very busy port for over three hundred years, and Robert Stenuit, the Belgian underwater archaeologist who led the expedition, writes of finding wrecks of all periods as well as modern Coca Cola bottles in the vicinity of the *Witte Leeuw*'s remains (ibid., 26). The excavation was perforce quite untidy, and a considerable quantity of eighteenth- and nineteenth-century Chinese exportware surfaced along with Wan Li (1573–1619) ceramics. The very bulk and uniformity of the rest of the Chinese porcelain is so convincing, however, that I have no difficulty accepting the vast majority of the porcelain as having been produced prior to 1613.

The ceramic load of the *Witte Leeuw* relates to both the iconography and the iconology of the early Chinese ceramics in the James River basin. First, the fact that in many cases the wares found in Virginia are identical to wares carried on the *Witte Leeuw* enables us to date the sherds in Virginia quite precisely to the late Wan Li period. Second, they may provide a clue to the Dutch presence in the James River basin, which is borne out in a circumstantial manner by documentary evidence and may explain the way in which this early seventeenth-century porcelain reached Virginia. Finally, the ceramics from an early Dutch East Indiaman allow us to hypothesize about

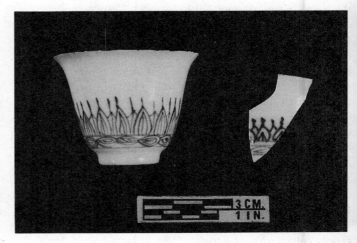

Fig. 2.9. Wine cup excavated from the *Witte Leeuw* (*White Lion*) (1613) with sherd from the Virginia Research Center for Archaeology

the nature of the porcelain to reach the Protestant west, and particularly Virginia, in the early years of the China trade. The last two issues relate to the iconology of the Chinese porcelain in Virginia and will be discussed below.

A stylistic comparison of some of the wares on the *Witte Leeuw* with the sherds found in the James River basin indicate that much of the porcelain found here on seventeenth-century sites is indeed late Wan Li. Perhaps the best known parallel between the sherds in Tidewater Virginia and the *Witte Leeuw* is a series of wine cups, some twenty of which were retrieved whole from the shipwreck, along with sherds comprising about twenty more. They are about forty millimeters high and about forty-nine or fifty millimeters wide. The cups are very fine (semi-egg shell) porcelain, carefully potted and neatly painted with a scroll design directly above the footring and a 'flame pattern' or spear motif above the scroll band. An identical cup about two-thirds complete was found at Kingsmill in 1955 and is now in the possession of the National Park Service at Jamestown. Sherds of this ware have been found on numerous other sites along the James, including Governor's Land (ibid., 156–7; personal communication, Merry Outlaw, Curator, Virginia Research Center for Archaeology, Yorktown; see fig 2.9). Excavations of a second East Indiaman, the *Banda*, sunk in Mauritius in 1615, confirm the early date of these wine cups, as does a still-life by Christoffel van der Berghe, dated 1617, in the Philadelphia Museum of Fine Arts, that depicts two identical wine cups.

A second ware frequently found on James River sites that surfaced in quantity from the *Witte Leeuw* is a bowl about 110 millimeters in diameter and about fifty millimeters high, with rounded sides and a slightly concave footring (fig 2.10). In counterdistinction to the finely potted wine cups, these bowls are poorly made, of coarse clay containing obvious impurities, and the footrings appear to have been cut off with a wire; unlike the footrings on almost all Chinese wares, however

Fig. 2.10. Bowl found on numerous seventeenth century sites in the James River basin c. 1610–25. Author's collection

crude, these show little or no effort at molding. Sand adheres to the footrings of all these bowls. The cobalt blue is watery in places but inky in others, and blobs of unrefined cobalt have burst through the heavy blueish overglaze, which is full of pinholes. The footring is surrounded by one or two plain bands of underglaze blue, and a similar line surrounds the outside and interior rim. In the center of the interior, a hastily painted flower can be discerned by the imaginative, surrounded by a blue band. The exterior is decorated by very badly rendered lotuses connected by tendrils and scrolls. The most complete bowl of this type so far found in Virginia was excavated at the 'enclosed area' at Flowerdew Hundred, but other examples have surfaced at two other seventeenth-century sites, Governor's Land and Eppes Island (van der Pijl-Ketel 1982, 156–7; personal communication, Jane Townes, Department of Anthropology, College of William and Mary, and Merry Outlaw, Curator, VRCA).

Other wares from the *Witte Leeuw* with counterparts in the James River basin should be briefly mentioned. A bowl decorated with large well painted peonies, leaves, and wide tendrils is represented by sherds at Jamestown, extremely finely potted and painted, and by a cruder example at Governor's Land (van der Pijl-Ketel 1982, 148–9). The rim-sherd of a large 'clapmuts', or shallow dish with flattened rim, decorated with a swastika pattern like that used opposite the monster masks on kraakware, was unearthed at Shirley Plantation in Charles City County, on the north bank of the James River (ibid., 110–11; personal communication, Theodore Reinhart, Department of Anthropology, College of William and Mary, Williamsburg). And the bottom of a two-chambered covered box like one found on the *Witte Leeuw* was excavated at Governor's Land. The Virginia example is decorated with a spray of long grasses, whereas the bottom of the box from the *Witte Leeuw* is decorated with thorn-covered branches. Recently, an entire footring of one of the deep cups, called 'crow cups' by the Dutch, decorated with beaded pendants on the interior and a bird on the rock' on the interior footring, was found on a site

survey at Flowerdew Hundred Plantation. Numerous examples of such cups were found among the artifacts from the *Witte Leeuw* (van der Pijl-Ketel 1982, 120, 124).

While the wares from the *Witte Leeuw* cannot be used to date all the Virginia sherds made in Wan Li's China, they do serve to establish an early seventeenth-century date for the cruder sorts of wares that are, in fact, the most difficult to date because they so little resemble the marked examples found in most museums.

Other facets of the iconography of Chinese porcelain can be studied only by reference to documentary sources either directly or indirectly. The symbols, both Chinese and Christian, that decorate the exportware can be studied in reference works on Asian and Christian iconography (Williams 1976; Ferguson 1961). Those students of material culture who would fathom the meaning of the scenes and stories that cover many of the export and domestic wares must have recourse to works on Eastern religions and their expressions in Chinese art over the centuries, as well as to Chinese literary sources. Finally, scholars who wish to use changes in landscape and figure painting on the ceramics as a means of dating the wares must study particular works on the history of Chinese painting and woodblock prints (cf. Ferris 1968; Shih 1976). The iconography of Chinese export porcelain in the James River basin can be understood only in reference to many documentary sources and monographs based on such documents.

Once the most elementary problems relating to the iconography of an artifact have been addressed, the discerning scholar will turn his or her attention to questions of iconology, the cultural symbolism of the artifact. He or she will attempt to discover the intrinsic meaning of the artifact to the society of which it was a part, in this case the world of international trade and the society of colonial Virginia. Only by recourse to documents and secondary sources based on the documents can the historical archaeologist, historian, or ceramicist comprehend the iconology of the Chinese export porcelain found in newly settled Virginia.

The very act of dating and identifying the thousands of Chinese export sherds unearthed in Tidewater Virginia gave rise to a number of questions relating to their iconology that can be answered only by consulting specific written sources. The majority of the sherds in four local archaeological collections can be dated either to the first quarter of the seventeenth century or to the period following the rebuilding of the kilns at Jingdezhen in 1681. The gap of fifty years between the early seventeenth-century ceramics and the extremely large quantity of Kang Hsi vessels found on Tidewater Virginia sites might have told us something about the nature of colonial Virginia society. But since no other artifacts exhibit a similar gap in their appearance on colonial Virginia sites, the iconological significance of the few Transitional wares found in the James River basin must be sought elsewhere. The chronological disposition of the Chinese export sherds can probably be explained entirely by porcelain's role as an object of colonial trade.

Much of the gap between the earlier and late seventeenth-century importation of Chinese export ware can be explained by the fact that the Chinese civil war made porcelain more or less unobtainable to the west between about the late 1640s and the early 1680s. Chinese history informs the student of iconology that the Manchu dynasty, which took control of most of China from the Ming partisans in 1644, failed to win complete control of the south coast and coastal waters until after 1683. In order to prevent Chinese trade goods from falling into the hands of the Ming partisans who controlled the waters of south China, the Manchus forbad all export trade (Fairbank et al. 1978, 216–17). Thus, in 1645, the English found Macao 'destitute of all sorts of commodities . . . but China ware' because of the rebellion (Foster 1906–27, 250–1; India Office Library, Factory Records, China and Japan, G/12/1, 'China. 1664, Voyage of the Surat Frigate to Macao'. Crown copyright material in the India Office Records is reproduced by permission of the Comptroller of Her Majesty's Stationery Office). In 1645, the Dutch, who had a factory in Formosa, began having difficulty filling their orders, and by 1657, the porcelain trade between the Dutch East India Company and Chinese merchants from the mainland ceased operations (Volker 1971, 54, 58–9).

Porcelain production proceeded during much of the Transitional period between the demise of the Ming and the rise of the Ching dynasties, but production was halted in 1675 by the sacking and burning of much of Jingdezhen during the Revolt of the Three Feudatories.[5] With the suppression of the mainland rebellion in 1680, the young emperor Kang Hsi appointed a supervisor to oversee production at the newly reorganized imperial kilns and abandoned the practice of using forced labor at the kilns, a source of much unrest. These changes revitalized the kilns almost immediately. In 1681, the Dutch East India Company recommenced the porcelain trade that was soon to flood the Continent with Chinese wares, and the British followed suit about fourteen years later (Kilburn 1981, 14–15; Medley 1976, 240–1). Thus history informs the student of iconology that the chronology of the Chinese export sherds found in Tidewater Virginia reflects porcelain's role as a commodity in international trade.

An understanding of the role of Chinese porcelain in seventeenth-century international trade raises a further question about the iconology, or cultural symbolism, of the porcelain that can be answered only by the documents: the manner in which the Virginia colonists obtained their porcelain. Since Virginia was a British colony, logic would seem to dictate that both the Wan Li and Kang Hsi exportware arrived in Virginia through the good offices of the British East India Company. But this surmise would be wrong; the documents clearly indicate that the Honourable East India Company did not import Chinese porcelain to London in quantity until the 1690s.

The records of the Honourable East India Company, many of which survive in London, clearly indicate that the British carried on a brisk trade in porcelain throughout the east during much of the seventeenth century. The English bought quantities of porcelain from Chinese junks that sailed to Java in the 1610s and 1620s and traded it in Asia, as far west as Persia, where they enjoyed trading privileges under Shah Abbas, who established the Ardebil Shrine (Foster 1906–27, 42, 208; Danvers and Foster 1896–1904, V, 246). They also used it as tribute to foreign rulers, and a number of references can be found in the records to porcelain brought back to England by officers and crew as 'private trade'.[6] But of all the surviving bills of lading for ships bound for London prior to 1650, none but those of the *James*, which sailed from Macao in 1615, and the *Catherine*, which left Macao in 1637, mention porcelain. And porcelain is conspicuously absent from the London sales listed in the *Court Minute Books* of the 1660s and 1670s. The only other known instance in which porcelain was officially dispatched to England illustrates its uncommon occurrence. In 1646, company factors loaded the England-bound *Eagle* with piece goods, pepper, indigo, and other unusual commodities, to which they added the twenty tubs of china brought by the *Hinde* from Macao, 'thinking that, as so much plate had been melted down in England during the Civil War, there would probably be more demand for such substitutes' than there had been earlier in the century (Danvers and Foster 1896–1904, II, 325; Morse 1926 (1646–50), viii, 14; see also Foster 1906–27, 250–1). The lack of demand for export porcelain in England before the 1680s awaits explanation, but until the 1690s, the English did not share the Dutch enthusiasm for the commodity (Godden 1979, 26). So East India Company shipping was probably not responsible for the presence of the early seventeenth-century exportware in the James River basin.

The presence of Wan Li export wares on seventeenth-century Virginia sites is difficult to explain at present. Based on the stylistic resemblance between the ceramic loads of the *Witte Leew* and the *Banda*, both Dutch ships, and the sherds retrieved from the early sites on the banks of the James, it is tempting to assume that Dutch traders brought the porcelain, as well as other commodities, to exchange for Virginia tobacco. The Dutch presence in Virginia since 1620 has been well documented, and John Pagan has shown that between 1640 and 1660, Dutch merchants established factories in Virginia and made themselves very useful to Tidewater tobacco growers. Nevertheless, we know little of the details of Dutch trade with Virginia before 1635; the relevant documents, such as the Amsterdam and Middleburg Notarial Archives of that period, remain to be studied. The absence of Chinese porcelain dating to the 1630s is also puzzling. Future documentary research in Dutch archives and English customs records may yield more information on the role of early seventeenth century Chinese porcelain as a commodity in international trade in Virginia.

The role of Chinese export porcelain as a commodity of trade explains the presence of the late seventeenth- and early eighteenth-century exportware sherds on Tidewater Virginia sites. And Chinese porcelain's role as a commodity in international trade in the late seventeenth century can be understood only with reference to such manuscript material as the records of the British East India Company. The India Office Records not only explain how the porcelain got to London; they also provide a partial explanation for the variety of wares found in the James River basin. Charles II, who returned to the throne in 1660, encouraged the passage of Navigation Acts whose enforcement effectively removed the Dutch from colonial trade and insured that almost all commodities manufactured in Europe or the east came in bulk through the port of London on British ships.

The extant records of the British East India Company reveal that the English did not start importing Chinese export porcelain to London as an official commodity until the 1690s. Furthermore, the importation of Chinese porcelain to London was directly related to the growing custom of drinking tea, coffee, and, to a lesser extent, chocolate in England and the colonies (Chaudhuri 1978, 406; Godden 1979, 26–7, 36, 119). The records of sales held by the East India Company illustrate the great variety of wares and of decoration on the ware brought into London, and a gradual shift to enormous quantities of 'ordinary ware' to meet the growing demand in England, Ireland, and the colonies.

In the first major porcelain sale for which records survive, the cargo of the *Sarah* yielded twelve beakers, ten 'rowl waggons' (tall, narrow vases) and two square bottles sold in different lots. But the merchant Gerrard Muyshen also bought coffee cups and saucers in lots of 2,100 and 913, and the following day, Paul Dominique bought 1,726 cups from the *Sarah* as well as twelve spitting pots. At a sale on January 6, 1696/7, of the *Dorothy*'s cargo, Mathew Long bought 2,360 tea cups at seven pence each and 2,100 at seven and one quarter pence each. These items were probably blue and white, because polychrome objects were designated 'painted' in the sales inventories (India Office Library, *Home Miscellaneous Series* 9, December 12, 14, 16, 18, 1696; January 6, 1697).

By 1704, the East India Company was offering a great variety of objects for sale, greater than it was to offer a decade later. At a sale of the *Union*'s cargo in 1704, you could buy a lot of seventy Dutchmen sitting, twelve Men on Sea Monsters, '21 ditto broke', sixty-five 'pulpitts with Paderies', three images with golden bellies and black faces, three Devils, and many other interesting forms. Other sales proffered roosters on rocks and boys on toads, some of which survive in museums in the United States and in Europe. But at the same sales, utilitarian wares predominated. Tea bowls were available in lots of 1,800 and 2,200 and their saucers in similar quantities, blue and white between three pence and six pence and painted ones between three and seven pence. You could also buy a lot of ten fine hubblebubbles (houkas) at sixty-one shillings, 173 painted tea pots at six shillings a pot, and 193 blue and white plates for one shilling each (ibid., 12, 30–67, 186–223; see 62–5 and 220–1 for types of figures). In 1704, the prices for the more extraordinary objects might have prevented their export to Virginia. Merchants had to make their mark-ups and pay freight for objects transhipped. Furthermore, the small numbers of

expensive peculiar forms almost guaranteed that they would make their way into specialized local markets and not into mass markets for Ireland and the colonies. But such assertions remain a surmise; few data on re-exporting survive from the William and Mary and Queen Anne periods.

The Company's sales of 1704 illustrate the wide variety of decoration and shape of even utilitarian wares of the period, a variety of which is reflected to some extent in the sherds from Tidewater Virginia. Even those staples of the trade, tea, coffee, and chocolate cups, were scalloped, ribbed, octagonal, square, and came in all sorts of color combinations: red, gold, and white, cream-colored bowls with red rims, black with gold rims, and so on (ibid., 35, 156, 206).

By 1712, however, the directors of the East India Company began a process of standardization that was to continue throughout the eighteenth century. The Company's *Dispatch Books* of that year specify the Company's order for ceramics was comprised of two categories: dinner services and beverage sets. The high volume items were 40,000 chocolate cups with handles, 110,000 tea cups with saucers, 6,000 tea pots, 10,000 milk jugs, and 2,000 sets of small sugar bowls, two to a set. The company directed the supercargoes not to buy 'large pieces such as jars, Beakers or great dishes or bowls' as they were out of fashion (quoted in Chaudhuri 1978, 408).

The trend towards standardization continued. A surviving sales catalogue of 1721 offers blue and white coffee cups in groups of 10,000 divided into five lots, 77,336 blue and white tea cups and saucers divided into twenty-seven lots, and other similar items (India Office Library, *Home Miscellaneous Series* 14, 196–205). Gone are the large ladies with odd hands, the pulpits with Paderies, and boys on toads. This standardization was occurring at the very moment when Tidewater Virginia began acquiring Chinese export porcelain in bulk. Given the nature of the East India Company's imports, it is no small wonder that, on most of our excavations, a monotonous array of utilitarian forms in blue and white and later polychrome Chinese porcelain confronts us. The records of the British East India Company help in large measure to explain why we find what we do on the banks of the James River and in Williamsburg.

The archaeological collections in Tidewater Virginia reveal that the quantity of export porcelain in the James River basin increased steadily from about 1715 to 1755 (fig 2.11). Local colonial inventories reflect the iconological implications of the increased number of Chinese export sherds dating from the 1720s and the 1730s; the export porcelain represents one manifestation of an improving standard of living that is reflected in local inventories.

In order to understand another facet of the iconology of the Chinese export porcelain, the role and frequency of 'China ware' in colonial Virginia households, the local inventories provide a valuable source. The James City County records, covering Jamestown and Williamsburg, were burned during the final days of the American Civil War, but a few inventories from Surry county and the entire surviving corpus of

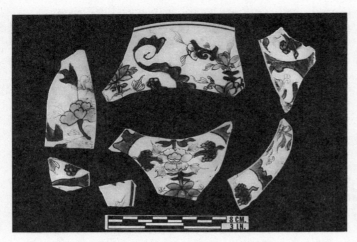

Fig.2.11. Sherds from Imari meatplate c. 1725. Jamestown National Historic site

inventories and wills from Yorktown, Virginia, have been transcribed. The Yorktown inventories are of particular interest in the absence of those from James City because excavations at several buildings in Yorktown yielded substantial amounts of Chinese export porcelain dating from the seventeenth century.

The Yorktown records provide no clue to the frequency and role of Chinese export porcelain in Tidewater Virginia prior to 1730. Between 1633, when the records commence, and the 1680s, the majority of the vessels mentioned in the inventories and wills have to do with preparing rather than consuming food. Some of the vessels mentioned were related to processing dairy products, but the majority were metal: pots, skillets on stands, frying pans, and copper kettles (cf. 'Inventory of John Hartwell', *York County Deeds, Orders, Wills* 2, 1645–49, 395). The inventories reveal a lack of interest in eating vessels in general; plates and drinking vessels seem to have had little value in the eyes of the appraisers before the 1690s, perhaps because the ceremonies surrounding the consumption of food were so much simpler than they were to become. By the 1690s, the Yorktown records reveal that this attitude had changed, but between the 1690s and 1717, there is not one mention of 'China ware' in the Yorktown wills and inventories.[7] Thus the documents belie the archaeological record in this instance.

By 1730, the Yorktown records indicate that the prevalence of Chinese export porcelain used for serving tea had increased markedly. Between 1730 and 1750, out of thirty-four tea services recorded in the inventories, twenty-two contained some pieces of Chinese export ware (Beaudry 1978b, 207–9). The inventories for Bacon's Castle, in Surry County, reveal a similar trend. By 1728, Arthur Allen III of Bacon's Castle, who died possessed of a tea pot, a coffee pot, and a chocolate pot of indeterminate material, also had eight china cups and a china plate. His father, who died in 1711, owned no equipment for drinking any of the stylish new beverages (Surry County Records, *Deed Book, 1715–30*, 807–10; *Deed Book, 1709–15*, 84–8). The Yorktown records indicate, however, that a

majority of its inhabitants drank from pewter and earthenware and ate off pewter, earthenware, or treen. This fact raises questions in view of the considerable quantity of export porcelain remains of cups, bowls, and plates predating 1750 that have surfaced in Yorktown and elsewhere in Tidewater Virginia.

The Yorktown records and local archaeological excavations confirm another of the iconological aspects of the Chinese sherds found in the James River basin. The exportware sherds made between 1690 and 1750 are an indication of the rising standard of living that affected the colony in this period (Carson and Walsh 1981, 45–7). There is a much greater mass of Chinese porcelain in the local archaeological collections dating to the 1750s than there is in those of the 1710s or the 1720s. The increasingly frequent use of specialized vessels made of Chinese porcelain is also reflected in the Yorktown inventories.

The Yorktown records also confirm perhaps the most significant iconological aspect of eighteenth-century Chinese export porcelain in the James River basin: Chinese exportwares as symbols of wealth. Of the twenty-two men and women who died in Yorktown possessed of Chinese porcelain tea wares between 1730 and 1750, all but one of them had estates valued at more than one hundred pounds sterling. Twelve individuals had estates of between £120 and £600, the rest between £601 and £2693, far above the norm for contemporary colonial Virginians (Beaudry 1978b, Appendix 3). The widespread distribution of sites yielding early seventeenth-century export porcelain at Jamestown appears to indicate that this particular luxury item was widely held. On this point the documentary record again confirms the archaeology. During the seventeenth century, Jamestown was inhabited primarily by affluent Virginians.

The study of Chinese export porcelain sherds excavated from sites in the James River basin illustrates the manner in which documentary research can illuminate artifacts from the historical past and elevate their study from the antiquarian and the particular to the historical and general. If archaeologists fail to carry their analysis of the artifact beyond the iconographical level, only dating the object and explaining its artistic symbolism to its own age, their work will lose much of its significance to scholars in other disciplines. The study of iconology, or the cultural symbolism of an artifact, is particularly significant to scholars of other persuasions. Thus, for example, the sherd of Chinese export porcelain becomes an important object of colonial trade to the economic historian. The presence of early seventeenth-century export porcelain sherds in the James River basin provides historians with an incentive to investigate further the early trade between the Dutch and the first two generations of settlers in Virginia. And the discovery of a considerable quantity of Wan Li porcelain and an even larger quantity of porcelain dating to the 1690s and later, raises questions for the social historian as well as the economic historian and the Chinese ceramicist.

Whatever the scholar's discipline, he or she can only

understand the socio-economics and thus the politics of seventeenth-century Virginia if his or her knowledge is grounded in the artifacts. And the artifacts can often be dated precisely and described iconographically only with the help of the written word. Ultimately, however, it is in the study of the iconology of the artifact, its 'intrinsic meaning' to the society of which it was a part, that the documents become indispensable. Therefore the archaeologist cannot be content to unearth, examine, and describe the artifact, or even to date it precisely and describe its artistic symbols. In order to achieve the full potential of his or her discipline, the historical archaeologist must use documents and the written word to place the artifact in its social, economic, political, and at times even its intellectual milieu.

Notes

1. The analytical scheme that underlies this paper is based on the work of I. Panofsky (1962): see 'Introductory', pp. 5–17.
2. See, for example, Garner and Archer 1972 and Honey 1933. My thanks to John Austin, Associate Director of Collections at the Colonial Williamsburg Foundation, for these suggestions.
3. A few examples must suffice. See Gordon 1977, 47–8. The Imari plate (no. 31) on p. 47 is a relatively early example dating c.1720. Blue and white examples of the same design abound and make its early date more apparent. The *rouge-de-fer* plate on p. 48 (no. 33) with turquoise roundel in the center is a typical ware of its type and would not have been made later than about 1730. See also Godden 1979, 135, no. 36. The vase pictured is typical of Kang Hsi ware made for the Dutch market following the resumption of trade in 1681. In 1974, David S. Howard published *Chinese Armorial Porcelain*, in which he established an almost infallible system of dating eighteenth-century services by categorizing the borders of the wares according to the dates of the armorials painted on the wares. The book is based on a decade of research and removes almost any excuse for misdating eighteenth-century Chinese export wares with borders.

   In another field, Herbert Cescinsky's *English Furniture* (1929) is often cited as containing a number of suspicious and married pieces. The chest of drawers on stand, c.1710, on p. 200, appears to have had its front legs replaced. The dating is probably early as well. Until recently, students of the decorative arts were not encouraged to digest dated work like Chippendale's *Cabinet Maker* and to work with inventoried pieces to insure accuracy of dating. Thus older books should be approached with special caution.
4. For an excellent summary of the stylistic relationship between the wares in the Ardebil Shrine collection and those on the *Witte Leeuw*, see 'Chronology of Kraakporcelain', in C. L. van der Pijl-Ketel, ed., 1982, 49–51. For a discussion of the evolution of styles in kraakware, see Oriental Ceramic Society of Hong Kong 1979, 34–6.
5. The revolt of the Three Feudatories, begun in 1673 and lasting eight years, was led by three Chinese generals who controlled semi-independent feudatories in southeastern and southern China against the second Ching (Manchu) Emperor, Kang Hsi.
6. On private trade, see Sainsbury, ed., 1907–38: 1644–9, p. 37; 1650–4, pp. 59–60; 1671–3, pp. 216, 261; 1674–6, p. 71. See also Godden 1979, 57–59.
7. Mary C. Beaudry points out that the first mention of 'china cups' in the Yorktown records occurs in 1717 (Beaudry 1980, 74).

Chapter 3

Documentary insights into the archaeology of smuggling

Peter R. Schmidt and
Stephen A. Mrozowski

During the seventeenth and eighteenth centuries New England's merchants relied upon smuggling to circumvent British attempts to regulate their economic activities (fig 3.1). This chapter draws upon a wide variety of documentary sources in constructing the cultural context of smuggling. Particular concern is focused on how smuggling techniques were refined and expanded as the British intensified their attempts to end the illicit trade during the decades preceding the American Revolution. Documents such as merchants' letters and other correspondence are employed to provide a detailed picture of the methods used to evade Royal detection. This chapter also contains a discussion of potential archaeological signatures of smuggling that may be useful in comparative research.

3.1 Introduction

The significant anthropological advantage inherent in historical archaeology is that it allows access to many more interpretative constructs than are available to prehistorians who are often without the corpus of culturally sensitive information contained in the documentary record. Through its study, the archaeologist can engage in the historiographic process whereby 'projected contemporary thought about past actuality . . . [is] . . . integrated and synthesized into contexts in terms of cultural man and sequential time' (Taylor 1967, 33). The construction of cultural context is the means by which cultural meaning is attached to any patterns that may be deducted from archaeological evidence. Furthermore, to meet conditions of anthropological and historical adequacy it is important to address problems of historical significance and to use the archaeology to uncover solutions that make important contributions to our ideas about how and why culture changed in the past. To insure this we must carefully research different historical documents and the literature of history to derive constructs that can be synthesized to build a complex cultural context for our archaeological excavation, be it a shipwreck, an Iron Age factory site in Tanzania, or a colonial privy in Rhode Island.

From various historical documents we may construct variable cultural contexts, out of which will come our synthesis and the systemic context in which behavior can be attached to the material world. With these concerns in mind, we now want to propose a problem that can be solved by a combination of documentary, terrestrial, underwater, and shipwreck archaeology.

3.2 Genesis of the problem

The problem that we will develop here found its genesis in an archaeological anomaly. Excavations in Queen Anne Square of Newport, Rhode Island, revealed three large trash pits, two of which dated to the mid-eighteenth century and contained French earthenwares as well as French brandy bottles and Dutch gin bottles (Mrozowski, Gibson, and Thorbahn 1979, 64, 116). Feature 1 at the Carr House contained 33% non-English ceramics, primarily French tin-glazed

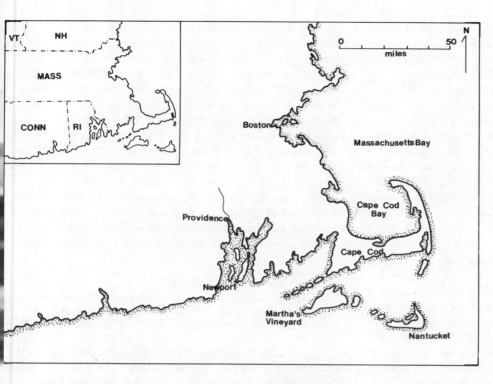

Fig. 3.1. Map of New England coast showing Newport and surroundings

earthenwares. The same feature also held a minimum of two pale blue, square-bodied bottles of a type that Noël Hume (1969a, 70) describes as French and the partial remains of a large Dutch gin bottle (Noël Hume 1969a, 62).

Excavations on the former Brown property in Newport revealed a second mid-eighteenth-century trash pit that contained two bottles identical to bottles described by Noël Hume as Dutch gin bottles. A third trash deposit partially excavated on Bridge Street during a salvage recovery yielded a French faience serving dish cover as well as remains of a Westerwald stoneware mug, a combed slipware plate, and a Chinese porcelain tea cup.

The archaeological evidence and historical evidence suggest that Newporters did acquire, use, and discard French ceramics and Dutch glassware before the Revolution. This observation agrees with Watkins (1973, 191), who emphasizes that 'ceramics of North America partake of far more than simply English traditions sprinkled with a few other North European ingredients.' If we look beyond Newport, we find that French and Dutch ceramics and glassware have been excavated from sites in Philadelphia (Liggett 1978; Cosans 1974), and in Salem, Massachusetts (Moran, Zimmer and Yentsch 1982), both centers of commercial shipping. In both of these colonial cities French or Dutch artifacts were recovered from what appear to be pre-1776 contexts (Liggett 1978, 33; Moran et al. 1982, 120–1).

These finds do not accord with the claim that the Navigation Acts effectively curtailed the importation of European, including French, painted earthenwares into North

American colonial ports until 1775 (Noël Hume 1969a, 140–1). But both history and historical archaeology tell us that the Navigation Acts were notoriously ineffective. They failed to limit the importation of other goods from Europe, especially via Dutch and French colonies in the Caribbean, during the eighteenth century. Moreover, the historical reputation of seventeenth- and eighteenth-century Rhode Islanders is that they were 'a set of lawless, piratical people whose sole business is that of smuggling' (Williams 1961, 140).

Archaeological evidence of the presence of Dutch gin in Newport prior to the Revolution accords with Pinson's findings that European wines and liquors were much desired and liberally consumed by Newport's elite in the fifty years before 1776 (Pinson 1980, 35). The more than moderate incidence of non-English ceramics in pre-Revolutionary trash pits suggests that a similar pattern of consumption may have existed for tableware. These two categories represent only a small proportion of the material culture of colonial America, but they are significant of consumer behavior by the elite and artisans in colonial port cities such as Newport. These goods acted as status markers in Newport society, and they also symbolically represented colonial American independence from British authority.

Another major source of non-English goods was the cargo of ships captured by privateers. Beginning in 1739, privateering became a major activity that employed the many artisans and mechanics involved in ship-related industries (Nash 1979, 165). The seizure of enemy ships and the sale of their cargo was a welcome economic boost for the many merchants who financed the outfitting of the privateers. Its unreliability, however, made privateering no substitute for the trade so necessary to maintain the rum distilleries of New England. Illicit trade was part of an adaptive strategy that allowed colonial merchants to maintain economic stability. Through duplicity they could insure a steady flow of sugar and molasses from the French and Dutch plantations in the Caribbean. They could also maintain control of the trade in quality goods while securing the finer items they desired. The circumstances surrounding the activity of privateers did not always afford the level of economic manipulation sought by the merchants of New England's cities. By periodically constricting the flow of much desired consumer goods, merchants could effectively influence prices, thereby manipulating the economic system for their own benefit.

The secondary literature on colonial economic life (e.g., Nash 1979; Bridenbaugh 1955; Andrews 1938) affirms that relatively little is known about the details and behavior surrounding the smuggling trade. Furthermore, how do we reconcile the dissonance between the archaeological evidence and the secondary histories on this period? We find that most historians of the illicit trade display considerable bias in their focus on major commercial commodities, such as molasses, sugar, rum, and tea. But what of the less visible and less economically important goods imported by the same ships that carried the primary goods?

Primary documents should allow us to see patterns of behavior associated with the smuggling trade into Newport, how and why that trade changed, and what goods were smuggled. But the documentary record is a fragmentary and limited one. Archaeology has the power to testify more concretely as to how goods were smuggled and why smuggling techniques changed through time. It can also furnish the material correlates of a set of behaviors that speak to a variety of issues ranging from economic manipulation by colonial merchants to the broader question of the relationship between dominance and resistance.

In harmony with the principles we set out previously, we began to examine the historical record, working primarily in the splendid archives of the Newport Historical Society. We sampled a variety of documentary domains, such as Merchants Day Books and Waste Books, in which the name of the purchaser is entered under the date along with the amount of purchase; payroll or receipt books of merchants in which they entered payment of debts, payment of artisans for work completed, payment of sailors, etc.; bills of lading, on which the goods being shipped are listed along with the vessel's name and master's name; invoices of goods shipped; letters of masters, agents, and factors to ship owners; receipts of shipments to local merchants and farmers; journals; probate inventories; command papers from ship owners to masters; and many other miscellaneous documents.

This preliminary study has provided us with a variety of cultural constructs that are best synthesized for the purposes of archaeology around the following questions. How did the

colonial smugglers conduct their clandestine affairs? If smuggling behavior changed, then what caused this change and how is the behavioral change manifest in the material record? With these questions answered we can then address the more significant question of why have the non-commercial goods been ignored in the literature of smuggling; what does the prevalence of smuggling suggest about the economic relationship between colony and mother country; what were the ideological prerequisites for such a relationship; and, can the material signatures of that ideology be applied historically and cross-culturally to provide a framework for studying the broader issue of dominance and resistance? First, we turn to the secondary literature to discern the primary trends in laws, economic life, and political relationships that provide the context for smuggling in colonial Newport and Rhode Island.

3.3 Historical background

Many colonial gentlemen sincerely believed that the clandestine traffic they pursued entailed no stigma of treason or loss of respectability, and a large portion of the citizens agreed with them.   (Bridenbaugh 1955, 64)

The history of Rhode Island smuggling goes back to the seventeenth century and the regular violation of the Navigation Act by Rhode Islanders. The Act of 1660 required that shipments to the colonies take place in English vessels and listed enumerated products from the colonies that had to be shipped to England; the Staple Act of 1663 prohibited importation of goods not loaded in England; the 1673 Plantation Duties Act closed a loophole, requiring that goods shipped from colony to colony could not be reexported to Europe; and the 1696 Act set up new enforcement machinery (Bigelow 1930; Andrews 1938, IV). These laws had little effect on commerce in the colonies, and violation of their provisions was commonplace. In that respect, virtually everyone involved in international trade was, technically, a smuggler.

By the beginning of the eighteenth century a customs service similar to that of England had been established. Significantly, Rhode Island was the last colony to enter the system (Williams 1961, 140). By this time Rhode Island merchants had already gained a reputation as aggressively resistant to any exercise of authority over their free trade, especially with the foreign islands of the Caribbean. Rhode Island participation in trade with the foreign islands increased rapidly between 1714 and 1724. In 1714, 50% of the incoming vessels from the West Indies came from Barbados and only 1% from a foreign possession; by 1724, 40% of the vessels returning from the West Indies came from foreign ports (Bigelow 1930, I, IV, 4–6). Protests from the British planters in the Caribbean finally resulted in the passage of the Molasses Act of 1733 that laid prohibitive duties upon the importation of foreign rum, molasses, and sugar into the colonies (McClennan 1912, 34; Andrews 1938, IV, 242).

The levy of 6d per gallon of molasses from the French islands, if enforced, would have had disastrous economic consequences for Newport. While Boston merchants felt the effects of enforcement in 1740 (Andrews 1938, IV, 242–4), the Newport trade in these illegal commodities continued uninterrupted. The distilleries of Newport obtained foreign molasses with no apparent difficulties from customs officials. Furthermore, during the 1740s, French goods were brought in legally by privateers who operated successfully out of Newport during King George's War, 1744–8.

It is clear, however, that the local merchants were aware of the law and that they realized that their active trade with the French islands was illegal; hence, there was some concern that their off-loading of goods not be observed by customs officials. For example, James Brown of Providence wrote to one of his captains in 1736 to warn him

> not to be too bold when you come home. Enter in the West Indies [west inlet between the mainland and Conanicut Island, avoiding Newport] if you can, and if you cannot bring too, down the River and send your Cargo. Some to Road Island, and some up here in boats, so as not to bring but a few hhds [hogsheads] up to my Wharff . . . (quoted in Bigelow 1930, I, V, 8)

This indicates that Rhode Island merchants were clearly involved in what was then and now considered smuggling. Furthermore, the duties collected by customs officers could not have paid for their salaries in that self-sufficient system. They lived in a style much beyond their means. The total customs duties in all of North America between 1733 and 1750 averaged only £350 sterling each year; the Molasses Act and Navigation Acts had been neutralized by successful evasion of the law (Bigelow 1930, II, III, 11). To be sure, smuggling and bribery were widely practiced, but smuggling was carried out without fear of reprisals.

Newporters continued to trade with the French islands with impunity into the 1750s. With the advent of the Seven Years War in 1756, trading with the French increased under Flags of Truce issued by the Rhode Island governor.

A major source of conflict between the British and the colonies developed from the widespread commerce that the colonies carried on with the enemy (Sachs and Hoogenboom 1965, 146; Bigelow 1930, II). New Englanders ran the Caribbean blockades at great risk but for significant profit. Newporters actively participated in this trade, simply continuing their open intercourse with the French that prevailed in the early fifties, when French traders could be found in Newport recruiting trade to Cape Breton and Cape François (Bridenbaugh 1955, 66). Much of this trade apparently had the official sanction of colonial officials, as customs officer Robert Robinson complained that Deputy Governor Ellery refused to assist customs and openly allowed Newport merchants to unload their ships on the west side of Conanicut Island (ibid.).

British efforts to suppress trade with the enemy increased in 1758 and 1759. By 1760–1 the British blockade was a complete success. Up until this time Newporters had carried out their trade without fear. Detection of smuggling in Narragansett Bay was difficult. The many islands, coves, and

rivers of the bay were easily accessible to Newport, situated at the head of the bay. Once goods were off-loaded on Conanicut Island or onto small boats west of the island, they were transported by boat to Rhode Island (Aquidneck Island), where they would be transported by wagons to the wharves and warehouses along Newport's waterfront.

All this changed in 1763. As the expenses of the war increased and British debt grew, the treasury realized that the North American deficits had to be covered and revenues increased (cf. Andrews 1938, IV, 217). In 1764, the treasury recommended harsh new measures to bring smuggling under control in the colonies. This was a critical turning point in resolve to suppress the trade that Newporters and other Rhode Islanders thrived upon.

British irritation over Newport's central role in smuggling led to the posting of H.M.S. *Squirrel* in Narragansett Bay in the winter of 1763–4 'for the enforcement of fair trade and the prevention of smuggling' (Bridenbaugh 1955, 259). The presence of a British warship in Narragansett Bay created an unprecedented stressful situation for smuggling. This and other related enforcement measures created an altogether different climate. The British resolve resulted in the Trade Acts of 1764, 1765, and 1766, the second Townshend Act that established the American Board of Customs Commissioners, and the Townshend Duties of 1767.

Pressure mounted in 1763 with the circulation of a letter to all governors reminding them of their responsibilities to enforce trade laws (Barck and Lefler 1958, 511). At the end of 1763 and early in 1764, the colonies prepared various memorials against the renewal of the Molasses Act. The Rhode Island petition admitted that 82% of its molasses came from foreign sources (Jensen 1968, 79–80) and that the Dutch colonies of Surinam and St Eustatius also supplied bills of exchange and some molasses. Nevertheless, the Revenue or Sugar Act of 1764 soon followed. Particularly obnoxious to Rhode Island were the new enforcement policies of the customs service and the new court of Vice-Admiralty to be located in Halifax. If enforced, the legislation meant dire consequences for the Rhode Island merchant/smugglers. Prosperous merchants such as Aaron Lopez, a Portuguese Jew who eventually grew to be Newport's most illustrious merchant prince, stood to lose their fortunes.

The Sugar Act reduced the molasses duty from 6d to 3d – still enough to make smuggling a profitable enterprise until 1766, when it was lowered to 1d. But foreign rum was prohibited. Certain wines, especially French wines, were subject to higher duties, as well as new duties of £7 per ton in wines of Madeira and the Azores (Sachs and Hoogenboom 1965, 159). In 1767, new duties followed upon glass, painters' colors, pasteboards, strawboards, milkboards, painted paper, tea, and various stationery papers (Atton and Holland 1908, 285). These were later modified in 1770, so that such goods manufactured in Great Britain were exempted (Atton and Holland 1908, 290). Silks and other fine textiles from France and the Orient were also heavily duted in the 1764 Act.

Particularly critical for the Newport merchants was the extension of the Hovering Act of George I into the colonies (Barck and Lefler 1958, 512); the Act stipulated that any ship within two leagues of the coast had to carry a list of goods. Failure to produce a list of verified goods meant possible confiscation of unlisted items.

The response of Newport merchants to legislative pressure and the presence of British warships was to increase their trade. The British sent men-of-war to Narragansett Bay to patrol, particularly after 1768. Tensions grew between 1763 and 1776, reaching their peak with the burning of H.M.S. *Gaspee* on June 10, 1773, in Narragansett Bay. The *Gaspee*, significantly, had been harassing the smugglers of Narragansett Bay; in the group that burned her were prominent merchants.

3.4 The problem revised

Smuggling was an integral and popularly accepted part of the Rhode Island economy during the early and mid-eighteenth century. Before 1763, smuggling had been conducted with caution but free of intimidation. There is little evidence to suggest that complex techniques of concealment were used prior to 1763 or that elaborate strategies or tactics were necessary.

The enforcement of British law in Narragansett Bay after 1763 abruptly changed conditions under which smuggling was conducted. We suggest that the stress caused by British attempts to suppress smuggling by the Newport and Providence merchants caused significant change in the way goods were concealed in ships. We also propose that careful analysis and synthesis of various documentary sources will show that adaptation in response to stress caused change in the locales used for smuggling and in the strategies and tactics used to avoid British officials.

3.5 Pre-1763 smuggling

The smuggling trade in tea and wine appears to have been active for the four decades after the Molasses Act was passed in 1733. In a letter from Mayne Burn of Mayne Co. in Lisbon to Johannes Roderick in April 1757, we learn that the Lisbon agents want 'to acquaint you that there is plenty of Bohea Tea to be had at about 2/ to 2/6 / pound on board'.[1] Agents regularly provided price lists to merchants such as Lopez, George Champlin, and the Vernons. Mayne also commented widely on the condition of grain crops in Spain and Portugal and provided comments on other items such as wines and fruits while soliciting business.

The Day Books of Aaron Lopez from the 1750s show that he carried on numerous transactions in tea, most of it Bohea tea obtained from the Dutch in the Caribbean.[2] We have found that on November 23, 1756, Lopez sold in his retail outlet one chest of tea.[3] This suggests that the original packing in chests still prevailed and that the origins of the goods were not concealed – either from customs or from the public. Merchants during the 1750s traded without fear of enforcement

at the Newport end. The Caribbean was a different matter, as the British presence during 1759 and 1760 in the Caribbean meant the virtual cessation of northern trade there by 1761 and 1762 (Bigelow 1930, I, VII, 65). This trend is hard to discern in the account books, however, for we see a surge of exotic goods in Lopez's Day Book in 1758: mohair buttons, shalloon, and silk romals were sold along with silk alamodes in 1759.[4] It is difficult to establish if these goods may have been shipped via Great Britain, but the extra freight, port charges, and some loss in drawbacks would have been adequate motivation for the profit-minded Newporter to circumvent those costs by smuggling. The early 1760s again experienced increased sales in mohair buttons after their ban, as well as in Barcelona silk handkerchiefs, coutreax [?], and even 'rich black Persian silk'.[5]

Lopez, however, was not directly involved in the Caribbean trade at this time. He sent few ships until the four he sent in 1766 (Bigelow 1930, I, VII, 19). These goods, then, Lopez obtained in trade with other merchants more active in the Caribbean, or he was having his whaling ships return with the goods. Lopez continued to deal in tea throughout the sixties, as well as China bowls and dishes.[6]

We see very little evidence for evasive tactics in the historical documents prior to 1763–4, when the British escalated their enforcement of trade laws to eliminate smuggling. Bigelow (1930 II, III, 6) says that the usual method of smuggling from Surinam and St Eustatius before 1763 was for a merchant 'to load a few chests of tea and a few bolts of duck between his hogsheads of molasses. This plan appears to have been very general' (ibid.). Bridenbaugh (1955, 66) echoes this, but claims that the tea and cloth were hidden among wine pipes; he also suggests that Lopez stopped doing this after 1763, but we know that only Lopez's whaling vessels touched St Eustatius or Surinam.

3.6 Strategies and tactics

There is clear behavioral change in smuggling after 1763–4. The stress caused by the presence of men-of-war and the fear of being seized and condemned compelled merchants to develop more clandestine techniques in their smuggling. It is here that we can investigate the material signatures of duplicity, thereby allowing us to operationalize a calculus of resistance and domination. Suppression of smuggling became a politically volatile issue; it reinforced, at an ideological level, the determination of local merchants to continue to prosper at the expense of the Crown. One consequence of this was greater caution in avoidance of official authority. We see great caution in owners' orders for this period. There are separate letters to factors in Surinam and St Eustatius (that can be thrown overboard if necessary) and detailed instructions about *how to smuggle successfully, without risk*. Instructions about smuggling techniques, absent from official orders, appear with increasing regularity after 1763. Adaptation to British enforcement can also be seen in the shift in geographical locales for smuggling in Narragansett Bay and the use of off-loading facilities outside the Bay.

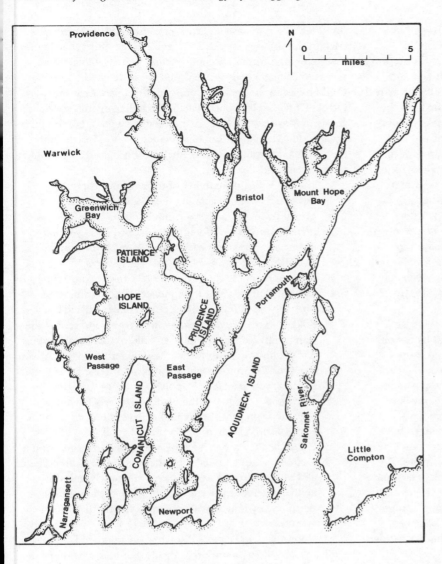

Fig. 3.2. Map showing enlargment of Newport area

Aaron Lopez made explicit his plan to evade detection in tea smuggling when he wrote during 1764 to his agent in Holland:

> have reason to think that the proceeds of such a Loading with the addition of some bills of Excg. being invested in Linseed Oyle & Bohea Tea, put up in Casks made English fashion to contain from 30 to 40 Gallons & shipped directly to St. Eustatia to the address of your Correspondent there . . . .   (Bigelow 1930, II, III, 6)[7]

Lopez admitted that his reason for packing illegal commodities in special casks was *to avoid risk* (ibid.). The size of the cask suggests that a tierce (of approximately forty-two gallons) was the container used. Letters from Lopez to his Amsterdam agents in the latter 1760s, however, indicate that hogsheads of sixty-three gallons capacity or larger were employed by him to transport illegal goods.

Lopez was not alone in his evasive tactics. The Browns of Providence began to employ similar devices in 1764 when the brig *George* was sent to Surinam, but cleared for Barbados. If Captain Whipple failed to purchase molasses at a reasonable price, then he was to buy Russian Duck, 'which you will pack into Dry melasses Hogsheads or other proper Package, and secret in ye most Effectual manner possible and proceed home' (Bigelow 1930, II, III, 7; Hedges 1968, 44–5).

Prior to 1763, the Narragansett Bay smugglers landed most of their illicit goods on Conanicut Island (fig 3.2) west of Aquidneck Island, where Newport is located. Small boats would subsequently carry goods across the bay where they would be collected by wagon for final transport into the warehouses of Newport. But British men-of-war in Narragansett Bay changed this pattern of smuggling. It became too dangerous to off-load on Conanicut Island because the smugglers risked detection and possible seizure. Newporters adapted to this stress by altering their tactics. Captain Whipple, in the employ of the Browns, received carefully detailed instructions from the Browns in 1765 about how to return from Surinam:

As times are we think we can once get the Brigg buy Conamicutt [Conanicut] without their knowing, in Newport, of her arrival Unload and send her Cargo pritty safely with much danger of being Seized but how the severity of the Officers may be by the time of your arrival we Cant Say, ... we Desire you'l Either Com in to the west end of the lite House (which is now in Very Good order) in the Ninte [night] or in the Secunnit way and proceed up as fast [to Providence] as you Can with the Vessill in Case the Wind is so as Can Come along as a man Can buy [by] Land, or other wise Lett your mate Mr. Hopkins on Shore to proceed to us as fast as possible, not stopping for Nite nor foul weither nor telling no person from wenth he Come and we will meet the Brig in Schows and as many hands as needful to unload. (John Carter Brown Library, Brown University, vol. 64 SF; Nicholas Brown & Co. to Capt. Abraham Whipple, 13 January 1765; Bigelow 1930, II, III, 16–17; Hedges 1968, 45)

The plan as set out by the Browns was that Whipple should pass to the west of Conanicut Island or pass by Sakonnet Point up the Sakonnet passage east of Rhode Island (now Aquidneck Island). Failure to make Providence would mean off-loading at night into small boats in either of these passages.

The reduction of the molasses duty to one penny per gallon in 1767 obviated any need to smuggle that commodity. But duties continued on other commodities, and rum from the West Indies was prohibited, thus encouraging smuggling. The Newport merchants continued their clandestine activities. By 1768, enforcement had escalated further, even though customs officers at Newport felt helpless. The Champlins were involved in the prohibited rum trade, as most merchants were, and took the following precautions to avoid British officials. George Champlin wrote to his brother in Newport from the West Indies in 1768:

take 18 or 20 thousand good sug. [sugar] and the Remainder of the Cargoes in Rum. If I get home by the 20th May as it appears here I shall go in the Secunnit way and desire you will leave me a letter at Clarks on Situwist [Sachuest] Point how to conduct if no danger can come in the Harbour say as usual otherwise at my Arrival there will acquaint you of it and you can send a small Vessel and take the rum out Run up the river with it take some Wood on deck and Cary it to Town and I can come a round in the harbour way with the Sug. which will be a Set of Ballast.   (Bigelow 1930, II, III, 22)[8]

The desire for French goods continued to run high after 1763. Some commodities remained attractive, such as sugar, because it was cheaper and of higher quality than what the British islands produced. French manufactured goods remained attractive to the elite because of their limited supply and distinctiveness. There is no indication that there was any abatement of illegal French goods into Newport in the years following 1763. In fact, merchants such as Aaron Lopez went out of their way to devise clandestine plans that would lead to the successful purchase and transportation of French goods back to the willing markets of Newport. The effort that Lopez invested in the formulation of schemes that might gain him access to French goods is illustrated in his detailed orders to Captain Heffernan, master of his sloop, *Lovely Lass*, on 24 October 1770, in Newport. The bill of lading openly consigns goods to Martinique. After first directing Captain Heffernan to proceed to Martinique, Lopez provided a set of instructions that is brilliant testimony to the behavior required to gain entry to the French port.

If there is any probability of trading your cargo to advantage without running the risk of a seizure, to prevent which, I am to recommend *you'll (before your arrival) stove most of your water casks, so as you may enter under pretences of distress.* Soon as you come with your Boat into the Harbour first apply to the Commandant to whom you are to present your request in want of Water. The Consequence of which will most probably be that he will direct you under the care of a Soldier to the Governor, to whom you are to repeat the same distressed situation as you did to the Commandant & I am no way doubtful that the Governor will grant you a permission to refit: when you have obtained that Liberty, you are then to apply to some of the principal merchants & acquaint them with what you have to sell: If they are want of it they will in course intercede with the Governor to grant you a permission to dispose of such Goods as they are in need of, which will once give you a sure change of a [illegible] trade; but if there should be a glut of such articles as you have, the merchants will neither intercede for you nor do I see any advantage in stopping any longer at that Port to run the risk of a seizure.[9]

Noteworthy in Lopez's discourse on commercial duplicity is the absence of any mention of goods that may have been purchased from the French at Martinique. This is undoubtedly purposeful, for an itemization of illegal goods to be purchased in his captain's orders would have been an unnecessary and obvious risk. Such orders were usually communicated orally from owner to master. In the instance of the *Lovely Lass*'s call at Martinique, the sale of goods to Martinique merchants, if successful, probably was not conducted in hard currency or bills of exchange. The transaction was very likely conducted as barter, with Heffernan trading goods mentioned in his bill of lading for French goods, perhaps wine, cloth, and ceramics of equal value.

We do not know if Heffernan succeeded in his Martinique ruse, but if the outcome left him with surplus goods, then he was instructed to sail on to St Lucia where he was to obtain rum, molasses, coffee, cocoa, and sugar at the cheapest price that would assure the best profits. If he failed to procure sufficient illicit goods at St Lucia, then he was to go on to other islands until he found the best market.

Less than one month after his departure from Newport, however, Captain Heffernan was in St Eustatius, the Dutch entrepot in the Windward Islands. The chance preservation of an account kept by Samson Mears, Lopez's agent in St Eustatius, suggests that St Eustatius was the primary port of destination for the *Lovely Lass* (see n. 9). In the last section of his orders, which are partly destroyed, Lopez told Heffernan to go on to St Eustatius where he was to deliver 'the annexed letter to mr. Samson Mears ... [who] ... may have some effects of mine to ship ...' Lopez further said to pay Mears whatever charges he incurred for storage of 'such effects as he delivers you' (see n. 9).

It is difficult to discern what goods made up the 'effects', but we see from other documents that this linguistic term was a euphemistic reference to illicit goods. Mears' account from St Eustatius indicates that Heffernan disposed of all nineteen hogsheads of codfish, all fifteen tierces of rice, 3,400 staves (400 more than listed on the bill of lading), forty barrels of fish (probably menhaden), a parcel of Danish money, 1,600 of 3,000 bunches of onions, and one of twenty-one cheeses. In return Mears supplied twenty-nine hogsheads of rum and a new mainsail, likely made with foreign duck (see n. 9). We do not know if the rum is the 'effects' or if other goods were handled under separate account with Heffernan and Mears. The annexed letter to Mears from Lopez undoubtedly refers to contraband goods. The mainsail purchase was planned in Newport for St Eustatius because of the higher quality of illegal, foreign duck. It is a virtual certainty that the contraband goods conveyed to Newport by the *Lovely Lass* compelled Lopez to instruct his ship's master 'if possible enter into the Harbour early in the Evening that we may have time to do the Needful with your Cargo' (see n. 9).

Lopez's explicit instruction to enter Narragansett Bay in early evening, rather than during the day, admits a concern to avoid detection by British men-of-war or customs officials. The early evening would allow sufficient time to unload and transport illicit goods during the night. The next day the *Lovely Lass* would have put into port with her legitimate goods.

It is apparent that by 1768 the coves and beaches of the Sakonnet passage were the preferred off-loading points, with small boats bringing products to shore. Customs records from the time indicate that this was not the only change that had taken place. Frustration of customs officers over the lack of government support and unified opposition by the local populace was acute in 1768. In a letter to the Commissioners of Trade, 22 April 1768, a customs collector in Newport lamented:

> want of support from the government here, and from the spirit that has prevailed so much of late throughout the colonies there are so many discouragements and embarrasments in an officer's doing his duty as to almost put it out of his power to behave with that fidelity ... that the service of revenue requires.[10]

Even when the Customs officers successfully discovered and seized goods, the items were sometimes robbed out of the customs warehouse,[11] as happened with molasses seized from the brig *Betsy* in 1768.

As stress mounted in the smuggling business, the Newport merchants began to develop dumping areas further afield, out of the immediate territory of the men-of-war and customs officials, as well as improved methods of concealment. Martha's Vineyard and Nantucket apparently became popular entrepots for illicit goods, although we know this only through the testimony of the customs officers (see fig 3.1). Ships sailing from the West Indies or Europe with illicit goods or commodities subject to duty would unload their cargoes at one of the two islands. Then the goods were loaded onto small fishing boats that sailed into Newport unmolested. As Newport customs officers became aware of this tactic, they obtained an order issued by the Commissioners 'to make seizure of all vessels and their cargoes that shall arrive from the said island of Nantucket without proper documents.'[14] The local customs officers informed the Commissioners that neither Martha's Vineyard nor Nantucket had the capacity to produce the mass of goods coming in on non-declaring ships from the two islands (see n. 12: 22 October 1768).

3.7 Discussion of changes

It is clear, then, that the Rhode Island merchants/smugglers adapted their behavior during the 1763–8 period to accommodate the increased efforts to suppress their trade. They began to secrete goods, such as tea, in casks that resembled English manufacture, so that when they returned from the Caribbean with false papers obtained at St Eustatius or some other port their cargo appeared to be uniformly English in character.

The use of molasses hogsheads (fixed at 100 gallons during George II's reign) for textiles similarly shows attempts to secrete goods more successfully in the holds of ships. The first documented instance we have of English-style hogsheads used for contraband goods is their use to convey French molasses from Hispaniola during the English embargo during the Seven Years War. This innovation arose out of the stress created by English attempts to suppress the colonial trade with the enemy (Bigelow 1930, I, IV, 57). Such changes should be possible to document in the archaeology of the period. Adaptations, such as secreting dry goods in containers for liquids, may represent a blueprint for conducting comparative research of similar situations in which economic stress brought about by political regulation brings about innovation in the avoidance of authority. The documents alert us to the possibility that there may be great subtlety in the cargo holds of wrecked ships. The necessity for careful analysis of the contents and form of all casks, hogsheads, tierces, and barrels is apparent. For pre-1763 vessels involved in the Caribbean trade, the evidence suggests that random goods, such as textiles, may have been scattered among the larger cargo or buried beneath the ballast.

We know from bills of lading that the Newport merchants sometimes transported European spirits directly to North America. The brig *Royal Charlotte* with William Pinneger as master sailed from Amsterdam during August, 1769, to Bona Vista, Newfoundland, with a cargo that included twenty-four cases of spirits such as gin and brandy.[13] These spirits likely made their way to Newport with a cargo of fish loaded in Newfoundland. Given the times, it is reasonable to suggest that these goods were probably repacked into hogsheads or other casks, possibly with the fish. Only six months earlier Pinneger had received elaborate orders, both false and genuine, from the Vernons. His genuine orders reflect the increased caution exercised by the Newport merchant/smugglers after 1763:

> it's best to Fill your lower hold with Rum take a few cask of Very good Sugars ... in your hatchway and Proceed here go in the Back side of the Island at Either End and Give us Intelligence these of as soon as Privately Possible, if you Meet with any Men-of-War or Cutter, as there is two In this Port at Present, you must say you Put in Distress for want of Provisions, Water or something Absolutely Necessary ... concealing Every Paper that may give the Least Intimation of your stopping here.
> (Bigelow 1930, II, II, 20–1)[14]

The pre-1763 illegal wine trade into Newport is difficult to document. The open operation of smuggling may have allowed the importation of French and non-exempted Portuguese wines in their original casks. But after the 1764 Revenue Act wines were subjected to heavier duties.

It appears that wine was illegally imported by shipping it in English-style pipes (126 gallons) so that the origins would be camouflaged. In 1759, Mayne in Lisbon supplied Johannes Roderick with 40,000 gallons (about 317 pipes) of white wine in English-style pipes, presumably to avoid duties on non-Madeira wine. In 1767, Aaron Lopez received an order from Mayne in Lisbon for 10,000 pipe staves, with their length stipulated at four feet ten inches, the English measure.[15] During November of 1768, we find that Lopez ordered 4000 double-length red oak staves from a local farmer.[16] These pipe staves may have been destined for the illegal importation of foreign wines. Ships of the period often carried coopers to make up hogsheads to receive West Indies rum and molasses, and many coopers worked in St Eustatius, where foreign wines could easily be transferred to the 'English' pipes. We see this as another important material by-product of adjustments in smuggling behavior to stress caused by increased enforcement.

Aaron Lopez actively pursued his illegal trade in wine, although not always in pipes. In the late summer of 1772, after the burning of the *Gaspee*, the pressure of British enforcement may have fallen off sufficiently to lull Lopez into incautiousness. Ezra Stiles (Dexter 1901, Vol. I, 270) comments in his journal entry of 25 August:

> The Man o'War yesterday seized his [Lopez's] vessel and wines by Accident and Folly of the people who in 5 row Boats were endeavoring the night before to run 91 Quarter Casks of Wine. The Vessel and Wines will be condemned – but it is said that they will be set up a Trifle and Lopez will bid them off at far less than Duties so that he can make his voyage good.

Stiles, in the same entry, commented extensively on the corruption of the local collector, Charles Dudly (ibid., 270–1); his commentary shows, however, that the outright bribery that prevailed in earlier times had grown more subtle, more circumspect. Lopez's captains, for example, were exempted from swearing at the Customhouse and made their entries without oath. The merchant prince's refusal to support the Non-Importation Agreement meant certain advantages with customs, and his largesse with Dudly was known to those who saw wines and fruits delivered to the Collector's house (ibid.).

The clandestine trade in tea was actively pursued throughout the period of heightened tension after 1761. Accounts of daily sales show a fairly constant activity in teas, most of which were never taxed. Along with tea came textiles from the Far East and Europe, as well as other goods such as Barcelona silk handkerchiefs, which are plentifully represented in the retail sales of Newport merchants until 1775.

The details of the illicit trade in consumer goods are, very clearly, elusive and imprecise. But there is sufficient evidence that we cannot conclude, as does Bigelow (1930, II, III, 4), that they are meagre. For the elite of Newport, illicit goods were, it seems, a critical part of their public display of status. The 1764 prohibition on hair buttons, for example, did not affect the continued trade in that commodity and the sale of mohair buttons in Newport (e.g., Lopez Day Books 1764–72). Nor did prohibitive duties on spirits and wine inhibit elite consumption. To the contrary the regulations stimulated ingenious innovations to avoid detection. Many of the changes in smuggling behavior that resulted from stress, such as fear of seizure and loss of income, have left material signatures that we should be able to discern in the archaeological record.

3.8 Smuggling in other contexts

The art of smuggling is an old one, but one that continues today. Although the context might differ, certain continuities remain. The coast of New England is still today a haven for drug traffickers who, like the smugglers of the eighteenth century, off-load their illicit goods from large vessels off-shore, to smaller boats that secrete the goods into port under the cover of darkness. During prohibition, these same tactics supplied much of the northeast with Canadian spirits.

In the Caribbean, smuggling goes on as always. In Grenada, for example, Tobias (1983, 383–400) found widespread recognition and acceptance of smuggling as a means of circumventing an economic system that offers limited opportunity. There is also status to be gained and reputations to be made in smuggling. Obtaining the goods many desire while outfoxing the authorities adds to the mystique of the smuggler's trade, a point much emphasized by Tobias (1983).

In Africa, as well, smuggling has long been a common practice. With the arrival of the colonial powers, however, the need for smuggling increased as it had in the American colonies. During the early part of this century in Egypt for example, the outlawing of the hashish trade, along with tight restrictions on both salt and tobacco, led to widespread smuggling in coastal areas as well as in the desert (Von Dumreicher 1931). British authorities went to incredible lengths to stop the importation of hashish along Egypt's coast. As these security measures grew in effectiveness, the Bedouin tribes were employed by traders to transport hashish overland through the Libyan Desert (Von Dumreicher 1931, 1–14). As the salt monopoly went into effect and duties were placed on food and tobacco, the British authorities had to contend with the corruption of their duty collectors. In many cases the British were actually successful in adding so much to the cost of contraband goods because of increased transportation outlays that the clandestine operations were brought to a halt.

In Kenya, the Portuguese, and later the British, once again were involved in stopping the smuggling of ivory (e.g., Thorbahn 1979, 1984). Here again we see attempts by a colonial power to regulate the exchange of a commodity. In this instance, however, the European market and its connections with the Far East actually added to the demand, thereby raising its price. Portuguese, British, and Kenyan smugglers alike were engaged in activities designed to circumvent the regulation of a highly marketable material. By employing intermediaries, the smugglers seldom ventured into the interior to obtain the ivory. The complexity of the system once again points to the breadth of its impact on the economy.

Even in Britain itself, smuggling was prevalent, reaching its height during the mid-eighteenth century (Atton and Holland 1908; Hoon 1938; Chatterton 1912). It was not uncommon during the 1740s for armed gangs of hundreds of men to accompany smuggled goods as they left the coast and were transported inland. Tea and French brandy were amongst the more common items smuggled. But the English smugglers worked under far more stress than their American counterparts. The customs service was much larger, more complex, and better equipped. In Newport in 1769, the collector begged for a boat to police one of the most active North American ports, whereas in the second half of the eighteenth century the English added boat after boat. Between 1763 and 1783, the number of armed cutters patrolling English shores nearly doubled from twenty-two to forty-two, and the tonnage, number of men, and number of guns increased by 300% (Hoon 1938, 178). When the commissioners added large boats, the smugglers resorted to light craft – useful in the shallows where the large boats could not run. Brandy runners used lug sails while the customs boats with ordinary sails often stood by, unable to follow.

The English smugglers developed a repertoire of techniques that resemble those of North America. The use of forged papers was common, as well as bribery of officials – especially the tidewaiters who stayed on a vessel until it was cleared (Hoon 1938, 255). Because the English customs service was more active and operated over a much smaller coastline, smugglers were more likely to be apprehended than the smugglers of New England. The English smuggler developed a variety of techniques to avoid detection, especially in the 1820s. Some of these techniques included structural modification of ships to accommodate illegal loads. The construction of false bulkheads to create special compartments was employed, and became so widespread that special officials were charged with

measuring the ship inside and outside to detect such hiding places.

3.9 Conclusion

The historical context that we have provided shows that smuggling in the two decades before the Revolutionary War was a complex behavioral phenomenon that was subject to change through time. It is a topic that has been reduced to simplicity in our historical literature, and it is an activity that leaves only a very fragmentary record because of its highly secretive nature. We have chosen to concentrate on those behaviors that most readily leave signatures in the material record. The use of false papers and the corruption of officials, however, are equally important and deserve much closer attention as part of a larger attempt to establish a more complex cultural context for smuggling in Rhode Island.

The political and ideological ramifications of smuggling activity, though, are perhaps most important to our historical identity. Smuggling and the conflicts that arose out of it were a significant contribution to the formation of an ideology of resistance to arbitrary political authority. The innovations that led to more successful techniques are material manifestations of the successful opposition to British authority; this success was an important prelude to the Revolution.

By looking at smuggling outside of New England we have seen both parallels and continuities. The role of the British as a colonial power is one theme that clearly runs throughout the examples discussed above. It may in fact represent a common thread of all colonial relationships. Attempts by the colonial power to regulate the economy of its colonies seems invariably to be met by resistance. Moreover, it would seem that resistance often crosscuts socio-economic lines while sharing widespread acceptance among the colonial population. In this sense, smuggling is not viewed as a crime but as a means of insuring economic stability, if not prosperity. From this perspective it then becomes an integral part of the economic systems as opposed to an isolated, short-term response.

While smuggling may be commonplace, as the Grenadian (Tobias 1983) example suggests, it does experience changes in purpose and intensity in response to outside pressures. In Rhode Island, colonial merchants altered and intensified their clandestine activities as greater British power was brought to bear on the problem. If our reasoning leads us to search for general principles that can be extended beyond the realm of our specific case studies, then surely parallels can be drawn between the adaptive behavior we have witnessed in eighteenth-century Rhode Island and other groups of smugglers throughout history. The use of clandestine measures visible in the construction of false compartments, camouflaged containers, and other techniques provides the archaeologist with a set of comparative constructs in the study of the changing technology of smuggling. Once the congruence between behavior and the material record is established, these principles can be applied to other eras and areas.

We have looked at history with the view that it provides

us glimpses of cultural process and of behavioral change that are important to understand because they impinge directly upon our ideas about who we are and how and why certain aspects of our culture have developed over time. We have found that each domain of historical documentation provides a distinctive, partial, and biased account from which we may derive a cultural construct. Day Books and Store Blotters, for example, provide selective but detailed merchandizing evidence for some categories of illicit goods and their volume through time; letters from ship owners to agents provide a different perspective, one that is more imbued with the strategies and tactics of the smuggling trade. Synthesis of these data allows us to develop a systemic context, wherein behavior and material culture are integrated. Once we have that systemic context derived from history and archaeology, then we may proceed to ask questions of anthropological value that archaeology can help to solve.[17]

Notes

1. Newport Historical Society, Vault A, Lopez Letter Books, Miscellaneous.
2. Ibid., Lopez Day Books, vol. 475; April–December 1756.
3. Ibid., Lopez Day Books, vol. 475; 23 November 1756.
4. Ibid., Lopez Store Blotter, 1759, vol. 475.
5. Ibid., Lopez Day Book, 1762, vol. 726.
6. Ibid., Lopez Store Blotter, vol. 726, June–July 1762.
7. Ibid., Lopez Copy Book, 1764–65.
8. Ibid., Champlin Miscellaneous Papers.
9. Ibid., Lopez Miscellaneous Papers, Letters, Box 168.
10. Ibid., Customs House Letter Book, 1768, vol. 90.
11. Ibid., Customs House Letter Book, 1768, vol. 90.
12. Ibid., Customs House Letter Book, vol. 90, 21 October 1768.
13. Ibid., Lopez Miscellaneous Papers and Letters.
14. Ibid., Vernon Copy Book, vol. 77.
15. Ibid., Lopez Letter Book, vol. 624.
16. Ibid., Miscellaneous receipts in Lopez Letter Book, vols. 632–6.
17. The authors would like to thank the School of American Research and the University of New Mexico Press for allowing us to reprint portions of an earlier article, 'History, Smugglers, Change and Shipwrecks', in *Shipwreck Anthropology*, edited by Richard Gould.

Chapter 4

Words for things: linguistic analysis of probate inventories

Mary C. Beaudry

Use of documentary evidence for vessel names reveals folk taxonomies held by early Americans. Such taxonomies can be helpful in understanding functional aspects of excavated ceramic assemblages. The methodology for textual evaluation of folk taxonomies is explored using examples from literary, documentary, pictorial, and archaeological sources in order to relate the object world of the past, which so often eludes definition, to the thought world of the past, because it is the key to understanding how Anglo-Americans incorporated everyday objects into their symbolic and social universe.

4.1 Introduction

I will illustrate, through an historical study derived from structural analysis of distinctions made in the context of modern-day linguistic performance, how historical archaeologists can attempt to reconstruct certain aspects of past systems of meaning that have direct relevance to the analysis and interpretation of archaeologically recovered material culture. The example is drawn from seventeenth- and eighteenth-century vessel terminology of the Chesapeake region and involves a combined approach using data from documentary, pictorial, and archaeological sources.

The basic rationale behind presenting such an example is to show that a linguistic analysis of documentary sources can provide useful information that can have quite practical application in historical archaeology. What this approach represents is a treatment of the historical record, of documents, in a very different manner than is usual in the field. By and large, historical archaeologists find the documentary record helpful as corroborative evidence for their discoveries or as a means of sketching in a broad overview of the cultural period with which they are dealing. This is, of course, the basic reason archaeologists turn to the historical record – or, more properly, start with it in the first place.

It need not, however, be the point at which they stop. What I hope to demonstrate through this study is that archaeologists can and should use the documentary record in much the same way that they use the archaeological record: through quantification (a method already employed by cliometricians in the realm of social and economic history) and textual analysis of selected elements of certain kinds of documents, new insights into the world of the past can be achieved. The classes of documents most useful to archaeologists pursuing this sort of analysis are generally those that deal specifically with items of material culture: account books, probate inventories, and wills are often the most helpful sorts of documents in this regard, although sales catalogs, advertisements, and pictorial sources are also of use despite the fact that they are slightly less amenable to rigorous quantification.

This study employed probate inventories as a point of departure for the delineation of functional variation in assemblages of foodways vessels found in probate inventories from Virginia and on sites in the Chesapeake, but could easily be extended to apply to other regions and the sites within them. The sample was divided into three time periods: Period 1 (mid-seventeenth century); Period 2 (the turn of the eighteenth century); and Period 3 (mid-eighteenth century). Each period was represented by approximately 200 inventories (Beaudry 1980, 59).

Probate inventories were examined for mention of foodways vessels of any sort, regardless of their composition. This was done in order to avoid potential bias by looking at only one sort of thing, such as ceramics. The terms for vessels as well as any adjectives or modifiers occurring in the inventory lists were extracted and analyzed according to their frequency at given points in time and according to changes that took place in their use or modification over time.

The use of modifiers was viewed as reflective of the meaning vessels had for their owners and users, or at least for the individuals operating within the colonial Chesapeake cultural system. In the case of inventory analysis, it became clear that adjectival distinctions were, like linguistic distinctions that mark terms through features such as aspiration and voicing, often binary in nature. That is, the modifiers applied to the vessels named by Chesapeake inventory takers tended to stress characteristics that in most cases were in direct opposition to one another.

Anne Yentsch, in a later chapter of this book, observes the occurrence of marked versus unmarked terms in probate inventories from Cape Cod. Marking occurred as a means of setting objects or terms apart from others, usually through modification or detail associated with them.

The concept of marking is drawn from the work of Joseph Greenberg (1966), in which he notes that in language there is often an internally conditioned neutralization denoted by an unmarked feature. On a phonetic level, voicing and aspiration are examples of marking, while unvoiced and unaspirated sounds are not marked. The unmarked feature has a higher frequency than does the marked and occurs in an unambiguous context (Greenberg 1966, 14, 21).

A marked category states the presence of a certain property 'A', while the corresponding unmarked category states nothing about the presence of 'A' and often indicates its absence. For example, *man* is the masculine unmarked term that implies the absence of the feminine, while *woman* is marked because it specifies the presence of the feminine (ibid., 25).

According to Greenberg, the 'ambiguous nature of the unmarked term' accounts for the fact that it refers both to the generic category as well as to the opposite of the marked term (ibid., 26). Hence, when a 'heterogeneous collection' of objects is to be named or enumerated, the unmarked or least marked term will be employed, in instances involving living things often as a surrogate for gender (ibid., 30). When gender terms are employed, the neuter category is most strongly marked and can be used in opposition to the masculine/feminine distinction (ibid., 39).

Yet another aspect of marking involves adjectival comparisons, in which marking is accomplished through comparative and superlative declension of the appropriate adjective. For example, in cases of normal size versus diminutive or versus augmentative size, the term for the normal sized object is unmarked, in contrast to both the larger and smaller items (ibid., 40–1):

smaller pot _____ pot_____larger pot
(marked) _____ (unmarked)_____(marked)

The alternative possibility of marking all non-normal sized objects against the unmarked term is seldom if ever employed:

pot _____ unusually small/large pot
(unmarked) _____ (marked)

Where adjectival opposites are used, marked and unmarked terms express relationships between features that are mutually exclusive: good/bad, long/short, wide/narrow, deep/shallow, and so forth. In many languages, the opposition 'good/bad' is not strictly binary but could be accurately rendered as an opposition of 'good' versus 'not good' (ibid., 52, 57).

In all cases the unmarked term represents the frequent or the taken for granted, and marking occurs in situations that present ambiguity. Many situations in English foster a contextual neutralization that suppresses marking (ibid., 53, 60). In the case of probate inventories, it is likely that the context serves to disambiguate much of what would be unclear in other situations and to render certain classes of marking superfluous (e.g., distinctions such as 'clean versus dirty'). Concomitantly, the inventory context necessitates a great deal of marking in other respects, most notably where value is concerned. This tendency gives rise to a higher frequency of marked and unmarked adjectival oppositions than of diminutive and augmentative markings, since evaluations presumably were made more on the basis of the inherent characteristics of given objects than on the basis of comparison. In other words, in inventories one encounters marking as a means of distinguishing things from one another but not necessarily as a means of directly comparing them to one another.

For example, a common distinction was made between objects that were small or large, old or new, and so forth. Such commonly made distinctions provide valuable clues to the ways in which objects were perceived and evaluated. Even more valuable to the archaeologist, however, are the clues that lead to precise definitions of vessel forms and functions. Such evidence appears when references to vessels are quantified along with their modifiers. Certain terms occur invariably with composition modifiers of metallic substances, indicating that they never occurred as ceramic objects. Other terms are seldom if ever modified, indicating quite clearly that the definition assigned to them was restrictive and strictly bounded. The inventories do not, however, provide the needed definitions, they simply offer the framework in which to pursue more precise and exact understanding of the terms and their referents.

Other sources must be consulted in order to corroborate the circumstantial evidence of the inventories. Most valuable in this regard are pictorial sources such as paintings and engravings that show everyday objects in use, cookery books of the seventeenth and eighteenth centuries giving instructions as to what vessel to employ for what purpose, and the occasional invaluable aid in the form of a dictionary or contemporary encyclopedic work. Evidence derived from all of these sources may be combined to yield functional data for foodways vessels that are as accurate as any we may hope to obtain. The importance of knowledge of this sort to historical archaeologists cannot be overlooked, for it informs our interpretive typologies, making them more responsive to the meanings and functions vessels served within the Anglo-American cultural system (cf. Chapter 5 below).

An example of the sort of encyclopedic work to which I refer above is Randle Holme's 1688 *Academy of Armoury*, a monumental compendium of symbols used in seventeenth-century armorial representations. In this most valuable but largely unknown work, Holme provides definitions for all sorts of everyday objects and even explains what they symbolize in terms of coats-of-arms. One page presents an illustrated household inventory with definitions of basic vessel terms such as *pot*, *dish*, *pitcher*, and so forth (Holme 1688). By incorporating this sort of information with an inventory analysis, the archaeologist comes one step closer to having confidence that he or she can assign appropriate definitions and functions to vessels that may have been used quite differently than we tend to assume.

Names for vessels are not presented in a systematic manner in the inventories and do not make up a taxonomy in the true sense of the word. Therefore, they are best considered as folk nomenclature rather than as a folk taxonomy. It is impossible to determine from inventory evidence whether, for instance, a plate was considered to be a kind of dish, or *vice versa*. It is clear that the term *ware* was inclusive of all types of cooking, storage, and serving vessels and sometimes of utensils, but it is difficult to trace any systematic relationships or levels of inclusion for the sorts of things that made up a '*parcel of — ware*'. The blank may be filled with '*earthen,*' '*stone,*' '*china,*' '*tin,*' '*iron,*' '*pewter,*' '*wooden,*' and so on.

A distinction, often implicit, was drawn between things to drink from and things to eat off or out of, especially if an individual vessel type could possibly serve either function. For example, a *bowl* may not be described as a *drinking bowl*, but, on the other hand, it might often be referred to as a *wine* or *beer bowl*, indicating its use as a beverage-serving vessel.

A core of vessel terms emerged from the inventories. These terms changed little over time. Changes tended to occur in the area of additions to the lexicon spurred by the presence of new kinds of vessels. More prevalent than changes in terms were changes in ways vessels were described or modified by the appraisers. The core terms appear in Table 4.1, which also indicates types of modifiers applied to the terms.

In the following section I discuss the modifiers used to distinguish vessels from one another. The modifiers are considered, in a general sense, more or less as 'principles of categorization' (cf. Beaudry 1978a). I then offer an explanation for the changes in modifier use over time.

4.2 Modifiers

After the core of terms used to refer to vessels in probate inventories had been isolated, ten categories of modifiers were selected for consideration. These were: composition, age, size, capacity, function, color, shape, weight, contents, and condition. All of these variables were of significance in distinguishing vessels from one another, especially with respect to distinctions within classes of vessels.

The appraisers' use of distinguishing modifiers to clarify evaluations was common in the inventories. The assumption upon which this analysis is based is that some of these distinctions were also made in day-to-day communication. Furthermore, it is assumed that all of these distinctions had cultural significance.

Table 4.1 illustrates the use of qualifying adjectives with the core list of vessel terms for the three periods of my sample. In this case, only presence (+) or absence (−) of modifiers is indicated in order to give an impression of the kinds of distinctions that were important to the inventory takers (e.g., *color* never seems to have been particularly worthy of note). This table also gives a rough indication of temporal change in modifier use.

Composition receives more frequent mention than almost any other variable. This is largely because substances varied in worth. For instance, in most cases metal vessels were appraised at a higher rate than similar ceramic items, the exception being examples of fine or scarce tea wares, which of course do not appear in the inventories until the eighteenth century. For metals, appraisal rates generally followed the scale of nobility of metals, with silver followed by pewter, brass, copper, and iron in value (gold occurs very infrequently and usually in the form of currency or as jewelry when it does). Since many articles such as tankards, porringers, and plates were made out of a variety of metals, distinctions between these were necessary, given the reasons inventories were recorded. It is noteworthy that unappraised inventories can sometimes be far less specific than appraised inventories, probably because the evaluations were based upon distinctions that had to be justified. In the same vein, the most detailed inventories often are those that specify a division of the testator's property among his or her heirs. Needless to say, in the latter case, the detail is inspired by the need to give an exact description of precisely which object, slave, or animal went to whom.

While the composition of vessels was usually mentioned in both seventeenth-century and eighteenth-century inventories, it was not a requisite distinction. The inventory samples reveal that all of the core group of vessel terms appear with no modifier at least once. If each term is to qualify as a lexeme, this should be so, for the term should conjure up a relatively specific image even without modifiers.

Table 4.1 *Modifier profiles for vessel terms: selected examples*

	Composition	Age	Size	Capacity	Function	Color	Shape	Weight	Contents	Condition
Basin										
Period 1	+	+	+	−	−	−	−	−	−	+
Period 2	+	+	+	−	+	−	−	−	−	−
Period 3	+	+	+	+	+	+	−	−	−	−
Bowl										
Period 1	+	+	+	−	+	−	−	−	−	−
Period 2	+	+	−	−	+	−	−	−	−	−
Period 3	+	+	+	+	+	+	−	−	−	−
Cup										
Period 1	+	+	+	+	+	−	−	−	−	−
Period 2	+	+	+	+	+	−	−	−	−	−
Period 3	+	+	+	−	+	+	+	−	−	−
Dish										
Period 1	+	+	+	+	+	+	−	−	−	+
Period 2	+	+	−	−	+	−	+	+	−	−
Period 3	+	+	+	−	+	−	+	−	−	−
Jug										
Period 1	+	−	+	−	−	+	−	−	−	−
Period 2	+	−	+	+	+	−	−	−	+	−
Period 3	+	+	+	+	+	−	−	−	+	−
Pan										
Period 1	+	+	+	+	−	−	−	−	−	+
Period 2	+	+	+	−	+	−	+	+	−	+
Period 3	+	+	+	+	+	−	−	−	−	−
Plate										
Period 1	+	+	−	−	+	−	−	−	−	−
Period 2	+	+	+	−	+	−	−	−	−	+
Period 3	+	+	+	−	+	+	−	−	−	−
Pot										
Period 1	+	+	+	+	+	−	−	−	−	+
Period 2	+	+	+	+	+	−	−	+	+	+
Period 3	+	+	+	+	+	+	−	−	+	+

It is interesting to note that in the inventories examined, *age* and *size* distinctions are generally those that carry a negative connotation: *old* and *small*. Evidently an item was described as new only if it was genuinely and noticeably unused and unworn. Of the tabulated material, very few examples carry the designation of *new*. It seems likely that wear upon an object was a striking feature that was frequently taken into account when value estimates were made.

On the other hand, it is not possible to attribute such differences to the relative poverty of many Chesapeake residents, as the total estate values in the sample reflect, for the most part, middling socio-economic status. Nor is it likely that there was much difference in the availability of material goods; kinds and quality of possessions at any given point in time are very similar within the three sample periods, but it is apparent that goods had to see long, hard use throughout most of the seventeenth century. By the middle of the eighteenth century, use of the term *old* diminished considerably, but its diminished use was not counterbalanced by use of *new* in object descriptions.

Size modifiers consisted of *large*, *small*, *great*, and *little*. The only other terms indicating size were *middling* and *less*. Both of these terms were most often employed in a comparative context. Since *middling* presumably referred to an average size (a normative pot, if such a thing may be said to exist), it does not show up in Table 4.1, in which only the large versus the small distinction is considered. It is evident that in the majority of cases, as is true of the age variable, the 'negative' side of the opposition small/large is emphasized. Again it would appear to be a choice related to a feature that significantly affected value, not necessarily diminishing it as is true for age or condition, discussed below, but marking certain objects as distinct from the norm. It is probable that people could afford and make use of 'small' versions of things more often than they could of their larger counterparts. This explanation seems to make more sense than attributing appraisers with a tendency to employ diminutive adjectives as *qualitative* evaluaters.

Capacity is of course related to size, but only those modifiers that refer directly to a measured volume were classed as capacity modifiers. These are for the most part liquid measures applied to hollow wares, ranging from one-half pint to several gallons. An occasional dry measure occurred as well, for example, *pound cannister*. Flatwares were never distinguished from one another in terms of their capacity; such a distinction would have no meaning.

An interesting aspect of capacity designations is their ability to serve as independent referents to vessel types. Terms such as *dram*, *quart*, *pint*, *pottle*, and *gill* occasionally appear on their own. Presumably they are drinking pots or measures, but appraisers may have meant to indicate a mug or tankard, perhaps even a jug. This phenomenon also occurs in the realm of age distinctions for livestock (cf. Beaudry 1980, 114–16) as well as with function markers for highly specialized vessels.

Occurrence of modifiers as independent referents serves to reveal what appraisers viewed as the *single most important feature* of an object. In a sense, the object was unique or distinctive because of this attribute. Therefore a capacity designation may stand alone, because the modifier itself becomes the referent for the omitted (understood) generic. As such it is a gloss for the composite lexeme of marker + generic.

This phenomenon can be classed as a form of description *via* metonymy. This is defined as the 'use of a word for a certain object or idea to denote another object or idea, the latter in some manner associated with the former, e.g., identifying the whole by use of a label for one of its parts' (Brown 1979, 257). Other kinds of modification through metonymy include the association of cause with effect and of a container with its contents. In the latter case, that of the use of a word for a receptacle to denote its contents, the two entities involved are perceived as bearing an immediate transitive relationship to one another. For instance, 'use of the word *dish* for food may relate to the conceptualization that food 'is contained in' dishes. If so the metonymic application of a word for a receptacle to denote its contents is based on a transitive relationship' (ibid., 264).

On the other hand, receptacles and the things ordinarily contained in them may come to be regarded as wholes: 'thus a dish and the food in it are thought of as one unit' (ibid.). The container and the thing contained therefore become parts of a whole, and through the expansion of the referent along a 'part of' path, the name of the container becomes the name for the whole. In the case of *dish*, the term denotes both the receptacle and the food in it as part of a single unit, and 'through a subsequent restriction of reference along a 'part of' path the thing contained takes the label of the whole thereby completing a name transfer from receptacle to *receptacle and contents as a whole* to contents' (ibid.).

Thus the compound labels that refer to a container plus its *capacity* are also subject to metonymic shifts through a form of reference restriction in which the modifier becomes the referent for an object previously denoted by the modifier plus a principal lexical item that denotes the class of things in which the entity is immediately included. The difference here is that the relationship between a container and its volume is not strictly a 'kind of' or 'part of' connection. There is, however, an element of physical contingency between container and its potential capacity, and it may be this relation, along with a presumed functional equivalence between vessels and their ability to contain measurable volumes, that makes the metonymic shift from container to *container and its capacity as a whole* to container's capacity. Furthermore, this may be more easily achieved in some contexts than in others, as in inventory lists, when it may be that the context in some way disambiguates what would otherwise be crucial distinctions.

Some vessels whose capacities are indicated did indeed function as measures. A few entries refer to *measuring pots* (not *cups*) and some simply to *measures* (presumably another example of a metonymic shift along the lines of functional contingency). Therefore it is easy to move from calling something a *pottle pot* (referring to a measure of two quarts), to glossing it as *pottle*. Not all vessels distinguished on the basis of capacity necessarily functioned as measures, but tankards and other receptacles for beverages were no doubt perceived in terms of exactly how much liquid they could contain – and therefore how much a person was likely to drink from them. Hollow ware vessels designed to receive solids or semi-solids were seldom thought of in this manner. Bowl capacity tended to be mentioned for punch or other *exclusively* drinking/serving beverage containers only.

The subject of vessel function was the most subjective as far as appraisers' descriptions are concerned. Function of course overlaps with capacity and presence or absence of contents to some degree. In the present study, however, I have elected to deal only with stated function or that which may be reasonably inferred, such as in the cases of *tea cups*, *soup plates*, *wash basons*, *pickle pots*, and so forth. This approach is intended to avoid guesswork and to prevent possible overemphasis of function-related modifiers.

Knowing what people did with their possessions tells us more about them than merely knowing what they had, and function modifiers employed by appraisers reveal not just emic but at times slightly idiosyncratic uses of objects. For example, keeping honey in a pitcher is an instance of a description prompted by the way a vessel was currently being used by its owner. This is somewhat different from naming and distinguishing vessels according to their assumed or intended function, as with tea pots, coffee pots, and chocolate pots, all of which possess rather similar attributes but have sufficient difference to allow immediate recognition of functional variation.

Use of functional modifiers as independent referents is common: *posset pot* and *caudle pot* become *posset* and *caudle*, *salt cellar* becomes *salt*. This syndrome, already noted for capacity modifiers, appears once again to be a result of the recognition of qualities unique to these types of vessels. Each of these examples reveals that the function intended for the vessels calls for a distinct shape, a norm around which there may be variations, usually decorative. In such cases it is true that 'form follows function' – or *vice versa*. At any rate, it can be said that posset pots, caudle pots, and salt cellars, all of which commonly occurred as ceramic items in addition to sometimes being made of pewter, brass, or silver, are relatively distinct vessel forms. Thus the use of *pot* after the qualifier *posset* is in a sense redundant, as the term *posset* conveys a sharp image as it is. It is clear that the function modifiers become independent referents or glosses because they call up only a narrow range of possibilities, making use of the generic term unnecessary. Thus a metonymic shift from container to contents (or intended contents) is achieved. In his 1688 *Academy of Armoury*, Randle Holme made a relevant observation in describing a *posset pot*: 'Its name shews its use and therefore of it shall say noe more . . .' (Holme 1688, Book III, 9).

While vessel composition remained an important variable throughout the seventeenth century and into the eighteenth, vessel function moved from relative insignificance to fairly great significance. This appears to be not only a result of the ownership of larger numbers of vessels made possible through the efficiency of the British pottery industry, trade, and local manufactures, many of which tended to be used for specialized purposes, but also of a general shift in attitudes about how vessels should be employed, especially in regard to serving (Beaudry 1979, 8–9).

This attitudinal shift parallels with some accuracy the broad trend towards specialization of serving vessels illustrated by Deetz in his 1973 article 'Ceramics from Plymouth 1635–1835: the archaeological evidence' and further elaborated in his book *In Small Things Forgotten* (1977). Prompted in the second quarter of the eighteenth century by the public's new fascination with matched sets, the pottery industry responded by producing a variety of special-purpose vessels that could be purchased as parts of tea sets or dinner services. Many of these types of vessels listed in the mid-eighteenth-century inventories are condiment or side-dish serving pieces (e.g., *sweetmeat glass*, *mustard pot*), as well as the ubiquitous accompaniments to the tea service: *milk* or *cream pot, sugar castor, sugar bowl, slop bowl, tea cannister*, and so forth (see Roth 1961; Beaudry 1978b; Beaudry 1980). Therefore, to a certain extent this increased emphasis on function in the domain of vessels is directly related to technological and behavioral changes.

Color and *shape* are variables that receive far less attention than do composition, age, size, capacity, or function. With little doubt this can be attributed to the fact that neither played much of a role in aiding appraisers in evaluating an object, although shape and color were at times useful as distinctions between very similar objects, or between objects whose composition did not differ, such as round versus square tin baking pans, or white and brown stoneware mugs.

Weight was important for metal vessels only. Iron kettles, skillets, and pots might be weighed in order to determine their value, usually calculated as so many shillings or pennyweights per pound. Other metals used in tankards, plates, dishes, cups, porringers, etc., were carefully weighed to the ounce and valued accordingly. As previously mentioned, valuations scaled highest for silver, decreasing for the baser metals. This use of weight as a variable in describing vessels reflects preoccupation with the mutable substances of which the vessels were made, over and above the vessel itself, its form, or its function. This notion of 'resource potential' of objects, clearly, was applied only to those items that could be transformed – usually by melting down the metal and recasting it in another form – but it helps to explain why relatively high values were given to various metal vessels whose poor condition rendered them unserviceable (see Beaudry 1978a as well as the discussion of condition modifiers below).

A vessel sometimes was specifically described as containing something, that is, as being *full of butter, with some oyle, of fatt*. Concomitantly, certain objects were occasionally described as *empty*. This contrast is considered to be more meaningful than the factor of whether or not vessels were always described in terms of their contents, since they seldom were. This variable is significant in that it does reveal, and is in fact directly related to, vessel utilization as well as to the types of non-perishable foodstuffs likely to be on hand.

By describing a vessel as *empty*, appraisers may have meant to indicate one of at least two situations: (1) direct contrast with other similar or identical vessels present in the same household, some of which had contents, or (2) special notice of a given vessel type when empty, because that type of vessel most frequently occurred *with* contents. The conclusions to be drawn from this are that certain vessel types were valued along with what was in them, even when the contents were not mentioned, and that the major function of such vessels was perceived as being *storage*, as opposed to preparation or serving.

Modifiers referring to *condition* of vessels were more likely to be negative than positive, indicating that an object was broken or damaged in some way, a factor detracting from its value – in some cases, rendering it totally useless, in others, relegating it to the scrap pile. Descriptions denoting

Table 4.2 *Frequency of function modifiers*

	Period 1			Period 2			Period 3		
	#	f	%	#	f	%	#	f	%
Bason	39	0	0	81	2	2.5	85	18	21.1
Bottle	29	3	10.3	213	3	1.4	170	9	5.3
Bowl	34	6	17.67	32	17	53.1	112	16	14.3
Cup	56	25	44.6	60	12	20.0	91	34	37.4
Dish	111	24	21.6	146	46	31.5	210	34	16.2
Glass	1	0	0	42	29	69.0	76	44	57.9
Jar	0	0	0	8	1	12.5	23	3	13.0
Jug	11	0	0	41	2	4.9	107	7	6.5
Kettle	117	1	0.9	127	2	1.6	194	77	0.04
Mug	0	0	0	61	1	1.6	71	0	0
Pan	197	176	89.8	398	337	84.7	369	299	81.0
Pitcher	0	0	0	2	0	0	3	1	33.3
Plate	31	3	9.7	153	7	4.6	256	19	7.4
Platter	10	0	0	7	0	0	0	0	0
Porringer	57	1	1.8	76	0	0	22	0	0
Pot	311	45	14.5	533	152	28.5	690	328	47.5
Saucer	16	0	0	7	0	0	55	0	0
Skillet	67	0	0	109	9	0	79	0	0
Tankard	15	0	0	96	0	0	15	0	0
Trencher	13	0	0	25	0	0	0	0	0

= number of entries; f = frequency of function modifiers;
% = percentage of function modifiers

exceptionally fine quality or workmanship, e.g., a *tite tub* or a *fayre wine cup*, were much rarer. These naturally indicate positive attributes that presumably made an object worth more than its average or run-of-the-mill counterparts.

4.3 Change in modifier use over time

Table 4.2 presents the quantified information about the frequency of modifiers referring to function in the inventory analysis. What is revealed is that certain terms were modified according to their functions with greater frequency towards the middle of the eighteenth century. This is interesting in light of developments in the ceramic industry that led to the production of more specialized vessel forms than had been known previously.

The marked increase in the frequency of function modifiers over time is indicative of the greater need to distinguish special function vessels from one another. This appears to have been accomplished by modifier use rather than through the addition of new terms to the lexicon. One of the most generic of vessel terms, *pot*, appeared frequently in the inventories of all periods, but the frequency of function modifiers increased from 14.5% in Period 1 to 47.5% in Period 3. This seems highly reflective of the trend to call new special purpose vessels by names indicating the special purpose for which they were intended: *mustard pot, sugar pot, tea pot, coffee pot, posset pot,* and so on.

The probate inventories likewise reflect a trend toward more individualized use of ceramics and other vessels. We can see this trend in the ways vessels were classified. To begin with,

items that were restricted to individual users increase in absolute quantities from the mid-seventeenth to the mid-eighteenth century:

Individual eating vessels	Period 1	Period 2	Period 3
bowl	34	32	112
dish	111	146	210
plate	31	153	256
saucer	16	7	55

Individual drinking vessels	Period 1	Period 2	Period 3
cup	56	60	91
glass	1	42	76
mug	0	61	71

However, vessels presumably more likely to be shared decrease:

Shared eating vessels	Period 1	Period 2	Period 3
platter	10	6	0
trencher	13	25	0

Shared drinking vessels	Period 1	Period 2	Period 3
flagon	18	17	1
tankard	15	96	15

This increase in 'individual' consumption items is interesting in itself, but even more revealing is the switch in classificatory focus from *composition* to *function* of vessels. This is especially true of those terms that are likely to be ambiguous. For instance, frequency of the term *pot* increased dramatically between Period 1 and Period 3 (from 311 in Period 1, to 533 in Period 2, to 690 in Period 3; see Table 4.3). In Period 1, 62.5% of all *pots* were described in terms of their composition. Composition markers had dropped to 21% by Period 3. A similar decline in the emphasis on composition occurred with the terms *bason, pan, dish,* and so on.

On the other hand, the emphasis on *function* increases (see Table 4.2), especially for the term *pot* but also for items such as *bason, glass,* and *pan*. (Composition of glasses, for obvious reasons, was never mentioned.)

This feature of vessel classifications is an accurate reflection of cultural concerns. *Pans* and most especially *pots* had many functions and took on a variety of forms. By the eighteenth century, ceramic pots became common (unlike *kettles* and *skillets,* which retained a very narrow range of meaning and occurred exclusively in base metals). The broad applicability of the generic term *pot* could accommodate many of the new forms that appeared in the eighteenth century but required marking to differentiate vessels. By the middle of the eighteenth century, appraisers tended to differentiate *pots,*

Table 4.3 *Frequency of composition modifiers*

	Period 1			Period 2			Period 3		
	#	f	%	#	f	%	#	f	%
Bason	39	22	56.4	81	36	40.5	85	21	24.7
Beaker	9	4	44.4	3	1	33.3	0	0	0
Bottle	29	11	37.9	213	63	29.6	170	14	8.2
Bowl	34	10	29.4	32	11	34.4	112	46	41.1
Can	0	0	0	11	2	18.2	28	20	71.4
Cup	56	22	39.3	60	30	50.0	91	25	27.5
Dish	111	80	72.1	146	72	49.3	210	75	35.7
Firkin	3	0	0	1	0	0	2	0	0
Flagon	18	6	33.3	17	6	35.3	1	0	0
Flasket	3	0	0	7	0	0	2	0	0
Glass	1	0	0	42	0	0	76	0	0
Jar	0	0	0	8	1	12.5	23	5	21.7
Jug	11	5	45.5	41	24	58.5	107	22	20.6
Kettle	117	101	86·3	127	102	80.3	194	102	52.6
Mug	0	0	0	61	28	45.9	71	20	28.2
Pan	197	113	57.4	398	107	26.9	369	68	18.4
Piggon	5	0	0	47	3	6.4	24	0	0
Pipkin	1	0	0	1	1	100.0	1	0	0
Pitcher	0	0	0	2	1	50.0	3	0	0
Plate	31	10	32.3	153	58	37.9	256	112	43.8
Platter	10	10	100.0	7	6	85.7	0	0	0
Porringer	57	13	22.8	76	25	32.9	22	4	18.2
Posnit	2	1	50.0	9	4	44.4	1	0	0
Pot	311	155	49.8	533	333	62.5	690	145	21.0
Rundlett	24	0	0	57	0	0	7	0	0
Salt	21	9	42.9	40	16	40.0	26	11	42.3
Salt cellar	25	6	24.0	24	4	16.6	11	3	27.3
Saucer	16	3	18.8	7	1	14.3	55	13	23.6
Skillet	67	35	52.2	109	74	67.9	79	44	55.7
Tankard	15	6	40.0	96	46	47.9	15	11	73.3
Tray	91	5	5.5	126	8	6.4	49	1	2.0
Trencher	13	0	0	25	3	12.0	0	0	0
Tub	58	0	0	151	1	0.7	181	0	0

\# = total number of entries for term; f = frequency of composition modifiers; % = percentage of composition modifiers

pans, and *basons* from one another on the basis of function plus other attributes. Such vessels intended for different functions may have been very similar in form, although they did sometimes differ dramatically in shape. Hence, although there was not a one-to-one ratio between form and function by the middle of the eighteenth century, the relationship between form and function was for some vessels far more arbitrary than it had been in the mid-seventeenth century. This is what is responsible for the shift to classificatory emphasis on function. Other variables remained significant, but by Period 3 of this study, these were likely to be combined with function modifiers as a further means of restricting the flexibility of certain vessel names.

The changing features of folk classification discussed in this chapter reflect configurations that Henry Glassie (1975, 161) attributes to the underlying internal abstract context of folk building in Middle Virginia. Folk builders succeeded in gaining control over a chaotic universe by repeatedly making decisions that favored the intellect over emotion and the artificial over the natural. Deetz (1979, 13) has extrapolated from buildings to other aspects of material culture – gravestones, ceramics, food preparation – pointing to a move from natural, open forms in the seventeenth century to a more intellectualized and artificial expression in the mid-eighteenth century. Shifts in folk classification seemingly originate from the same impulses that spurred Virginians to build symmetrical houses, acquire matched sets of dishes, and assign place settings, utensils, servings of food, and seats at table on an individual basis. Folk semantic domains of foodways vessels vividly depict the mediation in favor of the intellectual and artificial over emotion and nature. The increasing arbitrariness of Virginia folk classification reflects the psychological reality of Anglo-Americans confronted with a changing material and social universe. Shifts in emphasis, i.e., from 'natural' *composition* to 'arbitrary' *function*, indicate areas of concern – areas over which classifiers gained control by stressing more and more artificial, imposed, and restrictive modes of classification.

Chapter 5

A vessel typology for early Chesapeake ceramics: the Potomac Typological System

Mary C. Beaudry, Janet Long,
Henry M. Miller, Fraser D. Neiman,
and Garry Wheeler Stone

A tentative scheme for classifying vessel shapes excavated in the Chesapeake region of Maryland and Virginia is presented. The result, dubbed 'The Potomac Typological System' (POTS), links gradations of forms of vessels commonly excavated on tidewater sites to terms used in inventories and other documents of the period. Although many of the colonial terms also belong to the modern lexicon, their connotations and referents were not always identical in the past. The aim is not to produce a standardized, all-purpose typology but rather a preliminary foundation for comparisons enabling the exploration of what sorts of functional variability exist within and between assemblages. The important role of data from documentary sources in the interpretation of excavated ceramic material is also discussed.

5.1 Introduction

This paper is the result of a general dissatisfaction with the way in which archaeologists working on colonial Chesapeake sites (including the authors) have typically analyzed their excavated ceramics. Historical archaeologists spend considerable time excavating, sorting, and gluing together pots. Yet there is very little to show for it, save the contents of exhibit cases. While architectural data from a number of sites excavated in the Chesapeake are beginning to increase the understanding of the effects in daily life of demographic and economic instability (Carson, Barka, Kelso, Stone and Upton 1981) and of changing social relations among planters, their laborers, and their neighbors (Neiman 1980; Upton 1979), it is impossible to cite any similarly systematic contributions based on ceramic analysis.

The failure to impart much analytical utility to ceramics is the product of a number of factors. Some of these infect the discipline of archaeology as a whole. The lack of general archaeological theory and the failure to be imaginative make convincing attempts to connect the things dug up with other areas of past experience very rare (Leone 1978). Others are related to the often unhappy way ceramic data are cast once the pots are out of the ground. Categories are employed that, despite frequent assertions of an interest in past behavior, poorly reflect functional variation. The variety of such schemes in use makes comparisons between assemblages excavated by different archaeologists impossible. Finally, there is the failure to make good use of the documentary record with which we are blessed (or cursed).

Antidotes for the fear and trembling engendered by the call to make interesting connections and to manufacture fascinating hypotheses are hard to come by – so too are remedies for archaeology's theoretical deficiencies. It may be useful, however, to offer some suggestions about the categories used in the interpretation of excavated ceramics in the light of documentary evidence and about the use of the documentary record in archaeological research focusing on ceramics.

The immediate goal is to begin to systematize the chaos in the categories used to describe excavated ceramic vessels and the assemblages they comprise, in a way that will make the cultural dynamics behind them more accessible. The Potomac

Typological system (POTS) is the result. It is a first attempt whose ultimate purpose will have been served if it provokes historical archaeologists to begin to think seriously and critically about the analytical utility of the pottery typologies they currently employ.

5.2 Vessel typologies in historical archaeology

Discussions of typology have long had a central place in the archaeological literature. The importance of the topic is understandable, for archaeology pivots upon the initial ordering of data. The disagreement that runs through the literature concerns how one brings about that order. Does it exist in recoverable form in the data, or is it imposed by the investigator (Brew 1946; Spaulding 1953; Hill and Evans 1972; Doran and Hodson 1975)? Since these stump-infested fields have been plowed before, an extended discussion of the issues will not be undertaken here. However, let the cards be laid on the table at the outset. The authors sympathize with the second position: that all classifications are arbitrary. People impose categories, and hence order, upon objects to facilitate communication; this is as true of the archaeologist as much as it is of the people he or she studies.

The theoretical underpinnings of this view, which has found acceptance in a host of fields from physics to literary criticism, run something as follows. Despite our everyday notions, our world does not consist of independently existing objects whose nature is immediately known to the observer. In fact, this sort of immediate knowledge is impossible since any object, from a white saltglaze mug to a suspension bridge, presents the observer with a potentially infinite array of sensory data. If persons are to make sense of this bewildering variety of experience, they must pick and choose, recognizing certain features as significant and disregarding others. Perception is a creative process. People of different groups construct reality in characteristically different ways. Thus, the 'true' nature of the world is not to be found in the world itself but in the relationships that one chooses to perceive among the objects in it. An object is a mug and not a cup only because the observer chooses to recognize a rather limited number of features that make it so.

Obviously, from the researcher's point of view, there is no single best or true classificatory scheme for ceramics or for anything else for that matter. It is equally obvious that different classifications can and must coexist peacefully if we are to make the most of our data. Any system will have limitations that can be remedied only by the complementary use of other systems. For example, there has long been a working recognition of the fact that technological and stylistic attributes are best suited to the definition of units of temporal significance. *Termini post quem*, marker types, and the Mean Ceramic Date are all dating tools whose efficiency turns on the chronological significance of ceramic technology and decorative style. But if pots are to be used for more than dating sites and the features on them, some attention needs to be paid to function. Given the primitive state of research in this area, what is needed is a scheme that will allow the systematic description and comparison of assemblages and that, by attending to function in even a crude way, will allow a preliminary appreciation of just what sort of functional variation exists between assemblages in time and space. Since direct evidence for past use of ceramic vessels (e.g., knife marks on a plate) is spotty, the criteria used to assess functional variation must be indirect. They must trade on the physical and traditional cultural constraints on possible use. There are of course several ways in which such a measurement device might be constructed.

Archaeologists working on the colonial Chesapeake have long used shape to describe their ceramic finds. All of these workers have written about cups, mugs, pitchers, bowls, and who knows what else. By giving these items names, some sense is made of them (Tyler 1969, 6). The names are of course English, and, more important, the categories that they represent are those unconsciously employed in our day-to-day transactions, often supplemented by notions inherited from late nineteenth- and twentieth-century antiquarians and collectors. By naming objects from the past, they are made comprehensible in behavioral terms. They silently slip into our own familiar world so subtly that one feels little need for theoretical or methodological reflection. Problems can be expected.

The most glaring problem is consistency. The pages of even scholarly works on the pottery of a particular period show vessels that are given the same name even though they have significantly different shapes. Even worse, two identical vessels illustrated on different pages may be given different names. If individual authors have a hard time being consistent, there would appear to be little hope for a group of feisty archaeologists. One person's plate is another's charger and another's dish. If nothing else, this situation is embarrassing.

Complacency in the face of this situation may be a product of the way in which most archaeologists have until recently reported excavated ceramics. Either a few particularly complete or spectacular pieces are chosen for illustration, in which case the names given the vessels are unimportant since the vessels themselves are there on the page for public inspection, or sherd counts by ware are presented for each excavated context, in which case the question of shape is otiose. Occasionally the two approaches are combined.

The interpretive possibilities of data cast in either of these two forms are rather limited. It is difficult to imagine why one vessel that has by chance survived the passage of time relatively intact should possess more behavioral significance than one represented by only a few sherds. The relevance of sherd counts to the explication of past behavior is equally obscure. One needs to remember the obvious: the people whom archaeologists study worked with, ate from, and drank from whole vessels, not the sherds the vessels would eventually become. If archaeologists are interested, at the very least, in the systematic description of the way in which these folks lived, they need to consider every vessel represented in the archaeological record as well as some that are not.

When the desirability of systematic morphological description of the entire ceramic assemblage from a given period at a given site is recognized, inconsistency in the classification and naming of vessels ceases to be simply embarrassing and becomes intolerable. On a practical level, since one cannot illustrate every vessel from a relatively complex site, some naming (and/or verbal description) becomes unavoidable. Under such circumstances, unless there is some standardization in vessel nomenclature, inter-assemblage comparison is impossible. The need for explicitness to facilitate functional interpretation is one of the primary motivations behind this paper.

The analytical morass attendant on such inconsistency has not gone unnoticed, and attempts have been made to rid the field of the problem. One solution has been to discard traditional names entirely in favor of two categories that at least have the virtue of being unambiguous: flatwares and hollowwares. This is the Stoke-on-Trent approach (Celoria and Kelly 1973). In justifying this solution, its authors plead ignorance and understandable dissatisfaction with the fact that in recent numbers of *Post Medieval Archaeology*, 'a bewildering variety of vessels have been called dishes' (Celoria and Kelly 1973, 16). The authors also suggest that the flat/hollow dichotomy is legitimate by virtue of its use by seventeenth-century Staffordshire potters. Despite this historical validity, the wholesale acceptance of this two-term typology would send the baby out with the bath water. While the two terms may have served the potters' primarily technological concerns well, distinguishing those vessels that were usually press-molded from those that were thrown ('reckoned by their different breadths . . . or their contents [volume]') and stacked or nested for firing and storage, by themselves they can scarcely be considered useful tools in the functional explication of an assemblage. In a behavioral context, cups and butter pots, both hollowwares, have little in common.

A second sort of remedy is to attempt to give everyday and antiquarian terms, along with the fuzzy notions behind them, a degree of precision. Many people, for example, have called any two-handled vessel, roughly square in profile, with pint or more capacity, a posset pot. The name of course implies a very specific use, and the term was used in the seventeenth century. Unfortunately, it did not then apply to the wide class of vessels often described as such today. Small mistakes of this sort will inevitably distort the reading of individual excavated vessels, not to mention the interpretation of entire ceramic assemblages, especially when comparisons with documentary evidence are made.

Both the above approaches meet our criterion for typological adequacy. They allow for unambiguous assignment of new objects to their categories. In addition, the Stoke-on-Trent solution is adequate insofar as it accounts for the entire range of variability in the objects under study, and the second approach could be elaborated without much difficulty to the same end (and in fact has been by many).

Adequacy, however, is not the sole basis on which a typology should be evaluated (Binford 1972, 247). While any adequate typology allows the systematic description of similarities and differences between assemblages, not all are equally well equipped to make possible insights into the significance of this variability in the context in which the objects themselves were used.

POTS is one attempt to circumvent these problems. The distinctions made by colonial Virginians and Marylanders who named and described their neighbors' possessions in probate inventories were used as clues to where breaks of possible functional significance occur along the continuum of formal variation. The characterizations of contemporary terms that POTS offers were arrived at by considering variation in adjectives applied to the terms in a sample of Virginia and Maryland inventories and descriptions (verbal and pictorial) of the terms' referents in other contemporary sources. The categories used by inventory takers appear to have been based largely on three dimensions of formal variation: shape, size, and ware. Since the categories resulting from the intersection of these dimensions successfully mediated people's everyday interaction (behavior) with the objects denoted, they can serve as a reasonable basis for the construction of a functionally sensitive typology. Descriptions of the categories that comprise POTS provide a glossary for terms encountered in inventories, making more accurate comparisons between excavated and inventoried ceramic assemblages possible.

5.3 The use of documents in ceramic analysis

In putting POTS together, documentary sources have served as texts. In these sources, the manner in which their authors categorized a small part of the material world (which happens to be ubiquitous on archaeological sites) could be approximated. The application of POTS to an excavated assemblage, or any other sort of explication of archaeological material from an historical site, should also proceed with the documents in mind. Here, however, the archaeologist will be on more familiar ground, using the historical record, initially at least, as a source of data about the artifactual contents of the past. Doing history with objects is considerably easier and the results certainly more complete if the historical record is used to fill in the holes in the archaeological records and *vice versa*. Of more far-reaching importance, however, is the fact that, by using documents, one can ask more interesting questions about the things one excavates. These objects, in turn, can be expected to suggest more interesting questions about the documents. Documents do not provide archaeologists with a 'telephone to Glory'. Ignoring the documents, however, is at one's own peril. This point can be illustrated through several cautionary tales. Two widely held propositions, derived from archaeological sources, about the cultural significance of ceramics in seventeenth-century Anglo-America suffer quite devastating defects that are the inevitable result of the failure to take full advantage of the historical record.

The attempt to define socio-economic status through

ceramic assemblages is a genre that has gained considerable popularity in recent years, as historical archaeologists have struggled with the challenge to impart some anthropological or social-historical significance to their work. While explicit written statements on this topic (and many others) are rare in the study area, the proposition that in the seventeenth-century Chesapeake there was a strong correlation between the numbers and kinds of ceramics an individual possessed and his wealth appears to have some currency. Confronted with two ceramic assemblages from a pair of sites whose occupants are known through the historical record to have been of considerably different means, it is quite easy for one to attribute any quantitative or qualitative differences that he or she is able to define in the pottery to differences in the wealth of its owners, consider no other factors, and leave the matter at that.

This sort of analysis has been the bread and butter of prehistoric archaeologists for years. Whereas historical archaeologists are here treating assemblage variability as an index to wealth, prehistorians have traditionally treated it as an index to the presence of different tribes or cultural groups. In both cases percentage and/or empirical frequencies, calculated for a variety of artifact classes, are used as a measure of distance, cultural in one case and economic in the other, between the occupants of a number of sites. As Lewis Binford (1968, 1972), among others, has pointed out, this kind of approach severely limits the interpretive possibilities of the archaeological record and its potential to inform us about the past. The problem is that in both cases it is simply assumed that the contents of the archaeological record and its determinants are unidimensional. It would be surprising indeed to discover that any set of phenomena for which human beings were responsible was attributable to the operation of a single variable.

Theory aside, this particular projection of our own ethnocentric notion that the rich will invariably possess lots of pretty pots has another shortcoming. A cursory examination of the inventories indicates that it simply does not fit the seventeenth-century Chesapeake. Ceramics were optional for many of the early Chesapeake's wealthiest men. A case in point is Capt. John Lee, a Westmoreland County, Virginia, gentleman whose estate was probated in 1674. Lee was a quorum justice, the brother of a member of the Governor's Council, and, with an estate valuation in excess of 200,000 pounds of tobacco and twenty-four laborers, the wealthiest decedent appraised in the county during the seventeenth century. Yet Lee's collection of ceramics was exceedingly limited. The six quarts of oil and an equal amount of honey that the appraisers found 'In Capt. Lee's Chamber' may have been kept in a couple of earthen jars. Lee's kitchen contained three chamber pots, two old close stool pans, two porringers, and a chafing dish. But all these items, save the chafing dish, may well have been pewter, given their relatively high valuations. The chamber pots were worth fifteen pounds of tobacco each, and the two close stool pans and porringers were valued at forty

pounds for the lot, this at a time when butter pots, typically one of the most common ceramic forms, were worth only seven pounds each (Westmoreland County, Virginia, *Deeds, Patents and Accounts 1665–77*, 180). But even if one assumes in the face of this evidence that all these objects were ceramic, Lee's assemblage was modest indeed in terms of quantity as well as quality. Lee's inventory is characteristically detailed, containing specific entries for items as trifling as 'a small parcell of twine'. In addition, there are no non-specific entries like 'a parcell of lumber' or 'small things forgotten' for that matter, that might conceal ceramics. Nor was Lee married, so there are no pots hiding in an uninventoried widow's portion.

In Westmoreland County, Virginia, Lee was by no means unique. Mr Robert Jadwin, who died in the same year with a hefty estate valued at 46,749 pounds of tobacco, had no ceramics at all (Westmoreland County, Virginia, *Deeds, Patents and Accounts 1665–77*, 188). In fact, of the nineteen pre-1677 Westmoreland County, Virginia, inventories valued at over 20,000 pounds of tobacco, ceramics are not mentioned in seven. Of the remaining twelve, seven contain only coarse earthen and/or dairy-related forms. Typical of these for example is the inventory of Mr Richard Sturman (d. 1669), valued at 55,015 pounds. Sturman's only ceramic possessions were 'milke trays potts & panns' (Westmoreland County, Virginia, *Deeds, Patents and Accounts 1665–77*, 54). Another example, slightly lower down the economic scale, is Mr Daniel Hutt (d. 1674), worth 20,820 pounds, whose inventory contained the following uninspiring ceramic entries: 'crakd earthenware & a prcell of nales in it' and 'In the Milkehouse . . . a prcell old lumber' (Westmoreland County, Virginia, *Deeds, Patents and Accounts 1665–77*, 194).

What one might consider fine ceramics appear with certainty in only three of the remaining inventories: Roberts Nurses's 'prcell painted earthen ware' (1672), Nathaniel Pope's '2 juggs' (1660), and John Roasier's 'earthen porringer' (1661) (Westmoreland County, Virginia, *Deeds, Patents and Accounts 1665–77*, 198; Westmoreland County, Virginia, *Deeds, Wills and Patents 1653–9*, 8).

In Charles County, Maryland, settled like Westmoreland County, Virginia, in the 1650s, from 1658 to 1684 only 36% of the inventories of middling and wealthy planters list any ceramics (Walsh 1979, Table 2A).

On a practical level, these examples from the documents mean that a meager ceramic assemblage from a seventeenth-century Chesapeake site does not guarantee that its occupants were of meager means. This is not meant to imply that the appearance of vast quantities of porcelain and delft, for example, on a site suggests nothing about the wealth of its occupants. Quite obviously, it does. But once one realizes that ceramics were not *de rigueur* among the rich in the early Chesapeake, the interesting question is not whether rich people could afford more pottery than the poor, something anyone might have deduced without touching a trowel, but why some individuals chose to buy lots of fancy pots while many of their peers did not.

The second example is drawn from the work of James Deetz (1973, 1977). In attempting to develop a model for changing patterns of ceramic use in seventeenth- and eighteenth-century Anglo-America, Deetz noticed a dearth of nearly all but dairy-related wares on pre-1660 sites around Plymouth, Massachusetts. Drawing on Anderson's (1971) work on Tudor and Stuart English foodways he concluded, correctly, that eating and drinking vessels were generally not ceramic. Specifically, Deetz suggested that shared wooden trenchers and shared pewter and/or leather drinking vessels comprised the typical dining assemblage in early seventeenth-century Anglo-America. Deetz outlined two phenomena visible in the archaeological data after c.1660. The first was a general scarcity of ceramic plates, the second a gradual increase in the absolute numbers of ceramic drinking vessels. He concluded that wooden trenchers continued to be the norm for food consumption, that ceramic plates served primarily as decorative items in lieu of costly pewter, and that since trenchers do not survive in the ground, the increase in the number of drinking vessels might be taken as indicative of a general trend toward more individualized consumption of both liquids and solids.

While much of Deetz's (1973) articles relies on documentary evidence and the companion piece by Marley Brown (1973) is based solely on inventories, both suffer a preoccupation with excavated ceramics. Apparently when the inventory data were assembled for comparison with information from the ground, only entries for ceramics were systematically collected, a procedure not uncommon in the field. As one of the present authors (Stone 1977, 57, and below) has pointed out elsewhere, because archaeologists excavate ceramics they wish also to 'excavate' them from inventories. In the process, we often ignore the other forms listed there that comprised the larger context in which the ceramics had meaning.

Deetz's model was of course designed specifically for early New England. It may not be appropriate to attack it with data from the Chesapeake. Nevertheless, its applicability to all of Anglo-America is at least implicit throughout. The criticisms offered below, however, can be supported with data from New England as well.

The claim that trenchers were standard eating vessels is difficult to support, once one looks beyond the ceramic entries in the inventories. In the earliest Potomac entries, those taken in frontier St Mary's County, Maryland, 1638-50, wooden trenchers and dishes (other than Indian bowls used as utility vessels) were important only in newly established households – the households of recent immigrants or recently freed servants. In well established households, even of tenants, pewter predominated (Archives of Maryland 1887; Stone 1977, 60).

On the Virginia side of the river, the same pattern prevailed. In Westmoreland County, Virginia, in fourteen extant inventories taken during the decade following the county's incorporation in 1653, four contained *only* wooden eating vessels. Dishes and trays are mentioned specifically. In the rest, eating vessels were of pewter: saucers, plates, dishes, among other forms. In thirty-one inventories taken between 1668 and 1677 in the county, again only four listed eating vessels of wood, to the exclusion of other materials. And again all the rest contained pewter saucers, plates, or dishes.

The number of eating vessels, either in pewter or wood, was considerable. In the earlier Westmoreland County, Virginia, sample, Nathaniel Pope, with an estate worth c. £380, owned nine saucers, twelve plates, and thirty-six dishes, all of pewter. At the other end of the economic scale, George Poper, worth a paltry 1,035 pounds of tobacco, (c. £5) had three pewter saucers and three pewter plates (Westmoreland County, Virginia, *Deeds, Wills and Patents 1653-9*, 72). The pattern was the same in the later sample. Capt. John Ashton, with the second largest estate in the group, worth 94,000 pounds of tobacco (c. £470) owned fifty-one pewter plates, two pewter dishes, and '40 pewter dishes basons and pye plates' (Westmoreland County, Virginia, *Deeds, Patents and Accounts 1665-77*, 321-2). Francis Lewis, worth only 1,395 pounds of tobacco, the second poorest member of the sample, had three pewter plates and two pewter dishes. Men who owned smaller amounts of pewter typically supplemented their collection of eating vessels with wooden ones. Richard Sampson, a middling planter whose estate was not valued, had only three pewter dishes, but he also owned nine trenchers. Even the few planters who owned only wooden vessels owned them in quantities that suggest, given the small size of their households, that they were not shared. Henry Alday, for example, with an estate worth 5,840 pounds of tobacco (c. £29), had seven wooden trays, and Thomas Baron, whose estate valued at 394 pounds of tobacco (c. £2) made him the poorest individual in the sample, had four wooden dishes. (Westmoreland County, Virginia, *Deeds, Patents, and Accounts 1665-77*, 72; Westmoreland County, Virginia, *Deeds, Wills and Patents 1653-9*, 88). These examples could be extended, *ad nauseam*, from the St Mary's County, Maryland, inventories.

Clearly, then, the great majority of seventeenth-century Virginians and Marylanders were eating from pewter plates and not wooden trenchers, and eating vessels in either material were not being shared at the table in all save perhaps the poorest households.

This apparently had been the case in the most economically advanced areas of England since the late sixteenth century. In 1587, William Harrison, commenting on the effects of the price revolution, included in his famous three things 'marvelously altered in England within . . . sound remembrance' the appearance of quantities of pewter in the households of 'inferior artificers and many farmers'. The ordinary farmer had recently changed his 'treen platters into pewter', providing himself with a 'fair garnish of pewter for his cupboard' (Harrison 1968, 200-1). According to Harrison, a 'garnish' was comprised of twelve platters, twelve dishes, and twelve saucers (ibid., 367). Without doubt, the pewter vessels that proliferated in the houses of English yeomen were flatwares. It should not be surprising then to find Chesapeake planters following a pattern set by their ancestors in the previous century. Obviously the quantities of pewter plates in Chesapeake households make Deetz's suggestion that ceramic plates were displayed in lieu of pewter ones questionable.

If pewter eating vessels were numerous in the seventeenth-century Chesapeake, pewter drinking vessels were not. While the number of pieces of pewter a planter possessed was to some extent correlated with the size of his estate and household, the number of drinking vessels remained consistently small across the economic continuum. In Westmoreland County, Virginia, Nathaniel Pope had only four pewter drinking pots, and John Hiller, a planter of far more modest means (9,529 pounds of tobacco, c. £48), owned two drinking pots and three cups (Westmoreland County, Virginia, *Deeds and Wills 1660–1*, 16). Of the remaining six estates inventoried in the county between 1654 and 1661 in which pewter vessels were listed entirely by shape, none contained more than three pewter drinking vessels, although three of the individuals involved were more than twice as wealthy as Hiller. The pattern that emerges from the extant Westmoreland County, Virginia, inventories taken between 1668 and 1677 is similar. Capt. John Ashton, second wealthiest member of the group, had no pewter drinking vessels at all. Two middling planters had six each, and the remaining members of the sample owned three or less. Unless similar forms were present in ceramic or, in the wealthiest households, silver, the inevitable conclusion is that drinking vessels were being shared, if not with laborers, at least with neighbors when they came visiting.

It would seem that the increase in absolute numbers of ceramic drinking vessels noted by Deetz in the archaeological record towards the end of the seventeenth century might be taken to represent a trend toward more individualized consumption of beverages. But in social and religious ceremony, shared drinking vessels continued to be used as symbols of intimacy until the mid-nineteenth century (Stone 1977, 61–2).

5.4 Developing the Potomac typological system

The method behind the construction of POTS was unabashedly democratic. The authors have attempted to assign excavated forms to common categories and names derived from a number of documentary sources, most importantly probate inventories taken in Maryland (St Mary's County) and Virginia (Westmoreland and York counties) during the seventeenth and early eighteenth centuries. It appears that Englishmen in the Chesapeake took vessels from a wide variety of European potting traditions and applied relatively standardized uses and names to them. The functional significance of shape differences unique to a particular regional English folk culture may not have survived long on the Chesapeake frontier, where consumers could be less discriminating and where their needs were considerably altered. Similarly, some taxonomic distinctions with only regional distribution at home proved of little relevance to life in the Chesapeake, where they were discarded in favor of those that did.

In general, the process was akin to that by which

Virginians and Marylanders developed a distinctive vernacular architecture by drawing on a variety of English forms to combine and alter them according to local requirements. The general impression is that, as with architecture, the ways in which Chesapeake planters and New England farmers categorized their food vessels differed considerably in some domains. While there seems to have been significant variation between communities with different subsistence orientations in New England (cf. Yentsch below), such regional differences do not seem to have been characteristic of the Chesapeake (Beaudry 1980).

While many of the categories derived from the documents are fairly straightforward, some do require discussion.

Dish appears to have been used both as a specific and generic term. Randle Holme, an English artist who between 1640 and 1680 attempted to record and illustrate all of the symbols employed in English heraldry, provided a valuable source of information about seventeenth-century objects and their uses. Holme (1905, 4) listed the following terms under 'the several names of a dish':

A platter if large.
A dish, which [is] of a lesser sort.
A midleing dish.
A Broth dish, deeper bottomed than flesh dishes.
A Bason, is almost half round in the concave, . . .
A sallet dish.
A trencher plate or plate.
A saucer.

Holme's specification that a basin is 'almost half round in the concave' suggests that the term denoted a vessel different from the others. Elsewhere he pictures a vessel, round in plan, and labels it 'a dish, a platter, a saucer, a trencher plate'. Leaving basins aside then one can map 'the several names of a dish' in a tree diagram in which the lower levels are related to the higher levels by inclusion:

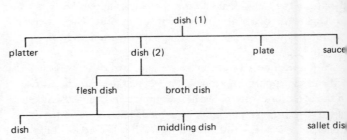

The arrangement of the terms in Holme's (1905) list is not accidental. They are given in order of decreasing size, a relation that obtains between the terms in the second row of the tree, from left to right. Depth was not a factor in distinguishing between terms at this level: *dish* (2) subsumes both *flesh dish* and *broth dish*. William Harrison looked at the matter in a similar fashion, noting in 1587 that 'dishes and platters in my time begin to be made deep like basins' (Harrison 1968, 367).

If the terms *platter*, *dish* (2), *plate*, and *saucer* denote vessels differing primarily in size (diameter), where do the breaks come? The anonymous author of *The Complete Appraiser* (1770, 42–3), published in the mid-eighteenth century, provides a partial answer in a table detailing prescribed weights and diameters for pewter plates and dishes. Plates run from 7¾ inches to 9¾ inches. Dishes range from 10¾ inches all the way up to 28 inches in diameter (Montgomery 1973, 135). Criteria similar to these were apparently in use in the seventeenth-century Chesapeake. Corduroy Ironmonger's 1675 inventory, taken in Westmoreland County, Virginia, listed dishes weighing 5.4 pounds each and plates weighing 1.5 pounds each (Westmoreland County, Virginia, *Deeds, Patents and Accounts 1665–77*, 243). The figures fit comfortably with *The Complete Appraiser*'s listing of the smallest dish at 1 pound, 12 ounces. One can infer that saucers, as the smallest members of the dish family, were of something less than c. seven inches in diameter, and that platters were the largest members of the group. *Platter* may have had other references as well. There is some evidence that it was on some occasions synonymous with *oval dish*. Holme makes the equation twice, noting that John the Baptist's head was served up to King Herod on an oval dish 'although some call it a platter' (Carson 1970, 44, 296; Holme 1905, 4). It would seem then that platters were *dishes* (2) that were either very large, or oval, or both. As the distinction between *platter* and *dish* was even then unclear, *platter* has been excluded from the POTS typology. All flat vessels greater in diameter than ten inches are defined as *dishes*.

As indicated, Holme (1905) made a distinction, echoed by Harrison (1968), between *flesh dishes* and *broth dishes*. The distinction does not appear in the authors' inventory sample, however, until the early eighteenth century, when it applies to plates. In 1756, William Wallet advertised in the *Maryland Gazette* that he would recast 'either flat or soup dishes or flat or soup plates' (Montgomery 1973, 135). Surviving pewter pieces from the period suggest that soup dishes and plates ranged in height between one inch and two inches. Rather than offer absolute criteria for soup dishes and plates versus flat dishes and plates, it is suggested that the distinction in an excavated ceramic assemblage be based on the objects in it. If the excavated material exhibits a continuum of depths relative to diameters, the distinction might best be ignored. If the distribution of shapes exhibits a break, however, the distinction may reflect functional differences and therefore be of utility.

Holme gives two functions for basins. He implies a food function by classifying basins as members of the dish family, and in this he was paralleled by many estate appraisers who grouped or found pewter basins with pewter dishes and plates. Holme also illustrates a barber's basin and a 'stand . . . used for to set a Bason on whilest washing . . .' (Holme 1688, 432, 438; 1905, 18, 18a). Both food basins and a great (wash) basin on a stand are listed in Robert Slye's inventory, taken in St Mary's County, Maryland, in 1671 (*Maryland Provincial Records, Testamentary Proceedings* 5, ff.152–90). While some basins may have been used for both dining and washing, archaeologists should try to determine the functions of the vessels that they recover from the find contexts of the sherds. At the Clifts site in Westmoreland County, Virginia, one of the authors excavated sherds of decorated basins matching plate fragments from early eighteenth-century contexts (Neiman 1980). At Rosewell, Noël Hume found undecorated wash basin fragments in a c.1762–3 pit (Noël Hume 1962, 203–7). In the Rosewell report, Noël Hume rightly grouped the wash basins with the chamber pots, while in Neiman's report on the Clifts site, the basins will be counted as dining vessels.

Apart from the problems presented by *platter* and *basin*, the sources used above describe a relatively straightforward typology for categorizing flat dining vessels. It is a comfortable typology as much of it remains in use today. But readers of seventeenth-century documents should be aware that alternate taxonomies were in use during that century. Some appraisers recorded many dishes and few plates. Others listed 'platters great & small' to the exclusion of both dishes and plates (*Archives of Maryland* 1887, 93).

Drinking vessels presented fewer problems. *Pot* is the most troublesome form as well as the most common. Fortunately Holme illustrates one pot shape – a pitcher-like form (Carson 1970, 14, 68, 196; Holme 1688, 167). The name also seems to have been applied to bulbous and squat cylindrical drinking vessels as probate and potters' inventories do not provide alternate designations. 'Drinking bowl' seems to have been applied to metal vessels only. Except in silver, *cup* was restricted to small containers. 'Pint cup' appears rarely in Chesapeake inventories, while (in pewter) drinking pots routinely appear in pint, quart, and pottle (two quart) sizes.

The procedure of naming by plebiscite bypassed most of the problems of describing food preparation vessels. Thus, all large pans are typed as *milk pans*, although some were used as wash basins and cooking pans. All dairy pots will be considered as *butter pots* until someone defines – in Chesapeake terms – the difference in form between a butter pot and cream pot. While excavated dairy pots vary in shape, the most important variable seems to be place of manufacture. Thus most North Devon pots have constricted shoulders (Watkins 1960, 45) while Flintshire pots are generally more cylindrical (Noël Hume 1976, 135). In a similar fashion, a seventeenth-century definition of *pipkin* has evaded these authors; it is assumed that the term encompassed most of the cooking pots excavated on Chesapeake sites. No other term identifiable as an earthen cooking pot appears in the inventories, and most excavated specimens are of one general shape.

Commonly used categories for summarizing excavated vessels have been too general. More gradations are needed to distinguish between shared and individual drinking vessels, and dining vessel groups oriented toward hominy and pottage versus boiled, baked, or roasted foods. The recommended categories are illustrated below. These are simplified groupings. It is realized, for example, that bottles were storage as well as serving vessels and that jugs of less than a pottle could be used for serving. In English America as well as in England, some families undoubtedly used pitchers as jugs and drinking pots as well as utility vessels. Without some simplification, however, summary would be impossible, and these categories represent the best fit achievable between the multifarious uses suggested by the documents and employable archaeological categories (fig 5.1).

The logical conclusion of an article such as this would witness the application of POTS to several excavated assemblages. Presumably, this would demonstrate the virtues of the typology by comparing ceramic assemblages from successive periods at the same site and from the same period at different sites. At the present time, however, such comparisons cannot be undertaken. Analyses of the excavated materials from St John's in St Mary's City, Maryland, and the Clifts Plantation site in Westmoreland County, Virginia, are still underway, although both will be used as test cases for POTS, along with materials from sites on the James River in Virginia. This typology is presented in its tentative form as a means of informing colleagues in historical archaeology of the direction this research is taking and in hopes of eliciting comments, suggestions, and shared information from others concerned with the problems of ceramic typologies and functional interpretations based on archaeological assemblages from historical sites.

5.5 Chesapeake ceramic forms and definitions

Ceramic forms discussed previously and listed in Figure 5.1 are illustrated and defined below. Groupings are determined primarily on the basis of vessel shape and only secondarily by vessel function. These groupings are not necessarily those used in the course of ceramic analysis, and infrequently excavated forms are neither illustrated nor defined. Probate inventories do, however, sometimes mention some of these unusual forms that are seldom found in archaeological contexts.[1]

Note

1. The authors would like to thank the following people for taking time to comment on this manuscript: John Austin, Norman Barka, Barbara Carson, James Deetz, William Kelso, Ivor and Audrey Noël Hume, Alain and Merry Outlaw, and C. Malcolm Watkins. All of the drawings in the text are by Janet Long. An earlier version of this manuscript was presented at the Jamestown Conference on Archaeology, Jamestown, Virginia, April 1979.

A SUGGESTED FUNCTIONAL DIVISION OF VESSEL FORMS FROM 17th CENTURY SITES

FOOD PROCESSING
(Cooking and Dairying)
Pipkin
Pudding Pan
Bowl
Milk Pan
Collander

FOOD AND DRINK STORAGE

Storage Pot
Jar
Bottle

BEVERAGE CONSUMPTION

Individual

(1 pt or less)
Cup
Mug
Jug
Footed Bowls

Communal or Individual

(More than 1 pt)
Mug
Jug
Drinking Pot
Flask

Serving

Pitcher
Ewer
Punch Bowl
Large Jug
Sillabub Pot

FOOD CONSUMPTION

Stews/Pottages/Soups
Porringers
Soup Plates
Small Bowls

Solid Food Consumption and Serving
Caudle Pots
Basins
Plates
Dishes
Saucers
Salts

HEALTH/HYGIENE
Galley Pots - Large
        - Small
Chamber Pots
Basins - Plain
       - Barber's

OTHER
Chaffing Dish
Candlesticks
Betty Lamp

Hollow Vessels for Liquids—1/8 size

CUP. A small, handled drinking vessel of less than a pint in capacity. In form, cups are closely related to drinking pots.

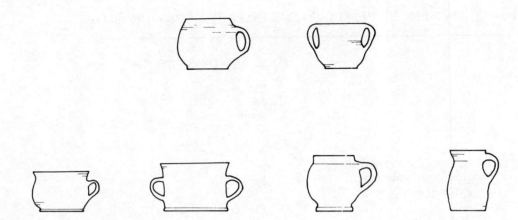

DRINKING POT. A one or multi-handled vessel, usually bulbous, but sometimes cylindrical in form, ranging in capacity from 1 pt to 2 qts or more. Cylindrical drinking pots are distinguished from mugs by being wider than tall and/or having two or more handles.

MUG. A single-handled, straight-sided drinking vessel, taller than wide, ranging from 1 gill (¼ pt) to 2 qts (or more).

JUG. A handled vessel of bulbous form with a cylindrical neck rising from a pronounced shoulder, with or without a gutter. In size, jugs range from small drinking vessels to large serving vessels. Jugs occur generally in refined earthenwares and stonewares.

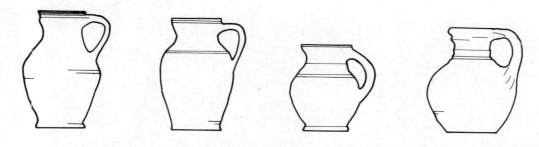

PITCHER. A handled vessel with bulbous body, having a flaring neck with a gutter. In America, used primarily in the kitchen and dairy. Pitchers occur in coarse earthenwares.

EWER. A handled, bulbous-bodied serving vessel, similar in shape to a jug, but with a narrower, elongated neck with a gutter or spout. Ewers occur in refined earthenwares or stonewares.

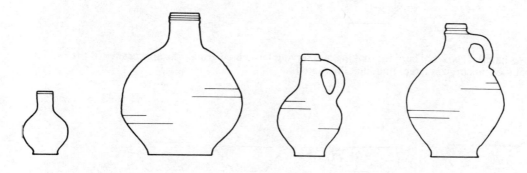

BOTTLE. A bulbous-bodied storage and serving vessel with a neck narrower than a jug or ewer, with or without a handle.

FLASK/COSTREL. A bulbous-bodied vessel with a very narrow neck, similar in form to a bottle, but having two ears or strap handles rising from the shoulder. A drink container carried by travellers and field workers.

SILLABUB POT. A pot with a spout, two handles, and sometimes a cover, for drinking and serving sillabub, posset, and wassail.

Hollow Vessels for Liquids and Semi-solid Foods—1/8 size

CAUDLE CUP/POT. A two-handled, covered cup, for making and serving fermented gruel. The appearance of the term caudle pot suggests that it occurs in sizes larger than that illustrated.

 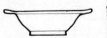

PORRINGER. A vessel usually hemispherical in shape and shallower in relation to its diameter than a cup or a pot. Porringers have at least one and sometimes two handles, either horizontal or vertical. Used for eating porridge, pottage (stew), soup, etc.

PUNCH BOWL. A hemispherical vessel with a plain rim. Punch bowls occur in refined earthenwares, stonewares, and porcelain. They range in capacity from ½ pt to several gallons. The smallest sizes were used by individuals for drinking punch and perhaps eating semi-solid foods. The larger sizes were used for making and serving punch.

BOWL. An open vessel with convex sides terminating in either a plain or everted rim or brim. Bowls have no footrings and occur only in coarse earthenwares. Bowls were used primarily in the kitchen and dairy.

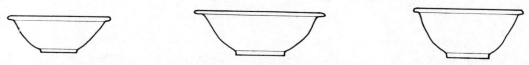

BASIN. An open vessel with convex sides, of greater width than depth, having a brim or everted lip. Basins occur with or without footrings but only in refined earthenwares and porcelain. These forms were used for washing, shaving and for dining.

Flat Vessels for Food—1/8 size

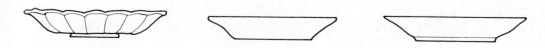

DISH. A serving vessel larger than 10 in either in diameter or in length, with or without a footring. Dishes were made in shallow and deep forms.

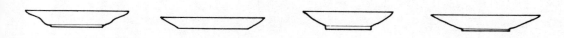

PLATE. An eating vessel from 7 in to 10 in in diameter, with or without a footring. Plates were made in shallow and deep (i.e., soup) forms.

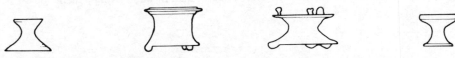

SAUCER. A vessel less than 7in in diameter, with or without a footring. Saucers were used for serving condiments (hence: sauce-r) and perhaps as small plates.

Miscellaneous Dining Forms—1/8 size

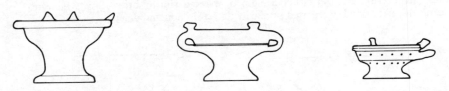

SALT. A pedestaled serving vessel in refined earthenware with or without supports at the rim.

CHAFING DISH. A coarse earthenware vessel on a pedestal with supports around the rim. Chafing dishes held coals used to warm food at the table.

Cooking Vessels—1/8 size

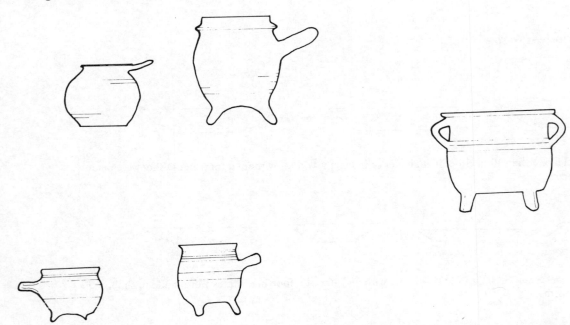

PIPKIN. An earthen cooking pot. Two varieties of pipkins have been excavated in the Chesapeake. The handled pipkin (above left) is a small, bulbous cooking pot, frequently with a rod handle. The pot/flesh pot (above right) is a cooking vessel with two ears and three legs. While the form is a metal one, it was occasionally copied in coarse earthenwares.

A VESSEL TYPOLOGY FOR EARLY CHESAPEAKE CERAMICS

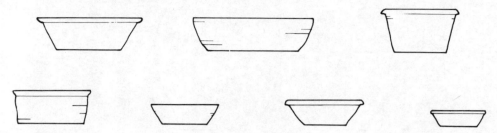

PAN/PUDDING, PASTRY, PATTY, ETC. A coarse earthenware cooking vessel, roughly in the shape of an inverted, truncated cone, less than 10in in diameter.

Dairy and Kitchen Vessels—1/8 size

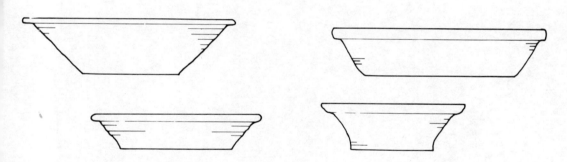

MILK PAN. A vessel roughly in the shape of an inverted, truncated cone, 10in or more in diameter. Used for cooling milk, as a wash basin and probably for cooking.

COLANDER. A pan-like, handled utensil with a perforated bottom. Colanders were used for making cheese, washing vegetables, etc.

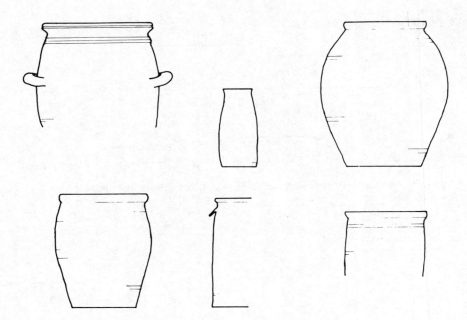

POT/BUTTER POT. A large, cylindrical or slightly convex-sided vessel, taller than wide, used for souring cream or storing butter, fat (lard), etc.

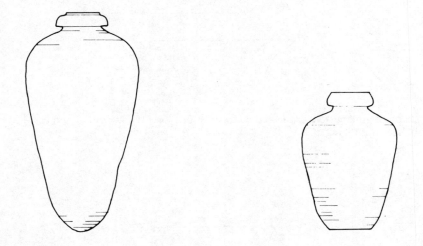

JAR. A large vessel, taller than wide, with pronounced shoulders and constricted neck, bearing a heavy, rounded lip. Jars were used for storing water, oil, beer, etc.

Hygiene-related Forms—1/8 size

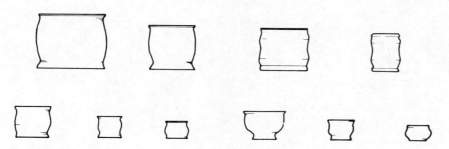

GALLEY POT. A cylindrical tin-glazed vessel with slightly flared rim and base. Large and small sizes may be distinguished. Used for drugs, ointments, cosmetics and, occasionally, condiments.

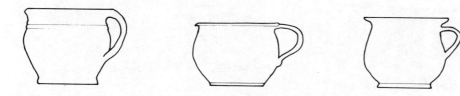

CHAMBER POT. A handled vessel with convex sides and a sturdy flared rim or brim. The eventual repository of the contents of all the above.

CANDLESTICK. A lighting device consisting of a hollow tube, a foot and/or a drip tray.

Part II

**Documents and the archaeologist:
the data base**

Chapter 6

Artifacts are not enough

Garry Wheeler Stone

An exhaustive and critical use of documentary sources by archaeologists is recommended. Probate inventories from the Chesapeake region of Maryland are used as the basis for reinterpretations of a number of common misconceptions about ceramic use and ownership by seventeenth- and eighteenth-century Chesapeake residents. The critical importance of considering materials that do not appear in the archaeological record in combination with those that do is emphasized.

6.1 Introduction

We weave our theories about the colonial past from materials that were never intended as historical evidence: tax lists, court records, pot sherds, or artifactual survivals. Constructing theory from such accidental and ambiguous evidence requires the greatest care. Hypotheses based on anything less than the critical use of all the relevant evidence are tenuous (Murphey 1973).

For no group of researchers are the problems of data interpretation more difficult than for archaeologists. The forces that determined (1) what materials were buried; (2) what buried materials survive; and (3) which of these buried materials archaeologists subsequently recover, are complicated and infinitely variable. In attempting to deal with excavated evidence, archaeologists are confronted with the difficult choice of interpolating habits and ideas from incomplete material remains or retreating to technological studies or mere description.

Fortunately, the archaeologist studying the recent Euro-American past has a wealth of other evidence available, including artifacts surviving in use or in museums, prints and maps, and ton after ton of written and printed documents. All of these sources must be used with discrimination, but, by combining the skills of social historian (or historical ethnographer) and archaeologist, the historical archaeologist may find evidence bearing directly on the non-material culture of the group he is studying and on the social and economic correlations of his excavated materials. Often documents provide the means for archaeologists to test hypotheses derived from excavated data; excavated data may provide the means for historians to test hypotheses derived from documents.

This paper is a plea for historical archaeologists to make more use of documentary evidence. It proceeds largely by suggestion, first discussing an example of the distortion possible when one kind of evidence is used uncritically, without resort to other data for hypothesis confirmation. The paper then illustrates some of the data that may be found in one legal record, the probate inventory. I make no attempt here to deal with the problems involved in trying to combine documentary and non-documentary evidence (see Brown 1973; Stone, Little and Israel 1973; Miller 1974a; Herman, Sands and Schecter 1973; and South 1974).

Folklorist Henry Glassie would disagree with my

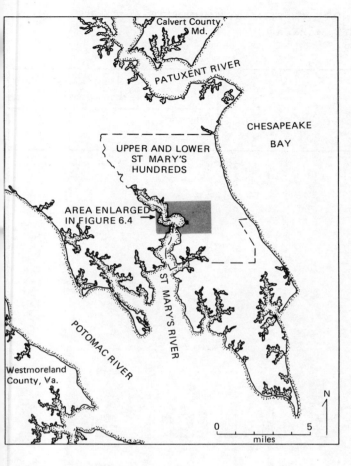

Fig.6.1. The area of the study

contention that extensive use of documents is essential for good historical archaeology. Glassie has written that

> a methodological limitation to print binds the scholar to studying only the handful of people who were literate. The artifact is potentially democratic; artifacts from the past are so abundant that they can be utilized to replace romantic preconceptions with scientifically derived knowledge.   (Glassie 1972b, 29)

This methodological hypothesis is the basis of Glassie's monograph, *Folk Housing in Middle Virginia: A Structural Analysis of Historic Artifacts* (1975).

An exhaustive survey of the Orchid-Gum Spring area of Louisa and Goochland Counties, Virginia, provided the data for *Folk Housing in Middle Virginia*. The survey recorded 338 dwelling units. Of these, 174, including house trailers, were modern and were excluded from further analysis. Of the remaining structures, Glassie implies that only twenty or thirty date from the eighteenth century. He discusses twelve eighteenth-century structures in detail.[1] On the basis of these *twelve structures*, Glassie presents a theory of eighteenth-century housing and cultural change. He applies these conclusions not just to Louisa and Goochland Counties, but to the entire area west of the Chesapeake Bay and east of

the Blue Ridge, from Albemarle Sound, North Carolina, to Anne Arundel County, Maryland.

Consciously revisionist, in one of his conclusions Glassie attacks the traditional stereotype of Chesapeake housing as the 'grandiose mansion or the humble hut'. Noting that in contrast to the lavish homes of northern merchants, the mansions of southern planters rarely were exceptional, he reports that a middling sort of wooden farmhouse typified the Chesapeake region. Glassie states that traditional houses had two or four rooms; few were larger or smaller. While Glassie notes that 'many, probably most of the smallest early homes have been reclaimed by nature,' he does not appear to consider this a serious research problem (ibid., 64–5).

By ignoring the processes that created his data, Glassie misuses his evidence to project a far too rosy picture of eighteenth-century housing. The forces that lead artifacts to survive above ground are as non-random as those that preserve buried evidence. Sturdy construction, economic suitability, and conformity to changing cultural values are all survival factors. Even the smallest structure Glassie describes appears to be a fully framed building, weatherboarded, with brick underpinnings, brick chimney stack, and glazed windows. None of the structures he illustrates seems to have originated as the cheap, impermanent structures that dominate eighteenth-century listings of Maryland tenant houses (ibid., 43, 153, 156). (Some of these weathered, gray buildings of riven clapboard and wooden chimneys lacked glazed windows and planked floors.)[2] If we want sociologically correct knowledge of folk housing, we must consult a democratic source. Fortunately, for the Southern Maryland part of Glassie's area of inquiry, such a source is available: a tax list that provides a housing survey as detailed as a modern census.

The Direct Tax of 1798 was a short-lived experiment in a federal real estate tax. The appraisers had instructions to record the dimensions, materials, and windows of every existing structure. They listed privies and hen houses along with tobacco houses and dwellings. The detailed descriptions of additions and sheds often make it possible to decipher the evolution of enumerated structures. Lists of lands and slaves extend the possibilities for sociological analysis.

For illustration, I have chosen the area with which I am most familiar, Upper and Lower St Mary's Hundreds, St Mary's County, Maryland (fig 6.1). These precincts made up a tobacco-growing district bounded by the St Mary's and Potomac Rivers and the Chesapeake Bay. Within this area, the tax lists include 128 dwellings (fig 6.2).[3] There is reason to believe that the lists included all structures of economic value. Many were appraised at only ten dollars, and some, though not all, derelict structures of 'no value' were included. The low appraisal of one unfinished building was justified by noting that it was 'not cover'd & without Windows, doors, or Floors'.[4]

Almost half of the hundreds' white population lived and worked in groups of buildings that had as their nucleus a one-room house. Some, with shed wings and exterior kitchens, provided perhaps four or five living spaces for the planter's

DWELLING[a] PLAN TYPES IN UPPER AND LOWER ST. MARY'S HUNDREDS, ST. MARY'S COUNTY, MARYLAND
1799

	Traditional plans One room deep		Transitional and Georgian Two rooms deep	
	One story		One story	Two story

	1 room N = 59 (46.1%)	1 or 2 rooms N = 17 (13.3%)	2 rooms + N = 52 (40.6%)				

Exterior[b] kitchens: without / with

Bar chart values:
- 1 room: 52 (39 without / with), + Shed: 7 (4)
- 1 or 2 rooms: 11 (4), + Shed: 6 (1)
- 2 rooms +: 31 (10), + Shed: 6 (1), 3[f]: 4, + Shed: 1, 2[g]: 6, 4[h]: 3, 4: 1

First floor[c] rooms:	1[d]	+ Shed	1or2[e]	+ Shed	2	+ Shed	3[f]	+ Shed	2[g]	4[h]	4
Structure[i] dimensions											
minimum:	16 × 12 (4)		24 × 14 (1)		32 × 12 (1)		34 × 16		20 × 26	30 × 32	44 × 38
maximum:	20 × 20 (3)		24 × 16 (15)		36 × 20 (1)		50 × 20		26 × 28	48 × 30	
modal:	20 × 16 (36)		24 × 16 (15)		32 × 16 (12)						
Materials											
brick:					3		2				
frame:	52		17		33		3		6	3	1
log:	7				1						

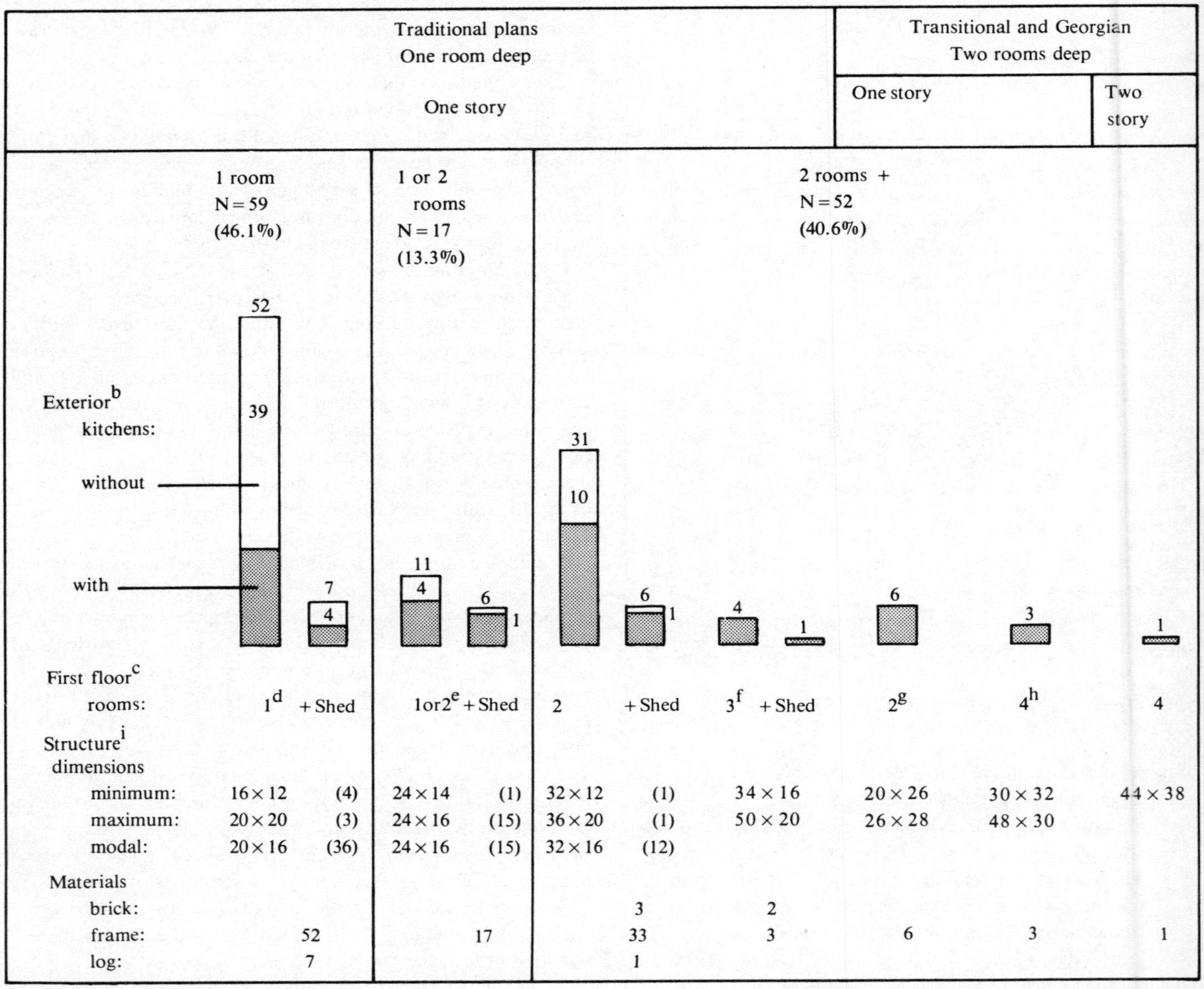

Fig. 6.2. Dwelling[a] plan types in Upper and Lower St Mary's Hundreds, St Mary's County, Maryland, 1799

[a] Dwellings: structures identified as dwellings, exclusive of specified slave quarters. The reconstruction of slave housing is complicated and beyond the scope of this investigation.

[b] Separate outbuildings.

[c] Exclusive of sheds. Surviving structures and manuscript sources suggest that St Mary's countians partitioned small houses less frequently than did the residents of Louisa and Goochland Counties, Virginia. I am greatly indebted to Cary Carson for his assistance in making these dimension/room determinations.

[d] Only one structure of this size (20'4" × 16'0") has been recorded with a two room plan (a large heated room and a small unheated chamber).

[e] Three plans seem to be present: one-room, two rooms, and one room and side passage. Seven houses of this size (length 22'6" − 29'; width 14'10" − 19'6") have been measured. One is a one-room structure. The other six have the one room and side passage plan. All date from the late eighteenth century or first half of the nineteenth century. The St Mary's County Orphans' Court valuations suggest an older plan of one heated and one unheated room. The 1780–1808 volume of Annual Valuations and Indentures lists ten 24' × 16' dwellings (exclusive of specified slave quarters). Partitions are specified in two. Since both were miserable dwellings, it is unlikely that either had innovative side passage plans. The eight other structures are described only as 24 by 16 feet.

[f] Four of these structures are two room or one room and passage structures to which additions have been added. The fifth is described in the *Maryland Gazette* as '54 by 20 with 5 rooms below and 3 above, with a brick chimney and two fire places; . . . [3 February 1774]'.

[g] The wider structures probably had side passages. One of the 20' wide dwellings survives. It lacks a passage.

[h] The smallest (see fig. 6.4: The Rev. Tabbs) was formed by doubling the width of a two room dwelling. The largest was a gambrel-roofed, brick-gabled structure of the second quarter of the eighteenth century. (See Henry Chandlee Forman, *Tidewater Maryland Architecture and Gardens* (New York: Bonanza Books, 1956), 95–100, 135.)

[i] Exclusive of sheds and porches. Bracketed numbers equal number of examples of those dimensions.

Sources: Federal Direct Tax of 1798, St Mary's County, Maryland, Particular Lists of Dwellings and Lands (Maryland Historical Society).

family. But a third of the area's total population lived in houses of one room, with an attic above. Only one two-story, double-pile, brick house was listed, and it was small in comparison with the mansions of the great Virginia planters.[5]

Figure 6.2 is a superficial analysis of these tax lists. (Its preparation, beginning with faded microfilm, took less than twelve hours.) Its only purpose is to demonstrate that archaeologists of whatever discipline ignore ethnography at their peril.

The information presented in Figure 6.2 has been simplified and rearranged in Figure 6.3 to correspond with the categories Glassie uses. Note that the two sources agree only that two-room structures were common. Few smaller dwellings survived in Glassie's survey area; few larger houses were present in St Mary's County in 1798.

What happened to eighteenth-century Chesapeake dwellings? They rotted, burned, or were torn down with appalling speed. Table 6.1 documents this process for one neighborhood of Lower St Mary's Hundred. Every dwelling recorded on Snow Hill in 1765 had disappeared or been rebuilt by 1803 (see fig 6.4).

When Glassie characterized tax lists and probate material as 'phantom' reflections of the past, he was of course, correct (1975, 11). What he failed to appreciate is how phantom-like his folk dwellings are, too. Standing derelict in a twentieth-century landscape, shorn of their inhabitants, furnishings, outbuildings, and fields, separate from the society and economy in which they functioned, these artifacts can provide questions, but reveal little by themselves. Only by juxtaposing *all* the ghostly images of the past can we examine the past in enough stereoscopic detail to understand its cultures. A surprising amount of documentary ethnographic material does survive.

St Mary's County is particularly well endowed with documentary materials describing housing. Surviving are the lists of the Federal Direct Tax of 1798, manorial documents, excellent probate records for 1658–1775, and detailed Orphans' Court valuations from 1780. While many areas do not have all of these records, some have others, including insurance surveys, newspaper advertisement files, real estate atlases, and deeds.

6.2 Sherds, inventories and the meaning of artifacts

The most important of these sources for the study of culture are the probate inventories made at the death of the head of a household. In Massachusetts these lists included real property, but elsewhere only movables (more subject to embezzlement) were enumerated. Inventories have to be used with discretion. They vary in quality and demographic coverage from place to place and decade to decade, but a good probate file, such as exists for St Mary's County before the Revolution, allows the scholar to observe almost every household in the community. When the enumeration was made room by room, it is almost possible to retrace the appraiser's steps around the dwelling and through the outbuildings (Main 1975; Smith 1975; Menard, Harris and Carr 1974).

For a decade social and economic historians, curators, and archaeologists have been using inventories to study seventeenth- and eighteenth-century America. But while the social historians, the ethnographers of this period, have used the data retrieved from inventories to study society (Main 1965; Jones 1970; Carr 1973; Kulikoff 1975), by and large scholars interested in material culture have used probate records only to study artifacts. We have used them to date artifacts, track their social incidence, and identify clusters of associated artifacts, but rarely have we made the step to studying culture through artifacts, a fault of which I am as guilty as anyone else (Brown 1973; Teller 1968; Chace 1972).

My research has focused on the increasing popularity of fine ceramics in eighteenth-century America. In large part, the popularity of delftware, porcelain, and the new stone-and-earthenwares was a reflection of Georgian taste. The eighteenth-century gentry wanted to be graceful, formal, and stylish. Tea drinking perfectly suited their requirements. It was novel and expensive. The clutter of accompanying artifacts and the tedious steps inherent in preparing and serving it encouraged formality. The imported and technically superb porcelains with which tea was associated seemed to be linked with man's increasing sense of control over his world. And the tea ceremony was a perfect social symbol. In contrast to the old communal tankard of ale, the individual cups and saucers of the tea service matched the gentry's increasing individualism. Simultaneously, these new habits advertised the social gulf between the elite and ordinary folk. A similar change occurred in dining equipage, as precisely matched sets of serving pieces, soup plates, and plates replaced heterogeneous collections of pewter and ceramics. These practices first became common in the 1720s. Tea quickly became popular among the urban middle classes, but in the countryside the tea etiquette

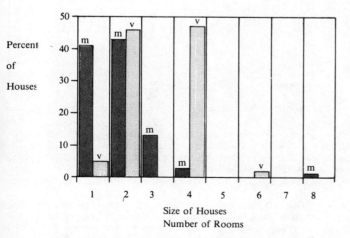

Fig. 6.3. Comparison of dwellings recorded in Upper and Lower St Mary's Hundreds, St Mary's County, Maryland, 1798 (m) with traditional structures surviving in the Orchid-Gum Spring vicinity, Louisa and Goochland Counties, Virginia, 1966 (v). (Maryland: exclude passages and attics; sheds counted as one room, Virginia: attics apparently excluded)

Table 6.1 *Impermanent eighteenth-century architecture: the housing on Snow Hill Manor c.1765–1824*
Few Tidewater structures lasted longer than one or two generations. Five dwellings stood on Snow Hill Manor in 1765. By 1803 every one had disappeared or been rebuilt. This attrition rate does not seem atypical. The fate of the Snow Hill structures shows why – where vernacular buildings are constructed of materials as perishable as unpainted clapboard – structures surviving to the present are almost certain to be a biased sample.

TENANTS TRACTS ACRES	c.1765[a] DWELLINGS OUT HOUSES	1798[b] DWELLINGS OUT HOUSES	1824–41[c] DWELLINGS PLAN OUT HOUSES	OCCUPANT CONST. DATE ACRES
Wm & Geo Hicks St John's 378*	old, large much decayed	none	28×30 2 rooms + side passage kitchen smoke house poultry house barn corn crib stable	Brome [owner] c.1816 378*
Mary Morris Paw Paw Fields 186	old, 28×18 clapboard clapboard kitchen tobacco house	18×16 log kitchen	?	Smith [tenant] 186
The Rev. Tabbs Chancellor's Orchard 143	good, 28×16 brick chimneys clapboard kitchen & quarter tobacco house	30×32 kitchen meat house	28×36 4 rooms log kitchen dairy log granary	Dennis [tenant] c.1770 208
John Baker Baker's Purchase + Inclosure 139	24×16 clapboard clapboard kitchen 1 other kitchen corn house tobacco house	28×16 kitchen meat house [dairy] house log house log corn house	26×30 2 rooms + side passage kitchen smoke house dairy quarters barn & stable corn house	Bennett [owner] 1803 195*
Thos Willinor Hardshift 80	none	'old Dwelling' 'no value'	none	[Brome, owner] 87
James Taylor Ivy Hills 52	old, 20×16 clapboard	none	none	[Smith, tenant) 29

* = owned additional land adjacent to Snow Hill.

Notes: Four of the 1765 tenements fell within the surveyor's standard formula for recording vernacular housing. The descriptions suggest that three of the dwellings and all the kitchens were clapboard structures with wooden chimneys. Only Mr Tabbs's 'good' house would have been weatherboarded. George Hicks's 'Large old Dwelling House much Decayed' fell outside the standard format for recording tenements (his father had been sheriff). The plantation outbuildings and his brother's large house were on their Church Point freehold land. These buildings had also disappeared by 1824.

The 1765 dwellings were above average for tenements (the Calverts gave long leases at low rents), yet three had disappeared by 1798. Tabbs had purchased freehold title to his land just before enlarging his house.

The confiscation, partitioning, and sale of the Manor during the American Revolution does not seem to have made an immediate impact on the quality of housing, but the extensive nineteenth-century improvements would not have been made without the change to fee simple ownership. Note how rapid obsolescence facilitated style evolution. All the 1765 buildings were one room deep. By 1816 three had been replaced by buildings two rooms deep. The new structures all had good brick chimneys and were faced with sawn weatherboard.

Sources
[a] Memorandum Book of Snow Hill Manor, Proprietary Leases, Hall of Records.
[b] Federal Assessment of 1798, Upper and Lower St Mary's Hundreds, Particular Lists of Lands and Dwellings.
[c] Annual Valuation of Real and Personal Property, 1807–26, ff. 94–5; ibid., 1826–41, ff. 200–1 [Brome: 1825, 1830]; ibid., 1826–41, ff. 125–6 ['Dennis': 1830]; ibid., 1841–64, f. 5 [Bennett: 1841]; Henry Chandlee Forman, *Jamestown and St Mary's: Buried Cities of Romance* [Baltimore: Johns Hopkins, 1938, p. 242 [Brome]); Henry Chandlee Forman, *Old Buildings, Gardens and Furniture in Tidewater Maryland* (Cambridge, MD.: Tidewater, 1967, pp. 200, 304 [Bennett]).

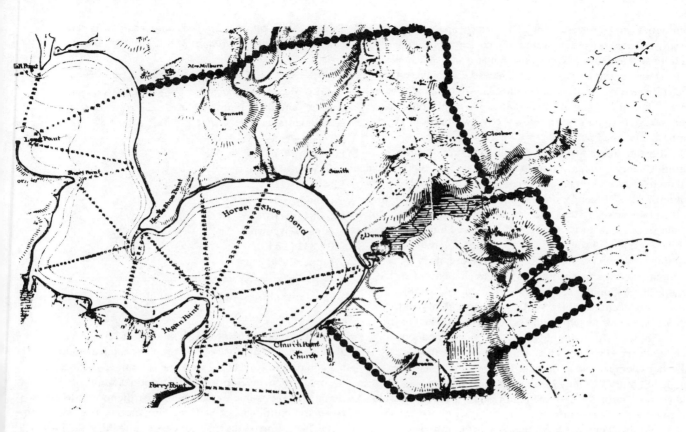

Fig. 6.4. Map of Snow Hill in 1824. approximate scale: 1 inch = 2500 feet. 1781 bounds of manor are shown by solid circles.
Source: National Archives Record Group 77, No. F27 (part).

remained restricted largely to the gentry (Roth 1961; Stone 1970; Stone, Little and Israel 1973; Deetz 1973, esp. p. 32).

Throughout the seventeenth century oriental luxuries trickled into England through Portugal and Holland, but in limited amounts that prevented widespread distribution. Even in the late seventeenth century, serious porcelain collecting was largely a queen's prerogative, but in 1700 this changed. In that year the Chinese first permitted the English East India Company to export large amounts of porcelain. Immediately, among England's aristocracy and mercantile gentry, exotic chinoiserie became extremely fashionable. By 1711 in London, 'China-ware' had become a fad, a fad so pronounced that it was ridiculed by social commentators (Syz 1969; Charleston 1969; Bond 1965).

I have studied two areas: Suffolk County, Massachusetts, 1680–1775, and St Mary's County, Maryland, 1730–60. Suffolk County is a particularly interesting area because in the early eighteenth century it included America's largest port as well as conservative rural townships.

The inventories suggest that Boston lagged behind London by about fifteen years. Porcelain does not appear in the sample until 1721, but within a decade it is present in a majority of merchant inventories. By then at least one merchant had booby-trapped his house with porcelain: William Welsted's inventory lists almost 150 pieces of porcelain (many of them gilded and enamelled) scattered about his living room, dining room, and master bedroom–sitting room. There were seventy-seven pieces and one large set of porcelain teaware, forty-eight porcelain dining vessels, three large bowls and basins of ambiguous function, and two decorative 'Images'. Welsted's inventory also lists seventy-three pieces of tin-glazed earthenware and thirty pieces of fine stoneware (Suffolk County, Massachusetts, *Probate Records 1650–1800*, vol. 27, 443). The prominence with which these ceramics were displayed and the relative care with which they were described indicate that porcelain and its European imitations had gained substantial social status. The use of fine ceramics spread rapidly. By the American Revolution fine ceramics probably were present in a majority of Boston households.

The diffusion of porcelain in Boston is highly correlated with economic status. For the 1730 sample, there is a 75% correlation between the presence of porcelain and the value of the inventory, as measured by the square of Pearson's correlation coefficient (Blalock 1960, 298). Yet this index is misleading: the most important factor is group identification. Wealthy merchants indentified with their English peers and therefore emulated them. In the same way, local economic groups dependent on the merchants or the royal bureaucracy – minor customs officials, book-keepers, and mariners – aped their betters and purchased porcelain as a cheap status symbol. Locally oriented townsmen were more conservative and traditional. They used luxury goods not as a way to achieve social status, but as a reflection of achieved economic status. The craftsmen and contractors in the 1730–70 urban sample had a mean inventory value of 350 pounds; 23% owned porcelain. The average mariner's inventory was only two-thirds as large, but 63% contained porcelain.[6]

Boston differed from the surrounding rural townships. Suffolk County yeomen and husbandmen saw that gentry ritual had no relevance to them, and consequently they ignored it. Not until the 1760 sample does a countryman appear with fine earthen tableware. Two yeomen in 1775 owned a few pieces of 'China, Earthen & glass,' but the values placed on these parcels (10 shillings; and 15 shillings, 7 pence) suggest that they contained only a few items. These vessels more likely functioned as attractive containers than as elements of social ritual (Suffolk County, *Probate Records*, vol. 74, 25–58).

In eighteenth-century St Mary's County, Maryland, patterns in the ownership of fine ceramics are similar. In the late 1720s, the inventories of two wealthy gentlemen, one a member of the Governor's Council, contain porcelain collections comparable to those of Boston merchants. The detailed St Mary's County inventories show that by mid-century, virtually all of the minor gentry – planters owning five to fifteen slaves – drank tea. One member of my sample, Samuel Caldwell (1752, f.558), seems to have owned everything – 'Dove Coloured' cups and saucers, sugar dishes, a cream pot, and slop bowls – his wife needed to set a fashionably complete tea table for a dozen (Maryland Hall of Records, vol. 15, 110–19 (Lowe), vol. 13, 79 (Bowles), vol. 79, 255–9 (Caldwell)). Most of his peers' wives could have entertained five or six for tea in a recognizable copy of elite style. But only two or three of the minor gentry families in the sample had enough ceramic vessels to set a dinner table, and, as in Massachusetts, the tea ceremony did not spread to the yeomanry.

Further down the social scale, among the small planters and tenant farmers, ceramic vessels appear in most inventories, but in small numbers and in completely utilitarian roles. Bottle jugs, milk pans, butter pots, and earthen plates are the predominant vessels. In the 1760s refined ceramics appear in modest homes, but only as colorful accents on a table otherwise dominated by pewter or coarse earthen. Delft bowls are the most commonly enumerated item. Tea, now less expensive, is found increasingly in small planters' inventories, but the lack of accompanying equipage indicates that it was used as a beverage and not the centerpiece in a social drama. A gentry ritual requiring leisure time and symmetry had been transformed into a popular taste for minor luxuries.

Table 6.2 did not appear in the first version of this paper, which was written to 'explain' a group of excavated ceramics recovered from the site of Capt. John Hicks's first house, St Mary's City, Maryland, by J. Glenn Little, III and Stephen Israel (see Stone, Little, and Israel 1973). In that draft I

Table 6.2 *Fine ceramics and tea equipage in thirty-seven household inventories from St Mary's County, Maryland, 1761–3*

Value of decedents' movable property and their approximate economic status	% decedents owning:	
	Fine ceramics	Tea equipage
£18–34 (n=5) (landless)	—	20
£38–61 (n=11) (landowners)	45	18
£86–304 (n=12) (small slaveowners)	42	25
£306–832 (n=10) (upper 25%)	89	89

Source: Inventories, Maryland Hall of Records, vols. 78–81.

correlated economic status with number of ceramic vessels and presence or absence of fine ceramics and tea equipage. The tea equipage was included with fine ceramics as a correlation factor. In some inventories the descriptions were so ambiguous that it was impossible to tell whether earthenware was coarse (slipware, mottle-glazed Staffordshire, etc.) or fine (i.e., delft or faience). I made the mistaken assumption that the presence of tea was equivalent to the presence of fine ceramics. And, while I tabulated the frequency of vessel forms, I neglected to cross-tabulate them by economic strata. Thus, I missed perceiving fully the cultural difference between a delftware bowl and porcelain tea equipage. Such artifact-oriented research has severe limitations.

The quality of the information we retrieve from inventories is very dependent on the skill with which we frame the questions. Usually, the more general the question, the more reliable the resulting answer. I am appalled to discover that because I dig ceramics as an archaeologist, I have tried, as a historian, to excavate them from inventories. The archaeologist's goal, after all, is not to count sherds, but to study culture. We should approach inventories in the same way, as students of behavior, not artifacts.

Inventories were designed to record the decedent's economic assets, and this is what they best reveal. They record artifact attributes accidentally, as elements of the object's value or as the result of a merchant's propensity to keep detailed records. Rarely are even the lengthy listings of fine ceramics detailed enough to permit comparison with excavated materials. A bowl may be described as blue and white. 'Tea pots, £1 16s' is even less informative. Thus a study with a technical focus (the distribution of porcelain) will sacrifice a great deal of the available information. From the viewpoint of a social historian or anthropologist, it is of minor importance whether a teapot was porcelain or stoneware. Even a telescoped entry such as 'Tea table & set 15 shillings' gives us the necessary information. It tells us that the decedent drank tea and that the equipage was on public display. We also learn the ratio of this asset to others in the decedent's inventory and to similar expenditures by his neighbors.

Despite this archaeologist's fondness for ceramics, some Americans lived, or appear to have lived, without them. The 1635 list of utensils recommended for Maryland immigrants did not include ceramics (Hall 1967, 95). During the first two decades, ceramics rarely appear in the inventories. Forty inventories survive for the period 1638–50. This is a small group, but Maryland's population was tiny, and the mechanics of preservation were random enough that the surviving lists are fairly representative. It is an extremely heterogeneous group, encompassing gentlemen, servants, and even a few non-residents.

There is no reason to believe that more ceramics were present in these decedents' households, but were not appraised. The lists are detailed. They give the impression that in a frontier economy of scarcity, decedents' administrators were hard pressed to compile inventories long enough to look presentable to the Provincial Secretary. They listed clothing piece by piece and included items as inconsequential as Indian baskets and wooden spoons. A few enumerated items were valued as low as one penny. In early Maryland, ceramics seem to have been optional. The same seems to have been true for early Massachusetts (see Deetz 1973, 23–6; Brown 1973, 43–5; Suffolk County, *Probate Records*, vol. 1).

These forty inventories list only a dozen ceramic vessels, largely jars and pans. Cooking containers were metal; the most common all-purpose vessel was the wooden bowl. Wood also was used for specialized dining forms, but pewter was the most important material for tablewares (see Table 6.3). (The only fine ceramic vessel listed is Governor Leonard Calvert's blue jug.) The almost complete absence of ceramic tablewares does not mean that these lists are lacking in cultural information. The dining forms specified – especially pewter – are as rich in cultural meaning as the eighteenth-century ceramics discussed earlier.

In order to facilitate comparison between economic groups, I arranged the decedents into three categories. These conform to three of the four ways an individual could belong to a household unit: as the head of the household; as an economic partner; or as an 'inmate' or boarder (indentured servant, wage laborer, or dependent sharecropper). The fourth category, that of family member, is not included as inventories were required only upon the death of the head of a family. As none of the inmates owned dining vessels, they can be excluded from further consideration.

The remaining comparison is between traditional household units and the frontier phenomena of 'mateships'. Mateships were partnerships of two or three men, generally bachelors, created to undertake the heavy work of clearing land and planting tobacco. As mates generally were newcomers or former indentured servants, a comparison of householders and mates is a rough comparison of the minor gentry and middling

sort with those of very modest means. The mean householder inventory was valued at five times that of the average mate.

Three observations about the pewter are especially relevant:

1. The collection is completely homogeneous. There are no distinctions, other than quantitative, between the forms owned by mates or gentlemen. The forms are flatwares for foods (platters, dishes, plates, and saucers), porringers and bowls for liquid foods, and hollow forms for drinking (cups, pots, tankards, and flagons). The only status distinctions are in silver and table glass (Governor Leonard Calvert owned a silver wine cup. Another gentleman owned a damaged silver can [mug] and a cellaret of drinking glasses.)

2. The ratio of food vessels to drinking vessels is five to one, and almost one-fourth of the listed drinking vessels are dram cups – tiny containers too small to be used for drinking water or cider. (This interpretation of vessel forms is based on those illustrated in Hood 1971.) While in some cases it is impossible to deduce the size of the households involved, in those cases in which a minimum number of members is known, there usually were fewer drinking vessels than household members. The probable explanation is that the drinking vessels present were shared. Two alternate hypotheses, that household members did not eat at the same time, or that gourds or comparable vessels were used for drinking, explain less of the evidence.[7]

3. Many of the vessels were designed specifically for sharing. Despite the ambiguity of the most common terms, a third of the vessels were described with enough precision, as dram cups, beer bowls, and a caudle cup, for us to assume that a majority had two handles.

These shared vessels were relics of a medieval European economy of scarcity, when not just cups, but architectural space, tools, draft animals, and land were shared intensively. While the pressure of scarcity was initially economic and political, its ultimate result was to create cultures with distinctly corporate characteristics (see Orwin and Orwin 1967, especially ch. 10).

In seventeenth-century Maryland, these corporate habits eroded rapidly. Unlike New Englanders, Maryland's frontiersmen never farmed the land communally. Tobacco planters were cash-crop entrepreneurs, but perhaps old corporate ways remained in the readiness of small planters to form mateships and in the apparent willingness of many former indentured servants to remain as sharecroppers within the households of their former masters. Certainly, at least in dining habits, an enormous gulf separated the shared drinking pot from the individualized tea and dining services of the eighteenth century.

This is only the imposition of meaning on isolated fragments of data. How could we convert these small questions and answers into problems large enough to reveal something worth knowing about the workings of culture? The first requirement is larger questions, and among them might be:

Table 6.3 *Pewter dining vessels in Maryland inventories 1638–50*

The presence and absence of pewter in 33[a] inventories

Inventory characteristics	Decedent's economic status			Total
	Householders	Mates	Inmate laborers, sharecroppers, and artisans	
Range	£372–6	£33–17	£42–7	
Mean	£126	£24.5	£19.5	
Number	12	8	13	33
Dining vessels				
None	1	4	13	18
Wood only	2	1		3
Pewter	9	3		12
(undescribed parcels)	(2)			(2)
(vessels specified)	(7)	(3)		(10)

Pewter dining vessels specified in ten inventories

Vessel form	Number of vessels		
	Householders	Mates	Total
Drinking			
cup	2	1	3
little	1		1
dram	2	3	5
caudle [spout]	1		1
beer bowl	2		2
pot	1	2	3
quart	2		2
pint	1		1
tankard	3		3
flagon	2		2
bottle		1	1
Eating			
basin	5		5
dish[b]	23	11	34
plate	17	7	24
saucer	17	3	20
porringer	19	6	25
salt	4	1	5
	102	35	137

Source: Archives of Maryland, 1887, vol. 4, *Judicial and Testamentary Business of the Provincial Court, 1637–1650.*
 [a] From a total of 40 inventories. Seven inventories, of transients, non-residents and persons of uncertain status, are excluded.
 [b] Includes platters. The term appears in only one inventory where it is an alternate designation for dish.

what is the relationship between the core areas of culture – ideology, family structure, socio-economic structure, etc. – and consumer goods?[8] When – especially for the working folk – do household objects become less technological means than social ends (Binford 1972, 23–5)? Is this change a result of economic forces (a rising standard of living and a better distribution system (Carr 1974, 139–45; 1973, 81)), or is it related to ideology and social structure? What were the effects of the 35-year depression in the tobacco industry, 1680–1715 (Menard 1974, ch. 6)? Did the standard of living decline, and was this related to late seventeenth-century political instability (Washburn 1957, 31–9; Morgan 1975, 213–70; Carr and Menard 1974, 293–331; Carr and Jordan 1974, ch. 6)?

Answers to these questions will not emerge from scrubbing sherds, but these are object-related questions that evidence from the earth can help answer. Trash pits do provide information about diet and consumer goods not found in inventories. Foundations and surviving structures retain evidence of style (and thus acculturation and style diffusion) not found in valuations and tax lists. Well preserved skeletal materials might explain the findings of demographers (Walsh and Menard 1974, 211–27). But alone, these materials are inadequate. Answering the questions above will require mastery of extensive information on material culture and complete familiarity with the research of social and economic historians.

Economic reconstruction (from probate records) can reveal what surpluses were available above the requirements of subsistence. Analysis (again of probate records) can show how these surpluses were invested (additional capital-producing goods, silver, clothing, and furniture were far more important status symbols than ceramics). Port books and merchants' accounts record available imports. Economic and style curves can be plotted against ideology, social structure, and political and religious tension (Rainbolt 1970, 411–34; Isaac 1970, 345–63). Such multivariate analysis will not be simple, but it is the only way to make an appreciable contribution to Euro-American ethnography – or to understand our excavated material.

Notes

1. Glassie 1975, chs. 3, 5; structures A, E, G, H, K, L1 AND L2, M, N, Q, R, V; pp. 43, 69, 72, 77, 81, 84, 87, 91, 97, 105; see also pp. 51, 64–5, 89.

2. Manorial surveys and Orphans' Court valuations frequently list clapboard. The valuations occasionally note wooden chimneys, and they are frequently implied by the absence of references to brick chimneys. The lack of glazed windows is clear from the lists of the Federal Direct Tax of 1798. We do not know how common were dirt floors, but during the period 1780–1808, the Orphans' Court appraisers described two tenements as having plank floors in only one room. (St Mary's County Valuations and Indentures, 1780–1808 (Hall of Records, Annapolis, Maryland), ff. 33, 40). For the Federal Direct Tax of 1798, see Figure 6.2. For one manorial survey, see Table 6.1.

3. Structures identified as slave quarters are not included in this figure. While most of these buildings are assumed to have been occupied by whites, at least one was occupied by a free black tenant. Others, dwellings on subsidiary plantations farmed by slaves, must have been occupied by the slaves themselves.

4. Particular list of dwellings: Dr Barton Tabbs.

5. 44′ × 38′ versus 73′ × 43′ for Carter's Grove, for instance; see Waterman and Barrows 1969, 104–6.

6. In 1779 an ounce of silver plate, the traditional English status symbol, was valued at 6 shillings, 8 pence. Thus a tiny teaspoon was worth about 2 shillings, and the values of substantial pieces like tankards began at £6. In contrast, an enamelled porcelain tea pot was appraised at only 6 shillings, and large bowls and punch bowls from 6 to 14 shillings. For prices for Suffolk County silver, see Cummings 1964. For c.1770 see pp. 230, 233, 235, 243, 247. Porcelain prices for the same period may be found in Suffolk County, *Probate Records*, vol. 68, pp. 470, 511; vol. 69, p. 53. For the remainder of the argument, consult Stone 1970.

7. Dutch paintings of the period show glass, ceramic, and pewter vessels being shared. Two paintings depicting gestures of the urban middle class with photographic detail are: Pieter de Hooch, *A Dutch Courtyard* (Washington, D.C.: National Gallery of Art, c.1660), two men share a Rhenish stoneware tankard; Jan Steen, *Tavern Garden* (Berlin: Gallery of Old Masters' Paintings), husband, wife, and young boy lunch casually under an arbor. The mother helps her son drink from a pewter beaker that she has just refilled from a large flagon. No other drinking vessels are present. As a specialized form ('loving cups'), English brown stoneware potters continued to throw two-handled cups until at least the middle of the nineteenth century. See Oswald and Hughes 1974, plates 98–100.

8. One hundred years separated the publication of a symmetrical code of conduct for the English gentry and the widespread appearance in the Chesapeake of symmetrical elite architecture. This culture lag is suggested by comparison of Henry Peacham's *The Complete Gentleman* with the correspondence of William Fitzhugh and the architecture recorded by Waterman (Peacham 1962; Davis 1963; Waterman 1946).

Chapter 7

The behavioral context of probate inventories: an example from Plymouth Colony

Marley R. Brown III

Probate inventories from seventeenth-century Plymouth Colony, Massachusetts, are used to illustrate the importance of examining the actors responsible for the written archaeological record. Both the limitations and potential of the source are discussed, and special attention is given to evidence within inventories that points to forms of behavior that are likely to be reflected in the subterranean archaeological record.

7.1 Introduction

Personal estate inventories have been successfully employed in a variety of historical studies, both in England and in the United States. Agricultural historians and cultural geographers have introduced these records into the analysis of field systems, crop usage, and livestock practices (Baker and Butlin 1973; Hoskins 1963; Rutman 1967; Thirsk 1955, 1957). Their counterparts in social history have searched them for data regarding domestic life, wealth distributions, and changes in the standard of living (Daniels 1973; Davisson 1967a; Emmison 1938; Havinden 1965; Jones 1972a; Main 1975; Steer 1955). In recent years, historical archaeologists have also come to realize the potential of probate inventories and are just now beginning the search for meaningful ways to incorporate these documents into specific research designs (Brown 1973; Stone 1970). As lists of an individual's property holdings at the time of death, inventories can provide remarkably detailed descriptions and valuations of household possessions, as well as information

about crops, livestock, foodstuffs, and land. If used properly, inventories can offer a basis for reconstructing the spatial contexts and functional dimensions of colonial American material culture. In addition, when compared with evidence from more traditional archaeological contexts, such as cellar fills, trash pits, and living surfaces, inventory data may be used to measure the relative completeness of assemblages recovered through excavation.

There are, however, those who question the value of probate records, particularly for the student of colonial New England society. Perhaps the strongest reservations in this regard have been expressed by the social historian Kenneth Lockridge. He has warned that

> There are great dangers involved in extrapolating from these documents to the society as a whole. Until many . . . issues are not only raised but resolved, the researcher into probate documents would do best to confine himself to a discussion of long-term changes within the peculiar minority of men who left wills and for whom inventories were recorded. And even in this case he must be cautious.

(1968, 517)

The limitations of any historical source are obviously defined in large part by the questions asked of it, and Lockridge intended his admonitions specifically for historians who use inventories to measure economic and social change during the colonial period.[1] Nevertheless, it does contain wise counsel for all inventory researchers, especially for those who would treat inventories as archaeological data. Of particular significance is Lockridge's call for the thorough evaluation of probate sources, as a step preceding their use in interpretation. Just as some archaeologists have stressed the importance of studying the formation processes responsible for the subterranean archaeological record (Schiffer 1972), historical archaeologists should recognize the importance of examining the factors responsible for the written archaeological record. With this in mind, several variables are reviewed that appear to have influenced the form and content of probate inventories from Plymouth County. While the focus is placed on the sample available for Plymouth, the variables discussed should be relevant to inventories from other areas as well.

7.2 Plymouth Colony inventories: limitations of the source

Although a handfull of inventories survive from the first decade of Plymouth Colony's history, they were not required by law until 1633. At a meeting of the General Court on October 28 of that year, legislation was enacted that specified the ideal sequence of events characterizing the probation of an estate. These were:

1   The issuing of a warrant by the Court designating certain individuals to take the inventory of the deceased's estate;
2   The compilation of the inventory by those designated;
3   The presentation of this inventory at a meeting of the Court of Assistants, and a swearing of an oath by the appraisers;
4   The swearing of an oath by the widow or other executor named in the deceased's will, or by the Court. (Shurtleff 1899, 17)

Once these steps were completed to the Court's satisfaction, letters of administration were granted, which allowed the executor to proceed with the distribution of the estate to the appropriate heirs. A time limit of one month following the estate holder's death was imposed by the law for the completion of these steps (ibid.).

The result of this legislation was a set of customary actions on the part of Plymouth Colony residents, consisting of their actual compliance with the law's provisions. Especially where it concerns the procedure of drawing up inventories, this behavior is very important to the evaluation of the content of these documents, and particularly the form that inventory entries take. Assumptions about this procedure, furthermore, are the basis for drawing inferences about the functional dimensions of material objects in Plymouth households.

Of course, not everyone complied with the law simply because it was on the books. In fact, Lockridge has estimated that, at best, inventories were recorded for less than half of the men dying in New England during the seventeenth and eighteenth centuries. If his figures are accurate, the problem becomes one of establishing who did leave inventories, and why? Lockridge suggests that individuals appearing in probate records represent a quite biased segment of the society, men who tended to be wealthier and more commercially and urban-oriented than most of the population (1968, 517). This latter conclusion has been questioned by Daniels in his study of inventories from New Hampshire (1973). He could find no support in his sample for skewing in favor of the wealthy. While there are definitely wealth biases present in the Plymouth sample, they are not nearly as extreme as those suggested by Lockridge. Inventories include a broad range of the social and economic positions present in the population as a whole (Brown 1973).

The question of what percentage of the Plymouth population actually left behind inventories can be answered only by comparing the total number of extant inventories with mortality rates in Plymouth during the same time period. At present, demographic data necessary for such a comparison are not available. Other demographic information is also important for a complete evaluation of the inventory sample. Age and sex biases are obviously complicating factors, since inventories are almost exclusively associated with old men. It is necessary to have an accurate estimate of the size and composition of the producing and consuming socio-economic units, the household that these old men headed, before it is possible to fully exploit the potential of inventory data.

7.3 Plymouth Colony inventories: procedural variables

To return to the behavioral context of inventory compilation, there are two general aspects of the appraisal procedure that seem to have had considerable bearing on the final form of these documents. They are: (1) the identity of the appraisers and corresponding questions such as: who were the appraisers? How were they selected? Were they compensated, and if so, how? and (2) the means employed by the appraisers to compile and organize the inventories, or questions such as: how did the appraisers go about their business when confronted with the contents of an estate? Were they shown the possessions by the deceased widow and/or executor? Was the estate specially arranged for the appraisers' visit? Were the widow's possessions included or excluded? Were larger estates organized in a room-by-room fashion for the sake of convenience?

In an attempt to answer some of these questions, the following information was recorded for each inventory consulted as part of a study of ceramics in Plymouth households during the seventeenth and eighteenth centuries (Brown 1973): the name and town of the deceased; date of death when available; the names of the appraisers; the date when the inventory was taken; and the date of the inventory's exhibition before the Court of Assistants. Also, cases of room-by-room designation, both partial and complete, were noted and room names listed. These data do permit some general conclusions to be drawn regarding the procedure of estate appraisal.

7.4 The identity of appraisers: selection and compensation

It was possible to discern fairly regular sets of men serving as inventory-takers within each town of the Colony. C course, these appraiser networks changed over time, but much overlap is evident. In fact, the deceased's place of residence can often be inferred from the appraisers' names appearing at the bottom of the inventory. Appraisers in Plymouth Colony were either kin and close friends of the deceased estate-holder, or men from his town called upon by the court. While often neighbors, these court-appointed appraisers were not necessarily friendly with or related to the deceased.

The rationale behind the selection of the latter appraisers is important, for it offers some insight into their qualifications for the job. In his inventory study of Plymouth Colony ceramics, Paul Chace assumed that 'favor with the current government and knowledge of the current economy' were the main criteria behind their selection (1969, 20). This speculation is partly borne out by the Court records. In March of 1634, the General Court granted towns the authority to choose three or four men to assess property for tax purposes (Plymouth County, *Court and Probate Records*, vol. II, 42). Soon after, this responsibility was assumed by the selectmen, a group of citizens elected yearly by the inhabitants of each town to serve in matters of local government. Selectmen lists are found in the court records by 1650, and when these rolls are compared to the set of appraisers active in individual towns during the same period, they closely correspond. Not all selectmen appear in the role of appraiser, and it seems that the General Court did call only upon those whom they considered most trustworthy. It is likely that the choice was also based on the knowledge of property values exhibited by these men. The ability to specifically identify and properly name material objects seems to have been an insignificant qualification in comparison to accuracy in the assessment of an item's worth. Indeed, many appraisers were illiterate, as is evidenced by the large number of inventories that show the marks of appraisers rather than their signatures. While they could recognize objects and estimate their value, these men could not describe them in writing. This literacy bias is important because it influenced the quality of object descriptions, and particularly the degree of detail present on the lists.

Closely related to the literacy variable is another aspect – the social background of the appraisers – that also contributes to the make-up of the inventories. Attitudes concerning the relative value of different classes of property had a definite effect on the adequacy of information about interior furnishings. This has led to a bias in favor of wealthier households within the inventory sample. During the first quarter of the eighteenth century, the growth of a class of merchants and mariners participating in the overseas trade can be observed in the inventories. The lists of these men contain the most detailed information regarding household possessions to be found in the entire sample. This detail is, of course, partly the result of the fact that a large portion of the assets of these estates were given over to movable property. An accurate appraisal of estate worth, therefore, necessarily included interior furnishings. The inventories of estates whose owner's wealth was mainly tied up in land and animals are, by contrast, less detailed with respect to household possessions, but very specific about land and livestock holdings. In addition, the inventories of both kinds of estates have, in most instances, been drawn up by relatives and friends who generally shared values regarding the appropriate investment of wealth. It is likely that these differing degrees of property being inventoried led to differences in the amount of effort expended in the description of it. In a sense, then, the commercial and urban orientation suggested by Lockridge does makes its presence felt within the Plymouth sample, as far as the detail and quality of object description is concerned.

Finally, it is possible that the kind of compensation provided the appraisers influenced the final product. During the seventeenth century, there appears to have been no formal payment of appraisers for each inventory compiled, although there are cases in the court records of individuals, who because of their frequent service in the name of the General Court, found themselves in financial straits. These men would petition to court for some kind of compensation, usually in the form of a lumped payment (Shurtleff 1852). By 1725, however, the column of 'debts owing from the estate' included the appraiser's fee, based upon a set percentage of the total estate value (Brown, unpublished data). It appears that this form of compensation also contributed to the bias in favor of detail in the description of wealthier estates.

7.5 The appraisal procedure: spatial and functional analysis

The aspect of appraisal procedure that is most important for functional analysis involves two interrelated assumptions: (1) that inventories were compiled in a consistent manner, according to the location of objects within the various rooms of an estate-holder's house; and (2) that the location of objects within the deceased's house, as perceived by the appraisers, is indicative of the activities in which they were employed.

With regard to the first assumption, Paul Chace, in his study of seventeenth-century Plymouth ceramics (1969, 36), considers it only logical to presume that inventories, especially of larger estates, were compiled in a room-by-room fashion. While there are enough explicit room-by-room inventories present in the sample to show that this organizing principle was indeed applied, these lists are almost exclusively associated with larger houses and wealthier estates, suggesting that the room-by-room scheme was useful for ordering extensive property holdings, but not necessarily employed in the inventories of small houses and modest estates. Even though it is possible literally to watch appraisers go in the front door and out the back when recording lists that have no explicit room designations, there is as yet no objective means for establishing room boundaries in these cases.

There is also evidence pointing to the use of classificatory principles other than location. Inventory entries that include, for example, 'pewter, brass, tin and earthen ware' are common. These entries indicate that appraisers grouped certain household items by material and function, rather than by location. By the middle of the eighteenth century, more extreme lumping appears, the most popular categories being 'outdoor moveables' and 'indoor moveables'. Inventories, then, are the product of a set of cross-cutting taxonomic principles; they do not simply reflect the sequence in which objects were encountered within the house of the deceased estate-holder, although this pattern is certainly observable in many inventories.

The second assumption is even more crucial than the first, in the sense that it provides the immediate basis for inferences regarding the function of household furnishings. It may be reduced to the proposition that the location of objects within a house is determined in large part by their use. When this proposition is combined with the first assumption, that appraisers recorded objects according to location, it becomes possible to define 'activity sets,' or groups of artifacts employed in related tasks, by observing the objects that lie adjacent to one another on inventory lists. These activity sets are at the same time 'activity areas' that may be used to establish room boundaries. This inferential procedure is facilitated by first outlining the activity sets found in rooms given on room-by-room inventories. Having postulated what might be called 'ideal room types' in terms of diagnostic activity sets, these may be compared to the activity sets reconstructed from non-room-by-room inventories. This is exactly what Paul Chace has done in his inventory study of ceramics, with some degree of success.

There are, of course, drawbacks to this line of inference that cannot be overlooked. It has already been pointed out that listing by location is complicated by other classificatory principles, namely by material and function. Related to this is the assumption that the location of household goods as perceived by the appraisers was not tampered with for the benefit of exhibiting the estate. It is apparent in some inventories that property was 'shown' to the appraisers by the widow or executor, and there is no reason to rule out the possibility that some preparation of the estate took place. One type of such housecleaning involved the possessions of the widow, the 'dower' that she brought to the marriage. There seems to be no hard and fast rule about their inclusion or exclusion from the appraised estate. In the seventeenth century, a few inventories specify that the widow's goods are absent, and by the early eighteenth century, separate lists make their appearance, under the heading 'widow's utensils'.

Another factor interfering with the inference of use from location is the practice of storage. In houses where space was at a premium, as was the case especially in seventeenth-century Plymouth dwellings, many activities took place in a single room. Not all objects, as a result, could be left in the places where they were used, but instead were stored out of the way until needed again. While Chace recognizes this storage variable, admitting that most objects had a storage area as well as an activity area, he asserts that:

> The storage area for many objects is standardized, learned, and habitually employed. It can be assumed that the storage area of each object is usually close by and handy to the area of its normal use. In most cases, an object usually would be stored within the same room in which it is employed. (1969, 37)

Although it seems reasonable that household utensils would be stored in the room of their use, there are no grounds for assuming that storage was habitual or necessarily standardized behavior shared by most households. In speaking of seventeenth-century Plymouth households and location of interior furnishings, John Demos has made the very reasonable point that:

> The need for some degree of orderliness and efficiency must have required constant attention to the disposition of objects . . . but there is no reason to imagine any set of principles common to every household. Indeed the objects themselves imply an opposite – a kind of easy flexibility, a willingness to improvise wherever necessary in order to make the best use of available space. (1970, 39)

7.6 Conclusion

Although it is dangerous to make any rigid assumptions about the degree of standardization characterizing the organization of space and use of domestic artifacts in Plymouth Colony during any one period of time, it is important to have some means of establishing functional domains from inventory lists. This is the only way to make these documents useful for testing explanatory propositions about the same kind of behavior drawn from more traditional archaeological evidence, such as those offered by Deetz from Plymouth (1973; 1977). While principles of spatial organization are explicit in a small number of room-by-room inventories, these same principles appear only as implicit orderliness on non-room-by-room lists. Until an objective method is developed for delineating spatial clusters in both types of inventories, functional inferences based on these documents will remain tentative at best.

This chapter has reviewed only a few of the variables affecting the observable form of inventory source material. There are many other factors that should be identified and described. The major value of probate records for archaeologists lies in the control of data they can provide, but this control will only be assured by the systematic investigation of the behavioral context responsible for the documentary archaeological record.

Note

1. Since Lockridge's statement and just after this paper was written for presentation at the annual meetings of the Society for Historical Archaeology in 1975, several reviews were published that examine in detail the wealth and age biases of probate inventories from New England towns (Main 1974, Smith 1975). These authors provide a clearer picture of the segment of the colonial population leaving behind wills and inventories, and even though distinct age and wealth biases are evident in their studies, they reaffirm the potential of these documents for a variety of analyses, as long as their limitations are understood and corrected by those employing them (Smith 1975, 110).

Chapter 8

Occupational differences reflected in material culture

Kathleen J. Bragdon

A model is derived from probate inventory analysis in order to test the archaeological proposition that the amount and quality of artifacts recovered from a site reflect the socio-economic status and occupation of the site's inhabitants. The artifact percentages that occurred in the documentary sources are compared against percentages of comparable items recovered from the home sites of a farmer and a tavern keeper in order to determine the degree to which such occupational differences have a discernible effect upon the archaeological record.

8.1 Introduction

One of the basic, yet largely untested assumptions in historical archaeology is that the amount and quality of artifacts recovered from a site reflect something of the social and economic status of its former occupants. While this assumption is clearly justified at a certain level of explanation, several studies, including those of James Deetz at Parting Ways in Plymouth, Massachusetts (1977), and Vernon Baker at Black Lucy's Garden in Andover, Massachusetts (1977), have challenged the overall validity and general usefulness of the concept, as it applies to sites occupied by non-Anglo-Americans. The model must also be qualified in order to account for occupational differences, which seem to contribute as much to the nature of artifactual remains at a site as do social and economic status.

The sites chosen for a study of occupational differences as they are reflected in material culture are the Joseph Howland site, the homestead of a well-respected yeoman farmer in Kingston, Massachusetts, and the Wellfleet Tavern site, on the north side of Great Island, Wellfleet, Massachusetts, the dwelling/tavern of a socially prominent individual named Samuel Smith. The differences in the material culture assemblages from the two sites, determined through functional analysis of the artifacts, are well aligned with evidence from probate inventories representing yeomen and tavern keepers and with what is known through historical documentation about the seventeenth- and early eighteenth-century occupations of tavern keeper and yeoman farmer.

8.2 The tavern in the late seventeenth and early eighteenth centuries

The consumption of alcoholic beverages was an integral part of seventeenth- and eighteenth-century life. The seventeenth-century farmer drank about a gallon of ale daily (Anderson and Deetz 1972). Wine also was consumed in large quantities, as indicated by the enormous yearly wine importation from the Madeira Islands (Duncan 1972, 48). The importance of alcohol in Puritan Massachussets is also indicated by the large amount of legislation concerning its sale and consumption (Pulsifer 1861; Shurtleff 1856).

As the dispenser of liquors, the character of the tavern keeper was also subject to much of this Puritan legislation. The house of Representatives for Suffolk County, for instance, voted in 1697 that 'each inn holder and retailer shall be persons of good repute and obtain the approbation of the selectmen before they first have their license' (Massachusetts, Commonwealth of, n.d., 122).

In addition, the tavern keeper needed a substantial amount of capital in order to pursue his occupation. Hugh March of Newbury complained, 'I was thereupon encouraged to dispense a large estate for the keeping of an ordinary, and a place which was purchased for it at a very dear rate' (Massachusetts, Commonwealth of, n.d., 76). According to the same source, in 1743, another tavern keeper, Thomas Stone of Weymouth, refused to keep a tavern any longer, because of the cost and harassment.

Laws specified the taverner's character and the services he was to provide. In 1671, the General Court of the Colony of New Plymouth enacted eight ordinances (Brigham 1836, 287–8):

1   No liquor was to be sold, or inn to be kept, except by license of the court.
2   The innkeeper was required to provide adequate bedding, pasture, and 'good beer.'
3   The innkeeper was required to sell beer for no more than 2s/qt or wine for 2p/qt, or 'strong waters' for more than it cost him for 'Butte or caske.'
4   The taverners were not 'to suffer any disorder, by excessive drinking in or at their house.'
5   Liquor was not to be sold on Sunday.
6   The innkeeper was required to report the names of any 'disorderly persons' to the court.
7   A committee was formed to enforce the regulations of the court.
8   The innkeeper was not allowed to serve servants, children, or Indians.

The food served in the ordinaries, inns, and taverns was similar to that provided in the home (Spitulnik 1972, 38). Alcoholic beverages, however, particularly the 'strong waters' and certain punches and egg drinks, were the province and specialty of the late seventeenth- and early eighteenth-century tavern. These special elements of the 'foodways' system required special containers and utensils as well (Anderson as quoted by Deetz 1973, 16). These objects made up the material culture assemblage characteristic of tavern activity.

8.2.1 Tavern assemblages

The most common forms of drinking vessels found in English taverns in the late seventeenth and early eighteenth centuries included (Hackwood 1909, 340–75):

1   the tumbler – for large draughts and heavy drinking
2   the tyg – for communal drinking
3   the bellarmine – a Frechen stoneware jug decorated with incised and molded masks and seals
4   the toby jug – a later form of jug formed in the shape of a fat human figure with a mug, pipe, and three-cornered hat

5   the posset pot – used for soups and stews as well as beverages
6   the blackjack – a leather drinking mug
7   the punch bowl – introduced into England with alcoholic punches such as arrack
8   the bombard – a large leather drinking vessel
9   wine and flip glasses

Pewter vessels were also common in English and Anglo-American taverns. John Wipple's tavern in Providence, Rhode Island (1674–85), was equipped with 'pewter basins, quart pot, pint pots, a tankard, pint pot, spoons, glass bottles and other dishes' (Field 1897, 29).

Other common drinking vessels included the mug and cup, made of such ceramic wares as Westerwald stoneware, dipped and white saltglazed stoneware, English brown stoneware, mottled ware, and combed, dotted and trailed slipware (Noël Hume 1969a; Barber 1970; Honey 1933). All of these ceramic types have been found on late seventeenth- and early eighteenth-century colonial sites in New England.

Many types of glass drinking vessels were also available in the colonial market during this period. References to 'Bristol Glass' appeared in Boston newspaper advertisements as early as 1704. These advertisements specified such forms as 'double flint wine glasses, common glasses, wormed wine glasses, decanters,' and other less common forms such as 'cruets and tumblers' (Dow 1927, 97–8). These advertisements imply that many forms and qualities of glassware were available to the public and could be bought in small quantities, or 'by the hogshead' (Dow 1927, 87).

The glass wine or liquor bottle was also available from the earliest periods of colonization. Most bottles were of English manufacture (Noël Hume 1961; McNulty 1971). The late seventeenth- and early eighteenth-century bottles were inefficient for 'binning' or storing wine, because of their shape, and were more often used as decanters or for drawing small quantities of wine from a larger cask or barrel. Noël Hume states:

> references to the importing of wine into Virginia in the colonial period are plentiful and show that it was transported both in the wood and in bottles. Merchants, having imported in the wood, were prepared to decant into bottles providing the purchaser supplied his own.
>
> (1961, 11)

In fact, it was the consensus that wine should be stored in large containers rather than in bottles for hygienic reasons. John Wright, an eighteenth-century physician, wrote:

> It hath long been our opinion, that good wine, particularly port, may be better conserved in a larger body of quantity than a quart bottle can contain . . . the glass quart bottle can be conveniently used in small families or tête-à-tête parties, but in larger companies, it seemeth probable that a greater quantity drawn off with a syphon would be finer, more free from the carelessness of decantation . . .
>
> (Simon 1927, 13)

Thus, although bottles were available, they may not always have been an important part of a tavern assemblage.

An equally important element of tavern behavior, with its own characteristic accoutrements, was the smoking of tobacco. Early references to such practice referred to it as 'drinking tobacco'. Taverns, drinking, and smoking were so inseparable in seventeenth- and eighteenth-century England that one social critic remarked, 'there is not so base a groome, that commes into an ale-house to call for his pot, but he must have his pipe of tobacco, for it is a commodity that is now as vendible in every tavern' (Bridenbaugh 1967, 195).

There were many early ordinances against smoking in public places, including taverns (Pulsifer 1861, 27, 36, 53). The practice of smoking became so widespread by the mid-seventeenth century, however, that most inn and tavern keepers provided pipes and tobacco *gratis* (Hackwood 1909, 331). Pipes were reused, after having been refired in a special rack in the oven. The 'recycled' pipes were used in the taproom, while the new pipes were reserved for 'parlour' customers (Penn, 1902, 151). Pipes, therefore, along with ceramic drinking vessels, glassware, and metal serving dishes, made up the basic 'material culture' assemblage of the tavern.

In summary, the documentary evidence suggests that the tavern keeper was a man of 'good repute' and some substance. He would have been expected to provide the following in his tavern:

1   vessels for the consumption of alcohol, including mugs, pots, cups, tankards, wineglasses, beakers, and serving vessels such as tumblers
2   serving vessels, including platters, bowls, bottles, pitchers, and jugs
3   clay tobacco pipes for smoking

Probate inventories from the estates of tavern keepers document such an assemblage of objects, in contrast to inventories of yeomen, which generally do not.

8.3 Probate analysis

Probate records, although not always dependable sources (cf. Brown 1973; Stone 1970), provide a large and readily accessible body of information concerning the use and importance of material objects. Systematic analysis of probate inventories of tavern keepers and yeomen farmers reveals differences in the patterning or occurrence of material objects, which should in turn reflect occupational differences.

Previous inventory studies have often been concerned with relating the amount and type of ceramics listed in the inventories to the economic status of the probated individual (Teller 1968; Carr 1973). Although there seems to be some correlation between wealth and the occurrence of certain ceramic types in the Plymouth Colony inventories (Brown 1973), the occupation of the individual often appears to have been an equally important determinant as to which items appeared in the inventories.

The inventories for the study included:

1   All inventories of yeomen of the town of Plymouth from 1690 to 1730 (the date of incorporation of the township of Kingston) and from Kingston from 1730 to 1750. Of these inventories 42 were chosen because of the location of the test domestic site, the Joseph Howland Site.
2   All inventories (19) of known tavern keepers from Martha's Vineyard (1690–1750). Inventories of only those individuals who were known to have kept a tavern for more than five years were chosen. The Vineyard inventories were chosen over those from Wellfleet (the location of the test tavern site, Wellfleet Tavern) as they constituted a larger sample. They were expected to be comparable to those from Wellfleet because of the similarity of the economy of the two areas.
3   Sixty-five inventories from Falmouth and the other Cape were also included as a control. It was considered possible that yeomens' inventories from domestic sites from Kingston and the Cape might differ, making a comparison between tavern and domestic inventories from the two areas less valid.

The results of the probate record analysis are summarized in table 8.1, a comparison among inventories of Plymouth tavern keepers with those from Martha's Vineyard and with domestic sites from Kingston. Objects and items associated with tavern activities, including bottles, wine glasses, serving dishes, and specialized vessels, as well as large numbers of tables and chairs, were in all cases more frequently listed in the tavern keeper's inventories than in those of yeomen. The occupational differences reflected in the probate inventories are also visible in the artifact assemblages of tavern and domestic sites.

8.3.1 The sites and their occupants

The sites chosen for the study are thought to have been the locations of different activities: the Joseph Howland site was a farmstead in Kingston, Massachusetts, occupied from 1674 to 1750 (Deetz 1960a, b), and the Wellfleet Tavern Site, located on the north side of Great Island, Wellfleet,

Table 8.1 *Mean variables per inventory, 1690–1750*

Variables	Kingston domestic		Plymouth taverns		Martha's Vineyard taverns	
	No.	Mean	No.	Mean	No.	Mean
Beds	132	3.3	11	2.8	25	1.5
Tables	51	1.1	6	1.5	49	2.7
Chairs	226	5.5	42	10.5	213	16.5
Desks	2	.04	0	0	8	.4
Candlesticks	21	.5	12	3	7	.35
Bottles	104	2.6	22	5.5	3,000	150
Wineglasses	20	.5	13	3.2	21	1
Earthenware	35	.83	52	13	20	1.4
Pots	174	4.3	26	6.5	20	1.4
Gallons Liquor	8	.02	0	0	969	43

Massachusetts, a tavern associated with the fishing and whaling industries of late seventeenth- and eighteenth-century Cape Cod (Eckholm and Deetz 1971).

8.3.2 The Joseph Howland site

The Joseph Howland site was occupied by Captain Joseph Howland and his son James. Joseph Howland acquired the lands at Rocky Nook in Kingston upon the death of his father John in 1672. By the terms of his father's will, Joseph Howland inherited 'the dwelling house at Rocky Nook together with all the outhousing, uplands and meadows, appurtenances and priviledges belonging thereunto' (Massachusetts Historical Society n.d., 72).

According to Joseph's biography, however, John Howland's house was burned in 1675, during King Philip's War (*Howland Quarterly* XIII, 4). Foundations of a partially burned seventeenth-century structure on the property said to be Howland's indicate that the information provided by the biography is probably correct (Hussey 1938, 11).

Joseph Howland built another dwelling on a different sector of the property within one year of the burning of his father's house (Deetz 1960a, 14). This dwelling was bequeathed to his son James in 1703 (Plymouth County Probate Records n.d., 43–5). The house and surrounding land were sold to Benjamen Lothrup in 1735, and the house continued to be occupied until approximately 1750 (Deetz 1960a; 1960b, 4).

Aside from his large land holdings, Joseph Howland owned (at least at the time of his death) very little personal property, as indicated by the probate inventory from his estate (Plymouth County Probate Records 6, 90):

An Inventory of the Estate of Capt. Joseph Howland late of plimouth deseaced taken and apprised by us the underwritten

Imprimis in his waring apparill & books	04	10	00
Item in armes at	03	06	00
Item in puter and brass	03	14	00
Item in one small silver Cupp	00	04	00
Item in one bed & furnetur to it & curtins	08	00	00
Item in two beds & furniture to them	07	00	00
Item in Iron potts & kettle hangers	01	00	00
Item in a grate table & forme & Cupbard & 4 Chests & a box	04	00	00
Item in Chairs one table & table lining & earthenware	02	00	00
Item in one saddle & pillion 2 sives	01	00	00
Item in New Cloath	03	00	00
Item in one pare of small stillards, Jarr	00	06	00
Item in 4 barrels & one Tubb	00	10	00
Item in Neete Cattle one yook oxen	07	10	00
Item in 4 cows	11	00	00
Item in 2 three year old sters at	03	00	00
Item in 2 two year olds & three calves	04	00	00
Item in 24 sheepe at	07	00	00
Item in two Mars at	04	00	00
Item 3 wine	00	18	00
Item in Cart & plow and tackling	00	15	00
Item in one spade on Frow one drawing knife & ax & sith	00	12	00
Item in one pestle & mortar & one saw 2 hows & other small Iron tools	00	13	00
Item in 2 spining wheeles	00	08	00

John Bradford
John Gray

Yet he appears to have been a prominent member of the community. He was appointed a treasurer's accountant in 1678, a freeman in 1683, and a selectman in 1684 (Shurtleff 1857, 25, 189, 196).

Joseph Howland's probate inventory suggests that although he was a respected member of his community, his 'status' was not reflected in his material goods, but rather in his lands. His large land holdings, which constituted most of his wealth, also reflect his primary occupation, that of farming.

8.3.3 The Wellfleet tavern

That Samuel Smith operated the Wellfleet tavern is suggested by a document dated 1731, in which he calls himself an 'inn holder' (Hogan 1971, 2). Oral history research done in 1970 reveals that a sign once hung outside his tavern, located on the north side of Great Island, that read:

Samuel Smith, He has Good Flip:
Good Toddy, If You Please.
The Way is Near and Very Clear,
Tis Just Beyond the Trees.

Positive identification of the Wellfleet site with Smith's tavern is impossible because of the destruction of the deeds from Great Island in a courthouse fire. Local tradition, however, and several indirect references to Smith's holdings on Great Island make such an identification feasible (Shurtleff 1856, vols. VI, VIII; 1857, vol. IX).

Wellfleet, for a time, participated in the thriving economy surrounding the hunting of blackfish and whales and the harvesting of oysters. Records of the Massachusetts General Courts describe the area in the early eighteenth century stating 'There is not its like for whaling and other fishing within the country, if within the province . . .' (Massachusetts, Commonwealth of, n.d., 10).

Samuel Smith invested in other trades, as did many other tavern keepers in commercial centers (Bridenbaugh 1938). He had a particular interest in the fishing and off-shore whaling industries for which Wellfleet was famous. The Plymouth Colony court records of 1754 state:

An agent was chosen to settle the petition of Samuel Smith, Esquire, to the general court, concerning Billingsgate Beach and islands (Wellfleet). Chose a committee to prosecute the Horwich people for carrying on the Whale fisher at Billingsgate.   (Pratt, 1844, 70)

Samuel Smith's interest in fishing and whaling, and the general economic prosperity of Wellfleet in the late seventeenth and early eighteenth centuries, probably explain the presence

Table 8.2 *Ceramic vessel forms*
(Joseph Howland site figures in upper quadrant; Wellfleet Tavern site figures in lower quadrant).

Ceramic Type	Plate	Plate/Pan	Pan	Pan/Dish	Dish	Lard Pot	Porringer	Cup	Mug	Mug/Beaker	Beaker	Jug	Bowl	Total
Mottled Ware								2	2					4
									15				1	16
Delft	9												4	13
	8												5	13
Sgraffito			2									1	1	4
			1		3								1	5
Slipware				2			1	11	2					16
			1	6				13	2					22
Brown Stoneware									2					2
									3					3
Nottingham														
									2					2
Fulham									2					2
									3					3
Saltglaze									4				1	5
									10			1	2	13
Gravel-Temp.			1											1
			1											1
Frechen												3		3
												3		3
Westerwald									6				2	8
									11			1		12
Slip-Decorated Redware							2			1			1	4
	1	11	20	1	3	5	17	3	5	1			4	71
Undecorated Fine Redware	2	2			1		5	2	4	4	4		10	34
							4		5	3	15			27
Undecorated Coarse Redware			19	17									4	40
			14	25									6	45
Total	11	2	22	2	1	17	8	15	22	5	4	6	21	134
	9	11	37	7	6	30	21	16	56	4	15	5	19	236

of a large tavern in such a relatively isolated spot as the north side of Great Island.

An oyster blight in 1760 (Whitman 1794, 119), and the growth of deep water whaling (Kittredge 1930), caused a decline in the Wellfleet economy. This led to the depopulation of Great Island and probably to the closing of Smith's tavern (Eckholm and Deetz 1971). His dwelling house, which was separate from the tavern, was moved to South Wellfleet in 1800.

Samuel Smith, like Joseph Howland, was a prominent member of his community. In 1735, he was appointed an agent to carry on the building of the new meeting house. In 1763, he was chosen the moderator of the first meeting of the newly formed Wellfleet. His title at that time was 'Esquire' (Pratt 1844, 123–4).

Socially, Samuel Smith and Joseph Howland occupied similar positions. According to Dawes (1949, 80–1) only three out of 3,440 freemen in the Massachusetts Bay Colony in the seventeenth and early eighteenth centuries were designated 'esquire' and only twelve had military titles. In addition, it is widely known that selectmen held the most important position in local government at that time (Wall 1965, 600).

Their occupations, however, were very different. Thus, variance in the archaeological assemblages from the Joseph Howland domestic site and the Wellfleet Tavern site should reflect these occupational differences, confirming patterns seen in the probate inventories.

8.4 Artifact analysis

The differences between the archaeological assemblages of the Wellfleet Tavern and the Joseph Howland sites were analyzed to determine: (1) vessel form; (2) percentages of ceramic types based on glaze and paste; (3) types of decorative motifs (any applied design); (4) types and numbers of glassware; (5) types and numbers of bottles; and (6) numbers of pipestems.

8.4.1 Ceramics

The vessels were counted and given a vessel form type through the analysis of rim and base sherds. Each base and rim was drawn; vessel forms were determined on the basis of comparison with the rims and bases of surviving vessels and through partial reconstruction of the vessels when possible. It was often difficult to determine precisely the vessel form, and in these cases a category such as plate/pan was employed.

Ceramic forms were found to include thirteen shapes, including pans, lard pots, pudding pans, baking dishes, plates, patty-pans, porringers, cups, mugs, beakers, and jugs. Pans, large pots, and baking dishes were most often associated with food preparation and storage, especially as it relates to dairying, an important subsistence activity of the seventeenth and eighteenth centuries (Deetz 1973; Watkins 1966). These vessels were designed for heavy use as indicated by the coarseness and solidity of the majority of the vessels of this type (Watkins 1950).

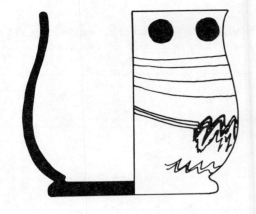

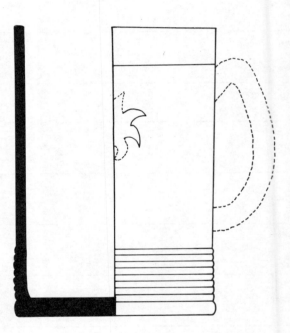

Fig. 8.1. Redware vessel forms from the Wellfleet Tavern

Comparison of the ceramic assemblages from the Wellfleet and Joseph Howland sites reveals differences in the vessel form totals and in the ceramic type percentages from both sites (Tables 8.2 and 8.3).

The Wellfleet sub-assemblage consists of a greater percentage of those vessel forms associated with drinking and fewer forms associated with food preparation and storage than does the sub-assemblage from the Joseph Howland site (figs 8.1 and 8.2).

The percentages of ceramic types in each ceramic sub-assemblage differ as well. Six of the eight most common ceramic types (treating fine and coarse redwares as two types) at the Wellfleet site are known to have been most often found in the form of mugs, jugs, beakers, posset pots and cups (Deetz, personal communication 1976). Only five such types

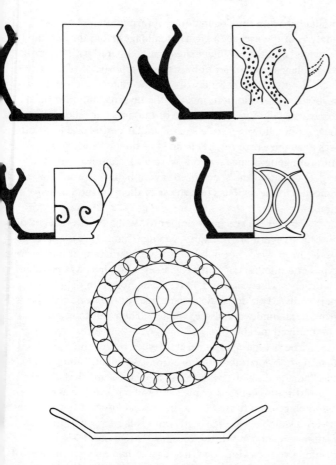

Fig. 8.2. Redware decorative motifs from the Wellfleet Tavern

Table 8.3 Summary of functional designations of ceramic vessel forms

Forms (Functional Designation)	Joseph Howland site	Wellfleet site
1. Utilitarian	44%	39%
2. Utilitarian/Service	16%	10%
3. Eating/Drinking	19%	21%
4. Drinking	21%	30%
Ceramic Types		
1. Redware	63%	63%
2. Coarse Redware	31%	43%
*3. Fine Redware	31%	20%
*4. Combed Slipware	12%	13.5%
5. Delft	11%	3%
*6. Westerwald	6%	7%
*7. Mottled Ware	4.5%	7%
*8. White Saltglaze	3.5%	4.5%
9. Sgraffito	1.5%	0%
10. English Brown Stoneware	0%	2%

Ceramic type associated with drinking vessels.

appear within the eight most common types at the Joseph Howland site (Table 8.3).

8.4.2 Bottles

A minimum of eight wine or liquor bottles was excavated from the Joseph Howland site. The vessels were identified through analysis of base and neck fragments. The basal fragments were generally of a dark green or black glass approximately 1–1.5 cm thick and had kick-ups ranging from 1.5 cm to 3 cm in height.

Eight neck fragments were excavated from the Howland site, all of which appear to have belonged to different bottles. These fragments had string rims neatly attached 0.3–0.5 cm from the mouth. The width of the string rims was approximately .5 cm, and the thickness of the glass in the neck fragments ranged from 0.3 cm to 5 cm. The diameters of the mouths and rims fell between 2.5 cm and 4 cm.

The minimum number of bottles found at the Wellfleet Tavern site was six (Pichey 1970). Diameters of the basal sherds ranged from 16 cm to 20 cm. The kick-ups were all less than 10 cm in height. The shallow kick-ups and the pronounced curvature of the body fragments date the bottles to 1685–1720 (Noël Hume 1961, 63–4).

8.4.3 Wineglasses

Three wineglasses were excavated from the Joseph Howland site. Eight rim sherds and three stem and base fragments were found. The rim sherds were of three types: a turned rim with an enclosed white band 0.3 cm wide encircling the edge; a turned rim with an enclosed white band 0.6 cm wide encircling the rim; and a turned rim with no band.

The stems included two with inverted balusters and knops, one stem having the knops separated by a collar. These stem forms were popular between 1695 and 1730 (Noël Hume 1969a, 190). In addition, one stem of four molded facets known as the 'Silesian' form, which was popular from 1710 to 1720, was retrieved (Noël Hume 1969a, 191).

At least thirty-two wineglasses represented by stems were excavated at the Wellfleet site. These included six basic types: one quatrefoil form popular from 1685 to 1705; one double-knopped form topped by a tear-drop knop; two molded pedestal 'Silesian' form stems, popular from 1715 to 1740; two straight-sided stems; eight inverted baluster and knopped forms popular from 1695 to 1710; and fourteen to eighteen double- and triple-knopped stems popular from 1700 to 1730 (Noël Hume 1969a, 191).

The numerous wineglass bowl fragments were thin and gently curved. Although difficult to reconstruct, the most common bowl forms from the Wellfleet site appear to have been the bell-shaped form with the raised rim and the form with a vertical lip above a marked shoulder (Pichey 1970; Noël Hume 1969a, 189).

Twelve dozen basal fragments were also recovered, all of which had folded feet, the most common form from 1680 to 1750 (Noël Hume 1969a, 189).

8.4.4 Tumblers and beer glasses

Fifteen pieces representing the bowls of at least three large drinking vessels were excavated from the Wellfleet site. The pieces are distinguishable from the wineglass bowl fragments by their size, thickness, curvature and design. Noël Hume describes similar finds as 'tumblers or beakers with small, molded diamond shaped bosses patterned over the walls, presumably to aid in the gripping of the vessel' (1969a, 187).

Such beakers were illustrated in the pattern books of Measy and Greene, English glaziers of the eighteenth century. These forms were available in two thicknesses and were designed for beer, wine, strong spirits, toddy, and flip (Watkins 1968, 154; Noël Hume 1968, 13).

8.4.5 Pipestems

Thousands of pipestem fragments were excavated from the Wellfleet site. These fragments, like those from the Joseph Howland site, may be dated to the period 1690–1740. The pipestem and bowl fragments excavated from the Joseph Howland site numbered in the hundreds. Application of Harrington's and Binford's dating formula to a sample of the pipestem fragments indicates that the largest percentage may be dated to the periods 1650–80 and 1710–50 (Deetz 1960a).

8.5 Summary of the artifact analysis

The tavern assemblage is characterized by: (1) a large number of vessels; (2) a large percentage of drinking vessels in relation to the total ceramic assemblage; (3) a large percentage of those ceramic types most often found in the form of drinking vessels; (4) large numbers of wineglasses; (5) specialized glassware; and (6) large numbers of pipestems.

Although not documented or tested, the fact that a high percentage of the local slip-decorated redware was found at the supposed tavern site suggests that such cheap but decorative vessels were purposely supplied for the use of discriminating but sometimes careless customers.

The domestic assemblage includes: (1) a high percentage of food preparation and storage vessels in relation to the total ceramic assemblage; (2) local redware of the predominantly coarse variety; (3) few wineglasses; and (4) pipestem fragments numbering in the hundreds, rather than in the thousands.

The 'tavern' assemblage in particular is in keeping with what is known from documentary sources about the common equipage of an inn or tavern. The high percentage of drinking vessels, the large numbers of pipestems, and the specialized glassware seem to be especially diagnostic. Such a grouping of material objects known to have been symbolic of, and most often associated with, the serving and consumption of alcohol, may be described as a functional grouping and may, like that of the probate analysis, be attributed to the specific activities of the tavern.

8.6 Comparative sites

Because a comparison between the assemblages of only two sites cannot be considered definitive, the material culture model based on the documentary information and on the analysis of the archaeological assemblages from the Joseph Howland and the Wellfleet sites was compared with the artifact assemblages from other published site reports.

Comparatively little work has been done on historic tavern sites. In addition, most of the taverns that have been excavated fall outside the range of the time period of this study. One report, however, of a site of similar period and location was available. Five reports from later time periods and/or different geographic locations were also examined with the expectation that the specialized tavern behavior would be reflected in the artifacts regardless of their location in space and time.

The tavern site most similar to Wellfleet was that of John Earthy's Tavern at Pemaquid, Maine (Camp 1975). Although vessel forms were not published, an examination of the ceramic types and numbers of bottles, glasses, and pipes was possible. In order to place Earthy's Tavern assemblage in the proper perspective, two domestic assemblages of the same time period from Pemaquid were also examined. The results are summarized in table 8.4.

The percentages of ceramic types from John Earthy's tavern are comparable to those from Wellfleet. Interestingly, the Pemaquid tavern assemblage also shows much the same contrast to the nearby domestic assemblages as the Wellfleet assemblage does to that from the Joseph Howland site. In both tavern assemblages, the sherd count is higher, and there is a higher percentage of those ceramic types associated with drinking vessels. Both tavern sites also had a larger number of wineglasses and pipestem fragments than did domestic assemblages with which they were compared.

Another possible tavern site of a similar time period is that tentatively identified by Cotter in his excavations at Jamestown (1958). The artifact assemblage from that site and a nearby domestic site are also compared in table 8.4. The tavern assemblage seems to be similar to that from Wellfleet, although it has fewer wineglass fragments than the compared domestic site.

Of the positively identified tavern sites, Wetherburn's Tavern, excavated by Ivor Noël Hume, at Williamsburg, Virginia, is the closest in time to the Wellfleet site. Although artifact lists were not published in the site report, Noël Hume does note that large numbers of wineglass stems, pipes, and drinking vessel sherds were found (1969).

The assemblages from four other taverns were also compared to that from the Wellfleet site. The sites included the Vereberg Tavern in Albany County, New York (Feister 1975), the Searight Tavern in southwest Pennsylvania (Michael 1973), the Man Full of Trouble Tavern in Philadelphia, Pennsylvania (Huey 1966), and the Orringh Stone Tavern in Brighton, New York (Hayes 1965). Although these sites differ from Wellfleet in time and location, their assemblages showed very high percentages of ceramics associated with food service and drinking, large numbers of vessels, and large amounts of glassware.

Table 8.4 *Sherd counts from Pemaquid and Jamestown tavern and domestic sites*

Pemaquid (Camp 1975)	Bottle Fragments	Winestems	Pipes	Redware	Slip-Decorated	Westerwald	Saltglaze	Sgraffito	Mottled Ware	Combed Slipware	Delft	Frechen	Gravel-Tempered
Structure 2 and 2A 1674–? John Earthy's Tavern	39	52	2,863	2,324	78	864	625	3	0	216	393	43	223
Structure 13 Dwelling 1680–1750	0	14	1,351	1,545	33	103	96	0	53	97	148	0	1
Structure 5 Dwelling ?–1696	2	0	180	432	0	32	302	2	0	35	243	0	4
Jamestown (Cotter 1958) Structure 19A, B Tavern 1694	320	3	586	101	4	52	1	3	0	52	130	31	17
Structure 21 Domestic 1680	4	55	31	62	0	0	0	0	0	0	33	0	56

8.7 Conclusion

In summary, the evidence from several tavern sites, from probate inventories, and from historical documentation suggests that the differences revealed by a functional analysis of the archaeological assemblages from the Wellfleet Tavern and the Joseph Howland sites, probable tavern and domestic sites occupied by individuals of similar social status, are not merely the function of that social position, or of wealth, but also the reflection of the occupations of each individual and the activities carried out at each site.[1]

Note

1. The author would like to thank the following people for their comments and suggestions on earlier drafts of this paper: James Deetz; Dwight Heath; Marley Brown III; and Vernon Baker.

Chapter 9

On the use of historical maps

Nancy S. Seasholes

Historical maps, defined as those drawn contemporaneously with the subject they depict as well as those reconstructed at a later date, come in many types. Because in the United States the types of historical maps available for urban areas tend to differ from those for rural, maps from these two areas are treated separately, using historical maps of Boston, Massachusetts, as examples of urban and of outlying areas of Massachusetts as examples of rural. As far as possible, the examples used in this chapter are based on real archaeological projects in order to show how historical maps can be used in archaeological research. Illustrations are given of how the information on historical maps can be assessed in relation to the purpose for which the map was made, the audience at which it was aimed, the bias of the cartographer, and the cartographic accuracy of the map. The types of maps discussed include: eighteenth- and nineteenth-century maps showing structures, directory maps, atlas maps, bird's eye views, plat plans, utility maps, maps for special projects, county maps and atlases, and reconstructed maps. For each, the discussion focuses on the kind of information that can be obtained as well as pitfalls to be avoided.

9.1 Introduction

In a field such as historical archaeology, where a major concern is the investigation of sites whose existence is already known, historical maps are an obvious source of information. These maps, which can be defined as those drawn contemporaneously with the information they depict as well as those that are later reconstructions of a given place at some specified time in the past, are invaluable not only in determining the location of specific sites but also in delineating settlement patterns and, where relevant, topographic changes. There are, however, some problems inherent in using historical maps as a documentary source. Some feel, for example, that many historical maps are inaccurate and should not be used as a reliable source of data, while others take the opposite view and too readily accept the information on historical maps as being invariably correct. This article is intended to help the researcher steer a middle course between these two alternatives as well as to serve as a guide to types of historical maps generally available.

Historical maps can be broadly classified not only, as suggested above, into those that are contemporaneous and those that are later reconstructions, but also according to type of map. Because in the United States the types of maps available for urban places tend to differ from those for rural areas, this article will treat urban and rural maps separately, using maps of Boston, Massachusetts, as examples of those for urban areas and maps of outlying regions of Massachusetts as illustrations of those for rural. In both cases, the discussion will focus first on contemporaneous maps and, since these map types tend to vary over time, will be organized chronologically starting with the earliest maps. Reconstructed maps for both urban and rural areas will be considered together in a later section. In all cases, the maps will, as far as possible, be discussed in relation to real archaeological problems in order to demonstrate the types of questions that can be answered by consulting historical maps as well as to point out some cautions to be observed when using such maps.

Before beginning this review, it is important to note that the information on any historical map should be evaluated in the same way as in any historical document, that is, by considering for what purpose the map or document was made and for what audience it was intended. Thus, a map sponsored by an advertiser might focus on information of particular interest to the sponsor at the expense of other types of information. Similarly, as will be illustrated below, maps made of Boston at the time of the American Revolution tend to show fortifications and troop emplacements and to omit the street layouts and residential buildings included on earlier eighteenth-century maps. Not only can the information on historical maps be affected by the purpose or audience for which they were made, but it can also be skewed by the bias of the cartographer or compiler. In the instance just cited, the early eighteenth-century maps of Boston that show structures were drawn by a mariner who tended to focus on maritime facilities such as wharves and gave little emphasis to major features of the landscape such as hills. To the factors already mentioned that should be considered when evaluating any historical document – purpose, audience, and bias of the author or compiler – there is a fourth consideration particular to maps: the skill and accuracy of the cartographer or compiler. Obviously a map that is drawn accurately to scale will be more directly applicable than one that is not, although even approximate representations or crudely drawn maps have their uses. In any case, the researcher should be aware of any inaccuracies or distortions in the historical map. In sum, then, the information on an historical map should not be accepted at face value but rather should be evaluated in the light of its purpose, audience, bias, and cartographic accuracy, as will be illustrated in the following survey of types of historical maps.

9.2 Maps of urban areas

9.2.1 Early maps

Beginning with an examination of maps of urban areas and specifically of Boston, historical maps of the Boston area date from its early exploration by Europeans in the late fifteenth and early sixteenth centuries (Winsor 1880, 37–40). These early maps are not really urban maps since they pre-date the first permanent European settlement of the Boston area in the 1620s and also because both they and most seventeenth-century maps of Boston were intended as charts to guide ship captains and therefore focus on coastal features rather than on details of the various settlements. Even though they are not strictly urban maps, however, these early charts are included in this discussion to indicate from what period historical maps of the Boston area date and also to suggest that even maps that are crudely drawn, often inaccurate, or on a small scale can have their uses. In the case of the Boston area maps, for example, they can be guides to former place names

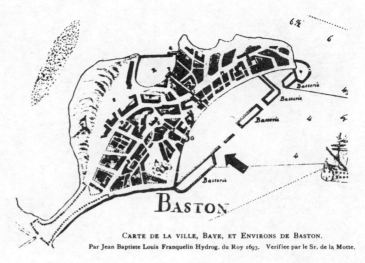

Fig. 9.1. The Boston peninsula from 'Carte de la ville, baye, et environs de Baston' by Jean Baptiste Louis Franquelin, 1693. Facsimile, n.d. (Courtesy of Massachusetts State Library)

now changed but important to know when consulting contemporary documents such as deeds.

9.2.2 Seventeenth century maps

More detailed maps of Boston itself did not appear until the end of the seventeenth century. One of the earliest of these was drawn in 1693 by the French hydrographer Franquelin and is shown in figure 9.1. A comparison of this map with one drawn in 1722 (fig. 9.2) indicates how inaccurate the earlier map is and yet, in spite of these distortions, it is a useful tool for historical archaeologists. The 1693 Franquelin map shows, for example, the layout of streets and buildings, and a careful comparison of this map with the one made in 1722 can suggest how much development took place between the two dates. The 1693 map also indicates the location of a fortified breakwater (marked by an unlabeled arrow, as are most features mentioned in the text on this and subsequent maps). This breakwater was built in the 1670s as a defensive measure but was soon allowed to fall into disrepair, as indicated on the 1722 map. Thus, in spite of inaccuracies, a late seventeenth-century map of Boston can be useful in tracing the city's development and in locating potential archaeological features.

9.2.3 Eighteenth-century maps showing structures

By the eighteenth century, map-making techniques were becoming more refined, and the maps themselves are consequently of greater value to historical archaeologists. Maps showing structures as well as street layouts, like the 1693 Franquelin map, were made with greater accuracy and detail. For Boston, the first of these improved maps showing structures was the 1722 map discussed above (fig. 9.2). It was drawn by a Captain John Bonner so it is not surprising that it has the maritime focus mentioned previously: wharves, shipyards, docks, and ropewalks are shown in careful detail but major

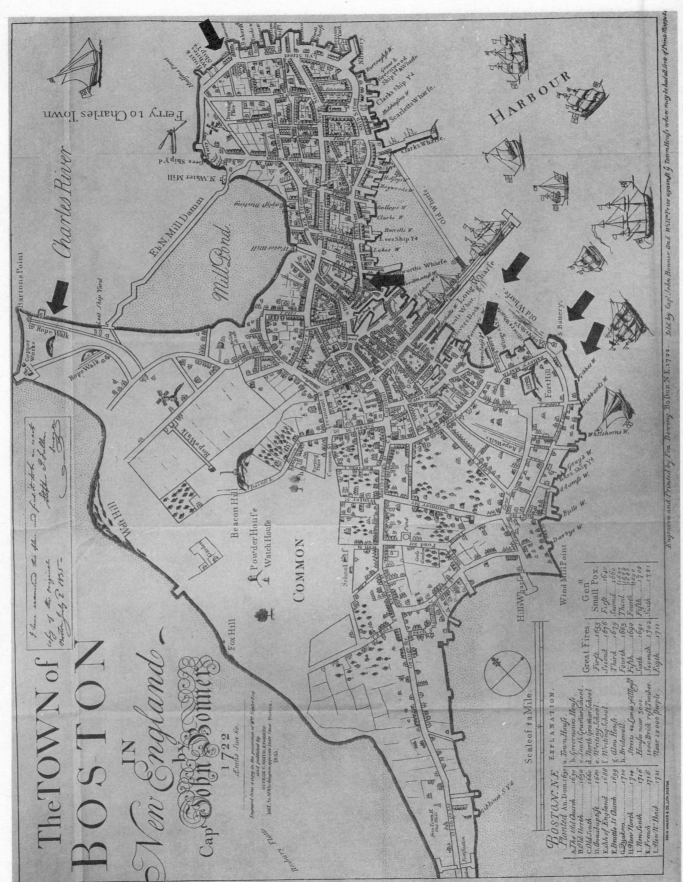

Fig. 9.2 The 1722 Bonner map of Boston: 'The Town of Boston in New England' by Captain John Bonner. (Courtesy of the Bostonian Society)

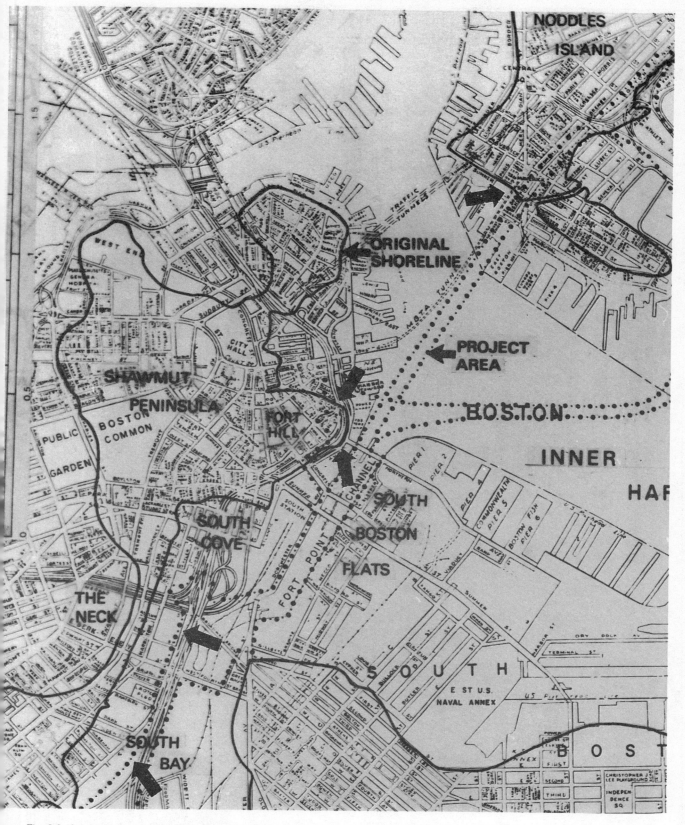

Fig. 9.3. Original shoreline of Boston and project area for a proposed third tunnel under Boston Harbor plotted on 'Boston City Base,' Boston Redevelopment Authority, 1980. (Courtesy of Institute of Conservation Archaeology, Peabody Museum, Harvard University)

Originally engraved in 1729. Reproduced in 1869.

'A New Plan of the Great Town of Boston in New England' by William Burgis, 1869 reproduction. (Courtesy of Massachusetts State Library)

Fig. 9.5. The 1733 Price update of the Bonner map: 'A New Plan of ye Great Town of Boston in New England' by William Price. (Courtesy of the John Carter Brown Library at Brown University)

hills, such as Beacon and Fort Hill, are only suggested. The usefulness of the 1722 Bonner map for an archaeological project was demonstrated by the documentary research for a proposed tunnel and highway in the Fort Hill district (fig. 9.3). The original shoreline has since been obscured by landfill, but the Bonner map made it possible to predict with reasonable accuracy the location of possible archaeological sites such as the foundations of the seventeenth-century South Battery (fig. 9.2). Another archaeological application of the Bonner map was the documentary research for the site of a hotel on the northwest corner of what were, in 1722, Ann Street and Mill Creek. Deed research and reconstructed maps indicated that the interior of this block had been dredged in the seventeenth century, but the Bonner map provided contemporary cartographic evidence that such a dock area really did exist.

Dwelling houses are depicted on the Bonner map from the front elevation only, giving the appearance that they have been toppled over backwards. Although the map is probably an accurate rendition of the density of settlement in the various parts of Boston, it should be noted that the number of houses shown is not indicative of the number actually standing. A twentieth-century antiquarian compared the number of houses in a specific section of the Bonner map with his own reconstruction, based on deed research, of the same area and found discrepancies in the number and placement of houses, thus concluding that the Bonner map is only a schematic representation. Thus, while the 1722 Bonner map of Boston is a good example of some of the uses of historical maps in documentary research, it is also a good demonstration of some of the cautions to be observed. In this case, the bias of the cartographer affected the type of information included, and some features are represented only schematically.

The 1722 Bonner map of Boston is also an illustration of another principle in the use of historical maps: checking the accuracy of one by comparing it with a contemporary map by a different cartographer, if such a comparable map exists. In the case of the Bonner map, its first appearance was followed shortly by the publication in 1728 of a similar map drawn by the cartographer William Burgis (fig. 9.4). There is common agreement that the Burgis map is a copy of the Bonner (Shurtleff 1890, 93; Reps 1973, 15; Benes 1981, 52) and thus the similarity between the two is not surprising, but there are also some instructive differences (figs. 9.2 and 9.4). In the case of the Fort Hill district, on the Burgis map Gales Shipyard and Wharf has been added between Gibbs Wharf and the South Battery and Greenleaf's Yard has become Holloway's, both changes that can be explained by new construction or transfers of ownership. More difficult to explain, however, is the omission, on the Burgis map, of the ropewalks shown in the Barton's Point area on the Bonner map; they could conceivably have been dismantled between 1722 and 1728 and this point might be established by deed research or tax records. If, however, they were omitted from the Burgis map by oversight, it raises questions about its accuracy, although the Burgis map

is generally considered the one more professionally drawn (Reps 1973, 15; Benes 1981, 52). Perhaps the most significant difference between the two is the greater amount of buildings, shown by cross-hatching, on the Burgis map. This presumably is an accurate reflection of the increased settlement of Boston between 1722 and 1728, but again, deed research might be able to establish whether the number of new houses implied by the Burgis map were actually built by 1728 or whether the map, perhaps because of its system of notation, gives an inaccurate impression.

This use of historical maps to trace changes over time, as illustrated by the foregoing comparison of the Bonner and Burgis maps, is one of the most important applications of historical maps in archaeological research. The comparisons need not be of different maps, such as the Bonner and the Burgis, but can also be of different versions of the same map. Boston is particularly fortunate in having a comparable series of an eighteenth-century map, in this case the 1722 Bonner map, which was revised and reissued in 1733 by its publisher, William Price, who then subsequently issued updated versions in 1739, 1743, and 1769. By comparing these various states of the Bonner map, one can thus trace development in Boston over a period of almost fifty years. The 1733 map (fig. 9.5), for example, uses cross-hatching to indicate new buildings, a device that makes it easy to ascertain areas in which streets and residences had been added. Thus one can see that between 1722 and 1733 development in Boston occurred in the Fort Hill district; in the South Cove area near Windmill Point, where new wharves, many with distilleries, had been built; near the Neck to the mainland; and especially in the West End near Barton's Point and on Beacon Hill near the original West Hill. The final state of the map was published in 1769 and although it shows some further development in all these areas, it suggests that more development took place in Boston in the eleven years from 1772 to 1733 than in the thirty-six years thereafter. The basic point here is that if one is fortunate enough to have an updated series of the same historical map, one can compare them to trace the development of the area as a whole as well as of specific sites.

The Price versions of the Bonner map are examples of yet another point alluded to previously: that the information on historical maps can reflect the interest of their sponsors. In this case, Price not only changed Bonner's method of indicating buildings, but he also added a cartouche, a long advertisement for the goods sold in his shop on Cornhill (located on the map by a pointing hand), an even longer historical text about Boston, and additional statistical information about the city (figs. 9.2 and 9.5). In each succeeding state, the advertisement, historical text, and statistics were lengthened until by the final state the surrounding text hemmed in the map on all sides. In this instance, Price's additions served more to make the map seem unattractively crowded than they did to alter the information on the map itself, but one should note that the contents of a map can be skewed by the interests of an advertiser.

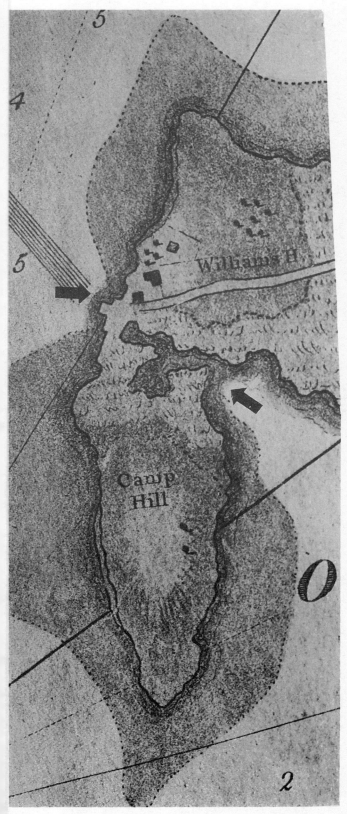

Fig. 9.6. Detail of Noddles Island from 'A Plan of Boston in New England with Its Environs. . .' by Henry Pelham, 1777. Boston, W. A. Butterfield, 1907. (Courtesy of Massachusetts State Library)

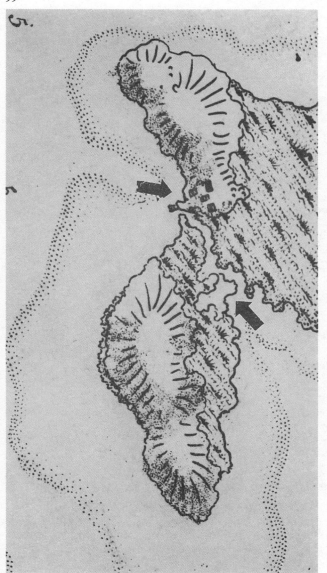

Fig. 9.7. Detail of Noddles Island from Boston Harbour sheet in *The Atlantic Neptune* by J. F. W. DesBarres, 1775. London, 1776 (Courtesy of Massachusetts State Library)

9.2.4 Comparable maps occasioned by an historical event
Sometimes one is fortunate enough to be doing research on an area for which many maps were issued on the same subject at about the same time, thus producing a useful set of comparable maps. The concurrent appearance of many similar maps is usually occasioned by an historical event and such was the case for Boston in 1775 and 1776 when the siege of the city at the outset of the American Revolution created a demand for charts of Boston harbor and maps of the city and its environs. These maps emphasize military fortifications and troop emplacements and, although they do show the layout of Boston's streets, they do not, as noted above, give as much detail about buildings as do the earlier Bonner and Burgis maps. The Revolutionary maps are useful nonetheless for locating military sites and also because many of them include

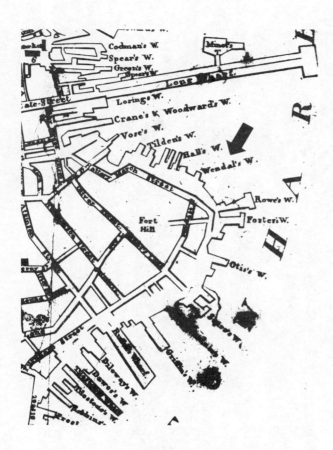

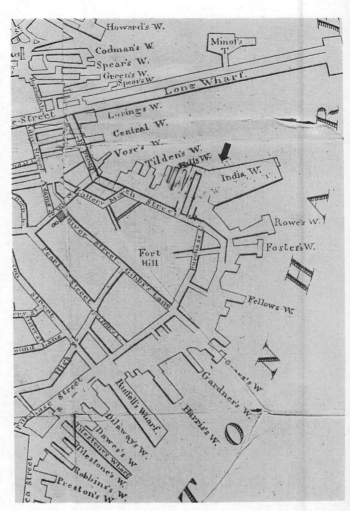

Fig. 9.8. Detail of Fort Hill area form 'A Plan of Boston from Actual Survey' by Osgood Carleton, 1796, for the *Second Boston Directory*. Boston, John West. (Courtesy of Massachusetts State Library)

Fig. 9.9. Detail of Fort Hill area and India Wharf development from 'A Plan of Boston from Actual Survey' by Osgood Carleton, 1803, for the *Boston Directory*. Boston, John West. (Courtesy of Massachusetts State Library)

areas outside Boston proper that had not previously been mapped in much detail, thus making them particularly helpful for archaeological projects in these areas. This was demonstrated in the case of research for the highway/tunnel project mentioned previously. Part of the alignment cut across what was originally Noddles Island (fig. 9.3) and, as one of the very accurate maps of this period makes clear, transversed the site of an eighteenth-century farmstead on this island (fig. 9.6). Although not directly relevant to this project, it should be noted that the cartographer, Henry Pelham, was a Loyalist, and his map tends to emphasize Anglican churches and parts of the Boston area with which he was familiar, such as Cambridge (Benes 1981, 55). This is not to say that his depiction of settlement on Noddles Island is inaccurate, but simply to reiterate the point that knowledge about the cartographer aids in the interpretation of an historical map. The eighteenth-century settlement on Noddles Island is verified by comparison of the Pelham map with another very accurate and complete map published at about the same time: the chart of

Boston Harbor by J. F. W. DesBarres (fig. 9.7). This chart was the result of a survey of the North American coast begun by the British in 1764 and hurried into publication to aid them in fighting the Revolution (Cumming 1980, 98–105; Loring 1980, 119–21; Evans 1969, 11–26). In the case of Noddles Island, the DesBarres chart corroborates that there was a farmstead on the south coast but indicates that the southeast portion of the island was entirely separated from the rest rather than just cut by a deep inlet, as shown on the Pelham map (figs. 9.6 and 9.7). In this case, the DesBarres chart, because it was the result of a long, careful, professional survey, is probably more accurate than the Pelham map, another instance where knowledge about the cartographer and the purpose of an historical map helps the researcher judge its accuracy.

9.2.5 Directory maps

The turn of the nineteenth century in Boston saw the introduction of a new type of historical map that has proved to be very useful for historical archaeologists: the maps included

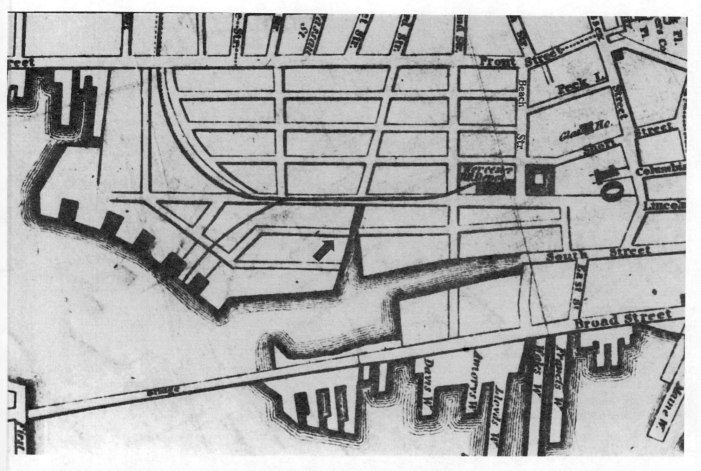

Fig. 9.10. Detail of South Cove area from 'Plan of the City of Boston,' 1837, in the *Boston Directory*. Boston, Charles Stimpson. (Courtesy of Harvard College Library)

in city directories. Directories, the nineteenth-century forerunner of today's telephone book, originally contained an alphabetical list of names, addresses, and occupations of all city residents and, later, also a classified list of businesses. Boston directories were published annually beginning in 1798 and each edition included a map of the city. Because these maps were intended to help locate street addresses, they show only street layouts and major public buildings rather than all structures and for this reason are generally less useful to the historical archaeologist than the series of eighteenth-century maps discussed earlier. Despite their limitations, however, directory maps can be applied to certain archaeological problems such as tracing and dating the enormous topographical changes that occurred in Boston in the nineteenth century as a result of major landfill projects. For example, a comparison of a detail of the map from the 1796 directory with a detail from that of 1803 (figs. 9.8 and 9.9) shows that by the latter year the India Wharf development had begun. Tracing these changes in the waterfront at the base of Fort Hill was important for the archaeology associated with the highway/tunnel project cited earlier (fig. 9.3) and, although construction and filling such as that at India Wharf can be documented through sources other

than maps (Cheney, Seasholes, Laden, Lewis, Krase, Woods and Gordon 1983, 54–6), the directory maps provide graphic confirmation of the written sources. An examination of the annual directory maps over a period of time would indicate in just which years various topographical changes occurred.

The use of directory maps to document and date topographical changes in a given area is probably valid when the maps in question are updated versions of the same map, as was the case in the example of India Wharf just cited. Periodically, however, the directory base map was changed, and caution should be exercised when comparing information from different base maps. For example, during the 1830s when the South Cove area was being filled, the map from the 1837 *Boston Directory* indicated that most of the area east of Front Street and south of Beach Street had already been filled and streets laid out (fig. 9.10), while the base map for the same year used in the *Boston Almanac*, a somewhat similar publication, showed that this same area still contained wharves extending east from Front Street served by an inlet running under Lincoln Street (fig. 9.11). Deciding which of these two maps is more accurate was important in the highway/tunnel project described earlier, where part of the alignment was in the South Cove

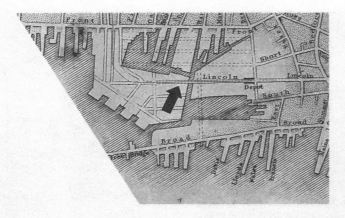

Fig. 9.11. Detail of South Cove area from 'Boston,' 1837, in the *Boston Almanac*. Boston, S. N. Dickinson. (Courtesy of the Bostonian Society)

it is, in fact, the more correct version. The basic point here is that while maps in city directories may be useful in tracing basic topographic changes, they may also contain some inaccuracies.

Another caution to be observed when using directory maps is that their representation is often stylized. This point is clearly evident in a comparison of the 1859 almanac map with a chart published in 1857 as part of the United States Coast Survey (figs. 9.13 and 9.14). One can assume that the latter map, because it was the result of a professional government survey, is the more accurate, and even a cursory inspection would indicate that this is the case. The Coastal Survey chart, for example, has a more exact representation of features such as South Bay and indicates the actual amount of landfill in areas such as Back Bay instead of showing proposed but not yet constructed streets as does the almanac map. Thus, for the highway/tunnel project, where it was important to date the landfill sequence in South Bay in the area east of Albany Street (fig. 9.3), the Coastal Survey chart was deemed the more accurate and the conclusions were based on it. The basic caution here is that directory maps may not always be cartographically correct and other maps should also be considered.

9.2.6 Nineteenth-century maps showing structures

Some of the limitations of directory maps can be avoided by using maps that show structures as well as streets. Such maps are, of necessity, on a comparatively large scale and, for a city

section (fig. 9.3) and thus the sequence of landfill in that area was of interest. One way to resolve the issue was to examine later versions of both maps; the 1838 *Directory* map shows the same amount of filled land as the 1837 (fig. 9.10) but the 1838 *Almanac* map indicates that the area east of Front and south of Beach streets had been filled since 1837 (figs. 9.12 and 9.11). Assuming that the landfill project had continued between 1837 and 1838, the *Almanac* map would seem more credible, although further documentary research could establish whether

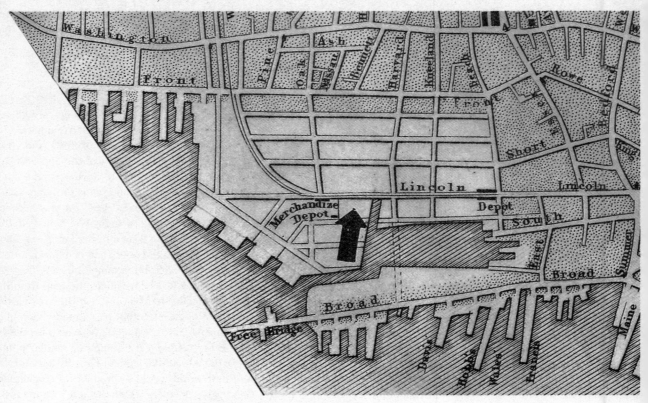

Fig. 9.12. Detail of South Cove area from 'Boston,' 1838, in the *Boston Almanac*. Boston, S. N. Dickinson. (Courtesy of the Bostonian Society)

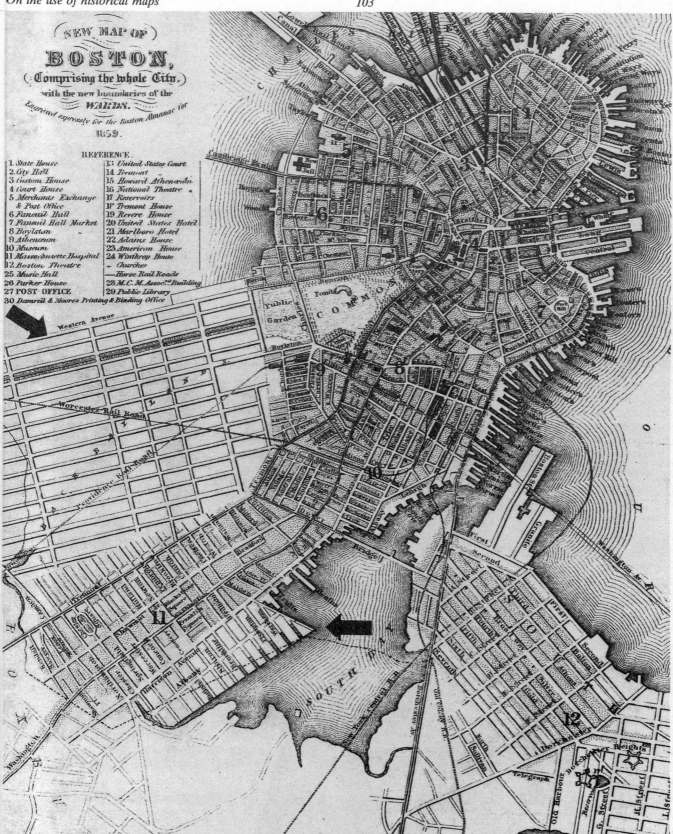

Fig. 9.13. Detail of South Bay, South Boston, and Back Bay from 'New Map of Boston comprising the whole city with the new boundaries of the Wards,' 1859, in the *Boston Almanac*. (Courtesy of the Bostonian Society)

A reconstructed map for 1798 indicated that the site included about ten lots containing houses or stores along Ann Street east of an alley (fig. 9.16), but on the Hales map these separate buildings are presented as one long wood structure (fig. 9.15). Thus the information on maps showing structures may need to be supplemented by additional research, in this case to verify whether the structures shown are individual buildings or a series of them.

The other two maps of Boston showing structures date from the mid-nineteenth century and, in contrast to the Hales map, do show individual buildings. By coincidence, both these maps were published in 1852, so some interesting comparisons are possible. The better-known of the two was surveyed by Henry McIntyre (fig. 9.17) and includes maps of neighboring cities as well as Boston proper. The buildings are coded as to type of construction material and the McIntyre map would thus appear at first glance to be an invaluable source for historical archaeologists. However, when the McIntyre map is compared with a similar map published in the same year – the map of

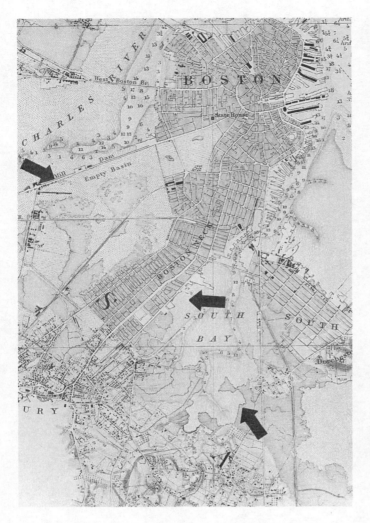

Fig. 9.14. Detail of South Bay, South Boston, and Back Bay from 'Boston harbor, Massachusetts, from a trigonometrical survey under the direction of A. D. Bache, Supt. U.S. Coast Survey,' 1857. (Courtesy of Harvard College Library)

the size of Boston, quite an undertaking to produce. Boston is thus very fortunate in having three such maps made during the first part of the nineteenth century. The first of these was published in 1814 as the result of a survey by John G. Hales. The Hales map differentiates between buildings of wood, indicated by diagonal shading, and those of stone or brick, shown by shading parallel to the façade (fig. 9.15), making the map very useful in assessing the archaeological potential of a given site. Since the Hales map is on a much larger scale than the directory maps discussed above, it is also an excellent guide to the topographical changes that had occurred by 1814. Despite all the advantages of large-scale maps of this type, however, they can have their limitations. The Hales map, for example, does not show every single individual structure but rather lumps together all structures built of the same material in a given area of a block. This problem became clear in the documentary research for the hotel project mentioned earlier.

Fig. 9.15. Detail of the Blackstone Block from 'Map of the City of Boston in the State of Massachusetts' by John G. Hales, 1814. (Facsimile from the Boston Redevelopment Authority)

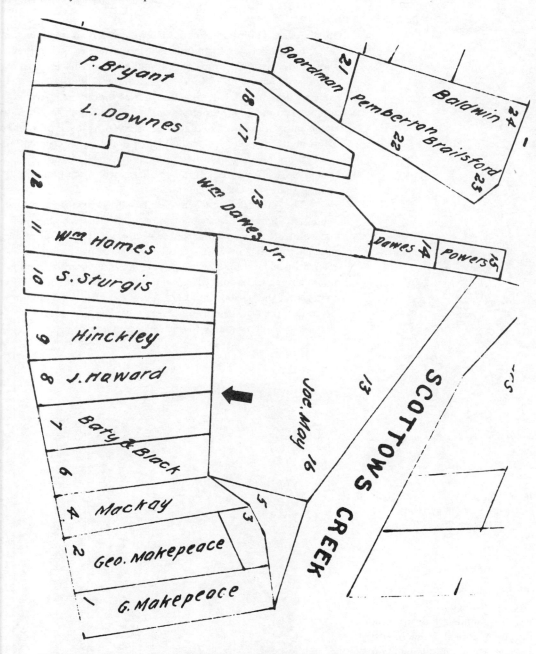

Fig. 9.16. Detail of the Blackstone Block in 1798 from a reconstructed map by Samuel C. Clough. (Courtesy of the Massachusetts Historical Society)

Boston surveyed by J. Slatter and B. Callan (fig. 9.18) – some of the inadequacies of the McIntyre become apparent. The two maps have differences in notation and some outright discrepancies. One possible explanation for these discrepancies might be that the McIntyre map was surveyed considerably earlier than the Slatter and Callan and, for some reason, its publication was delayed until 1852. This explanation seems plausible when comparing the Boston Wharf Company's landfill north of First Street in South Boston. The company had begun filling this area in the late 1830s and, as both the McIntyre and the Slatter and Callan maps indicate (figs. 9.17 and 9.18), in 1852 was still in the process of creating a large wharf area.

Although both maps show the same general wharf configuration, the Slatter and Callan indicates that two arms of the wharf were complete by 1852 while the McIntyre shows a large unfilled area still existing between the arms, thus giving credence to the idea that the McIntyre map was surveyed earlier than the Slatter and Callan although not published until the same year. More research about the cartographers themselves would be needed to establish whether this is actually the case, but the basic point here is that even the most carefully surveyed map may contain inaccuracies, and comparison with a similar contemporary map is always desirable.

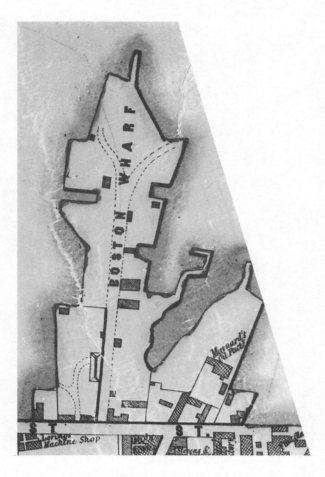

Fig. 9.17. Detail Boston Wharf Company area from 'Map of the city of Boston and immediate neighborhood' by Henry McIntyre, 1852. Boston, H. McIntyre. (Courtesy of Massachusetts State Library)

9.2.7 Atlas maps

By the late nineteenth century another type of map showing individual structures became available: the maps in insurance and real estate atlases. Atlas maps are a cartographic source generally known and used by historical archaeologists, yet there are cautions to be observed when employing even these familiar materials. As implied above, late nineteenth-century city atlases can be divided into two types – insurance and real estate – and, while both contain comparable information, there are also significant differences between them. Insurance atlases for major eastern American cities were first published in the 1850s (Wright 1983, 1). These atlases were sponsored by fire insurance companies and were intended to help these companies assess the fire risks in the buildings depicted. Thus, insurance atlas maps generally indicate construction materials, features such as stairs, roofs, and skylights, and, most important for the historical archaeologist, building use. The first insurance atlas for Boston was published in 1861, the second in 1867, and then, starting in the mid-1880s, at about ten year intervals. Real estate atlases, which for

Boston were published at about five year intervals beginning in 1883, have some basic similarities to insurance atlases in that they, too, are books of maps generally on a large scale, often fifty or 100 feet to an inch, and indicate the building construction material. Real estate atlases, however, were intended to indicate property ownership and so the owner's name rather than the building's use is given for each property. Knowing the ownership is useful when doing deed research but is often not much help in determining land use, so for archaeological research insurance atlases will often be more helpful than real estate.

The difference between these two types of city atlases can readily be demonstrated by a comparison of maps concerning the hotel site mentioned earlier. The 1883 Bromley real estate atlas of Boston shows the site divided into at least ten lots owned by at least nine different persons and, by color-coding not visible in black and white, indicates the construction material of the various buildings (fig. 9.19). The 1885 Sanborn insurance atlas (fig. 9.20), however, not only gives more detailed information about construction material (again

Fig. 9.18. Detail Boston Wharf Company area from 'Map of the City of Boston, Massts' by J. Slatter and B. Callan, 1852. New York, M. Dripps. (Courtesy of The Boston Athenaeum)

generally working in partnership with a business agent. When starting on a new town, the agent would try to sell enough advance orders, often through the local newspapers, to finance the project, and then the artist would make a street-by-street survey, sketching each building as seen from the direction of the hypothetical view. The sketches were then combined into an overall perspective drawing, the resulting work lithographed, and then distributed to the subscribers (Ruell 1983, 6–8; Reps 1984, 3–23, 39–58). The views so produced were promoted for a number of reasons: as works of art and suitable wall ornaments; as reference works that served as both maps and directories; as important historical records; as mementos for former residents and visitors; as advertisements of a town's manufacturing facilities or tourist attractions; and, perhaps most often, as appeals to civic pride (Ruell 1983, 6–8; Reps 1984, 61–3). One might think that the attempt to serve such a variety of interests would lead to distortions of the information in a drawing, but this is apparently not the case. Although there were isolated instances where a view included buildings planned but never actually constructed, careful studies have concluded that bird's eye views are usually an

Fig. 9.19. Detail of the Blackstone Block from *Atlas of the City of Boston*, vol. 1: *Boston Proper* by George W. Bromley, 1883. Philadelphia, George W. & Walter S. Bromley. (Courtesy of Massachusetts State Library)

color-coded and not apparent in black and white) but also indicates that the lot shown in the Bromley as owned by G. Collamore was occupied by a five-story hotel with a market on the first floor; the lots owned by Freeman and Rockwell were covered by a four-story building with a market on the first floor and a sign painter and carpenter on the upper floors; the Squire lot was occupied by a four-story building with a wholesale provision firm on the first floor and a clothing manufacturer above; and so forth. Thus, as these examples make clear, insurance maps are often preferable to real estate maps in determining land use at a particular site.

9.2.8 Bird's eye views

There is yet another type of nineteenth-century map that shows structures: the bird's eye views that were very popular in the second half of the century. These perspective drawings of a town as if viewed from the air are not maps in the strictest sense but are included in this discussion because they are comparable to several types of historical maps and are a cartographic source useful to historical archaeologists. Bird's eye views were typically drawn by itinerant specialized artists

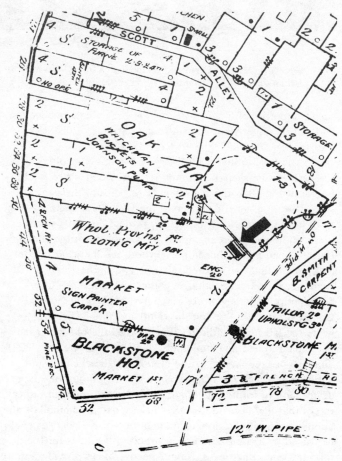

Fig. 9.20. Detail of the Blackstone Block from *Boston, Massachusetts*, vol. 1, by Sanborn Map Company, 1885. New York, Sanborn Map and Publishing Co. (Courtesy of Harvard College Library)

Fig. 9.21. Detail of Fort Point Channel area from 'View of Boston Massachusetts 1880' by H. H. Rowley & Co. Ithaca, New York, Historic Urban Plans, 1970. (Courtesy of Massachusetts State Library)

accurate portrayal of a city or town at the date of publication and can therefore be used as a reliable source of historical information (Ruell 1983, 8–9; Reps 1984, 67–72).

The application of bird's eye views in archaeological research can be seen in a comparison of two views of Boston, one drawn in 1880 and the other in 1899. Both these views show Boston as seen from across the Fort Point Channel and were useful for the highway/tunnel project discussed above because the proposed alignment went right down the channel (fig. 9.3) and it was thus important to trace the wharfing-out and landfill that had created this waterway. The 1880 view, for example, shows that in that year there were a series of nondescript buildings on Russia Wharf next to the new Congress Street bridge (on the righthand side of fig. 9.21), while the later view indicates that by 1899 the old wharf had been filled in and new buildings erected on the site (fig. 9.22). Similarly, a comparison of the area along the channel south of Summer Street in the two views shows the amount of filling, destruction of former buildings, and rearrangement of railway tracks that had occurred by 1899 in order to accommodate the building of South Station. Although these same changes could be traced by a comparison of insurance atlas maps for the relevant years, the bird's eye perspective views provide a more graphic, and to many, more comprehensible version of the information on the maps.

Despite their many advantages, however, there are some

cautions to be observed when using bird's eye views. Not only do some include buildings drawn from projected plans though never actually constructed, but the drawings of existing buildings are often stylized versions of their actual appearance. The Russia Wharf Building, for example, has in reality much more detail than the box-like structure shown on the 1899 bird's eye (fig. 9.22). Distinctive or very important buildings, however, are often drawn resembling their actual appearance, as is South Station in the 1899 view (fig. 9.22). Thus, while bird's eye views are generally a reliable source of information about the appearance of a city or town at the date of publication, more research may be necessary to establish the actual appearance of the buildings depicted.

9.2.9 Specialized maps

The discussion thus far has covered various types of historical maps available for American cities in the eighteenth and nineteenth centuries: maps showing street layouts and structures, directory maps, atlas maps, and bird's eye views. The remainder of this section on urban maps will focus on some specialized maps that may be particularly useful to the historical archaeologist but may not exist or be relevant for all cities. The first such map type is one that is particularly germane to Boston, a city that, as noted before, has undergone enormous topographical changes because of landfill projects. The extent of these changes has occasionally been recorded by plotting the

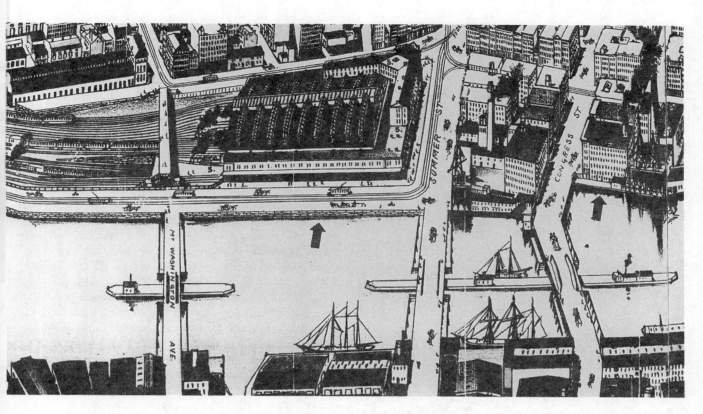

Fig. 9.22. Detail of Fort Point Channel area from 'Boston 1899' by A. E. Downs. Boston, George H. Walker, 1899. (Courtesy of Massachusetts State Library)

original Boston shoreline on a contemporary map of the city. One example is the map for the highway/tunnel project cited many times already (fig. 9.3) that shows the original shoreline drawn on a 1980s base map of Boston. There are also, however, historical maps showing topographical changes, one of the most useful of which is a map published in 1895 that not only plots the original shoreline on the city street map of that year but also shows the wharf lines for 1795. This map was very helpful in assessing the archaeological potential along another alignment of the aforementioned highway/tunnel project. A segment of the 1895 map appears in fig. 9.23: the numbered blocks are in the project area, the 1630 shoreline is indicated by the heavy black line, and the 1795 wharves and shoreline by heavy dashed lines. From this it is apparent that blocks 9 through 12 and some of blocks 7 and 8 are on land in existence since the seventeenth century, most of blocks 13 and 14 contained wharves by the end of the eighteenth century, and blocks 6, 15, and parts of 7 and 8 were filled in the nineteenth century. Although a map such as this that shows topographic changes is obviously a valuable source of information for a city like Boston, such a map would not exist for a city that had undergone little or no topographic modification.

Some types of specialized maps, however, are just as available for other cities as they are for Boston. One such type are the plat plans for specific parcels of land. These plans are generally the result of a survey made at the time a property is sold and are intended to establish the exact boundaries of the parcel. They therefore emphasize lot lines, often name the owners of abutting properties, and, on occasion, show the location of buildings. Other features are usually omitted unless they have some relevance to the location of the property lines. Such a case was found in the course of the documentary research for a proposed hotel in downtown Boston. This hotel site was comprised, in part, of many eighteenth-century house lots all given rights to a common well and a 'necessary'. These rights were always cited in the deeds to these lots and although measurements to the well and privy were not part of the legal descriptions, location of these features was apparently an integral part of the relevant properties. Thus, when the entire parcel was sold in 1833, a plat plan made at that time included the well and privy, an occurrence of great help to an archaeologist trying to locate such features in the field. Even the more usual plans that show only lot lines are clearly useful for locating historical boundaries and are a cartographic resource that should not be overlooked.

Other specialized maps that are particularly useful to archaeologists are maps showing the location of utilities. Present-day utility maps are familiar to archaeologists and often essential when excavating an urban site, but there are also historical maps of various city utilities. For Boston, maps showing the location of water pipes, gas pipes, and sewers began to be published in the 1840s and appeared periodically

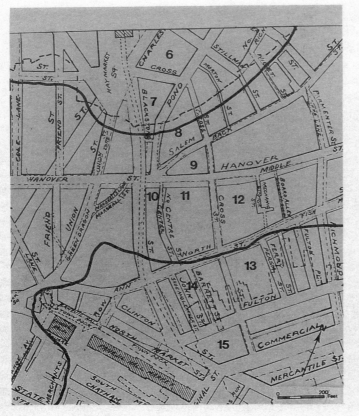

Fig. 9.23. Detail of Third Harbor Tunnel project area from 'Plan of Boston Showing Changes in Street and Wharf lines, 1795 to 1895' by Charles C. Perkins, 1895. (Facsimile from the Boston Redevelopment Authority and courtesy of Institute of Conservation Archaeology, Peabody Museum, Harvard University)

throughout the rest of the nineteenth century, usually in connection with improvements to the water works or sewer systems. There are also late nineteenth-century maps showing the location of conduits carrying underground electricity, telephone, telegraph, and other electrical lines. Although not all these utilities are still in their nineteenth-century locations, the maps are nonetheless very useful to the archaeologist trying to assess the disturbance in a given area.

Yet another type of specialized map available for urban areas is the plan of a special project. For Boston, there exists a wealth of nineteenth-century maps showing landfill projects, wharf areas, railway lines, subway tunnels, parks and recreational areas, and the like. These maps are often on a large scale and are invaluable to archaeologists doing research on areas covered by such maps. In addition, some of these developments took place over an extended period of time and are the subject of a number of maps, making it possible to trace the course of a given project. Although such maps do not always exist, they are an important resource, and an archaeologist working on a site that was the focus of a major nineteenth-century special project would be well advised to

ascertain whether there is an historical map of the project and the area.

9.2.10 Twentieth-century maps

The discussion thus far has focused on historical maps of Boston from the seventeenth through the nineteenth centuries and has examined a number of map types. The twentieth-century cartographic sources for Boston are less varied, however: most maps of the city are street guides and do not show structures, though both insurance and real estate atlases continued to be published. Plat plans are also still made, as are plans of special projects, although the latter tend to remain in the offices of the private firms involved rather than being made available in public archives as is the case with many nineteenth-century project plans. Perhaps the most accurate twentieth-century maps of Boston are those resulting from regular United States government surveys: the Geological Survey (USGS) and the Coast and Geodetic Survey (USC&GS). The former maps are issued as named quadrants on a scale of 1:24000 making it possible to indicate individual structures in outlying sections although not in urban areas, which are designated by shading and show only street layouts and major public buildings. Coastal charts are intended to facilitate navigation and therefore do not focus on land features: the charts of Boston Harbor show only street layouts and structures visible from sea, such as tall buildings and smoke stacks.

Perhaps the main reason that the twentieth-century cartographic record of Boston seems less rich than the nineteenth is that in many instances nineteenth-century cartographic skills have been replaced by the aerial camera and photogrammetric plotter. Aerial photos exist of the city from a variety of heights and angles and now even form the basis for updating the Geological Survey maps. Thus an archaeologist needing twentieth-century cartographic information about a site in Boston may be restricted to a few types of maps and may eventually have to consult a photograph.

9.3 Maps of rural areas

Having concluded the discussion of urban maps, the next section of this article will consider maps of rural areas in the United States and will, as stated at the outset, use maps of areas in Massachusetts outside Boston to show how these map types differ from those made for cities.

9.3.1 Seventeenth-century maps

The early maps of rural Massachusetts date from the seventeenth and eighteenth centuries when the state was first settled. Unlike the early maps showing Boston, which tend to be small-scale charts of the whole coast, early maps of rural areas are often relatively large-scale plat plans of land grants or of 'divisions', the allocation of a town's land among its early residents. A good example of this type of map is a 1708 plan of the town of Sudbury, Massachusetts (fig. 9.24). Although it is

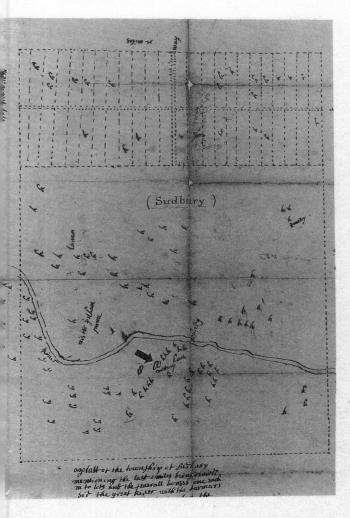

Fig. 9.24. Map of Sudbury [Massachusetts] probably by John Brigham, 1708. (Courtesy of Massachusetts State Archives)

9.3.2 State-mandated maps

The cartographic record of rural Massachusetts is especially complete at the end of the eighteenth and beginning of the nineteenth centuries thanks to two resolves passed by the state legislature requiring each town to conduct a survey and file a plan. It should be mentioned that in Massachusetts, as in all New England states, the term 'town' refers to an area, not a settlement. All the land in a state is divided among cities and towns whose borders are contiguous; there is thus no unincorporated land, and a town may contain several centers of settlement as well as a large amount of rural area. The practical effect of the Massachusetts resolves, therefore, was to require that all the land outside of Boston be mapped.

The first of these resolves was passed in 1794 and required that the town plans be on a scale of 200 rods to an inch. The result was to be a map of the state that would 'facilitate & promote such information and improvements as will be favorable to its [Massachusetts'] growth and prosperity' (Massachusetts, Commonwealth of, 1794, 202), apparently a reflection of the interest in internal improvements then current in the United States. Besides town boundaries, each plan was to include rivers, bridges, county roads, churches, court houses, ponds, waterfalls, mountains, factories, 'mills mines and minerals' (Massachusetts, Commonwealth of, 1794, 204), and iron works and furnaces. Most of the plans filed were in manuscript rather than published form and for that reason cannot be relied on for accurate measurements. They are, nonetheless, a valuable source of information about early road systems, industries, and public structures and have obvious archaeological applications. A 1794 plan was used, for example, in tracing the history of a mill site located in Lancaster, Massachusetts, during a power line survey. Documentary sources indicated that the mill had been built in the 1720s but had later fallen into disuse at an unspecified time. The fact that this mill was not shown on the 1794 plan of Lancaster suggested that the period of disuse had begun before that date.

The other state resolve was passed in 1830. It required that the plans be drawn on a scale of 100 rods to an inch and, in addition to the features specified in 1794, show all roads, public buildings, ferries, shores, harbors, islands, hills, meadows, and woodlands. Most maps in the Massachusetts 1830 series were printed rather than remaining in manuscript form and, although it was not required by the legislative directive, most of these printed maps show all residences as well as public buildings in a town. Figure 9.25 is a detail of the 1831 map of Chelmsford, Massachusetts, and an illustration of the amount of useful information, such as the location of canals, turnpikes, taverns, and industries that was included on these plans. In this case, the map was used for the historical research in connection with a proposed highway in the Chelmsford–Lowell area and shows that the project area contained a house on Wood Street. The date of construction of this house, which is still standing, is disputed, but the 1831 map confirms that it was certainly in its present location at that date.

highly schematic, a plan such as this can still be very helpful to the historical archaeologist. In this case each house in Sudbury is indicated by the letter 'h', and this information could be used not only to locate house sites but also to delineate settlement patterns. For example, the general layout of houses on the east side of the river (at the bottom of the plan) has been verified by the research of a twentieth-century historian (Powell 1963, facing 76). It should be noted that knowledge about the cartographer is as important for schematic plans like this one as it is for more finished maps; the Sudbury plan, for example, was probably drawn by a man who lived on the west side of the river, where the residents had been petitioning for their own meeting house on the grounds of distance from the existing one (marked with an arrow), so it is possible that the number and location of houses on the west side were deliberately altered, although historians believe this is not the case (Benes 1981, 59). The basic point here is that even plans that are highly schematic and not drawn to scale can contain information useful to the historical archaeologist.

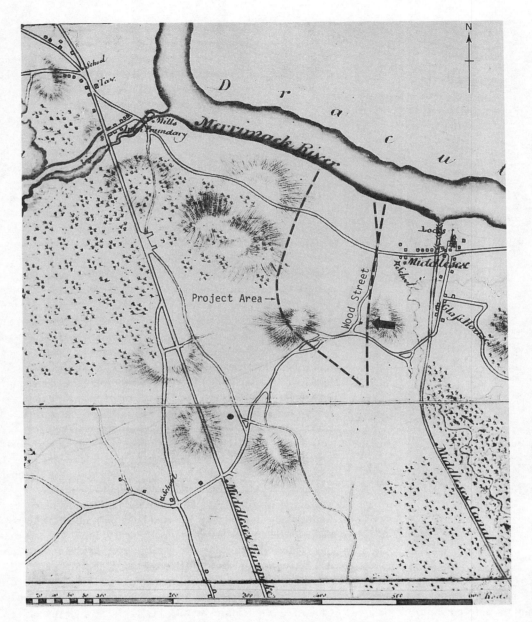

Fig. 9.25. Detail of Middlesex Village area from 'Plan of the Town of Chelmsford in the County of Middlesex' by John G. Hales, 1831. (Courtesy of the Massachusetts State Archives and Institute of Conservation Archaeology, Peabody Museum, Harvard University)

9.3.3 County maps

By the middle of the nineteenth century, a new type of map became available for Massachusetts as well as for other parts of the country – county maps. These were large wall maps that were popular in the period from 1850 to 1880 and were sold by subscription in a manner very similar to the promotion of bird's eye views (Reps 1984, 56–7). In New England, a county map contained maps of all the towns in the county and included much the same information as the 1830 series maps but with the additional advantage that the property owners were named. An example is the map of Windsor,

Massachusetts, taken from the 1858 map of Berkshire County, Massachusetts (fig. 9.26a and b). The 1858 map of Windsor was useful in the archaeological investigation of two sites in that town: the Weston farmstead on the Savoy Road and the Nichols blacksmith shop on Windsor Hill. The 1858 map shows the Weston farmhouse and gives a good indication of its geographical relation to other farms in town (fig. 9.26a). And the larger-scale detail of Windsor Hill that was also typically included in county maps shows the exact location of the blacksmith shop as well as other buildings in the town center (fig. 9.26b). County maps are not infallible and some of the

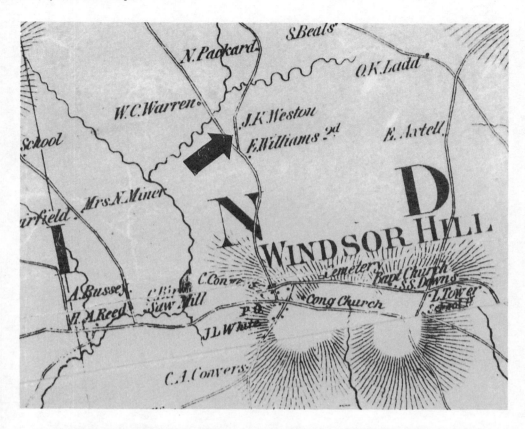

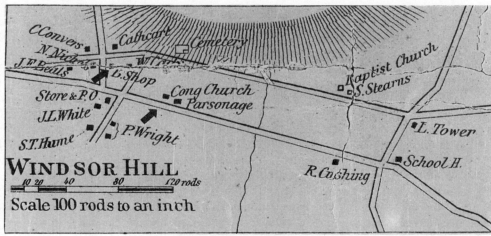

Fig. 9.26 (a and b): Detail of map of Windsor and of Windsor Hill from 'Map of the County of Berkshire, Massachusetts' by Henry F. Walling, 1858. New York, H. F. Walling. (Courtesy of Massachusetts State Library)

suggestions made earlier for verifying the information on historical maps can well be applied here. Similar maps, for example, sometimes exist and when possible should be compared with county maps to point up any discrepancies.

A somewhat different version of a county map was produced in the mid-nineteenth century for cities like Cambridge, Massachusetts (fig. 9.27). This map is similar to county maps in that it names the larger property owners and shows the boundaries of their lots, but is also like the mid-nineteenth-century maps of Boston such as the McIntyre

and Slatter and Callan (figs. 9.17 and 9.18) in that for smaller properties it simply shows the structures but does not name the owners. The Cambridge map is on such a large scale that it is an excellent guide to archaeological and historical features such as the North Cambridge cattle pens (fig. 9.27).

9.3.4 Atlas maps
By the end of the nineteenth century, the large county and city maps showing property ownership had been replaced by real estate atlases. The maps in county atlases were similar

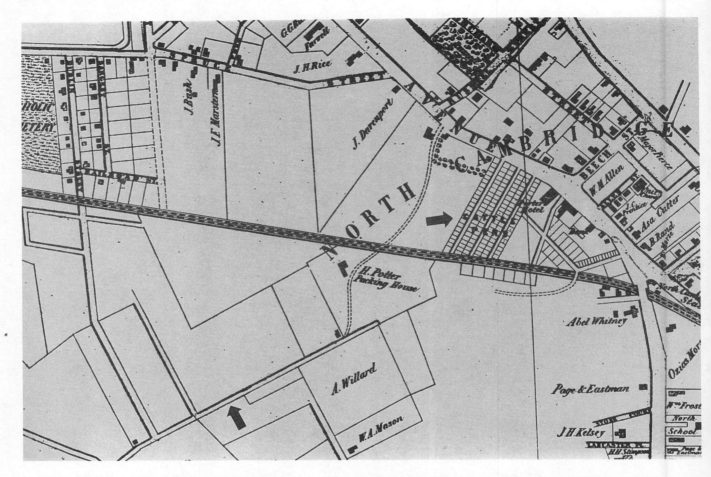

Fig. 9.27. Detail of North Cambridge from 'Map of the City of Cambridge, Middlesex County, Massachusetts' by H. F. Walling, 1854. (Facsimile from the Cambridge Historical Commission)

to those on the county wall maps: the map for each town indicated all houses, named the property owners, and was supplemented by large-scale details of town centers. These detailed maps usually showed lot lines and the actual configuration of houses and for that reason are very useful in archaeological research; for larger towns there might be several full-page detailed maps supplementing the basic town maps. The atlas maps for cities tend to be all of the large-scale, detailed type. The 1879 atlas for Lowell, Massachusetts, for example, shows that since 1830 some additional structures had been built in the project area for the proposed highway mentioned above, including a large barn or other outbuilding associated with the Bowers house on Wood Street (figs. 9.28 and 9.25). Atlases such as this continued to be published into the twentieth century, and successive editions can be compared in order to trace and date changes in a given area in much the same way that was suggested for directory maps of Boston (figs. 9.8 and 9.9).

9.3.5 Bird's eye views

As in the case of cities, there are also bird's eye views for some outlying areas of Massachusetts. One example is the 1877

view of Cambridge (fig. 9.29), which is drawn from a different perspective than the Boston views discussed above (figs. 9.21 and 9.22). The Boston views were compared with each other in order to trace development in a given area, but it is also possible to compare a bird's eye with a conventional map of the area and obtain the same type of information. Thus, a comparison of the 1877 bird's eye of Cambridge with the 1854 detailed map of that city shows that by the later year the North Cambridge cattle pens were gone but extensive brick works had been built in the area bounded by Raymond, Walden, and Dublin (now Sherman) streets that had been empty in 1854 (figs. 9.29 and 9.27).

9.3.6. Specialized maps

There are also plat and other types of specialized plans for outlying areas. For the projected highway in the Chelmsford–Lowell area, for example, it was necessary to ascertain the date of construction of some historic buildings abutting the project area. These buildings had been part of a county training school and architects' drawings as well as a plan showing construction dates were found in the county commissioner's office. The point here is the same as that for

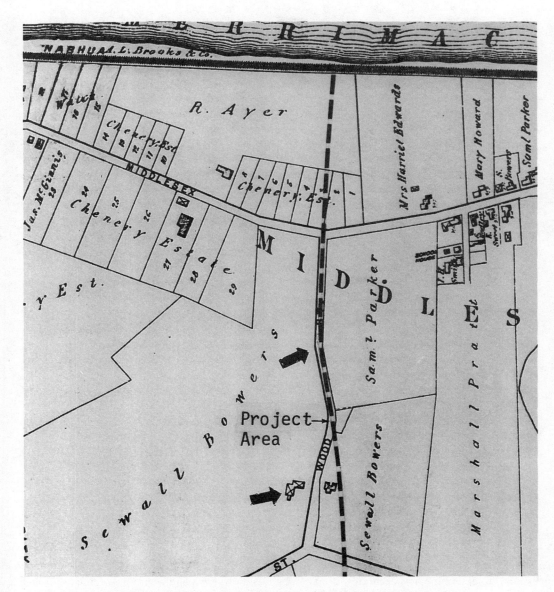

Fig. 9.28. Detail of Middlesex Village area from *City Atlas of Lowell, Massachusetts* by G. M. Hopkins, 1879. Philadelphia, G. M. Hopkins. (Courtesy of Massachusetts State Library and Institute of Conservation Archaeology, Peabody Museum, Harvard University)

urban areas: specialized plans are often on a large scale and contain useful information, so if an archaeological project is located on the site of a former special project, it is worth the researcher's time to seek out any relevant plans that may exist.

9.4 Reconstructed maps

The final section of this chapter concerns reconstructed maps – maps drawn at a later date about a given place at a specified time in the past. Because the problems inherent in using reconstructed maps apply equally to maps of urban and rural areas, maps from both areas will be considered together, again using maps of Massachusetts as examples.

The first problem in dealing with reconstructed maps is to determine whether the map is, in fact, a reconstruction. The

answer is generally obvious: the cartographer's name and the date of publication are usually clearly stated as part of the map title, which sometimes also identifies the historical sources on which the map is based. Nevertheless, there are reconstructed maps such as one for Lexington, Massachusetts, made, as stated in the border design, for the 'United States Bicentennial' in 1975 but entitled only 'Plan of the Town of Lexington in the County of Middlesex, 1775'. In this case, the bicentennial attribution is an indication that the map is a reconstruction made in 1975, but knowledge of the historical maps of Lexington would be necessary to establish whether this is so or whether the map is based on a map originally drawn in 1775. The point here is simply that in dealing with historical maps, some supplementary research may be necessary to determine

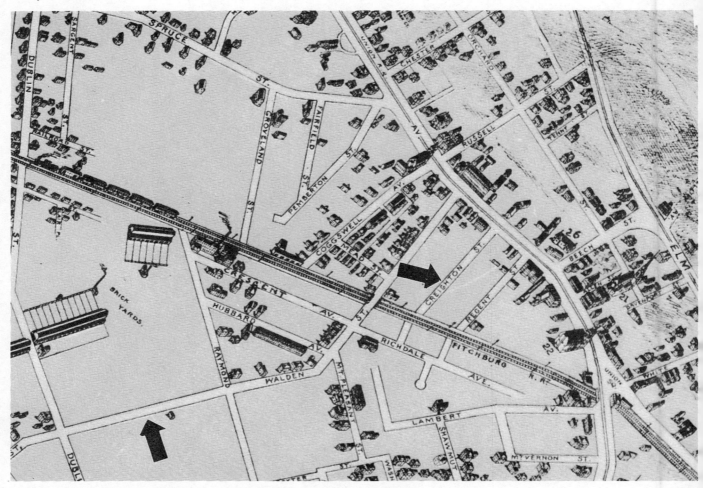

Fig. 9.29. Detail of North Cambridge from 'City of Cambridge, Mass. 1877.' Boston, Franklin View Company, 1877. (Courtesy of Cambridge Historical Commission)

whether a map was drawn contemporaneously with the events it depicts or is a later reconstruction.

Once it has been established that a map is actually a reconstruction, the next question is to determine how accurate it is. Reconstructed maps are typically made about subjects for which no contemporary maps exist but about which there are sufficient historical data to enable such a reconstruction to be made. Thus a reconstruction is as good as the research on which it is based, as the following examples will illustrate.

A favorite subject of reconstructed maps of Boston is the property holding of the earliest settlers. These maps are made possible by the existence of a document called the *Book of Possessions*, a description of all property holdings in Boston in about 1643, and thus, because they are all based on a common source, one would expect the reconstructed maps to be very similar. This is not the case, however, as the maps shown in figures 9.30 and 9.31 indicate. Both maps purport to show Boston as described in the *Book of Possessions* and both show an area later known as the Blackstone Block, the site of the hotel project mentioned several times previously. Since no contemporary maps of this area exist, both reconstructed maps were potentially useful for tracing the history of the hotel site

and it was thus important to determine which of the reconstructions was the more accurate. Documentary sources agree that some of the Blackstone Block area was originally a marsh, but just how much and where the original shoreline lay are questions that are obviously open to interpretation, as demonstrated by the differences between the reconstructed maps. (For another reconstruction of the original shoreline on this block, see the block immediately west of Block 10 in figure 9.23.) In the case here, George Lamb, the cartographer of the map in figure 9.30, specifically disclaimed that he had reproduced the 1645 shoreline (Lamb 1881), thus giving more credence to the map in figure 9.31, drawn by Samuel C. Clough. There are other significant discrepancies between the Lamb and Clough maps, particularly the location of the various properties (in figure 9.31, the Clough map, 51 stands for the holdings of Thomas Marshall, 52 for John Lowe, and 53 for Henry Symons). Again, it is helpful to know that the lot lines on the Lamb map (fig. 9.30) were thought to be 'purely imaginary' and requiring 'almost entire revision' and that Clough himself was motivated by a desire to improve on Lamb's work and to make a more correct map of the *Book of Possessions* (Clough 1919, 251). Clough is known for the

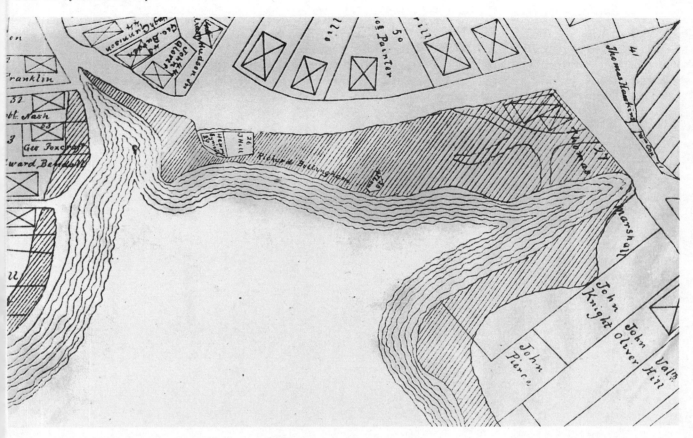

Fig. 9.30. Detail showing the Blackstone Block from 'Old Boston compiled from the Book of Possessions' by George Lamb, 1881. Boston, Trustees of the Boston Public Library, 1881. (Courtesy of Massachusetts State Library)

Fig. 9.31. Detail showing the Blackstone Block from 'Map of the Book of Possessions' by Samuel C. Clough, 1927. *Publications of the Colonial Society of Massachusetts* 27: between 12 and 13. (Courtesy of the Colonial Society of Massachusetts)

thoroughness of his historical research and for his cartographic skill, and so his map is probably the more accurate and was, in fact, used for the research on the hotel site. The point to be observed is that the accuracy of a reconstructed map can be evaluated by obtaining some information about the sources on which it is based or about the cartographer who compiled it.

The Lamb and Clough maps demonstrate another problem of reconstructed maps – what could be termed 'reconstructive license'. This term can apply to the position of roads or other features mentioned in the documents but not precisely located, but on these two maps it concerns the placement of the houses on the lots. The documentary sources describe the size of the lots and thus imply the position of the lot lines, but do not specify where a house was situated within the lot. Thus, Clough's and Lamb's placement of most houses abutting the street (figs. 9.30 and 9.31) are arbitrary decisions by the cartographers and may be more a reflection of their ideas than an indication of where the seventeenth-century houses were actually located. Therefore, in using any reconstructed map, one should be aware of what information is based on actual research and what reflects the discretion of the cartographer.

9.5 Conclusion

This chapter has reviewed a number of types of historical maps – both contemporaneous and reconstructed – for urban and rural areas in the United States. The objective has been not only to serve as a guide to the many types of historical maps that are available, but also to indicate what kinds of archaeological information can be obtained from such maps and what pitfalls should be avoided. Since the examples have all been based on maps of Boston and other parts of Massachusetts, it is entirely possible that in other parts of the country there may be types of historical maps not covered in this article. In such cases, the maps can be evaluated in the same way as the maps discussed here: by assessing the purpose for which the map was made, the audience for which it was intended, the bias of the cartographer, and the cartographic accuracy of the map itself. With these considerations in mind, it is usually possible to obtain useful information from almost any historical map.

Chapter 10

Military records and historical archaeology

Lawrence E. Babits

Two types of documents unique to the military, orderly books and impressment receipts, are analyzed in light of the information they provide that can be useful to archaeologists. On a site-specific level, orderly books record specific depositional episodes relating for the most part to waste disposal. Quantification of such entries yields evidence of patterned behavior reflecting seasonal factors as well as the size and duration of occupation. At the regional level, impressment receipts can be used to discover the names of persons who often fail to be recorded in other, more usual sorts of documents. Such information helps the archaeologist to reconstruct an accurate estimate of a region's population and aids in predicting potential site locations for regional surveys.

Imagine an archaeologist who unknowingly fails to collect all artifact types during excavation. Interpretations made from the incomplete data will include errors. If the missing materials are not recovered from a number of sites, interpretive errors would be magnified and reinforced by the cumulative effect of cultural blindness (Thomson 1979, 4) and repeated miscalculation. In historical archaeology, many types of documents are systematically overlooked, although documents are a crucial part of the cultural material composing the record of a site. The use of certain military documents can identify patterning in the archaeological record and suggest how representative of the population within a region the documents may be. Documents generated by the military can aid archaeological interpretation and provide a check on historical representation.

For archaeologists, the underlying assumption is that documents reflect patterns in the archaeological record because both documents and the archaeological record are the result of human behavior, which is also patterned (Deetz 1970, 110; South 1977, 88). Military documents have been used rarely by historical archaeologists except in those cases where the documents referred to a specific site (Grimm 1970; South 1974; Stokinger et al. 1978, for example). Just as archaeologists have moved from site-oriented research to regional analyses (Smith 1976; Price and Price 1978; Lewis 1980), they should recognize that the use of a range of military documents can provide information useful in interpreting archaeological sites. A range of military documents can provide information normally unavailable to historians or to archaeologists who restrict their attention to site-specific records or to civilian documents alone.

Although numerous military sites have been excavated, only a few archaeologists have utilized the available documentary sources to develop more than information related to the site under investigation. This limitation was partially a result of funding aims, but some of the responsibility rests with archaeologists who did not deal with documents in the same way that they dealt with artifacts. Archaeologists recognize artifact types because they represent patterned examples of behavior identified through refining analyses.

Critical analysis of documents, however, has been limited because archaeologists usually are not trained as historians, do not have archaeologically trained historians doing their research, or limit their research to the site in question. In contrast to the notion that a single artifact does not represent a class of artifacts, documents dealing with a single site may represent several different classes of evidence. Comparison of a single artifact with those from other sites will help to define the range of the artifact's special characteristics and the information it can impart. Comparison of the various documents with those relating to other sites can reveal patterns because the range of similar material being examined is greater (Wilmsen 1968, 168).

Once archaeologists begin to apply standard archaeological methods of analysis to the documents, excellent results are bound to occur. Traditionally, historians have utilized a standard group of documents, and such a practice has produced a largely homogeneous kind of history (Wood 1974, 68). Modern and pre-modern societies have produced a large amount of varied documentary evidence that should be analyzed just as artifacts are. In some cases, an archaeologist may be even better equipped to analyze documents for purposes of archaeological interpretation than a historian.

If documents are analyzed as if they were artifacts, they fall readily into classes: civil, religious, and military. These classes, in turn, can be subdivided into more specific groupings of documents; for example, probate inventories, wills, deeds, and tax records in the class of civil documents (see table 10.1). Each of these subclasses of 'docufact' can be treated as an entity and examined to obtain a generalized picture of what it contains (Main 1975, 580–1; Stone 1977, 63). The subclasses can also be examined with reference to a specific site to generate an impression of the site's occupants. Unfortunately, the site-specific approach exists in a theoretical vacuum unless the broader generalized study of the subclasses is also presented. In most cases, there are simply not enough different documents within any one subclass to provide a range sufficient to detect patterning. Consequently, all of the documents relating to a single site are usually treated as a single class: documents.

Table 10.1 *Classes of documents*

Category			Information
Types			Documents
Classes			Civil
			Personal
			Church
			Military
Subclass			
Civil	*Personal*	*Church*	*Military*
Probates	Letters	Baptisms	Manuals
Wills	Diaries	Marriages	Orderly Books
Deeds	Account	Deaths	Court Martial Records
Taxes	Books	Minutes	Impressment Receipts
Court Records			Muster Rolls
Indentures			

Military documents are subclassed very easily. Orderly books, court martial records, participants' records and letters, impressment records, and muster rolls all form subclasses within military documents. When examined with a single site in mind, there are usually too few documents for comparative purposes within any one subclass. As a result, military documents are often lumped together. Patterns of human behavior are thus difficult to detect because of the small sample size and because the range of subclasses is too small when examined with regard to only one site. Since the range of documents is also varied, the researcher is further hampered in detecting patterns when all the documents are simply lumped together.

In this chapter, the documentary subclasses under examination are orderly books and impressment receipts. Orderly books were maintained on a daily basis to record orders received from higher authority and issued or passed on from the unit maintaining the record. They constitute the official record of the unit. In addition to the orders and announcements of higher authority, orderly books also note such activities as courts martial, disposal of wastes, and assignment of duties. Each entry was identified by date and location, thus providing the firm controls for space and time required for historical analysis (Binford 1964, 168; Deetz and Dethlefsen 1967, 83).

Impressment receipts are the by-product of an army's efforts to provide supplies for itself. In the eighteenth century, necessities such as food and equipment often did not arrive at the military unit requiring them. In the absence of regular channels of supplies, an army would resort to taking whatever was needed from the local populace, a practice known as impressment or foraging. In order to provide a semblance of legality to the procedure, receipts stating what was taken, its value, from whom, by whom, when, and where, were issued to the person whose material was confiscated. These impressment receipts could then be turned in by the civilian for cash or to satisfy tax obligations. In some cases, they were used as currency during a time when money was in short supply. As the foragers issued receipts for the material, they also maintained a record of their own, detailing the accumulation of items seized for the use of the army.

The records maintained by the foragers provide some unusual insights into the representativeness of those materials usually consulted by historical archaeologists during a documentary search. This examination of representativeness will be limited spatially to that part of the North Carolina piedmont now comprising portions of Guilford, Caswell, Rockingham, and Stokes counties. The time period is limited to February and March 1781. By limiting the time and area, it should be easier to show that military documents provide information for identifying socially, spatially, and archaeologically a portion of the civilian realm.

The counties in the study area are shown on the Collett map of 1770 and the Mouzon map of 1775 (figs. 10.1 and 10.2). Within the counties, the cultural features include the county

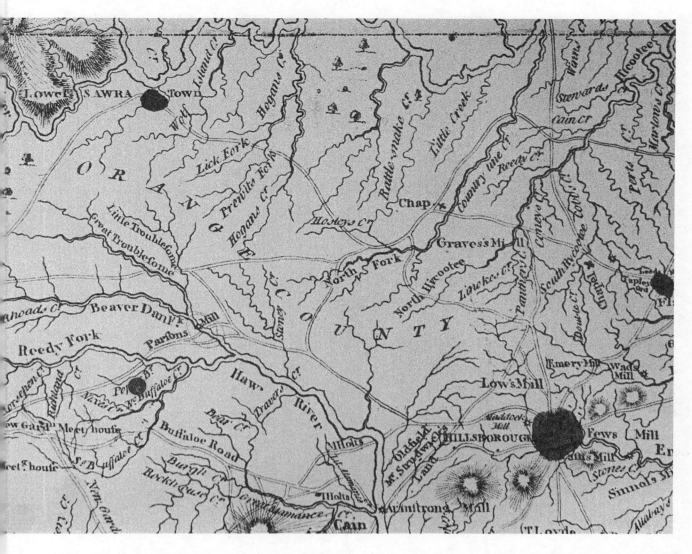

Fig. 10.1. The study area as shown on the 1770 Collett map. Taken from Collett, John, 1770, 'A Compleat Map of North Carolina from an Actual Survey'. North Carolina Department of Cultural Resources, Raleigh, North Carolina

eat, towns, some meeting houses, mills, ordinaries, and the location of the leading citizens. Other than these names, the maps are largely devoid of cultural features, apart from roads connecting settlements.

As the army moved, local militiamen and special regular military units were delegated to collect supplies. The army was remarkably indifferent to a potential supplier's socio-economic status and took what it needed from anyone who possessed the appropriate materials. This system, together with the record of materials taken, meant that people who were not recorded formally as part of the local population found their way into a distinct body of documents.

Under the heading of Treasurer and Comptroller Papers–Military Papers, the North Carolina Archives preserve receipts for supplies impressed by American forces. It is possible to get an impression of who lived within an area of military operations by noting date and location on the receipts.

This information enables the researcher to draw a radius about a central collection point. Since the supplies that form the data base of this study were impressed at mills, the mills form central points. The area within the circle could be described as the 'field' of the mill (Cassels 1972, 215). Mills do not operate without grain, and those persons whose grain was seized at a mill define the minimum population for the field around the mill.

In February and March of 1781, a Lieutenant Colonel Mountflorence impressed 464 bushels of grain from ninety-two different people at eight mills. Only one of these mills appears on a contemporary map, and only one additional mill is mentioned in other documents. The cartographic sources provide only a twenty-five per cent sample of the mills recorded by the foraging party. Not one of the individuals in the impressment records appears on contemporary maps. A similar twenty-five per cent figure is obtained when the names of

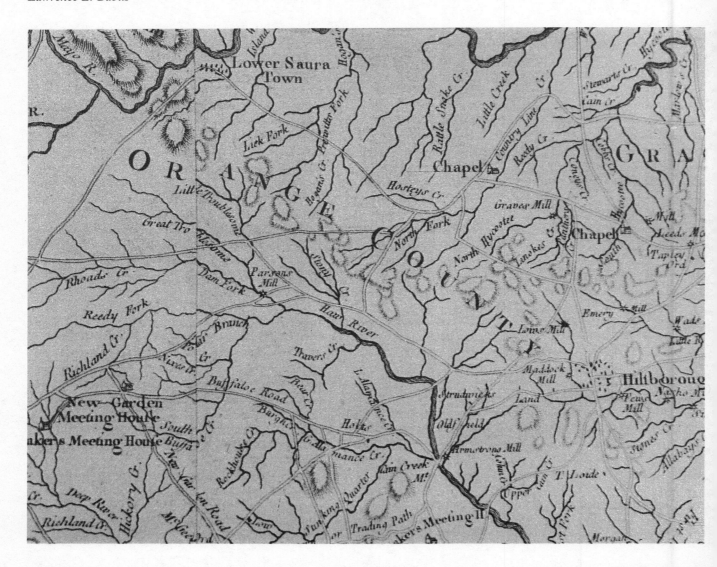

Fig. 10.2. The study area as shown on the 1775 Mouzon map. Taken from Mouzon, Henry, 1775, 'An Accurate Map of North and South Carolina'. North Carolina Department of Cultural Resources, Raleigh, North Carolina

impressment victims are matched against the formal documentary evidence of the *State and Colonial Records of North Carolina* (Clark 1895–1907). Of the ninety-two names (obvious duplicates were counted only once), sixteen (nineteen per cent) appear in the index to the *Records*. In the case of these records, the lack of inclusion is certainly understated because a check was made only for the name. No attempt was made to confirm that the indexed name was that of a person from the appropriate county, or whether the entry in the *State and Colonial Records* correlated with the time period of the impressment records.

In order to derive a better figure for determining representation, a comparison with county level documents was made. The documents included tax and census records, deed book indexes, wills, and the one county history available. There were two sets of tax records for Surry and Caswell Counties. In 1772, fourteen (thirty-nine per cent) of the forty-four Surry

County names were noted (Johnson 1957). By 1777, only twelve (twenty-seven per cent) were recorded (Johnson 1974). Caswell County has a better representation in that ten (thirty-one per cent) of thirty-two were recorded in 1772 (Johnson 1957) and sixteen (fifty per cent) in 1777 (Johnson 1974). Guilford County tax records for the period were not available. Much lower figures were obtained when the names were compared with the 1785 census. Surry County had only eight (eighteen per cent) of forty-four and Caswell County three (nine per cent) (Register 1973). Again, Guilford County records were not available.

The will indexes provided similarly low figures of three (seven per cent) of forty-four for Surry County, four (twelve per cent) of thirty-two for Caswell (Linn 1974) and two (twelve per cent) of sixteen for Guilford County (North Carolina Archives, Wills, *Secretary of State Papers*, n.d.). In part, the low number of names recorded in wills and in the 1785 census may reflect outmigration from the counties in the case of the census and individual longevity in the case of the wills, since the record was followed only to 1825.

Initially, it was assumed that the impressment figures would relate fairly closely to land ownership, because owners would be growing the grain later taken by the army. A check of land entries for the counties disproved this assumption, although it did aid materially in locating those mills not shown on contemporary maps. In Surry County, little more than one-third (fifteen out of forty-four, or thirty-four per cent) of the names were found in the land records. In Caswell County, only ten of thirty-two (thirty-one per cent) were landowners. Guilford County showed an identical percentage since only five of sixteen (thirty-one per cent were identified as owning land (North Carolina Archives, *Secretary of State Papers*, n.d.). Two factors may be at work here. First, tenant farming has long been a feature of Southern agricultural practice (Land 1976, 240; Reid 1976); second, the person given credit for the grain may have been a son, younger brother, or even an overseer for the actual landowner.

Only one county history containing a large amount of information on the eighteenth century was available. Caswell County's history (Kendall 1976) recorded the names of only three of the thirty-two people noted by the military.

Although the people represented by inclusion in the Mountflorence impressment record are a non-random sample, the document is nevertheless of great utility. Few of the individuals recorded appear in other documentary sources. Since the historical archaeologist draws on written materials, considerable bias must be assumed. The twenty per cent representation of impressment document names in the *State and Colonial Records* is hardly a true reflection of the total number of inhabitants of a county, and by extension, of the potential archaeological sites within the area. Even when the county records are checked, the representation in any one list rarely exceeds thirty-five per cent. Those who are represented in the more commonly consulted types of documents, such as court orders, wills, deeds, tax and census lists, are a minor portion of the entire populace.

When all the lists were combined to inspect for names mentioned in the impressment lists, sixty-one per cent of the ninety-two names were found. This adjusted total, however, still omits thirty-three per cent of the individuals, all of whom were males. Women, children, indentured servants, and blacks are seldom mentioned; only one woman, a widow, is mentioned in the impressment lists. One must therefore be cognizant that the reconstruction of a county's population through this combined method is, in the end, representative only of white males who were probably property owners.

If historical archaeologists excavate the houses of prominent persons, the more conventional consultation of site-specific documents such as deeds, wills, census records, and the like, may be justifiable. Since there is at present a trend towards making the sample of archaeological sites more representative of the actual past population (this has been brought about by the development of cultural resource management plans required by law), a method combining a number of documentary sources, especially military documents that yield unexpected information on population distribution, will provide a more complete data base. The usual cartographic evidence shows very little of a region's resident population; the official records often display a cavalier lack of concern for the less affluent and the unimportant. Since any interpretive sampling based on cartographic and state records alone is unlikely to provide information on more than a very small percentage of the population, a check of county records should also be included. Even this more intensive documentary survey is likely to omit up to sixty per cent or more of the total population of white males.

A more representative overview of a population might be obtained by examining a body of documents relating to an entire social group. Such a record exists in the form of military orderly books. Just as the impressment receipts illuminated a wider range of the regional population, orderly books can provide information about different attitudes of varying social strata and, specifically, about the creation of the archaeological record.

The orderly books utilized in this study have been taken from the period 1755–82. This twenty-seven-year period encompasses the French and Indian War as well as the American Revolutionary War, both times when large-scale military activity resulted in the production of numerous orderly books. It is not certain exactly how many orderly books of this period have survived to the present day. There are over ninety books in the Library of Congress (Sellers et al. 1975, 141–50), seventy in the National Archives (White and Lesser 1977, 2), thirty-nine in the collections of the American Antiquarian Society (undated list of the AAS orderly books), and at least 196 in the New-York Historical Society (Anon. 1977). Various local and state historical societies and state archives have many more. An estimation of five to six hundred orderly books might be reasonably correct, although more continue to be located and identified.

The sample used here consists of orderly books produced by British, Provincial, and American forces during 1755–63 and 1775–82. The orderly books thus represent two discrete temporal samples that have been consolidated for the purposes of this presentation. Statistically, they do not show any difference in patterning over time (Babits 1981, 191). The spatial area in which these books were initially recorded ranges from Canada to Georgia and from the Atlantic seaboard to the Appalachian Mountains. This spatially defined area is better known as Anglo-America, although minority groups were present.

Table 10.2 presents an abstraction of the orderly book references to offal (waste material) and to privies. The references apply to burial, burning, or other methods of waste disposal that would have created archaeologically visible remains. Since the references are dated, it was possible to identify the season and to perform statistical tests on the

Table 10.2 *Orderly book citations by season and camp duration, 1755–82*

Season	Camp		Bivouac		
	Privy	Offal	Privy	Offal	Total
Spring	4	2	0	0	6
Summer	51	39	17	2	109
Autumn	4	10	1	0	15
Winter	4	5	0	0	9
Total	63	56	18	2	139

monthly distribution of waste-related citations. Of the 139 references to waste-disposal behavior, a statistically significant majority (109) were found to have been issued during the summer months of June, July, and August. A more detailed examination of the dates also showed that the citations were more likely to be recorded at sites occupied for longer than ten days (camps) than in short-term occupations (bivouacs) (Babits 1981, 206).

The relationship of seasonality and camp duration to the disposal of waste products resulting in the formation of archaeological features such as privies and trash pits corresponds well with the observations made by Yellen (1977, 135), who felt that camp duration resulted in increased activity, and the conclusions of Gibson (1979, 13), who felt that seasonal cleanup was related to preventive medicine and resulted in the burial of refuse. Neither Gibson nor Yellen were able to offer statistical verification of their observations because their samples were either too small or their time range too limited to detect enough instances of patterned waste-disposal behavior. In this respect, table 10.2 provides the basic data to verify Gibson's observations; verification of Yellen's conclusions has been presented elsewhere (Babits 1981, 206).

Waste-related features are found on many archaeological sites, and they often contain a large assemblage of material (Noël Hume 1975, 142; Stokinger et al. 1978, 6.1). To date, no one has published an analysis of waste-related features from several similar historical sites, although inter-site comparison of features has been done with useful results (Binford 1967). Such a study could concentrate on detecting seasonality and verifying site duration and then move toward a comparative analysis of the artifacts contained within the features.

This summary has dealt with the identification of patterning in military documents as it relates to particular archaeological features termed trash deposits and privies. Discussion of waste-related behavior is missing from most civilian documents, but the archaeological record reveals that similar seasonal patterning and duration of site occupation is true of some civilian archaeological sites as well (Blades 1977, 57; Mrozowski 1981; Lewis 1977, 31). In these cases, ranging from New England to South Carolina, archaeological features

related to waste disposal were noted, providing confirmation that behavior recorded in military documents (e.g., seasonality, occupation over ten days, covering of refuse on a daily basis) were practiced also by civilians who did not record their actions.

Features are only one component of a larger archaeological entity, the site. Archaeological sites are routinely compared, and prehistorians have been quite successful in identifying many relationships among sites within a region (Gumerman 1971; Hassan 1979; Wood 1971). While the actual number of sites within a region must be regarded as finite, identification and location of *all* sites is difficult. The sites that are not identified are usually those with sparse, less prominently preserved remains. In many cases, poor-visibility sites may reflect occupation by poor, low-status individuals (McDaniel and Potter 1978, 7). Military documents can provide useful information for the archaeologist dealing with a poor-visibility site by identifying some of the people and placing them on the landscape at a certain time and within a certain general area. In this respect, military documents provide a check on the typical written sources utilized by historical archaeologists. In order to relate this information dealing with the correspondence between military documents and potential civilian archaeological sites, a digression into eighteenth- and early nineteenth-century military organization is relevant.

The military is, and was, a hierarchically arranged organization (Spindler 1948, 277; White and Lesser 1977, 1). The eighteenth-century military hierarchy mirrored the civilian social hierarchy in America and, for some time, that of nineteenth-century America as well. Military rank was usually awarded to those persons who held comparable civilian rank (Anderson 1979, 15; Bailyn 1971, 139; Main 1965, 213; Lender 1980, 35; Sellers 1974, 153). Whether or not this civilian rank was a result of wealth, literacy, kinship, or any other factor is unimportant here. It is important, however, to note that military rank was awarded, with ascribed status (Spindler 1948, 277), to those persons who had achieved a near-equal rank in the civilian social hierarchy. The military was organized into a formal hierarchy clearly delineated in manuals in use at the time (Riling 1966, 6).

On the broadest level, military ranking can be divided into two groups: officers and enlisted personnel. In theory, officers were gentlemen and enlisted personnel were the more common sort (Wood 1974, 73). One can also see that the line was drawn between those who were literate and those who were not (Barker 1976, 33; Corvisier 1979, 140, 170, 180; Hayter 1978, 3), although there were some privates who could read just as there were some officers who could not.

The upper-class officers imposed their will on the lower-class enlisted personnel through the medium of military orders. The officers issued orders, recorded them, and made a formal record of what happened during their service. In keeping orderly books, the officers served as unwitting ethnographers for their enlisted men. It is possible to detect from the wording of orders related to waste disposal that enlisted men had a distinctly different outlook towards the disposal of waste material than did the officers. This is exemplified by the following:

> The General also forbids in the most Positive Terms the Troops easing themselves in the ditches of the Fortifications, a Practice that is disgraceful to the last Degree. (Showman 1976, 268)

This reporting is biased because it is seen in terms of the officers' point of view, but the contrast between concepts of waste disposal is clear.

When dealing with documents it must be remembered that a high percentage of the population outside the one-time Puritan educational stronghold of New England were illiterate (Lockridge 1974, 56; Matthews 1976, 56; Schofield 1973, 68; Vann 1974, 290). Typically, those who were literate were placed above those who were not. Those who wrote have left a remarkably homogeneous view of their contemporary world (Wood 1974, 68). This view is biased and distorted when it describes those who could not write. In some respects, this is good, because it provides useful information about the relationship between two social classes. In other respects, the bias has led some to interpret Anglo-America as having been homogeneous, which certainly cannot have been the case.

The orderly books indicate that the two groups of people, officers and enlisted men, had radically differing ideas about the proper disposal of waste materials. The officers were in a position to see that their views were acted upon by the enlisted personnel – who perhaps did not share their views – because of the hierarchical nature of the army command structure. In issuing orders and noting their reasons for giving them, the officers have left what is often an explicit statement of the opposition between their own views and those of the enlisted men. They have thus articulated a simple dichotomy between the literate, upper social strata and the illiterate, lower social level of eighteenth-century Anglo-American society.

Since the lower strata of the army represented by the enlisted personnel were drawn from the corresponding lower strata of civilians, differences similar to those between officers and enlisted men should be seen in the civilian realm. If the officers generally were literate, and enlisted personnel generally were illiterate, then there will be more documentation generated by the literate upper level of civilians. The lower strata will be underrepresented, being, for the most part, mentioned only in passing in the records created by their social betters. Yet, as this study has shown, such passing and often inadvertent references are invaluable clues to the behavior and lifestyle of the majority of Anglo-Americans about whom the records are otherwise so frustratingly silent.

Through this examination of a range of military orderly books, it has been possible to demonstrate that the patterning that we normally attribute to the depositional processes creating the archaeological record may also be discovered in written sources. Specifically, it has been shown that orderly books' references to the disposal of waste followed a pattern based on duration of site occupancy. Further, the references were also seen to be seasonal. This knowledge of occupational duration and seasonality, derived from contemporary documents, can provide a series of hypotheses to be tested against refuse-related features on archaeological sites (e.g., seasonality, notions of socio-economic status and its relationship to literacy, etc.).

Additionally, archaeologists' usual approach to documentary research has been shown to be flawed. Within the upper North Carolina piedmont, some twenty-five to thirty-five per cent of the males mentioned in military documents do not appear in any other contemporary civil accounts. These otherwise undocumented men lived somewhere within a fairly small area easily defined by the impressment records. They must have contributed in some way to the archaeological record. Unless this undocumented third of the male population is accounted for, regional surveys will not be accurate. Survey models must incorporate techniques for locating sites of these individuals, sites that most likely are of as low focus and visibility archaeologically as they are from a documentary perspective. Therefore, archaeologists must take into account the potential of records to inform us about both the literate *and* the non-literate segments of the population.

A combined approach to documentary analysis has distinct advantages for regional site location studies. Furthermore, the information gleaned from military documents provides a successful demonstration that imaginative use of a largely ignored body of documents pertaining to certain aspects of colonial American life can add a new dimension to our understanding of the past.

Chapter 11

**The material culture of the Christian
Indians of New England, 1650–1775**

Kathleen J. Bragdon

By using an ethnohistorical approach to the analysis of probate
documents recorded by the Christian Indians of southern New England,
it is possible to examine the degree to which acculturative influences
affected the material life of native New Englanders. The Indian
inventories, wills, and account books provide evidence that the
Christian Indians were not merely 'red Puritans' but members of a
unique series of communities differing both from their own forebears
and from the surrounding English population.

Ethnohistory, the discipline devoted to reconstructing the past
cultures of non-literate peoples through the use of documentary
sources and historiographic techniques, has been responsible
for correcting our view of the nature of native life in southern
New England after European exploration and settlement.
Recent ethnohistorical studies have emphasized both the
previously underestimated effects of early peripheral contact
with Europeans and other native peoples (Ceci 1982; Brasser
1971), as well as the enduring nature of native configurations of
belief, perception, and behavior (Simmons 1986; Bragdon
1981).

Nevertheless, the Indian way of life in the two centuries
following contact with Europeans, and especially after their
conversion to Christianity, is still poorly known, partly as a
result of the neglect of the topic by scholars, and partly because
the documentary record is fragmentary. One view of Christian
native life during this period is represented by Alden Vaughan
and Daniel Richter, who argue that it was among the Christian

Indians of southern New England that 'transculturation' was
most complete (1980, 32). It is the purpose of this paper
to examine this view in the light of native material
culture.

The natives of southeastern New England, known in the
seventeenth century as the Massachusett and Pokanoket, lived,
at the time of contact with Europeans, in coastal regions
stretching from what is now the New Hampshire border, south
as far as northeastern Rhode Island, and including the
Elizabeth Islands, Nantucket, Martha's Vineyard, and Cape
Cod (see fig. 11.1). While much remains to be learned
concerning their pre-contact subsistence patterns, it appears
that the Massachusett were semi-sedentary horticulturalists,
who relied heavily on wild game, shellfish, nuts, fruits, and
seasonal greens. In the sixteenth century, they occupied both
protected inland locations and coastal settlements, the latter of
which may have developed in response to sporadic contact with
European exploring and fishing parties and which were
probably sustained as much by marine resources as by corn
agriculture (Ceci 1982).

The first Europeans to come into contact with the Indians
of southern New England were fishermen, explorers, and later,
traders. When the transport and display of the Indians
themselves was not feasible, these early harbingers of Western
expansion brought back material objects created and used by
the Indians to describe them to those who remained behind.

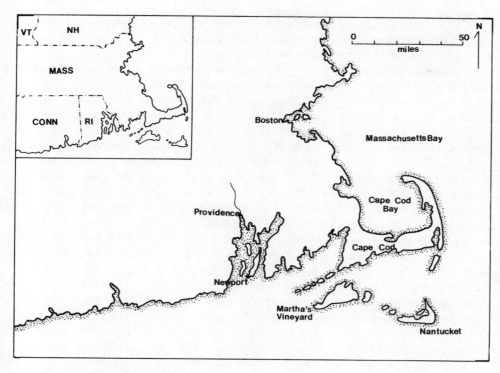

Fig. 11.1. Southeastern New England

The Sloane collection, part of the British Museum's holdings, includes a number of 'curiosities' sent by Adam Winthrop, the son of the first governor of Massachusetts Bay, back to England, to convey an idea of what Winthrop believed was representative of Indian culture. Among these were a spoon and bowl of the knot of a tree, out of which 'they eat their succatash, which is venison, fish & Indian corn boiled together', 'A fine, large Indian basket made by an Indian Queen', a fishing line, and 'a mattump or braided strap by which they tye their children to the bark of a tree as soon as born' (Museum of Mankind, London, ms.).

The arrival of the English settlers in southern New England resulted in heavy losses of Indian life through disease and warfare. Weakened by attrition and overwhelmed by the influx of settlers, many Indians sought or were coerced into seeking Christianity, such that by the late seventeenth century, most of the surviving Massachusett-speaking peoples were concentrated into a number of small permanent Christian communities known as 'plantations' or praying-towns. The communities were governed by a system derived partially from traditional native custom and partially from English law. Indians were taught to read and write in their own language and sometimes in English, and within their communities, kept many of the same kinds of records found in English settlements of the same period.

Among these records are deeds, wills, and accounts written in the Massachusett language (Goddard and Bragdon in press). The Massachusett texts and probate records written in English by non-native appraisers, along with account books

kept in English by merchants on Martha's Vineyard and Nantucket, form the main body of information concerning material culture among the Christian Indians. Knowledge of changes in that domain can in turn guide our understanding of changes and continuity in other, less tangible aspects of native life.

Along with the usual sorts of bias to which the public records of English communities are subject (Main 1975; Smith 1975), the use of the inventories, wills, and accounts of the Indians has additional pitfalls. Underregistration, reported by Smith (1975, 108) to approach twenty to fifty per cent among English households, was even more pronounced among Indian decedents. During the period 1720 to 1760, in Natick, for example, at least 400 deaths were recorded, yet only twenty-five per cent were probated. There remain only a score of native wills and estate accounts as well.

In addition, the distribution of native probate records was decidedly non-random and seems to have been a function of the proximity of Indians to English settlement, the value and amount of Indian land, and the way in which the land was held. In those communities, such as Natick, where land was the chief source of income-producing property, and where individual ownership of land by Indians was institutionalized early, probate records for native decedents were relatively common. In Barnstable, Plymouth, and on the Islands, probate records were less frequent and probably represented only the wealthiest of the natives.

Perhaps a more severe bias was the fact that except for the cases where documents were probated in Massachusett

(Goddard and Bragdon, in press, docs. nos. 7, 64), all Indian estates, and all transactions involving Indians, were recorded by non-natives.

Although the very existence of inventories describing native estates speaks to their separation from aboriginal cultural traditions, the inventories, wills, and account books provide evidence that the Christian Indians were not merely 'red Puritans' but members of a unique series of communities differing both from their own forebears and from the surrounding English population.

The increasing sophistication of our understanding of the nature of cultural contact and change calls in turn for a reevaluation of the ways in which artifactual remains reflect cultural change in other aspects of native society. The concept of acculturation, or transculturation, that posits a progressive departure of a subordinate cultural group from traditional ways in favor of those of a dominant culture with which it has come into contact, has long since been abandoned in favor of a more sophisticated way of understanding cultural change; one which focuses instead on the creative reworking of new concepts, objects, and practices by both groups in contact, a process occurring whenever groups come together, regardless of their original similarities and differences. At the same time, we have become increasingly aware of the ways in which dominated or oppressed groups within a larger society, such as the Christian Indians, manipulate symbols, both tangible and intangible, in order to preserve and maintain distinctiveness as individuals and groups. The material culture of the Christian Indians of southern New England as described in surviving records illustrates change and continuity as well.

On the most elementary level, inventories, wills, and accounts document the survival of a number of traditional objects and 'tool-kits' among Indian families, in contexts that suggest that these objects had a significance beyond that of heirlooms. Several native inventories from Natick note the presence of items of native manufacture such as 'barks', baskets, 'tump' lines, snow-shoes, and skin leggings. Barks, described by Gookin and others (1806, 151), were bark boxes of several sizes used to store grain and even to carry water. Since these, and many of the other objects listed, were heavily used and relatively fragile, their presence in eighteenth-century inventories suggests that they were still in use at that time and that the skill of their manufacture had not been lost.

Leggings, or 'Indian Stockings' described by Roger Williams as made of 'Deer skin worn out', (1936, 205), were found in at least one Natick Indian inventory (Middlesex County, *Probate Records*, 65), probated in 1759. The mattump, or carrying strap, another native implement, was also found in a native inventory from Natick (Middlesex County, *Probate Records*, 7003 (1746)).

Other objects described in the inventories may have been of either native or European origin, including pigeon nets, eel pots, and snow-shoes (Williams 1936, 116; Marten 1970, 26). Some items, although known in English inventories, seem to have been associated more commonly with Indian use. These

include the samp mortar, used for grinding corn, which remained a staple of native diet in the eighteenth century (Marten, ibid.).

The nature of traditional southern New England native basketry and the origin of block-stamped splint basketry (McMullen 1982, 1983; Brasser 1975; Speck 1947) can be clarified through analysis of native and non-native inventories. According to Frank Speck, splint basketry in southern New England is of native origin. He cites as evidence for this the undoubted aboriginality of cane-splint basketry in the southeast (1947). Brasser disagrees, arguing that splint basketry was a craft introduced to the Delaware by Swedish immigrants as a cottage industry in the eighteenth century and diffused to the New England Indians (1975).

Seventeenth-century records from New England mention at least two types of baskets, 'wicker' baskets, and 'Indian' baskets, as well as 'Indian bags' (e.g. Middlesex County, *Probate Records*, 1, 17–18 (1653); 2, 4 (1661); 2, 47–51 (1661)). Natives in southern New England made twined bag-like containers of hemp and basswood fiber (Willoughby 1935, 248–53), utilitarian as well as fine. These were probably the 'bags' mentioned in the inventories. Indian wicker 'baskets' may have been stiffer containers made of rush or husks twined on a rigid twig frame (ibid., 354). The missionary John Eliot introduced several crafts to the Christian Indians, including the manufacture of baskets, possibly the 'wicker' of the early inventories (Eliot 1647 (1834), 59). These would have been closer to traditional basketry than the splint baskets introduced later, although the early introduction of the craft may explain the aboriginality of the traits within the basket-making complex (Speck 1947).

Wampum use is suggested by the presence of skeins of 'wompanpeaque and suckonhock' listed in two native inventories from Natick (Middlesex County, *Probate Records*, 21335 (1749); 00016 (1742)). Seventeenth-century sources indicate that 'suckonhock' referred to the 'black' or purple beads, which were the most valuable native currency (Williams 1936, 236). In the eighteenth century, wampum was manufactured by coastal Algonquian-speaking peoples, including the Leni-Lanape, Niantic, Shinnecock, Scaugticook, and others, for sale to the Iroquois. It was also traded to the northern Algonquian peoples such as the Malecite, Penobscot and Abenaki. No wampum-making tools appear in the inventories, and the beads may have been acquired by native soldiers during the campaigns against the French in 1735 and 1742, or purchased for eventual trade to the Iroquois. A third possibility would be that the beads were kept as 'heirlooms' by the more traditional Natick families.

The dwellings of the Indians of southern New England encompassed a surprising variety of forms and materials during the historical period. In the early decades of contact, perhaps most of these were variations on the traditional wigwam. The majority were constructed of woven mats, with the addition of introduced elements such as metal door and window hardware, wooden doors and door frames, and other architectural features

(Williams 1936). Later structures included all manner of wooden buildings. By the middle of the eighteenth century, a variety of traditional and Anglicized house forms were occupied by Christian Indians (Anon. 1802; Freeman 1807; Crèvecoeur 1782, 101). Elizabeth Little notes the occurrence of nails, clapboards, and other building materials and tools in Indian inventories of Nantucket (1980), which suggests that some natives were constructing frame houses for themselves, as was also true at Wellfleet in 1747 (Massachusetts, Commonwealth of, Archives, 33, 29a). Many of the earliest frame houses consisted of a single room open to the rafters, with a dirt floor, and a hole in the roof that served to let smoke out, similar in form, if not in material, to more traditional native structures (Dwight 1821). Historic native house form in southern New England can serve as an example of the development of innovative forms that were consistent with other changes in native culture.

In Natick, traditional dwellings continued to be constructed until well into the eighteenth century, for a 1749 map depicting the locations of houses in the community noted the presence of twenty-five wigwams (Livermore 1749). Travellers on Cape Cod in 1802 found that at least half of the natives of Mashpee lived in wigwams as well (Anon. 1802). Some of the native dwellings characterized in inventories as 'huts', 'cottages', or even 'tents' were probably transitional dwelling house types such as those described above (e.g., MXD 0489; Anon. 1802, 4).

These wigwams and early wooden dwellings were filled with a variety of traditional and adopted objects. Ezra Stiles' 1763 drawings of a Niantic wigwam show it furnished with a number of pieces of English furniture, including a chest and a table and chairs (Sturtevant 1975). Inventories for Natick, Cape Cod, and the Islands suggest that native household interiors were similar in many respects to that described by Stiles.

Earlier studies (Bragdon 1979; Little 1980) indicate that native material culture in the eighteenth century differed in several respects from that of the English. Most obviously, the Christian Indians had fewer objects, and most were of less value than those of the English of the surrounding area. In Natick, the Indians kept less livestock, engaged in less dairying activity, and stored fewer dry goods. The kinds of food vessels described in their inventories indicate that their diet consisted of a higher percentage of stews and pottages than did that of the English (Bragdon 1979, 138). The natives owned fewer draft oxen, and only one or two had plowing tackle. On the Islands, the natives owned few 'income-producing' items such as whale-boats, fishing boats, calashes, and heavy ship tackle (Little 1980). At the same time, the inventories suggest that the Indians practiced a seasonally varied, multi-based economy and commanded many skills.

This view from the inventories is consistent with what we now of native economy from other sources. The Indians engaged in trade in baskets and brooms from the 1640s on (Eliot 1647, (1834), 49). They gathered and sold berries and other crops, and sold the produce from their own gardens to

Table 11.1 *Comparison of Natick and Nantucket native inventories, 1700–60*

Category	Natick (n=40)	Nantucket (n=10)
Livestock		
Sheep	0	1
Horses	8	9
Poultry	0	2
Swine	12	5
Cows	16	3
Oxen (yoke of)	1	1
Total	47	19
Per capita %	<1/person	1.9/person
Farming equipment		
Light farming	24	37
Heavy farming	6	15
Total	30	52
Per capita %	<1/person	>5/person
Furniture		
Bedsteads	8	17
Chairs	45	51
Chests	26	16
Tables	15	10
(Side)boards	1	7
Stools	0	3
Total	95	104
Per capita %	<2.5/person	>10/person
Ceramic/glass/cutlery		
Hollow vessels (preparation & consumption)	47	111
Flat vessels (preparation & consumption)	30	51
Spoons/forks	21	32
Total	98	193
Per capita %	<2.5/person	>19/person

local merchants (Biglow 1830, 36). Many derived income from day labor, in house service, or from seasonal farming (Allen 1730; Starbuck 1683–1766). On the islands, most of the men were engaged in the fishing and whaling industries (Freeman 1807, 51; Crèvecoeur 1782, 126).

The native inventories from Natick and Nantucket allow us to compare Indian and non-Indian material culture and economy. Systematic comparison of the two largest bodies of probate inventories surviving for Christian Indian communities in the eighteenth century is also useful in identifying differences between native communities that crosscut the general similarities described previously. Table 11.1 illustrates the differences between Nantucket native inventories and those of Natick, taken during the same time period, for several different categories of material culture.

While the eighteenth-century inventories of natives in the rural farming community of Natick and those living on Nantucket shared many similarities, there were discernible differences as well. As was noted in an earlier study (Bragdon 1979), Natick Indian houses, foodways, clothing, and other material objects, if not wholly traditional, were distinct in the aggregate from those of their English neighbors. Little reached a different conclusion, arguing that the surviving inventories of Nantucket Indians were hardly distinguishable from those of non-Indian Nantucketers (1980, 32).

Such differences in the inventory samples of the two groups may reflect basic differences between the economies of the farming community of Natick and maritime-oriented Nantucket, as well as the fact that the smaller sample of island inventories is biased towards the wealthier natives. It is further possible that the Indians of Nantucket were more fully integrated into the island economy because of their skills in the whaling trade and the shortage of labor on the islands, and probably because the isolation of the island required greater interdependence between the two populations than was true in Natick. It would appear that the natives of Nantucket were unusually wealthy, and many came from families whose members held positions of authority in both traditional and newer native political structures. The Indians of Natick, by contrast, were extraneous to the local economy and were perceived of as barriers to agricultural expansion. Their isolation, both cultural and economic, is reflected, one might argue, in the 'non-English' nature of their material possessions.

The actual historical situation was more complex, however. Evidence in the form of first-hand reports and writings by native speakers of Massachusett indicate that the language was spoken and read for two generations longer on Nantucket, Martha's Vineyard, and possibly some of the communities on Cape Cod, than in Natick. By 1729, a committee from Harvard determined that few of the Natick Indians could read Massachusett, although some could read English (Winthrop et al. 1729, 576). In 1798, no speakers of Massachusett could be recalled to the memory of Stephen Badger, minister to the Natick Indians since 1749 (Badger 1835, 38). In contrast, writings dating to 1787 are found on Martha's Vineyard (Goddard and Bragdon, in press), and Englishmen on Nantucket recalled attending religious services held in the native language at mid-century (Macy 1835, 257–58).

Other contrasts between the Indian communities of Natick and those of the islands included the strength of the native churches in each area. Church membership in Natick declined after Eliot's death in 1689 and with the deaths of the first and second generations of native converts. In 1750, only fifteen individuals were members of the local congregation (Natick C.R., n.d.). On Martha's Vineyard and Nantucket,

and in Mashpee, church communities flourished and supported a number of native ministers (Simmons 1979; Ronda 1981). These congregations, although Christian, conducted their services in Massachusett and preserved a number of traits of traditional native meetings (Bragdon 1983).

The political structure of the native communities was similarly distinct. Native rulers on the islands and Cape Cod frequently came from traditionally powerful elite lineages, and in some cases inherited their office in traditional fashion (Conkey, Boissevain and Goddard 1978, 177). New positions within the communities modeled after English prototypes in New England were often merged with traditional functions or named by native terms once describing similar functions (Bragdon 1981, 134). On Nantucket, the position and rights of the sachem, the traditional leader of the native communities, remained intact under another name, sachems receiving tribute in the form of credit from the local storekeeper accumulated through labor and goods provided by other men who were 'subject' to the sachem (Little 1980, 28). The Christian Indian town meetings were similar to traditional native decision-making, where emphasis was placed on consensus.

Native land use and land tenure on Martha's Vineyard, Nantucket, and in Mashpee were likewise distinct from English practice. Communal land-holding and communal use of resources were characteristic of native land use until the nineteenth century (Bragdon 1981, 114). Land was passed down through the community, with each member having the right to take what was needed and with land returning to the communal holdings at the individual's death (e.g., Massachusetts Archives, 30, 347–9; Pease 1885).

At the same time, changes in the native language, Massachusett, testify to the universal way in which objects of non-native origin had permeated the experience of the natives of the Islands. Although the language survived on the Islands until the early nineteenth century, loan words from English are documented in Massachusett from an early date (Bragdon 1981, 71–2). Many of these refer to animals, foodstuffs, clothing, and other objects with which the Indians had no experience or for which they had no analogous replacement. A 1749 will written in Massachusett by the Gay Head woman Naomi Ommaush bequeathed a number of articles of clothing to relatives, including a 'petticoat', and a 'calico dress', as well as a 'blanket', 'pewter dishes', and 'pewter spoons' (Goddard and Bragdon, in press, doc. no. 7). The act of bequeathing material goods itself also seems to have been an innovation in native culture, associated with English concern with inheritance.

Ownership and use of English material goods, animals, and plants had important symbolic significance to many natives as well. Graves of what were probably Christian Indians were excavated in Natick in the 1820s. Several of these contained objects of English origin, including beads, spoons, and bottles (Biglow 1830, 15–16), interred with the deceased in spite of a Christian prohibition against grave goods. While Christian Indians used English objects to express non-Christian ideas about the afterlife, they also manipulated them in the same wa as did the English surrounding them. An extended quote from the petition of Samuel Abraham, a native of Natick, written in 1726, illustrates the importance that owning an 'English-style' house had for him:

> whereas I have a great desire to live more like my Christian English neighbors, than I have hitherto been able to do; being weary of living in a wigwam . . . and whereas I have a great desire to continue here under the gospell, which I hope I should be able to do with more comfort and satisfaction, if by any means I could be able to build such a house, as the English live in.
>
> (Massachusetts Archives, 31, 135)

The implications of these findings for material culture studies are various. Out of necessity, archaeologists rely on material remains to make judgements about the effects of contact, whereas these examples show that possessions of the Christian Indians only faintly reflect the reality of change. The major documentary sources describing aspects of their material life, probate records and account books, point out the inconsistencies between material culture and other cultural domains. Even though the Christian Indians of Natick appear to have retained a much more prominent assemblage of traditional objects than did their counterparts on the Islands, many other contexts in which native identity was re-defined and perpetuated, such as language and political organization, were preserved much longer by the Island natives than by the Natick population.

In short, these records and the material world they document serve to demonstrate both the multi-faceted nature of the acculturative process and the many ways in which objects reflect that process. To argue as some have done that the Christian Indians of southern New England were 'transculturated' by the mid-eighteenth century is to misrepresent both the complexity of the change and the product of the change itself.

Chapter 12

Anthropological title searches in Rockbridge County, Virginia

*Henry Langhorne
and Lawrence E. Babits*

A regional approach to the use of documentary sources concerning land ownership is recommended as a means of reconstructing land-holding patterns over time as well as familial ties that affect the transfer of real estate. In this case study, land transaction records from nineteenth-century Rockbridge County, Virginia, were the focus of intensive as well as extensive research. The results of the study revealed that certain types of land transfers, e.g., from father to daughter, were far more common than had been suspected. The relative frequency of such transfers indicates that consanguinial ties in the female line were highly significant even within a strongly patrifilial kinship system. Reconstruction of familial links therefore becomes an important factor in research designed to provide the background for regional archaeological surveys.

Although the recovery of artifacts is indispensable to archaeology, many historical archaeologists may be guilty of overlooking a body of evidence just as vital to the reconstruction of past lifeways as excavated materials. In commenting on the goals of archaeologists, Irving Rouse suggests that an archaeologist should reconstruct 'the lives of extinct people from their remains' (1972, 1). While documentary evidence available to historical archaeologists has traditionally been used to verify land ownership and occupational period, we have found that an analysis of documents may provide answers to questions about a site or region that are difficult, if not impossible, to determine from excavations and artifactual analysis alone.

There has been a tendency in historical archaeology for documentary research to be merely a system for verifying the analytical results derived from excavation (South 1977a, 23). We feel that limiting documentation to the role of 'handmaiden of archaeology,' to paraphrase Marley Brown (1977, 4; Noël Hume 1975, 19), is quite an injustice to the information it may provide. Documents provide keys to the relationships of the people in our study of western Rockbridge County, Virginia, that are impossible to determine from the meager archaeological record.

The use of deeds in documenting and reconstructing the lives of largely illiterate and now dead people can very easily be likened to the analytic and synthetic approaches used in dealing with artifactual assemblages recovered from any site. As Rouse defined it, the analytic approach recovers 'all possible kinds of remains in an effort to learn the nature' of the site (1972, 4). This approach should necessarily include documents as the component parts of the remains to be examined. The parallel of the archaeological analytical approach in deed searches could be the title search, simply a determination of the owners of a tract of land and the changing value of the land through time.

According to Rouse (1972, 4), the synthetic strategy of archaeology requires that one

recover ... the kinds of remains needed to learn about people ... This approach brings together the pertinent bits of archaeological evidence with facts drawn from other sources and uses them to synthesize a picture of peoples, their lives, and time.

It is from this synthetic perspective that the deed searches began. The goal has been to identify relationships among the people who inhabited the research area. A simple chain of title would not attain the goal. Only through analysis of the study area as a whole could relationships among numerous people, plots of land, and generations be identified. It is through the analysis of the region that the interrelationships among landowners and their relatives could be determined and a picture of one aspect of their lives made clearer.

In the past, historical archaeologists have usually attempted to trace the chain of title for the site under investigation. This process has some utility in identifying the owners of the site, and, possibly, the changes in the size of the property. As with historical archaeology generally (Baker 1979, 4), this is a site-specific approach. Prehistorians (Cassels 1972; Gumerman 1972; Webb 1974; Wood 1971), and to some extent, historical archaeologists (Babits 1981; Bartovics 1975; Lewis 1980; Price and Price 1978), have begun looking at regions to better understand the archaeological sites under investigation. Such studies have revealed a great deal about population density, methods of exchange, and land use.

Just as a site-specific approach treats a site as a single entity, so too does the chain of title for a single tract produce a narrow, isolated view of the land. As part of the regional study being conducted in Rockbridge County, Virginia, students in a Washington and Lee University field methods course in historical archaeology were assigned the task of tracing carefully defined tracts of land ranging from 200 to 500 acres.

This paper summarizes the work of eighteen Washington and Lee anthropology students involved in over 1,000 hours of data collection in the Rockbridge County court house. The research involved tracing the titles of over 120 tracts of land, covering more than 5,000 acres (of an original 8,800-acre research area) and recording specified information contained in the deeds.

Specifically, the students were to record each property transaction for the land in their area back to the patentee. They were to record the name of the grantor (seller), grantee (buyer), and the adjoining property owners. The students were also directed to check the relationship of the grantor to the grantee and to note whether or not the parties involved signed their own names to the documents.

Each student had Friday afternoon off, plus rain days and one free day. Results were varied as students were successful or not depending on their own enthusiasm and perseverance. There were some problems. The court house had suffered from four fires (in 1787, 1796, 1864, and again in the 1890s) (Morton 1980, 148; Barbara Bowyer, personal communication, 10 June 1981). Some records are missing, misfiled, or stolen. Generally, the records are remarkably intact, especially for a small southern county seat lying in the path of northern infantry during the Civil War. Time limitations placed on the students through excavation requirements also caused difficulty in completing some searches. This difficulty was compounded because the court house was closed on weekends.

Still, this exercise in regional historical research produced some outstanding results. Some 395 transactions were recorded involving wills, sales, and indentures. These were classified as to the relationship of the persons involved, data, and type of transaction. Interpretation is still underway, but preliminary results presented here are revealing.

Of the records available, the deeds proved to contain the most important information: acreage; value; names of former owners; and, in some cases, the relationship between grantor and grantee. Since the parties involved had to sign the deeds, literacy could be estimated by the presence or absence of a mark or signature. Sometimes there is evidence that the owner was bankrupt or heavily in debt because a special commissioner was appointed to auction off the land. The description usually identified adjoining property owners as well, allowing some analysis of marriage patterns.

Literacy studies outside of New England have been somewhat limited. As part of the deed research, attempts were made to determine literacy. The students performing the search were irregular in recording this information. Nevertheless, when literacy was computed for those who reported it, evidence of literacy did increase through time. This was to be expected. What was not expected is that, as late as the 1840s, some landholders were unable to write their names. Large landholdings in Rockbridge County were not necessarily associated with educational levels requiring the ability to sign one's name.

In addition to the deeds, the court house records also included wills that helped define the relationship between owners and heirs, the personal and real estate of a person, and the value of the property. Birth and marriage records, where available, helped define important interpersonal relationships across generations and between adjoining tracts of land. These documents make it possible to show that a deed search, as an examination of documentary artifacts, is not an exercise devoid of personality, because people from the past were being drawn into the present via these documents.

An example of this can be seen in one title search in which a property was found to have changed hands from father to daughter. The father clearly thought little of the daughter's choice of a husband, because he specified that the property was to be hers alone and in no manner was it to be considered as part of the husband's holdings. If the wife were to die before her husband, the property would go to any daughters produced by the marriage.

Typically, the procedure involved started with the location of the property and the determination of the current owner in the tax index maps. Since this was a regional study, the lists within certain districts were simply copied and assigned to students. The students searched through the index to the grantees and located the current owner's purchase. This deed listed the grantor and the deed by which the grantor came into possession of the property. Following this procedure,

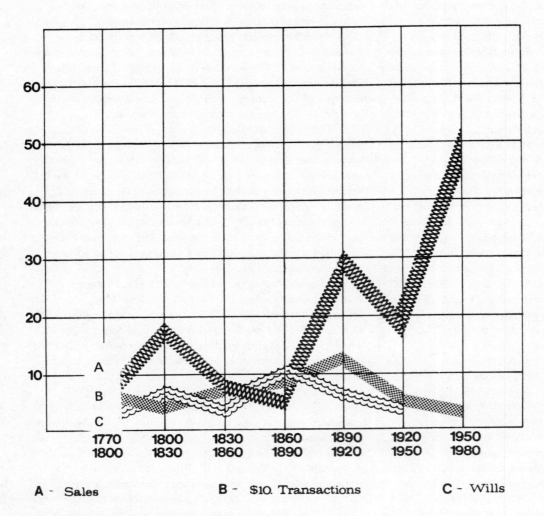

A - Sales   B - $10. Transactions   C - Wills

Fig. 12.1. Frequency of land transfers over time

it was possible to trace the title back to the patentee, or original owner.

Occasionally, there was a break in the listing of former owners when a special commissioner was appointed. In these cases, it was necessary to search through the 'commissioner records.' The information contained in this class of documents usually bridged the gap between owners and gave additional information about incidents of bankruptcy or lack of heirs.

There was a general tendency for the acreage of tracts to increase as they were traced back in time. This is especially noticeable in transactions before 1930. Tracts tended to be merged with adjoining tracts. This enabled students to trace several modern tracts as a single property. Since two or more students might end up tracing the same early tracts, a means of verifying the accuracy of the data recovery was accidentally built into the research strategy. The trend toward larger parcels of land is logical if one considers that, as time progresses, tracts are divided and further subdivided into smaller acreage because the land is less available while the population has grown. By

manipulating the boundaries, the accumulation of acreage, the names of the owners on adjacent tracts of land, and the geographical features of the area, the original tracts for the patentee can be determined. Occasionally, a deed book or a plat book will contain a survey map, but this is not the rule.

Ideally, the entire project should probably be done with a computerized plotting system. The tracts are usually described by their boundaries. The boundaries are delimited by angles from North in distances of poles. A plotter would substantially reduce the problems of tract sizes, but one was not available. Additional research is continuing in applying this mode of analysis to the regional study in an effort to represent land tract borders graphically.

Further analysis will be drawn from the data accumulated through the deed searches. These are a comparison of transactions through time, the types of transactions through time, the types of transactions involving relatives, and male versus female acquisition patterns. Emphasis was placed on the people involved in the transactions, because the students were being trained as anthropologists. The land and documents were vehicles that enabled the researchers to reach people in the past.

Figure 12.1 shows the frequency of transactions through time. There is a steady growth in the number of land transfers, with a slight peak between 1800 and 1830. Census data show that the county population increased steadily over time, apart from a sudden growth spurt between 1820 and 1840 (Sisk 1980). This growth rate is also reflected in the archaeological record, because most sites identified as 'early' in the western part of the county seem to date from the 1820–40 period rather than the eighteenth century (Cole 1980). A second growth period began about a decade before the Civil War and continued to climb to a peak in the 1890s. This was a result of the dislocations

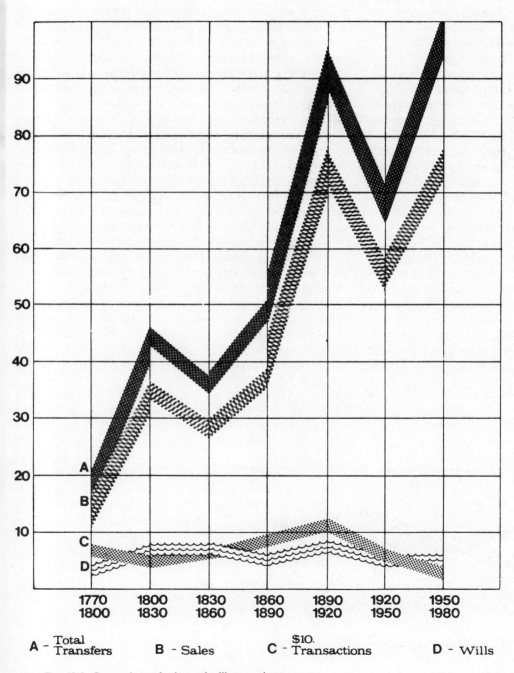

Fig. 12.2. Comparison of sales and wills over time

brought about by the Civil War that brought about many sales of property. A boom in the iron industry in the last decade of the nineteenth century prompted the highest number of property transactions for the entire century.

Additional reasons for increased land sales are being sought in the county records as well as in general histories of the period. Economic and demographic data are still being analyzed to consolidate impressions derived from this partial study of the deeds. Among the possible causes yet to be investigated are land speculation, decline or rise in the use of slave labor, introduction of the James River Canal transport to the area, and the effects of increased harvest potential after the invention of the McCormick reaper.

Figure 12.2 is a comparison of sales and wills as the means of transferring property. In the initial period of the study, some land was still unclaimed, and families could continue to expand their holdings. Later, parents were able to will land to their children. This is reflected in the steady rise of will transfers that contrast sharply with the rapid rise in land sales. The difference between sales and wills may be a result of one of two factors. First, outmigration of sons seeking their own land further west cut down on the number of transactions via wills. This can be documented from various wills that were examined. A second factor is related to overall population increase, which prevented new lands from being available for purchase. There was no new land in Rockbridge County. The end of available land for patenting can be seen as occurring between 1810 and 1830. As younger people came of age, they moved out of the county, and the parents continued to farm the land. When they died, the land went to the son or daughter still in the county. Similar practices were observed in New England in the seventeenth century (Greven 1970, 155–7).

As an indicator of this activity in Rockbridge County, the Cunningham and Taylor families serve as ideal examples. The two families occupied adjoining parcels of land on the northern slope of House Mountain. In 1807 and 1808, members of these families intermarried. Later, the new families moved west to Shelby County, Kentucky. In 1817, when the senior Cunningham died, disposal of the land was finally accomplished by selling the Cunningham homestead to the Moore family. The Moores were also adjoining landowners, and one Moore son married a Cunningham daughter. Interrelationships of this type would not normally be identified during the course of a single title search because they involve three different families on as many tracts of land.

By 1860, sales increased in comparison with will transfers, probably because landowners began to consolidate property and make it better suited for their own uses. Additional study should follow up on this interpretation and compare acreage held before and after this period. It is our interpretation that the sales involved transfers of bottom lands, acquisition of water sources, and, in some cases, avoidance of bankruptcy. The continued rise is probably the result of disruptions in the economic situation caused by the Civil War. The rise was also helped by a boom in the local iron industry and resulting land speculation. Apparently, a large number of people had profited by the mistakes of others, and more tracts were being handed on via wills than previously. The land boom, however, masks the importance of will transfers and inheritance during the last half of the nineteenth century. A modest rise in land sales is also noted for the period after World War II; this may be the result of families moving away from Rockbridge County. The sale of land served as the vehicle for their escape, providing them with the funds to leave. Population decline is reflected in the census data as well.

Figure 12.2 also presents information about the type of property transfers, but it includes two different types of sales. A special indicator shows the transmission of land for cash in the amount of $10.00. The fee appears to be a ritual price for land transferred between relatives, since it does not correlate to

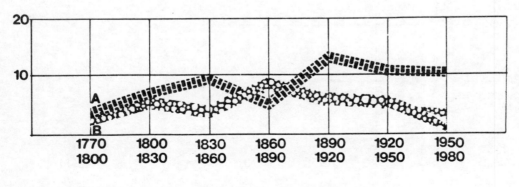

A - Father-Son　　　　**B** - Father-Daughter

Fig. 12.3. Transactions over time between fathers and their sons or daughters

the amount of land involved. It may well be that these small-fee sales were designed to avoid complications and taxes associated with inheritance proceedings. Even within the total number of related persons involved with transfers, wills were apparently not always highly regarded as a means of transferring property.

Figure 12.3 shows the transactions, through time, between fathers and their sons or daughters. The reading of numerous wills suggested that there might be a large number of property transfers between fathers and daughters. There is little indication that there might have been a matrilineal bias to land transfer via inheritance. It is interesting to note that the values for female and male descendants do parallel each other until 1890. Reasons for the sudden downward shift in frequency of transfers to females are not known, but they may be related to the Victorian ideal of male dominance so prevalent in the latter half of the nineteenth century. Another reason may be the shortage of males immediately after the Civil War, although the local census data indicate that this situation was not at all severe in Rockbridge County.

There are several other patterns that are suggestive. For example, there appears to have been a tendency for property to pass down solely through the female line in some families. It is difficult to assess this trend, although the birth and marriage records do provide some limited assistance. The major problem lies in coping with the name changes associated with daughter marriages. There are some examples of father–daughter–granddaughter transactions in which the land remained in one matrilineal line despite the changes of name through marriage. In at least two cases, the granddaughter sold her inherited property to her mother's brother, an action that may be indicative of a latent kinship network not previously suspected.

Exchanges between cousins are equally difficult to detect at this stage of the research. The major problem here is the lack of genealogies and family reconstructions. Before 1850, birth and marriage records were poorly kept, and many names do not appear. After 1870, records are fairly good, with marriage and birth records containing a great deal of information, including parental names of both spouses. This has permitted clarification of some relationships, but earlier examples remain muddled.

There is no question about the practicality of regional deed searches. Archaeological evidence is supplemented by the court house materials. The records provide people to populate the land. The data have the potential of producing very strong, perhaps distinct conclusions about the regional study area. Data from the deeds may be the only accurate means of humanizing the archaeological materials that have been recovered. Oral tradition is also being utilized, but there are discrepancies and exaggerations present in this source that do not exist in any of the documentary sources.

In the future, approaches using archaeological, oral, and documentary sources will attempt to shed more light on western Rockbridge County. At present, the tip of the iceberg reveals that chain of title searches are not really productive in terms of time and energy when compared with the results obtained from a regional search of property records. The larger regional study suggests a great many additional questions that can be asked of the records as well as of the archaeological data. These questions can be used to formulate distinct hypotheses that, in turn, can provide the data-recovery operations with specific goals and directions. In this respect, the initial regional documentary search has proved most illuminating.

Part III

Ecological questions in historical archaeology

Chapter 13

Farming, fishing, whaling, trading: land and sea as resource on eighteenth-century Cape Cod

Anne E. Yentsch

This chapter focuses on variation in the material culture of the people who inhabited the Cape Cod peninsula of New England in the eighteenth century. These were men who made their living by harvesting both the land and the sea, as farmers, whalers, fishermen, and coastal traders. Their wives and children helped them procure a living, defining as they did so a subsistence pattern that is today described as exemplifying Yankee ingenuity. The subsistence pattern was resilient, persisting into the twentieth century; information concerning it was conveyed in oral tradition kept alive among generation after generation of families living in small hamlets, villages, and towns.

Information on the use of land and sea as a resource was also encoded in probate inventories. This information is the central focus of the study described here, which, as it progressed, became an exercise in historical anthropology with an anthropological consideration of social organization and reciprocity. Reciprocity was an integral element in the shared social matrix of daily activities in the community and embedded in the native representations, or folk classification systems, used by the eighteenth-century Cape Codders to build models of their universe containing explicit *and* implicit guidelines for social action. This social action included strategies for procuring a living in an environment situated at the edge of the sea.

13.1 Introduction

Cape Cod is a narrow peninsula that intrudes into the Atlantic Ocean from the southeastern corner of Massachusetts (see fig. 13.1).[1] Its ever-changing shoreline discloses its close relationship to water, tidal fluctuations, winds, and weather. Beginning in the 1630s, men created smaller, dispersed

settlements further and further away from Plymouth yet still within the confines of Plymouth Colony. As the population moved outward from Plymouth, tiny Cape Cod villages grew up nestled among glacial ponds and rolling hills on sites protected from winter winds and storm tides. The families who resided on the Cape informally divided their region into three areas: the lower or outer Cape, the mid-Cape, and the upper Cape. Today, inhabitants of the Cape still speak in terms of these three broad localities. The origins of the division are lost, although local folklore confirms its existence.

The folklore of the Cape, both that which is conveyed orally from one generation to the next and that which was encoded in local histories written in the nineteenth and twentieth centuries, also conveys information about a change from an agricultural to a maritime economy that took place in the eighteenth century. A history of Nauset states that seven men from Plymouth, 'impressed by the abundant forest and rich soil' moved their families to the outer Cape (Lowe 1968, 12–13). An agricultural orientation is also conveyed in statements by W. C. Smith in his *History of Chatham*: 'All these early settlers were tillers of the soil ... they devoted their lives to agriculture' (1971, 91). Evidence of a change in orientation appears, however, in a documented plea for tax abatements filed in 1776 by Wellfleet townsmen, who noted that their land yielded insufficient corn to feed people, that ninety per cent of the population was involved in whaling, and

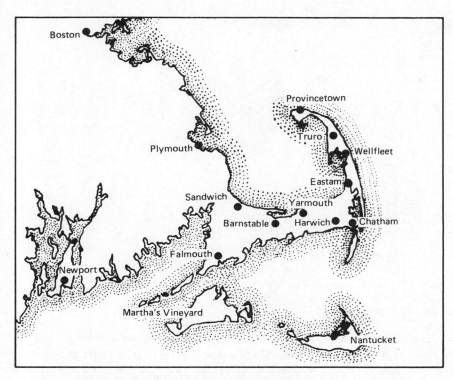

Fig. 13.1. Map of Cape Cod and Islands region showing study area

that the remainder were oystermen (Freeman 1858, vol. 2, 669). Supposedly the outer Cape was once as fertile as the upper Cape, but the farmers who settled on the further reaches of the Cape peninsula stripped the soil and then, disappointed in farming, turned to the sea for a living. Their up-Cape neighbors were, by comparison, more prudent managers of the soil whose farms continued to be productive.

The narratives of the late eighteenth and later centuries convey an unfavorable opinion of the farming conditions and the soil on the outer Cape (Dwight 1821, Letter X, 57–8; Thoreau 1849–57, 48–9). Ethnocentric, perhaps, these writers did not recognize a difference between their conservative environmental perspective and the anti-environmentalist beliefs of earlier, colonial people wherein land and sea were seen as ready provisioners of earthly goods for man's use. The latter view, as noted by Tate (1984b) was one that guided early Anglo-American use and treatment of land and sea resources. Reading the later statements, one gains an impression of disbelief in them that Cape men could willingly have let their limited agricultural resources become impoverished. Yet, as Tate points out, 'Historians have all but uniformly concluded, too, that the colonists practiced a crude agriculture of low yields that quickly destroyed soil fertility, largely basing that conclusion on an uncritical acceptance of the testimony of European travelers and a first generation of American agrarian reformers who wrote at the end of the colonial era' (1984a, 2). If scholars also have taken this perspective, perhaps it is *not* surprising to find it encoded in local traditions about early life on Cape Cod. Unanswered in the earlier descriptions of the region, the question still remains: what really happened on the

outer Cape? and might probate inventories contain useful evidence for studying the interaction between culture, social action, and the environment?

The preliminary study reported here was undertaken during the summer of 1975. The objective was to test for the presence of information among a set of historical documents often considered to be relatively unbiased presentations of household possessions, i.e., probate inventories, to see if these contained information that would confirm or disprove the local traditions about culture change on the outer Cape. Glassie, for example, had described inventories as 'unintentionally informative' and suggested that they were less apt to be biased than other texts prepared with a different objective (Glassie 1975, 10).

Glassie's observation was accurate. Probate inventories (see fig. 13.2) provided a singularly informative point of departure for an exploration of the culture of the people who once inhabited Cape Cod. The insights they provided were not limited to the elite members of society, but covered a far broader spectrum. Today, few realize that free black families were living in quiet obscurity in Cape Cod towns like Chatham during the early eighteenth century. The probate inventory of Felix, 'a Negroe man' who drowned in 1743, is evidence that these families existed (Barnstable County Probate Records 6, 351). Unfortunately, the inventory and other records filed in the Barnstable Court during the settlement of his estate also reveal that the simple material objects his family used and owned were sold to pay debts to the white inhabitants of Chatham, that his estate was depleted, and his family exploited by the legal maneuverings of his Anglo-American neighbors

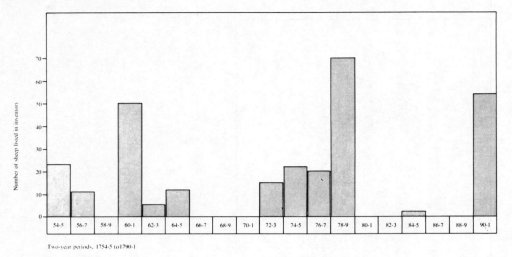

Fig. 13.2. Size of the largest sheep herds shown in probate inventories by two-year periods from 1754 to 1790. Note the dramatic decrease in herd size during the 1780s after British naval raids for provisions in the Cape Cod region began in 1778

and fellow townsmen. 'Unintentionally informative' is a good description of probate records; poignant at times, they reveal a range of attributes characteristic of the social relationships and social structure of Cape Cod society.

Probate inventories proved to be rich in ethnographic detail that disclosed the social texture of daily life. While the study is not conclusive nor fully reported here, the subtle differences the inventory data revealed were worth examining. The study suggests that probate inventories contain information about the material culture of the past that can be welded to that procured from traditional archaeological excavation to produce detailed anthropological descriptions of past social action. The study was also a first step in understanding the necessity for and the methods appropriate to historical anthropology – an avenue of scholarly inquiry now seen as theoretically distinct from both historical archaeology and social history, requiring its own methods and strategies.

Gradually the initial research design was expanded. Initially, the major premise was that material culture, as a product of cultural behavior, would be patterned, and that this patterning would both stem from and reflect non-material aspects of culture. But because the concept of culture used was not based on materialist ideas, but on interpretive philosophies, other elements came to the forefront than those that pertain to adaptation. Starting as a simple study of the effects of environment upon Anglo-American culture, a concern with meaning, native representations of society, and other more subjective aspects of culture emerged as a focus. This chapter reflects this.

The report begins with a consideration of the nature of probate inventories, looks at them as a data base analogous to archaeological sites, lays out a method of analysis, places the communities studied in an environmental framework, and discusses the information in the inventories in terms of basic subsistence patterns and the relationship of these to the

environment. Then it moves beyond this surface level of information to a deeper level relating to the structure of the society. Of interest here were the ways in which the words within the inventories revealed basic assumptions or ideas of the way things were, what the inventories told of folk classification systems (i.e., native representations) and reciprocity. Overall it seemed that the minute details of daily life, even trivial details concerning the possession of $\frac{1}{3}$ of a saw, $\frac{1}{2}$ of a sow, or part of an old boat, were among the more important elements in gaining an understanding of how the quality of life varied between households of the outer Cape and those of the upper Cape. The choice was more than that between farming, fishing, whaling, and trading, between land and sea, and more than simple adaptation. Those eighteenth-century families who chose to stay on Cape Cod, not moving inland, made a decision that affected the form of their culture for generations to come. As indicators of cultural process, their possessions revealed the web of interconnectedness that tied their society together.

13.2 Observations on the nature of probate inventories

In most societies the transferral of property from the dead to the living is an orderly process. In New England, if a person died intestate the estate was divided according to Biblical law: a double portion to the eldest son, the rest to the other heirs. *All* other heirs were supposed to share equally. One element in the orderly process that distributed material possessions to the heirs included the preparation of an inventory.

Normally the inventory was taken within a week after death. In unusual circumstances it was compiled later. There was a three-month mourning period during which the inventory had to be made. On the same day that the will and inventory were exhibited at court, each of the will witnesses and inventory appraisers came to court, gave their oath that the words spoken were truly spoken, that the words written were read aloud to the dying person, and that the inventory was accurate. If no signature existed or if only a mark, such as initials, was on the paper, when the dying man was known to be able to sign his name, then full and detailed explanations were recited. Information concerning any problems, such as items not placed on the inventory, were brought before the court by interested parties in the community. The process was orderly, communal, and difficult to circumvent (Burns 1763; Main 1972; Jones 1977; Yentsch 1980).

Simply put, probate inventories were lists of things that people owned. They included notations of land, houses, livestock, rights to business ventures or to undivided lands, rights to the unborn offspring of livestock, money due as debts, and material objects of all kinds. The few obvious exceptions were perishable items like chicken eggs or things that could not be sold readily. Women's property was excluded when it was readily discernible as feminine property or specifically designated within the inventory as property brought to the marriage by the widow when it might be confused with male possessions.

Accompanying estate accounts listed debts to and from the estate. These frequently listed the reason for the debt: care in sickness, entertaining, a shroud, a coffin, wine and figs for the funeral, wintering a cow, provision of clothing, laundering, watching, and mourning. Together, inventories and estate accounts illustrate the economic network, the reciprocal system of goods and services exchanged, within the colonial community. Together they provide access to a body of information relating to social organization and basic subsistence activities not otherwise obtainable.

Still, probate inventories present only fragmentary information about objects found in Cape Cod households of the past. Although they were intended to list the possessions owned by someone at death, these lists do not include all the items ever owned by an individual nor even all the items contained within the house. Because items perceived as perishable or unworthy of enumeration may have been essential to daily life, this fragmentary aspect of the inventory data is worth further consideration. Two sources of information useful in this regard are merchants' inventories and archaeological assemblages.

In the early years of Plymouth Colony, bees, poultry, and firkins of butter were often enumerated (Yentsch and Stein, in preparation). Notations of bees, poultry, and butter disappear in the eighteenth century. Seventeenth-century inventories list trays, baskets, milk pans, colanders, jugs, crocks, chamber pots, and other things that in the eighteenth century were lumped under the broad categories of woodenware and ceramics. It makes sense that these items were still in use and, in fact, a dozen chamber pots were among the assemblage recovered by Eckholm and Deetz at the Great Island Tavern site on the outer Cape at Wellfleet (Eckholm and Deetz 1971). Chamber pots and other ceramic items also appeared in the inventory of a Harwich merchant, John Smith, dated 1795. Clay pipes appeared only in this merchant's inventory and in one other Cape inventory, yet 9,090 pipe stem fragments alone

were retrieved from the Wellfleet site (Rockman and Rothschild 1984, 118). Clearly the absence of an item in an inventory does not mean it was never owned or used by members of any particular household.

Other examples can be cited. Perhaps household pets were considered members of the household and were not, strictly speaking, property that could be alienated and sold from an estate. They were almost never listed, although Mastromarino (1984) writes eloquently of dogs' lives in the colonial era, and I have seen dog skins in a Middlesex tanner's seventeenth-century inventory. With the exception of a few deerskins, moose skins, or swan-skin blankets, entries pertaining to wildlife were also rarely seen. Although seventeenth-century documents indicate that wild resources were frequently used, and gulls were caught for bait up through the nineteenth century by building small houses, presumably of Indian derivation, as traps (Thoreau 1849–57), English trapping devices such as fox traps and tunnels were represented in only 5% of the Cape inventories. Nor do these list wild ducks, geese, or heath hens. Matthiessen (1959, 66–9) tells of the survival of heath hens on Cape Cod into the 1800s until they became extinct because they were both available and edible, while Governor Winthrop's text, quoted by Matthiessen (1959), provides evidence that they were a common food fed to Boston servants two hundred years earlier. Similarly faunal analysis for remains found at several Plymouth Colony sites indicates a high frequency of waterfowl among the recovered skeletal materials and is evidence that these also were part of the regional diet, if only on a seasonal basis (Olsen 1972). Thus the results of faunal analysis and documentary research on foodways indicates the necessity for integrating archaeological data with observations gleaned from probate documents.

It is true that the absence of an item on the inventory listing implies its absence from the household, but to assume its absence or non-existence because it is unmentioned in an historical text is to speculate about the past. Here again, archaeological research is useful in debunking historical speculation by demonstrating, for example, the occurrence of certain things such as the presence of tobacco pipes and the existence of chamber pots. Especially useful in this regard is the analysis of ceramic vessel forms. Many vessels such as chamber pots and mugs can be distinguished in an archaeological assemblage that are not listed in inventories unless the inventory belongs to the estate of a merchant. Perhaps because the quantities of goods they sold were not sufficiently large to be set apart from ordinary household objects, there is limited evidence in the body of the text that an inventory taker has listed goods belonging to a small shopkeeper. Yet the inventories of large merchants stand out: John Smith's saleable goods, quantities of ceramic items no one could mistake for ordinary, even extraordinary, household possessions, included 100 teapots, thirty-eight sugar pots, sixty cream jugs, and sixty tea cups (Barnstable County Probate Records, vol. 28, 15–21).

It is in merchants' inventories, then, that one finds details on ceramics, clay pipes, implements used to make, dye, and decorate clothing, gunflints, provisions such as sugar, tea, chocolate, and spices. Presumably these items appeared in merchants' inventories because the inventory takers perceived them as income-producing objects. Because the sugar and spices were present, it can be readily inferred that the merchant's wife might have used them in her cooking. Still, it seems equally possible that her neighbors also cooked with sugar and spices bought from the merchant's stock, just as their husbands smoked the clay pipes he also sold, and the entire household used chamber pots obtained from the same source. This point is made because some researchers take an inventory as representative of the total material goods owned and used by a family. Therefore, if spices are absent, the homemaker is viewed as preparing simple, spiceless food – a fact often equated with food preparation techniques of the households placed lower on the social scale (Carr and Walsh 1976; Carson and Carson 1976).

While keeping in mind that the data from inventories are fragmentary, they are still analytically useful. Bowen's 1975 analysis of the faunal assemblage from the Mott Farm, excavated by James Deetz and Marley R. Brown III, makes this point clearly and concisely. The Mott Farm site was located on Narragansett Bay and inhabited by sheep owners noted for raising, grazing, and breeding fat mutton to be sold at market (Bowen 1975). The faunal assemblage contained only a small percentage of material from sheep. Bowen was able to resolve the contradictions presented when reading the archaeological evidence (suggesting minor dependence on mutton) against the documentary data through a detailed examination of probate inventories. Thus even their biases do not preclude their use as a data source for observations about the past in a manner complementary to techniques used to analyze materials recovered from archaeological sites. Inventory data can also be viewed as analogous to archaeological data.

13.3 Inventories as data sets analogous to archaeological sites

On the basis of research at Plimoth Plantation in the 1960s on the feasibility of using probate inventory data to procure additional information about the seventeenth century to use in museum programs, Deetz concluded that these could be subjected to analysis akin to that used on archaeological assemblages (Deetz 1970). They do differ in some respects. Unlike the assemblages from many archaeological sites, the constellation of objects found in a probate inventory represents a single household and is therefore always analogous to a one-component site. Each inventory bears the date it was taken, and most contain information on the residence of the person whose possessions the inventory lists. The tight date assigned each inventory, therefore, controls the dimension of time while the geographic designation controls the dimension of space. Demographic information, derived independently through family reconstitution, permits one to determine how long a family or household existed as a social entity (Wrigley 1966). Thus patterns derived from inventory analysis reflect the household possessions of a specific, known family over an unambiguous span of time with a clearly delineated starting point (i.e., date of marriage) and a known spatial location. These attributes permit many kinds of analysis. The focus in this chapter is a synchronic study designed to delineate regional differences in subsistence patterns on Cape Cod to test the validity of information conveyed in oral traditions.

Despite the growing use of inventory data by social and economic historians in New England and the Chesapeake (Jones 1980b, 248–9), the use of inventory data as the equivalent of archaeological materials is still uncommon. Students of material culture have not created techniques for their analysis and use similarly sophisticated to those developed by social and economic historians. In fact, many historical archaeologists have let the skilled use of documentary sources remain in the hands of ethnohistorians or anthropologists such as Cohn (1971), Rosaldo (1980), and Sahlins (1981, 1985) whose interests lie outside their native culture; they have not developed similar techniques of their own for studying American derivatives of European culture. Trigger's 1980 denunciation of the anti-historical perspective that pervades the study of prehistory can readily be said also to characterize much of the field of historical archaeology. Most historical archaeologists use inventories primarily as they use other documentary sources of information, i.e., as ancillary information sources intended to *support* information obtained from field excavations.

The specific problem with inventories is, perhaps, that one must take them as symbolic of an archaeological site. The words must stand for the artifacts, i.e., for the broken bits of pottery, glass, clay pipes, butchered bone, rusted iron nails, and common pins found in the ground. The inventory itself must arbitrarily represent the site with the order of words the equivalent, in a very general way, of spatial designations (see Brown, ch. 7 above, for an expanded discussion of spatial aspects of inventory data). This requires thinking of inventories in a slightly more complex way than is required for an artifact found in a specific level within a designated unit. The problems involved in their analysis are also slightly different from those one encounters in most archaeological research, but, at the most basic level, the problems are simply ones of technique; probate inventories and archaeological sites are analogous sets of data (Yentsch 1980, 28–36, 102–52; Yentsch 1983).

The patterns that emerge from inventory analysis, in this chapter, are based on information comparable to that which might be obtained if one were to excavate seventy-five sites on the outer Cape and ninety-one sites on the upper Cape, each with tightly defined spatial and temporal dimensions and limited to single-component occupations. It is neither financially feasible nor humanly possible to do this within a reasonable period of time. Hence one attribute that sets inventory analysis apart from more traditional archaeological research is the intriguing problem of quantity.

The quantity of inventory data available in county court houses in New England distinguishes inventory analysis from more traditional archaeological research in the Northeast. The sample size in archaeology is necessarily small because of the high cost of excavation, yet if historical archaeologists are to be able to make predictions based on data found archaeologically, they require a larger empirical base than excavation alone can provide. This base could be provided through inventory analysis. And, if one knows a region well through the use of inventory analysis, it is far easier to place an archaeological site within it in terms of its relationship to other potential sites. At the same time, biases in reporting procedures for estates suggest that under-registration of inventories, especially for those in the lower income levels of colonial society, was prevalent in certain areas of New England (Smith 1975; Main 1974).

Another thing that is problematic centers on the duration of the household. There is nothing in an inventory that can serve as the equivalent to an artifact from a site that gives a *terminus post quem* (i.e., date after which something happens). What serves in its stead is the marriage date for the couple who act as the male and female heads of the household. The customary procedure was for an individual to accumulate a few personal possessions while single, usually only a few tools, some livestock, or wearing apparel, and linens or kitchen goods if one were a woman. The unmarried state was perceived as deviant behavior, and single people of marriageable age were expected to marry, so single individuals married in their twenties. With rare exceptions, unmarried, single individuals did not form households or live alone. Thus, the normal accumulation of material possessions began with marriage and the formation of a household.

It is not difficult to correlate inventory data with family reconstitution charts providing information on dates of marriage, births, deaths, and occasionally geographic mobility. The specific techniques of family reconstitution, developed by French historians, are detailed in Wrigley (1966); they were used by social historians such as John Demos (1970) and Philip Greven (1970) in the 1960s and form the basis of much research in New England family history at present. They can be readily adapted for use by historical archaeologists, as demonstrated by Yentsch (1975, 1980, and 1981) and illustrated in Chapter 1 *above*. With the use of collateral documents one can gain a very close approximation of the period when a household identified with a probate inventory came into existence.

13.4 Methods of analysis

Initially the data were divided into four arbitrary categories representing a quarter of a century apiece, but because of the small sample size for the first quarter inventories (three for Falmouth and five for Truro–Provincetown), the periods 1700–24 and 1725–49 were lumped together. The procedure used in their analysis insured that results would be comparable across community boundaries while the placement of the communities represented (i.e., adjacent to the mainland and at the tip of Cape Cod) provided an opportunity to

assess the impact of small-scale environmental differences on household possessions and subsistence activities.

Initially, the number of times an item appeared in an inventory set, rather than the number of pieces represented, was the basis for establishing its representation in the community. Three cows enumerated in one inventory were viewed as a single 'cow'. The number of cows tallied were divided by the number of inventories in each set to obtain the percentage of households owning cows. This step gave an indication of gross similarities or differences across community boundaries. If one community had different dairying practices than another, this might initially show up in the percentage representation. A town where 80% of the inhabitants owned cattle was significantly different from one in which only 20% owned cattle. While recognizing that similarities (i.e., two towns each with 80% representation) could also mask differences, this preliminary study uncovered sufficient variation between the two regions of the Cape – upper and outer – that it highlighted the maritime adaptation or orientation of the latter region. While more detailed analysis was postponed until a later phase of the study, some similarities were the focus of attention in 1975.

It was recognized that similarities could also mask differences, and it seemed unwise and insufficient to take equivalent percentages of particular items contained in households at face value. In two communities, while 20% of the inhabitants might own cows or chairs or weapons, there could still be significant differences: the size of dairy herds could vary from town to town, the number of chairs, beds or tables could be more or less on a per person basis, and the ownership of armaments might indicate a dependence on the traditional weapons of hand-to-hand combat (e.g., swords, rapiers, cutlasses) or on the more sophisticated guns useful in long-range warfare and in hunting. Thus, whenever the artifact clusters appeared to be equivalent, the individual items within them were subjected to closer scrutiny.

Through this two-stage process, differences in lifestyle emerged. It became apparent that in the early eighteenth century, swords and cutlasses were more favored weapons among the men of the outer Cape, present in 25% of the inventories in contrast to the 9% shown among the upper Cape households. Differences in ownership of maritime-related items indicated that different spectrums of the marine resource base were being developed or utilized in each area (see section 13.8). Differences in household possessions prompted Deetz, when told that a deacon in Truro possessed more than seventeen chairs, to suggest that the outer Cape folk could properly be called 'The Chair People'. The differences were not limited to chairs alone, but were also seen in beds, bedsteads, tables, and other household accoutrements. Thus in the early eighteenth century, 36% of the Falmouth families had candlesticks compared to 6% on the outer Cape; 80% used pottery cooking and eating utensils compared to 62%; more than 84% had a pot or pots compared to 68%; 100% had beds as opposed to 83%. Yet pewter was not as prevalent, present in only 80% of the inventories in contrast to the 94% found at the Outer Cape. Tables with these data were later used as a control by Bragdon (1977) in a detailed study of differences between the material culture of taverns and farmsteads. The differences observed suggest that significant variations in day-to-day routines characterized the lives of these people, without identifying the social factors responsible for the variation.

When reading inventory analyses written by economic historians, it was clear that none of the economic, quantitatively framed approaches permitted a ready analysis of the pattern of ordinary social action that characterized the daily life of families, or consideration of seasonal rhythms and their effect on individual, household, or community behavior. Yet these were aspects of the past that interested me as an anthropologist. By placing a fine-grained lexical grid over each inventory that pinpointed technological objects and isolated those things associated with day-to-day living, some objects that reflected differences in subsistence patterns appeared, as did some that suggested status differences. The lexical grid consisted of assemblages, clusters of objects, that could be linked to specific activities. While recognizing that some things could be used in more than one activity and that others might be used in ways that varied from the norm, the categories of objects were based on the most likely use, given their semantic definition according to eighteenth-century accepted usage as given in the *Oxford English Dictionary*.

The context was the entire inventory. The categories lumped together items whether they were used indoors or outdoors. What was deemed important was whether or not the presence of an item suggested behavior associated with central themes: sleeping, storage, fireside cooking, food procurement and storage, use of maritime resources, environmental relation-ships, cloth production (the spinning–weaving complex), and so forth. For example, a fish pan, salt, an eel pot, or a cod hook were all things used in the procurement, preservation, and preparation of food resources from the sea. These were among the items considered part of the maritime cluster.

Some objects appeared in more than one cluster; there was overlap. For example, while a fireplace and its tools were integral to food preparation, the fire itself also produced light and warmth. Corn in the sheaf, corn in the ears, corn barns, corn riddles and sieves, meal bags, and grist mills were all objects that comprised elements in the corn sub-assemblage, and denoted a resource base emphasizing grain cultivation. As seasonal indicators, corn in the sheaf and corn in the ears told of the sequence of agricultural activities and were part of another cluster distinguished from structures such as grist mills and barns contained within the building assemblage. Livestock and crops formed separate clusters because they designated different farming activities and varying agricultural foci, yet they were subsumed at a more general level because, when analyzed in terms of seasonal cycles, they revealed a different aspect of household activity than when kept separate.

The household was considered the minimal, primary unit, in terms of both economic activities and social organization.

One question is to what extent certain subsistence activities affected the day-to-day activities in the home. In a demographic study of southern women, Carr and Walsh (1977) described the effects of a labor-intensive economic system based on tobacco-growing upon the lives of women. At the same time, Carson and Carson (1976) described the life of southern families and noted that little spinning or weaving was done in southern households. In fact the image presented contrasted sharply with observations I gained through reading the early Plymouth Colony inventories. Was there a qualitative difference to the standard of living in the southern colonies that arose because of lack of time, brought about by the labor required to grow tobacco, or was the difference a result of other, culturally-based beliefs about what women or men should do and could do? Might there be analogous differences in New England communities dependent on the sea? Was there something related to the utilization of marine resources that might also have affected the pattern of daily life on the outer Cape in unforeseen ways? What was the interaction between utilization of marine resources and dependence on resources found ashore, especially those procured through farming? These questions underlay some of the preliminary analysis as I sought to understand the effect of environmental factors on the eighteenth-century towns situated on Cape Cod.

13.5 Micro-environments and Cape Cod towns

Cape Cod is a narrow, glacial peninsula extending forty miles into the Atlantic Ocean. Buffeted by storm winds from winter gales and a strong surf along its outer beach, it is a landscape that, in John Hay's words, 'moves and changes' (1969). There are many evocative descriptions of its land; the outer Cape especially is beautifully described by Thoreau, by Beston, or by Hay.[2] Geologically, the historic period environment of the Cape and Islands consisted of gentle hills formed by the glacial moraine, deep ponds or kettle holes, outcrops of glacial erratic boulders, the outwash plain, moors, shifting sand dunes, swamps, bogs, streams, salt marshes and tidal creeks, tiny harbors, barrier ponds, steep sea cliffs or marine scarps, sand bars, tidal flats, and shoals given vivid names by early sailors.

During the seventeenth century the Cape was divided into five settlements: Sandwich, Barnstable, Yarmouth, Eastham, and Chatham (or Monomoy). By the late seventeenth century, these primary towns were divided into precincts that became secondary townships. By the late eighteenth century, with the exception of the political incorporation for Bourne, the 'budding' process was complete. Falmouth was laid out in 1686; Truro was founded in 1709. The Provincelands (now Provincetown) were given tax-exempt status in 1727, prompting a spurt of growth in that tiny community on the tip of the Cape that lasted less than a decade (*Collections of the Massachusetts Historical Society* (hereafter *CMHS*), series 1, vol. 8, 196–201).

Part of the Cape and Islands region, Falmouth, Truro, and Provincetown, shared certain features with other settlements. Cape and Island towns lacked the hills and

Table 13.1 *Land holdings on Cape Cod, Massachusetts, c.1786, derived from tax tables in the Massachusetts State Archives.* The classes of land shown in the table: tillage, English mowing, fresh meadow, salt marsh, pasturage, woodlands, improveable and unimproveable, are classes of property taken directly from the tax list and described as such in the list.

	Upper Cape			Mid Cape			Outer Cape		
Acres utilized for:	Barnstable 1639	Sandwich 1639	Falmouth 1686	Yarmouth 1639	Harwich 1694	Chatham 1712	Eastham 1651	Truro 1709	Total Acreage
Cultivation									
Tillage	957	1,135	954	883	603	615	1,301	1,046	7,494
Animal Husbandry									
English Mowing	130	227	57		18	10		2	444
Fresh Meadow	295	497	126	30	216	10		3	1,177
Salt Marsh	2,262	1,231	332	1,249	396	321	1,388	413	7,592
Sub-total	2,687	1,955	515	1,279	630	341	1,388	418	9,213
Pasturage	3,890	4,520	3,537	3,736	2,762	1,768	1,776	58	22,047
Woodlands	2,551	1,438	2,285	962	2,060	23	114	487	9,920
Acreage utilized c.1786	10,085	9,048	7,291	6,860	6,055	2,747	4,579	2,009	48,674
Improveable Acreage	8,801	6,433	5,379	5,106	5,836	1,089	123	2,122	34,889
Total farming land available	18,886	15,481	12,670	11,966	11,891	3,836	4,702	4,131	83,563
Unimproveable Acreage		7,156	1,954	5,811	1,804	1,202	10,043	2,648	30,618
Total Acreage/Town	18,886	22,637	14,624	17,777	13,695	5,038	14,745	6,779	114,181

mountains of northern New England and they lacked the rock-bound shores of the towns situated north of Boston. Formed by the glaciers, the ice sheets of the Pleistocene, the soils of the Cape were created by a stony debris. Its podzol, a sandy glacial till ranging from a few inches to several feet in thickness, is the most well developed in New England and usually less than six inches in depth (Chamberlain 1964), but it is exceedingly fragile.

Cronon, in a 1983 study of ecological relationships between man and land in New England, notes that Englishmen lacked 'an intimate understanding of the habits and ecology of other species' of living things (Cronon 1983, 37). Tate suggests that this lack of understanding was partially the result of a world view wherein the New World was seen as 'a source of extractive wealth, a treasure bin of commodities' (1984b, 9). The folk classification system used for taxation stresses the potential for income in its division of lands, not an awareness of it as a natural habitat. Cape men carved it into eight different classes (tillage land, English mowing land, fresh meadows, salt marsh, pasturage, woodland, unimproved, and unimprovable) that reflected their perception of its use as an agricultural resource. Falmouth contained more acreage suitable for pasturage than any other town in the region with the exception of Chilmark on the western tip of Martha's Vineyard, but in

Table 13.2 *Comparison of land-holdings used for subsistence*

	Cape Cod		Truro		Falmouth	
	Acreage	%	Acreage	%	Acreage	%
Tillage	7,494	14.75	1,046	42.48	954	13.08
Eng. mowing	444	.87	2	.01	57	.78
Fresh meadow	1,177	2.32	3	.12	126	1.73
Salt marsh	9,213	18.13	413	16.77	332	4.55
Pasturage	22,558	44.40	511	20.76	3,537	48.51
Woodland	9,920	19.53	487	19.78	2,285	31.34
Total	50,806	100.00	2,462	99.92	7,291	99.99

terms of tillage was roughly equivalent to Truro (see tables 13.1 and 13.2). One would expect these differences to have had an impact on the things men used to wrest a living from their surroundings as they sought to weld land and sea together.

Each and every town in the region was a coastal community under a marine climatic influence. Their climate was warmer in winter and cooler in summer than inland regions of New England. Spring came late; autumn, especially the days

Table 13.3 *Census data for Cape Cod towns (c.1765)*

	Families		Men over 16		Boys		Women		Other		Total
	Freq.	Average size of household	Freq.	%	Freq.	%	Freq.	%	Freq.	%	
Upper Cape:											
Barnstable	481	5.43	631	24	623	24	1,301	50	55	02	2,610
Sandwich	263	7.57	460	23	469	24	1,015	51	47	02	1,991
Falmouth	217	7.54	418	26	365	22	816	50	38	02	1,637
Mid-Cape											
Yarmouth	450	5.95	651	24	667	25	1,327	50	33	01	2,678
Harwich	420	5.70	545	23	593	25	1,243	52	11	0.005	2,392
Chatham	196	5.82	267	23	292	26	578	51	3	0.003	1,140
Outer Cape:											
Eastham	311	5.90	426	23	431	23	974	53	3	0.001	1,834
Wellfleet	211	5.32	301	27	252	23	562	50	2	0.002	1,117
Truro	221	5.40	324	27	279	23	586	49	4	0.003	1,193
Provincetown	95	4.78	142	31	99	22	211	47	2	0.004	454

Table 13.4 *Livestock holdings on Cape Cod, Massachusetts, c.1786, derived from tax tables in the Massachusetts State Archives*

	Upper Cape						Mid-Cape						Outer Cape[1]				Regional Total	
	Barnstable		Sandwich		Falmouth		Yarmouth		Harwich		Chatham		Eastham[2]		Truro			
	Freq.	%	Freq.	%	Freq.	%	Freq.	%	Freq.	%	Freq.	%	Freq.	%	Freq.	%	Freq.	%
Livestock																		
Cows	670	32	592	30	370	31	457	31	318	23	239	29	519	33	157	41	3,322	30.52
Oxen	343	16	298	15	194	16	302	21	276	20	146	18	290	18	101	26	1,950	17.92
Neat Cattle	530	26	608	30	279	24	305	21	301	22	196	24	396	25	70	18	2,685	24.68
Horses	166	8	154	8	114	10	99	7	137	10	70	8	164	10	36	9	940	8.63
Swine	358	17	349	17	221	19	288	20	359	25	177	21	212	14	23	6	1,987	18.26
Sheep[3]	n.s.		n.s.		1,456		n.s.		n.s.		367		333		(Well.) n.s.			

[1]No figures are shown for the Province Lands

[2]Includes data from Wellfleet; sheep figures represent only Wellfleet

[3]Because these were not entered for most of the towns, the percentages that sheep represent in the livestock holdings were not calculated for any town

identified as belonging to the 'Indian harvest', brought the most predictable weather: cool, crisp, and bright. The land was visited in winter by severe coastal storms, or *nor'easters* that brought steady rain and dampness for days at a time. Foggy weather, gray and damp, was frequent in late spring and early fall. Summer afternoons brought strong westerly breezes, evening mists, and cloudy *sou'westers*.

No one knows when the inhabitants of the Cape and Islands began to use sea-faring terms to describe their weather and their houses. Certainly from the outset it was the sea that connected the isolated settlements on the outer reaches of New England with the larger, pre-modern world. Seaborne vessels, sloops, shallops, and canoes derived from Indian prototypes, using the bays, sounds, and harbors as a transportation system,

were more important in the Cape and Islands region than any extant system of English roads or Indian paths.

Cape and Island towns were small communities characterized by face-to-face interaction. Although some were clustered and some were dispersed, with the exception of the town of Sherburn on Nantucket, none of the settlements had population densities that reached urban proportions. Information on population (table 13.3) from the 1764 census reveals a similar age and sex structure for the communities, although Truro had a slightly larger number of men over sixteen (27% as opposed to 26%), while Provincetown had a larger number (31%). Additional information on land, livestock holdings, buildings, vessels, and other taxables for the Cape and Island region is presented in tables 13.1, 13.2, 13.4 and

Table 13.5 *Personal property on Cape Cod, Massachusetts, c.1786, derived from tax tables in the Massachusetts State Archives*

	Upper Cape			Mid-Cape			Outer Cape[1]		
	Barnstable	Sandwich	Falmouth	Yarmouth	Harwich	Chatham	Eastham[2]	Truro	Total
Dwelling Houses	312	227	185	277	272	114	278	116	1,781
Barns	184	118	93	133	165	47	115	40	895
Buildings worth £5 or less	45	0	2	20	0	0	20	0	87
Grist mills, saw mills, & tanneries	8	12	8	10	13	6	11	2	70
Shops	26	28	30	10	10	10	0	0	114
Warehouses	2	0	1	1	0	0	0	0	4
Wharfage-superfootage	60	0	0	0	0	0	0	0	60
Factorage	10	0	0	0	0	0	0	0	10
Cider	0	0	0	0	0	0	0	0	0
Stock in trade at 6%	80	?[3]	186	100	286	50	20	?[3]	722
Oz. plate	721	585	298	99	55	0	30	0	1,788
Vessel tonnage	389	359	240	478	155	1,117	393	not shown	3,131

[1]No figures were provided for the Province Lands
[2]These totals include personal property for Wellfleet men; Wellfleet separated from Eastham in 1763
[3]These figures were illegible on the original

13.5. This information also suggests that there were microenvironmental differences that affected subsistence patterns.

13.6 The data

The data base was comprised of all probate inventories filed in Barnstable County at the Barnstable County Probate Court, Barnstable, Massachusetts, for individuals who resided in Falmouth, Truro, or Provincetown during the eighteenth century and whose place of residence was shown on their inventory. Since neither of these towns was incorporated until the end of the seventeenth century or early in the eighteenth century, earlier inventories from Sandwich, Barnstable, Yarmouth, and Eastham were also used to establish the seventeenth-century base of material possessions. These towns were the original settlements, comprising larger geographic areas from which the newer towns were split as time progressed.

The inventories from Falmouth formed one set and represented the upper Cape; the inventories from Truro and Provincetown formed another set and represented the outer Cape. The former sample contained ninety-one inventories, ranging in value from £9-00-00 to £5,672-00-00 with a mean of £749-00-00 and a median of £340-00-00. The outer Cape sample contained seventy-five inventories ranging in value from £8-00-00 to £5,221-00-00 with a mean of £484-00-00 and a median of £223-00-00. These inventories included several that were women's, and represent men who were single, married, young, and old. In other words, they span the different segments of the society that lived in the towns. No inventories for Indians were included; none were part of the sample.

Table 13.6 *Range of wealth for probate inventories in the upper Cape and outer Cape Samples, 1700–1800, in pounds sterling*

	Outer Cape		Upper Cape	
Wealth range	Frequency	%	Frequency	%
0–25 (£)	4	5	6	7
26–50	6	8	6	7
51–75	5	7	6	7
76–100	2	3	4	4
101–150	13	17	10	11
151–200	5	7	1	1
200–299	9	12	10	11
300–399	9	12	5	6
400–499	4	5	3	3
500–750	9	12	13	14
751–1,000	0		6	7
1,001–1,500	5	7	11	12
Over 1,500	4	5	10	11
	75	100	91	101

Table 13.6 gives a breakdown of the distribution of wealth among the households represented by the inventories and indicates that the upper Cape households had higher wealth levels. Since both areas were settled at the same time, however, by members of the same English culture without any discernible differences in status, the variation in the wealth levels on a per household basis is believed to reflect an environmental effect. Through happenstance, people settled in areas of the Cape that provided a better opportunity to be

self-subsistent using the traditional English barnyard complex of domestic animals and the farming techniques of old England. Over successive generations, families in these communities grew wealthier, whereas those families who located where there was less opportunity for agriculturally based increases in wealth were faced with a different set of options. This is a complex issue, not fully resolved in the data discussed in this chapter, but it would be incorrect to infer that the differences that appear among the outer and upper Cape households result solely from differences in wealth. Other processes were also at work.

The first step in sorting out this problem was to look at the information in the inventories to see what it revealed about the division of labor in colonial society. By analyzing the various clusters, the division of labor involved in the production and distribution of products appeared; the interdependency of the colonial household and community could be read. This was immediately apparent when one considered the spinning–weaving complex.

Weavers were men who were taught their art by a master craftsman. Yet at the household level those objects belonging to the spinning–weaving complex also revealed that among many Cape Cod families spinning was a female task done within the home. Woolen bedding and clothing, of course, cross-cut all ranks of society and were used by both young and old, married or unmarried, male or female members of a household. It was not as informative an item within the cluster as were looms (used by men) or different types of wheels (used by women).

There are texts that tell us something about the lives of weavers in England and note the fact that some of these men travelled about the countryside stopping first at one home to weave cloth and then at another. Even if these documents did not exist and one could only analyze the inventories, the fact that weaving was a specialized task could be inferred from the sparser representation of looms on a per household basis. Among upper Cape families, for example, while 81% of the probated estates listed various wheels for spinning, and there were 1.21 wheels per household, looms were found in only 36%. On the outer Cape, looms were found in an even smaller percentage of households (23%).

Thus differences in material possessions at the household level begin to reveal differences in behavior among members of the household, while other differences in material possessions of a household, when juxtaposed against the backdrop of the community, revealed a range of activities characteristic of the community. Relationships that might be linked to the use of maritime resources began to appear. And, extending this further, differences in material possessions at the community level also suggested differences in the subsistence patterns of particular towns and villages.

It was apparent, for example, that there were significant differences in the possession of objects related to the spinning–weaving complex within the Cape Cod region that, in turn, implied the existence of regional specialization. Table

Table 13.7 *Possession of specific objects related to spinning and weaving in Cape inventories, 1700–1800[1]*

	Outer Cape		Upper Cape	
	Frequency	*%*	*Frequency*	*%*
Sheep	34	45	44	48
Wool	15	25	26	29
Flax	9	15	18	18
Yarn	15	25	21	23
Looms	12	23	33	36
Wheels	30	49	62	68
Combs	3	5	12	13
Cards	8	13	21	23
Reels	1	2	20	22
No contents related to spinning– weaving	18	30	18	20

[1]The prevalence of lumping categories in the outer Cape inventories, i.e., entries that read 'all the household goods', etc., prevented a thorough analysis of this cluster for all estates. Percentages shown were computed for those estates which contained no lumping category for goods within the home. Note that the categories are not mutually exclusive and that percentages were derived by determining the proportion the value in the frequency column represents of the total sample for each community.

13.7 reveals that households on the outer Cape peninsula were less apt to participate in any task related to the spinning-weaving complex than were the families living in the upper Cape towns of Falmouth, Barnstable, and Sandwich. Only 49% possessed one or more spinning wheels while only 23% owned a loom. Although they did raise sheep, the outer Cape households did not possess the necessary implements to turn sheep wool into cloth with the same frequency as upper Cape households. At the very least, this suggests that there was a qualitative difference between women's lives in the two different parts of the Cape Cod peninsula, but it also raises the question as to whether scheduling activities between maritime-related tasks and those associated with raising sheep, arising from seasonal/environmental factors, presented outer Cape men with an irresolvable scheduling conflict. For example, did participation in the late summer and fall blackfish drives or the winter cod fishery preclude weaving?

At the same time, the fact that sheep were raised in both areas (see table 13.9) complicated the issue. If sheep were raised in both areas, but only one contained large numbers of households with the equipment necessary to shear sheep, procure the wool and then process it until it became cloth, what did the other region do with its sheep? Again, an interdependency among communities was suggested, and the

Table 13.8 *Percentage of households owning livestock as shown on 17th-century Cape Cod inventories*

	Upper Cape Sandwich– Falmouth (n=22)	Mid-Cape Barnstable– Yarmouth (n=55)	Outer Cape Eastham (n=10)
Cows and heifers	91	84	100
Oxen	27	51	60
Bulls	23	20	0
Other cattle	91	86	100
Horses	55	56	90
Swine	59	71	90
Goats	5	3	0
Sheep	32	47	70
Fowls	9	2	0
Bees	5	10	36

existence of reciprocal systems of economic activity could be reasonably postulated.

Further regional diversification between the outer and upper Cape communities is also apparent in both crops and livestock holdings, although here it must be delineated against a pattern of change over time that can be seen in both regions. An emphasis on dairy farming, revealed by the presence of cows and heifers, was characteristic of all Cape communities in the seventeenth century. If anything, the outer Cape inventories suggest a stronger dependence on animal husbandry as a core element in subsistence, but the smaller number of inventories may be skewing the trend in that direction.

The small sample of inventories dating between 1700 and 1724 for both regions indicates a continuation of the pattern shown in table 13.9: cows and heifers were owned by almost all. Most men also owned oxen, mares, swine, and sheep. Judah Butler had a bull and rights to twenty sheep, but he is the only one of eight who did not own any dairy animals (Barnstable County, *Probate Records*, vol. 3, 51).

Table 13.9 *Comparison of livestock holdings* listed in outer Cape and upper Cape inventories, 1700–1800*

	1700–49[1]		1750–74[2]		1775–1800[3]		1700–1800[4]	
	Frequency	%	Frequency	%	Frequency	%	Frequency	%
COWS & HEIFERS								
Outer Cape	11	44	4[5]	16[5]	10	40	25	33
Upper Cape	20	80	25	18	24	69	60	76
OXEN								
Outer Cape	7	28	1[5]	4[5]	8	32	16	21
Upper Cape	8	32	8	19	9	26	25	27
OTHER CATTLE								
Outer Cape	10	40	14	56	7	28	31	41
Upper Cape	15	60	17	55	15	43	47	52
HORSES								
Outer Cape	12	48	7	28	7	28	26	35
Upper Cape	14	56	19	61	13	37	46	51
SHEEP								
Outer Cape	13	52	11	44	10	40	34	45
Upper Cape	13	52	18	58	13	41	44	48
SWINE								
Outer Cape	14	56	12	48	5	20	31	41
Upper Cape	17	68	18	58	17	49	52	57

**Note:* Since these are not mutually exclusive categories (i.e., an individual might have owned animals belonging to one or more of these categories), the percentages shown represent the number of inventories in the total sample that listed cows, swine, horses, etc.

[1]The outer Cape sample size is 25; the upper Cape sample size is 25

[2]The outer Cape sample size is 25; the upper Cape sample size is 31

[3]The outer Cape sample size is 25; the upper Cape sample is 35

[4]The outer Cape sample size is 75; the upper cape sample size is 91

[5]Cows, heifers, and oxen were more frequently enumerated under the lumping category of 'all the cattle' on inventories from the outer Cape during this period than during others. This has undoubtedly biased the frequencies shown here

Table 13.10 *Percentage of wealth held in livestock, 1700–1800, for probate inventories from outer and upper Cape towns*

	None	£1–10	£11–20	£21–30	£31–40
Upper Cape					
1700–24	—	67	33	—	—
1725–49	8	72	16	4	—
1750–74	11	62	17	3	7
1775–99	22	64	11	3	—
Outer Cape					
1700–24	—	80	—	—	20
1725–49	23	41	27	9	—
1750–74	15	45	40	—	—
1775–99	48	48	4	—	—

As shown in tables 13.8 and 13.9, this pattern of livestock holdings changed during the eighteenth century as Cape families adapted, over successive generations, to the Cape's natural habitat. Throughout Cape communities there was a decrease over the years in the frequency of dairy cattle listed in the inventories, but the decrease was greater in the outer Cape communities, where the numbers declined from 100% to 45% from 1775 to 1800. Where once outer Cape farmers had raised more horses, sheep, swine, and oxen than their upper Cape neighbors, the situation was reversed. Larger and more diversified stocks of animals were maintained on the upper Cape farms. By 1800, outer Cape households raising swine had decreased by 28%. Barely more than half the inventories (52%) for outer Cape inhabitants listed livestock; 48% had only between one and ten pounds sterling invested in barnyard animals (see table 13.10); 48% had none.

Overall, the number of oxen per household changed least, perhaps because oxen had a more generalized use than horses. They not only drew plows and prepared fields for crops, but were an important means of transportation, invaluable in drawing heavy cartloads of whale blubber from the beach to the try-house or in hauling seaweed from the shore to the field. As late as the twentieth century, oxen, not horses, were used for activities that drew men onto difficult terrain – salt marshes, tidal flats, swampy areas. This was explained by a local informant who noted that it was better to use oxen because if an ox broke a leg or was otherwise injured in a swamp or marsh, it could be shot and used as food. The potential for accidents always existed while working in rough terrain, but something could still be salvaged (Yentsch 1974b).

As Thomas notes (1983), horse meat was culturally taboo and had been for centuries among English settlements. The terrain of the outer Cape was, overall, less tame than that of the gentler lands that lay beneath the upper Cape towns, and sturdy beasts were required, sturdy beasts that could accidentally die and then be used as food. By interweaving information from various sources, the consistent presence of oxen in the inventories became understandable. The fact that ownership of oxen comprised a conservative, less changing element in the culture while other types of livestock holdings changed dramatically was no longer inexplicable.

Conversely, changes in the sheep holdings on the upper Cape – the lower numbers in the third quarter of the eighteenth century – were explicable once one knew that the sheep herds were subjected to depletion by British raids on Woods Hole and the Elizabeth Islands during the Revolution. During the month of September 1778, Major General Sir Charles Gray sent a fleet to Holme's Hole, procuring 10,000 sheep from Martha's Vineyard (Banks 1911, vol. 1, 367–83). Approximately 4,000 animals were taken from Naushon, Nashawena, and Cuttyhunk, and many of these belonged to upper Cape and Dartmouth families who maintained herds on these islands (Emerson 1935). Sheep may also have been used to provision patriot forces. The effects of wartime activity on livestock holdings in the area were significant. Sufficient increase among the sheep holdings to offset these losses, by natural population growth, could not have occurred during the sampling period and are a major cause of the variation in the size of the herds of sheep depicted in figure 13.2

The decrease in livestock holdings on the outer Cape was paralleled by a change in agriculture. Crops of corn and rye dropped from levels of 31% and 27% respectively to a nominal 8%. Wheat, oats, barley, beans, turnips, potatoes, and flax disappeared. The only increase seen was in the number of orchards, which grew from 4% to 13% representation in the inventories by the last quarter of the eighteenth century (Table 13.11).

In summary, we have considered two regions of the Cape that were similar in many ways at the beginning of the eighteenth century, and have seen that evidence in the probate inventories records an alteration in the use of land-based resources, with these decreasing on the outer Cape, increasing on the upper Cape in terms of corn production, and otherwise remaining relatively stable for other elements in their system of diversified agriculture. The pivotal phase occurs in the second and third quarters of the eighteenth century, and a decade-by-decade breakdown of the inventory data would probably pinpoint it precisely. Whether or not the decrease is a result of the depletion of the fragile soils that overlay the outer Cape peninsula, causing destructive erosion and a subsequent decline in agricultural productivity, or whether it results from a scheduling conflict with maritime pursuits, is not yet clear.

The clues in historical texts are suggestive. A seventeenth-century description of whaling brings the question of seasonality to the forefront in the statement by an anonymous Cape inhabitant that 'all or most of us are concerned in fitting out boats to catch and take whales when *ye season of ye year serves*' (cited in Clark 1887c, 27). Conflict in scheduling is implied in Whitman's 1794 observation that Wellfleet men, engrossed in navigation, would be able to create gardens were their attention not otherwise diverted (*CMHS*, 3, 117–25). Differences in the care of land resources are suggested in Dwight's 1821 journal entry noting the melancholy cornfields

Table 13.11 *Crops shown on outer Cape and upper Cape probate inventories, 1700–1800*

	Outer Cape						Upper Cape					
	1700–49		1750–74		1775–1800		1700–49		1750–74		1775–79	
Crop	Freq.	%	Freq.	%	Freq.	%	Freq.	%	Freq.	%	Freq.	%
Corn	8	31	5	21	2	8	5	20	6	19	12	34
Rye	7	27	6	25	2	8	2	8	2	6	4	11
Wheat	5	19	1	4	0		0		0		3	9
Oats	3	11	0		0		2	8	2	6	2	6
Barley	0		0		0		2	8	0		0	
Hay	5	23	1	4	2	8	4	16	3	10	7	20
Beans, turnips, potatoes	2	8	2	8	0		2	8	5	19	6	18
Flax	4	15	4	16	0		7	28	4	13	7	20
Orchards	1	4	4	16	3	13	1	4	0		1	3

of Truro, the fences unable to protect against cattle, the forsaken air that clung to the Truro fields, while noting that these lands are said in ancient times to have produced fifty bushels of maize to the acre and from fifteen to twenty bushels of wheat' (1821, 59). This theme is continued further.

Henry Kittredge in *Cape Cod: People and Their History* (1930), wrote about Provincetown, 'from the earliest times the inhabitants, following the example of visiting fishermen, fell upon the trees, turned their cattle loose to graze on what clumps of vegetation still struggled for existence on the denuded hills, with the result that the grass was demolished as fast as it grew'. John Hay in *The Great Beach* also quotes another unnamed gentleman who noted that while a law passed in 1739 'forbade the pasturing of cattle on the sand hills, the Court might as well have forbidden the winds to blow or the sun to shine' (1963, 38). By the late nineteenth century, when Henry David Thoreau visited the area he was 'surprised to hear of the great crops of corn which are raised in Eastham, notwithstanding the real and apparent barrenness', and he quoted a man who described the Chatham soil in the *Collections of the Massachusetts Historical Society* for 1802 (series 1, vol. 8, 145) as doubtful 'because it would not be observed by every eye, and perhaps not acknowledged by many'. Thoreau concluded that 'all an inlander's notion of soil and fertility will be confounded by a visit to these parts and he will not be able, for some time afterward, to distinguish soil from sand' (1849–57, 46).

The impetus that destroyed the soil could have been agricultural in origin or maritime related. Farmers must have cleared land to plant and plow, but many of the trades related to maritime industries also needed extensive supplies of lumber. This also effected deforestation. Further work is needed to clarify whether it was agricultural activities or maritime resource requirements that led to extreme deforestation on the outer Cape. Still, no matter what their original objective was, the fact that outer Cape men had paid little regard to the fragile nature of the original Cape ecosystem leaves little doubt that this did affect in some way the

dependence on the resources of the sea that the outer Cape families adopted and that this, in turn, distinguished them from the families living on the upper reaches of the peninsula, close to the mainland. This may be why the inventories also show that the wealth possessed, on the average, by upper Cape families was greater than that of most outer Cape households. But, paradoxically, the inventory analysis also reveals that maritime implements do not appear over time among the outer Cape inventories; they disappear. Even as the blackfish disappeared from Cape Cod waters in 1737, 1738, and 1739, maritime tools of the trade disappeared from outer Cape inventories (see fig. 13.3).

It is likely that this was a result of alterations in work patterns that arose as the labor economy shifted its base with emerging capitalism, and reflects this as much as it reflects the shift from coastal to oceanic fishing grounds as Cape Cod men followed the whales north to Arctic waters and the Davis Straits. Equally interesting is the interdependence among households characteristic of a folk tradition that can be seen within the elements of the maritime cluster, and the way this and other elements of the folk classification system used in the inventories yielded information on ways people perceived their world and divided it into manageable units. What appear in this portion of the analysis are clues to the distinctive shape of pre-industrial society in the New World that rested on a world view or belief system that also disappeared, on a world view embedded in Richard Mather's 1635 description of 'mighty fishes rolling and tumbling in the waters, twice as long and as big as an ox' (Clark 1887c, 26).

13.7 The emic quality of probate inventories

Although mention has been made of the need to interpret the meaning of an object by placing it within the social matrix in which it functioned, this has not been emphasized. The analysis presented here has concentrated on observations derived from the use of a lexical grid, but up to this point the use of the grid has been etic. The analysis, in other words, has been etic, yet

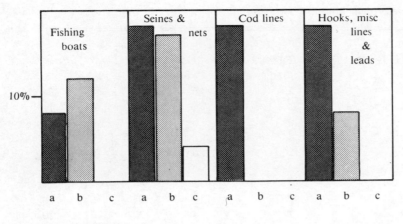

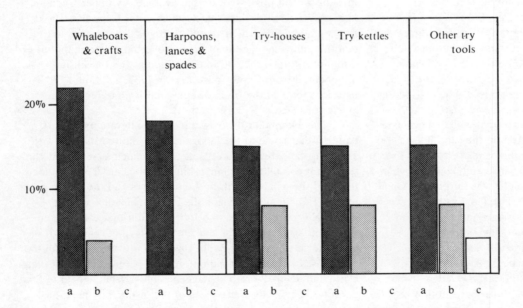

Fig. 13.3. Percentage frequency of entries pertaining to fishing and whaling implements as shown on probate inventories filed for residents of Truro and Provincetown, 1700–1800

the kind of information conveyed in probate inventories can be broadly described as falling into both etic and emic categories.

Etic analysis is, in fact, an appropriate way to describe most of the analysis done to date with probate inventories. Beaudry's 1980 doctoral dissertation and her research leading up to it are notable exceptions (Beaudry 1978a, 1978b, 1979, 1980). In etic analysis, probate inventories are used to explicate theories developed by quantitatively based economic historians; the inquiry centers on supposedly objective attributes of the objects listed in the documents. The focus is not the intrinsic

relationships that the objects held for people of the seventeenth and eighteenth centuries.

Yet there are two levels of analysis that enable one to interpret material culture, whether observations are derived archaeologically by excavation of historical sites or whether these are procured through an analysis of documentary materials. These are the etic and emic levels, and they should be kept analytically distinct. The terms are drawn from linguistics and more specifically from the terms *phonetic* and *phonemic*. *Phonetic* refers to all the possible sounds that humans can make, and the list is rather long. *Phonemic* refers to all the meaningful sounds that form elements of any given language, and, for any given language the list, while varying with reference to the potential sounds available in the phonetic list, is limited. Emic analysis thus refers to an interpretation that considers things in terms of their meaning to the people who use them (Pike 1954).

Etic classifications useful in archaeology are those that distinguish one soil type from another or one ceramic type from another. They represent discriminations imposed by an observer amongst a variety of data that permit one to classify information into usable categories. As such they are essential. They are analogous to the word clusters used in the lexical grid. The clusters, or assemblages or objects, observed in the inventories could be used to analyze the material culture of any society such as the maritime Chuckchi, the Vikings, or the Northwest Coast Indians. Because the grid is lexical, however, it has further implications for the recovery of knowledge about material objects from another time that relate to emic analysis.

The emic quality inherent within the inventories also conveys information about the subsistence orientation of households on the Cape. Shifting from a consideration of inventories as etic evidence about material objects and what objects reveal about culture, it is equally insightful to look at inventories and the words they contain in a slightly different way, to place them under an emic grid. What changes is not the word clusters, or lexical grid, but the focus.

Inventories contain lists of objects, but they are also documents created from words. And, since the grid is lexical, its categories are drawn from the semantic system of the seventeenth and eighteenth centuries, representing a series of folk classifications or discriminations. In other words, the grid contains an emic perspective that is drawn directly from the eighteenth century, a time when word meaning could be very different from the meaning we associate with the same word today.

The way pre-modern people used and structured their language, or the words they used in the probate inventories, reveals more about the eighteenth-century world than appears if the words are taken at face value as equivalent to those in use today. The words in the inventories are residual pieces of a bygone world-in-action in which they played a major role, providing classificatory schemes that were the basis for and one means of organizing the cultural categories used to structure the eighteenth-century English world. As Englishmen transplanted into another world with a differing environment containing strange and new flora and fauna, people had to name these things. In England, the word *corn* signified any grain. In the New World, maize also grew and was grown, in fact, by the Wampanoag and Mashpee Indians whose territorial lands encompassed Cape Cod. As Englishmen learned to cultivate this Indian plant, they renamed it, making it familiar by incorporating its essence (i.e., its Indian origin and its similarity to English grains) in the label *Indian corn*. All of the early

probate inventories invariably specify *Indian corn* when referring to maize.

Sometimes it is difficult to assess the composition of livestock holdings in terms of the etic grid because domestic animals could also be listed simply as 'the beasts' or 'the creatures'. Today, hearing these particular words, one would more quickly place the beasts and creatures deep in the forest and consider them as a wild resource. The question that arises is how were words selected? Why were domesticated, barnyard animals called beasts and creatures?

The inventory taker, in viewing an object and writing down an appropriate term for it, scanned the possibilities inherent in his day-to-day language, and chose an appropriate word. Occasionally his purpose was to make things appear less valuable, or, when a stranger died in town, the purpose could become a listing of every single item so that these could be distributed through the community as payment for the villagers' time and effort in caring for the stranger in his sickness, for digging the grave, and for celebrating the funeral. The inventory of Moses Bartlett reveals that his sea chest was broken open and his goods distributed (Plymouth Colony, *Probate Records*, 1678, vol. 4(1), f.7), for the inventory taker carefully noted who had the drawers and who possessed the gloves. Captain Forster's possessions, listed in minute detail, were used to pay the Widow Eldredge for entertaining the man and his servants, while Elisha Hedge was paid for his 'trouble and charge' of both the captain and his servants during Forster's illness and subsequent death (Barnstable County, *Probate Records*, vol. 1, 1–2).

The manipulation of terminology for items listed on an inventory represents a decision made by the inventory taker that situated the objects described within a culturally construed field of meaning. The words the inventory taker chose created a folk classification of the objects in his text identical to that which he used in everyday activities. And, in the values ascribed to certain objects, there was also a hierarchical taxonomy presented. Folk taxonomies and classification systems are emic. They relate directly to the schemes used by people as they interact with one another to represent reality, sustaining and providing cultural categories that organize reality.

Within this language, the inventory takers marked (or set off) categories of special significance. For example, their terms 'livestock', 'beasts', 'creatures' and, to a lesser extent, 'cattle', are unmarked terms. They are categories that can include horses, sheep, swine, bulls, calves, or lambs. In contemporary use, the term *man* is unmarked, for it can stand for men, women, and children alike. Marked terms make more fine-grained discriminations than do the unmarked terms.

This is clearly revealed when one looks at the unmarked term 'cattle' that was used, especially in the mid-eighteenth century on the outer Cape, as a lumping category (see also Brown, ch. 7, above). What kinds of cattle were there? First, drawing on terminology defined through reference to the *Oxford English Dictionary*, there were cows (female bovines) that have reproduced) and heifers (female bovines capable of reproducing but that have not yet given birth) and farrow cows (no longer able to give birth). There were calves (young, uncastrated male bovines), steers (castrated male bovines), oxen (castrated male bovines aged eight years or more) and bulls (uncastrated male bovines). Each word represented a different and specific term for an animal that could be subsumed under the more general, unmarked term *neat cattle*. A similar taxonomic scheme that discriminated among animals based both on age and reproductive capabilities was used to distinguish among the sheep (rams, wethers, ewes, lambs, yearlings, shearlings), the goats, the swine, and the horses, although in this latter group other elements that related to speed were also introduced (see Leach 1966, Beaudry 1980).

On the outer Cape unmarked terms were the norm for livestock, but on the upper Cape men used marked terms even to the point of designating which cows were farrow. This discloses in a way that parallels and strengthens the interpretation gained from a count of the raw numbers of animals present that a farming orientation dominated the community. On the other hand, on the outer Cape the marked terms were used for maritime implements: herring net, oyster rake, mackerel seine, whale lamp, etc. These marked terms did not appear among the upper Cape inventories. Instead more general labels such as *fish net* would be recorded.

Linguists generally agree that where language differs, it represents differences in thought (Eastman 1975). Language is responsive to communication needs, and where the need increases or a great focal emphasis surfaces for a cultural unit, one can expect to find more language differentiation. The fine-grained terminology used in listing maritime implements displays the focal orientation of the outer Cape communities towards the sea, whereas on the upper Cape the fine-grained terminology exists in relation to livestock. It is likely that in the southern colonies, after slavery became focal, one would encounter the use of fine-grained terms used in the lists of slaves appraised in the inventories. These shifts result from specializations developed as part of the subsistence pattern that evolved in each region. The fact that similar classification systems were used to describe taxable land, on the other hand, indicates a shared set of assumptions.

The words used in the inventories to describe livestock provided access to information about the meaning of farming and its deep-seated role in the culture. Agricultural terms were not limited to descriptions of livestock in probate inventories, but were extended to become metaphors describing resources found in the world of the sea, thus linking it with the land. The whales that men from Truro hunted off the New England coast were called by names agricultural in origin: the cachalot, or sperm whales, were divided according to a representation that consisted of male whales, or bulls, female whales, or cows, and young whales, or calves. A Nantucket Islander purportedly looked out to sea in 1690 from Folly Hill at a spouting whale, and with uncanny foresight stated, 'there is the green pasture in which our childrens' grandchildren will find their bread' (Macy

1835, 33). Further extending the idea of sea as pasture was the presence in Nantucket and Vineyard Sound of shoals and reefs named for barnyard animals (e.g., sow and pigs reef, hen and chickens reef, etc.). This was done through a folk taxonomy in which classificatory terms used in agriculture were also utilized to describe marine life, i.e., the nomenclature of the land and its farms was imprinted on the oceans.

13.8 Reciprocity and shared resources

One of the primary characteristics of pre-industrial society is the material basis on which reciprocal systems operate. Goods and services were exchanged in lieu of money and circulated among the community in a reciprocal system of shared responsibility. There are hints of this in a 1753 vote at the Truro town meeting that, 'if any person shall take a boy under 10 years old to drive blackfish or porpoises, he or they shall have nothing allowed for the boy; and that when any black-fish or porpoise shall be driven ashore and killed by any number of boats of the inhabitants of this town, if one man or more shall insist on having the fish divided to each boat, it shall be done' (Freeman 1858, vol. 2, 556). Whaling was a communal enterprise undertaken initially in the late summer and early fall. Proceeds were divided according to a system of shares; marks of ownership akin to marks on domestic animals allowed to roam free were recorded and used (cf. Clark 1887c); whale cutters and whale viewers were appointed as town officials.

The communal quality of early whaling appears clearly when one looks at the distribution throughout the community of the implements that formed the maritime cluster. No individual possessed the complete assemblage of tools necessary to catch and kill the whale and to process its blubber. One person alone could not accomplish the task proficiently and groups of men are invariably shown in artists' depictions of the process (see figs. 13.4 and 13.5). Nor could one individual or even one household take the risk involved in the outlay of equipment. Furthermore, the danger involved in this pursuit was mitigated by community involvement and shared responsibility.

During the later summer months, when squid were present and the mackerel schools were plentiful, came the season when the blackfish appeared in Cape Cod Bay; men kept watch over the shimmering water for the first telltale glimpse of the herd and for sightings of right whales. Whaleboats, light craft manned by five to seven men, were on the beaches ready to launch. The harpoons or whale irons used to fasten the whale to the line were kept handy as were the lances, similar in appearance to an eel spear, that men plunged into the whale to kill it. Men held shares or portions in the whaleboats. Entries that read '1/6 of one whaleboat and oars' were commonplace, although some might own as much as a half a craft. The tools, however, were owned on an individual basis. The task was to either kill the whale and tow it ashore or in the case of porpoises and blackfish, to herd or drive them into the shallow waters, to strand them on the beaches and sandflats as the tide ebbed (see fig. 13.5). There the animals

197. HENDRICK GOLTZIUS: *The Whale.* 1598. Haarlem, Teyler's Stichting

Fig. 13.4. A woodcut by Hendrick Goltzius of 1598 showing a beached whale and preparations for procuring its oil (Haarlem, Texler's stichting).

were slaughtered; every able-bodied man and boy participated. The outgoing tide washed away the blood and swept the surviving mammals back to sea.

The next step was to peel the whale blubber from the body with a whale spade, to cut the blubber into small pieces (five inches by twelve to eighteen inches) termed horse pieces, and then to mince it with a tool similar to a scythe. The then 'lean whale' was left on the beach to rot while its blubber was placed in large kettlers, or coppers, where the oil was 'tried' from the blubber by boiling for several hours. Afterward the oil was cooled and stored in wooden casks (Macy 1835). These tasks too possessed potential danger. Nathaniel Harding Atkins fainted and died at age eight-four in Truro in 1741 by falling into one of the large kettles 'of boiling, hot oyle and was scalded in a most miserable manner' (*Boston Newsletter* 23 July 1741) leaving his heirs 'all his right in tryhouse kettles, coolens and mauliping tools' (Barnstable County, *Probate Records*, vol. 5, 64). The danger was shared as were the tools. Fred Lumbert possessed a try kettle and trying instruments (ibid., 311) while Richard Rich owned four (ibid., vol. 6, 332). Thomas Paine, Esquire, owned the whalehouse lot (ibid.,

vol. 4, 10–11) while Nathaniel Atkins claimed the whalehouse itself (ibid., vol. 5, 165). Other men possessed the carts and oxen used to transport the blubber from beach to tryhouse, or held shares in the schooners that took it to the Boston markets.

Men thus shared the investment required to fund this labor-intensive folk industry by dividing the tools among a number of families and by allocating the profits to individuals based on their participation in the activity itself in terms of skill required and resources possessed.

The industry was not dependable and this too was probably a factor in the shared base of personnel and resources on which it developed. Men knew only the season when the squid and whales appeared in Cape Cod waters; oral tradition upholds this unpredictable or catch-as-catch-can quality to the venture in tales of church congregations dismissed during sermons at the sight of a whale offshore (Clark 1887a, 295; Kittredge 1937, 174). In a form of community tithe, some towns even voted the minister his share in the profits from whales (Thoreau 1849–57, 54). The fact that the clergy received shares in the venture testifies to the multi-stranded penetration of the activity into the fabric of town life on the outer Cape and

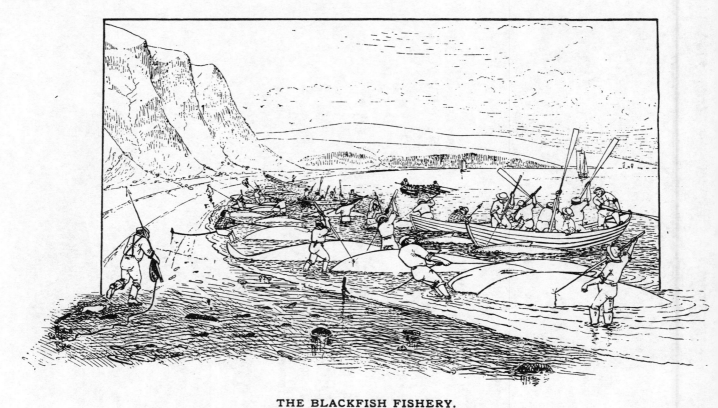

THE BLACKFISH FISHERY.

The capture of a school of blackfish in Cape Cod Bay. (Sect. v, vol. ii, pp. 295, 307.)

Drawing by H. W. Elliott, from a sketch by J. S. Ryder.

Fig. 13.5. Sketch of the nineteenth-century practice of driving blackfish ashore to procure their oil as done at Cape Cod, Massachusetts. Reprinted from *The Fishes and Fisheries Industry of the United States*, vol. 5

at Nantucket. This penetration was mirrored in the dispersed holdings of whaling-related gear found in the probate inventories of the men living on the outer Cape.

A similar mode of production structured the fishing industry, although it took into account habits of specific genera of fish. Fishing nets and seines for bass, herring, and mackerel were owned communally. This stood in sharp contrast to fish hooks, cod lines, and leads, which were individually owned. A description of the behavior involved in seining and cod fishing explains the different patterns of ownership and also makes clear the point that much of what we need to comprehend, even in something as simple as an entry in an inventory, is information pertaining to the background, or social matrix, of an object that forms the context in which it exists. It is difficult to extricate even as small a thing as a fish hook from the matrix of its social world and then find its meaning, for the meaning exists in the informing context of culture. This is conveyed in nineteenth-century sketches of fishing techniques analogous to those of the eighteenth century (see figs. 13.6 and 13.7).

Seines were large nets, often hand-knit by the village women. These were dropped into the water and dragged in towards the boat in such a way that the open portion gradually narrowed and shut, enclosing a large number of fish. Several tons of fish might be caught in one haul (Clark 1887b). The

labor required for this undertaking was considerable. The technique was such that no one individual could be given credit for catching a particular fish. Men were allotted shares in the haul; seines were owned on a communal basis. George Whitford had one-half of a bass net and one-half of a mackerel net at his death in 1730 (Barnstable County, *Probate Records*, vol. 5, 131–2).

Cod fishing, on the other hand, was done off boats by men who worked in shifts (Clark 1887b). One group of men would fish from the side of the boat while the second group dressed the cod already aboard. It was possible to count the fish hooked by a fisherman. The local practice was to pay each man on the basis of the amount of fish caught. Given this social matrix, or informing social context, it is not unreasonable to find that while seines and nets were shared among a group of households, hooks, lines, and leads were the possession of particular individuals. And, when Christopher Strout died in 1715, the inventory taker noted the presence of an old cod line worth two shillings, six pence (ibid., vol. 3, 243).

As illustrated earlier in figure 13.3, the maritime emphasis revealed in the inventories of households located on the outer Cape sharply decreases from 1750 to 1800. The change may be explained by the shift to an off-shore fishery in the 1730s resulting from the depletion of the alongshore whale

THE MENHADEN FISHERY.

Haul-seine fishing at Long Island, 1790 to 1850; taking out the fish.   (Sect. v, vol. i, pp. 341, 368, 371.)

From sketch by Capt. B. F. Conklin.

Fig. 13.6. Sketch of men seining for menhaden in the nineteenth century. Reprinted from *The Fishes and Fisheries Industry of the United States*, vol. 5

THE BANK HAND-LINE COD FISHERY.

Hand-line dory cod fishing on the Grand Bank.   (Sect. v, vol. i, p. 126.)

Drawing by H. W. Elliott and Capt. J. W. Collins.

Fig. 13.7. Men in individual boats surrounding a mother ship and fishing for cod in the waters off New England in the nineteenth century. Reprinted from *The Fishes and Fisheries Industry of the United States*, vol. 5

fishery as the herds of right whales, diminished by overkillings, no longer came into Cape Cod Bay. The disappearance of the blackfish in 1737 signalled the approach of this era; by the 1740s more than a dozen whaling vessels were outfitted in Provincetown for voyages to the Davis Straits. This, however, is only a partial explanation. Throughout the latter half of the eighteenth century and well into the nineteenth century, the probate records describe outer Cape men as mariners and seafarers. Their probate inventories contain few material possessions that would readily reveal that these men went to sea; many times the only indication is the designation of someone as a 'mariner' or 'seafaring man'. An occasional compass, navigational text, or sea chest are the primary material remains that provide clues to a continued maritime orientation.

There are many other historical documents that clearly and unequivocally state that the sea provided a living for outer Cape men. In fact, fishing remained a major industry into the twentieth century, and its history is well documented in *Reports of the U.S. Fisheries Commission* (see especially the reports for 1873 and 1887). Perhaps as the area of maritime use changed from alongshore to offshore oceanic waters, or when the summer fishing grounds in the North Atlantic began to attract Cape fishing vessels, the lifestyles of mariners became more transient, and it is this transient quality that is reflected in the few craft-related objects they owned at death.

Equally responsible, however, was a change in the broader economic system that affected the outer Cape region. The era when maritime implements disappear from the inventories also coincides with the period when gravestone motifs on the gravestones in cemeteries of outer Cape communities changed from motifs produced by folk craftsmen residing in Plymouth to a pattern identified as originating in urban Boston (Deetz 1968). Families on the Cape did not begin to purchase goods in Boston solely because it was more fashionable to do so; it is more likely that marketing ties relating to the fishing industry shifted their locus. Urbanization, even in fragmentary form, began to affect the outer reaches of the Cape.

One hypothesis would be that as this happened outer Cape men became part of an economic system in which major capital investments were made by entrepreneurs residing outside the local Cape community. The older, kin-based system was transformed. Seamen began to move in a social field along lines of friendship and by utilizing technical knowledge, the traditional kin-based matrix shrank. Men sought individual economic advancement, and while they still worked in crews, the membership of these crews did not necessarily persist over time nor was it fixed or based on kin ties. As this happened, it is possible that opportunity for upward social mobility decreased, and this in turn may be reflected in household contents; at the same time, with control of the industry in the hands of a few wealthy individuals, there was no need for the workers to own technical implements. In other words, the men on the outer Cape lost the communal shape of life, based on

Table 13.12 *Frequency of inventory entries revealing patterning in maritime possessions*

	Ship's gear	Vessel shares	Navigational devices	Fishing equipment	Whaling implements
Upper Cape					
1700–24 (n=3)	0	1	0	0	0
1725–49 (n=22)	1	2	1	3	1
1750–74 (n=31)	3	9	2	1	2
1775–1800 (n=35)	1	5	1	2	0
Outer Cape					
1700–24 (n=4)	1	1	1	3	4
1725–49 (n=21)	2	2	6	10	11
1750–74 (n=25)	1	1	0	6	2
1775–1800 (n=25)	1	1	1	1	1

village reciprocity, echoed in inventories listing one-half of a bass seine, a part of a cow, a portion of the mainsails, one-sixth of a whaleboat or one-third of a mortising ax (see table 13.12).

That the lives of outer Cape men differed from those of the men who lived on the upper Cape is suggested by the inventory data. The method of analysis contained two steps: one for establishing similarities and differences on a broad scale and one for investigating at a more microscopic level those clusters that seemed equivalent. Table 13.12 gives the frequency of inventory entries for maritime-related items owned by households in both regions of the Cape and shows that households in both areas used the sea as a resource base, but it also indicates differences in the way they did so over time. There were differences in the strategies people adopted for securing material wealth from the ocean waters surrounding Cape Cod.

The sea has been described in terms of four separate foci visible in eighteenth-century maritime activity. These include the alongshore fisheries; men who utilizes this domain spend their day at sea, but return to shore and to their homes each night. The men who utilize offshore fisheries such as George's Bank go to sea for longer periods of time. Whalers, for example, in the second quarter of the eighteenth century, claimed this domain as their own, spending up to six weeks at sea in forty- to fifty-ton schooners and sloops. The deep water mariners sailed international waters and were part, at a very personal level, of a broad-based Atlantic economy spanning the world's oceans. By the end of the eighteenth century, men on whaling ships sailed to the coast of Brazil and further south (Macy 1835). The participation of Truro men in this type of maritime venture can be seen in their death records on homeward voyages from Spain, Senegal, Sweden, Russia, and the northwest coast of America (Treat 1891).

The remaining maritime domain was that of the coastal trader who might work the waters in the immediate vicinity of his home harbor, but who was equally apt to be found anywhere along the eastern seaboard and in the Caribbean, carrying cargo as fragile as eggs or as durable as pine boards. A closer look at the Falmouth inventories shows that there were few possessions that related to whaling or to cooperative seining for fish. In a series of lectures, C. W. Jenkins (1899) told of Falmouth men who spent winters in the Carolinas and along the Georgia coast procuring lumber that they then sold in New England come spring, carrying south with them in the fall other goods to sell or trade. In 1802, there were some thirty Falmouth vessels involved in this type of coastal trade. And it is this kind of maritime venture, in all its minute detail, that is revealed in the contents they possessed at death: traders' stocks, provisions, and shares in sloops. These possessions stand out in the Falmouth men's inventories. Names of vessels in the inventories as, for example, the *Two Brothers*, recall the shared quality of these ventures, and this is coded into local Cape lore. Captain Charles Davis, of Falmouth, while talking of what he had been told, asked if I had seen any evidence of the practice whereby 'old boys would get together and finance a voyage' (Yentsch 1974b).

To trade one must possess a surplus of some kind, something that can be bartered or sold for cash. Here perhaps the more stable farming environment and economy that formed the subsistence base for the upper Cape community was a crucial element, enabling successive generations of men to build up small surpluses that they could then risk in an 'adventure in the venture'. The things they sold, the sugar, coffee, chocolate, wooden bowls, deerskins, wool, butter, and cheese, do not seem the things of which fortunes were made. Out of these small beginnings, visible in inventory contents of upper Cape men as early as 1672, when Nicholas Davis, trader of Barnstable and Newport, died at sea, grew larger and larger commercial ventures reaching eventually to the China seas. Merchants and mariners, they were never as wealthy as the men of Boston, Salem, and Newport who owned fleets of ships. Yet neither did they ever suffer the massive losses of kith and kin at sea that periodically devastated the outer Cape towns well into the nineteenth century.

13.9 Conclusion

There is a thread throughout this chapter present from its first inception that hovers around the question of a rhythm to life, dictated not by man or culture, but suggested by nature. This is the question of seasonality, and the conflict imposed by the requirements of agricultural activities and the rhythm of life in the sea. There is a complexity to maritime commerce. Oceanic resources are never certain; their time of arrival never predictable. Yet with the spring and the gradual warming of ocean waters, herring enter the streams to spawn, the mackerel rise from their winter abode, the striped bass and bluefish move northward following a temperature gradient to their summer feeding grounds. The winter ocean comes alive, teeming with life that possesses a rhythm of its own, creating scheduling conflicts with the farmers' needs to plant crops, hoe, weed, and harvest.

While the cod fishery in Massachusetts Bay was a winter activity, and the herring were caught in the late fall (October to December), the other marine resources were most available in the spring, summer, and early fall. Bass were caught from May to November. The offshore whales were in northern waters during this period as well. Schools of mackerel arrived in the spring, becoming more abundant in the late summer. The blackfish came in July and left in late November or early December. Lobsters were most plentiful in spring and early summer. The swordfish reached northern waters in July and August. Thus the ecological system of Massachusetts Bay had a timetable that could be useful in understanding the sequence of subsistence change on the outer Cape.

The scheduling conflict was solved in two ways by eighteenth-century Cape and Island residents and solved in such a way that maritime pursuits achieved dominance. One strategy proceeded along age-ranked lines. First, from the age of twelve to fourteen, able-bodied men went to sea until they were forty-five to fifty years old. Second, young men under twelve, certainly those under ten, and those over fifty, stayed home to work the land. There is evidence of this in the different descriptions of Cape Cod communities printed in the *Collections of the Massachusetts Historical Society* in the late eighteenth and early nineteenth centuries.

A second strategy consisted of altering the traditional agricultural complex of activities so that those given priority were agricultural activities that required less attention, particularly less skilled attention, during critical periods of the year, especially the months of late spring, summer, and early fall. This involved the inclusion of extensive pastoral husbandry into the regional subsistence base wherever local resources permitted. It also included planting crops that were not labor intensive and, in addition, limiting the hoeing and weeding that would have maintained a higher yield of productivity. In turn, the land was left fallow for longer periods than was the norm elsewhere. One can see the contrast in a description of Truro agricultural practices that reveals:

> The soil in every part of the town is continually depreciating, little pains being taken to manure it. Not much attention is paid to agriculture ... The method of tilling the land is this: After ploughing, it is planted with Indian corn in the spring, and in July is sowed with rye. The hillocks formed by the hoe are left unbroken, and the land lies uncultivated six or seven years, at the end of which it goes through the same course of cultivation.
>
> (*CMHS*, 1974, series 1, vol. 4, 195–203)

This was a lazy, pragmatic form of agriculture that contrasted sharply with practices elsewhere in New England and in Great Britain (Bidwell and Falconer 1925; Russell 1976; Thirsk 1967).

Also included in this strategy was a diminished concentration on animal husbandry that required skilled, male labor. Certainly a few dairy cattle, several cows and a heifer, continued as essential elements of the subsistence activities of many households, but these were animals that were primarily kept and cared for by women. Swine, in parts of townships where they could be left to forage, were still raised. Herds of grazing sheep, which required the care of men and a more extensive support technology than swine, became less prevalent on the outer Cape. There was a concomitant lessening of spinning and weaving activities by women in the outer Cape homes.

In fact, in a society where most able-bodied men were at sea for large portions of the year, the requirements on women for working the land and raising animals to maintain a subsistence level of production may have served as a deterrent to the pursuit of other, domestic activities.

Thus one begins to see a picture of the interrelatedness of the past emerge from an anthropological analysis of probate inventories that emphasizes the reciprocity between man and nature, between man, woman, and child, between young and old. The oral tradition of farming communities replaced by maritime communities as the soil became depleted is not confirmed by this analysis. There are hints that men used the sea from the onset of settlement on the Cape. It might be more accurate to think of the Cape's subsistence base as primarily agricultural yet supplemented by communal fishing and shared resources, replaced by a maritime resource base complemented, in turn, by particular farming activities and a limited use of other wildlife resources. The relationship between colonial culture and the Cape habitat is not precisely defined, for it is intricate; its parameters are merely suggested by the inventory entries. These could be further defined using additional archaeological and historical sources.

In conclusion, while inland visitors such as Dwight and Thoreau implied that the farming practices of Cape Codders were strange, the complex picture that emerged began to fall into place when a holistic view was imposed. Initially Cape Cod households participated in a subsistence system that used the sea's resources for food and transportation, that used the land's resources in numerous age-old English ways, and that even drew on the interface between land and sea, on the salt marshes and tidal flats, for support. Cape Cod men were farmers, fishermen, and whalers. Notwithstanding the fact that they did not fully understand ecological relationships, cutting wood from forests that covered the sand dunes, leaving the sand free to blow and drift across more fertile fields and marshes, these men and their families used whatever perceived natural resources were at hand for sustenance, creating differences as they did so between outer and upper Cape families. The evidence for these subtle differences in lifestyle is contained in the interrelationships that exist among inventory entries, encoded in the words inventories contain, words that link objects to activities pursued in daily life, revealing American folk perceptions of land and sea.

Notes

1. Versions of this chapter were presented in 1977 at the 10th Annual Conference of the Society for Historical Archaeology, January 5–7, Ottawa, Canada, and at the 1977 meetings of the Northeastern Anthropological Association, Providence, Rhode Island. Robert Jay, A. D. Van Nostrand, James Deetz, Captain Charles Davis, Mary C. Beaudry, and Larry McKee provided helpful comments and criticisms.
2. There are a number of good histories of both individual towns and of the Cape Cod region itself. Freeman (1858) is one such history. Some of the earlier topographic descriptions are contained in the *Collections of the Massachusetts Historical Society*, series 1. Vol. 3 contains reports on Barnstable (pp. 12–17), Wellfleet (pp. 117–25), Nantucket (pp. 153–61), and Truro (pp. 119–26). Volume 8 covers the remainder of Cape with Sandwich (pp. 119–26), Falmouth (pp. 127–8), Dennis (pp. 129–31), Yarmouth and the south side of Barnstable (p. 141), Chatham (pp. 142–53), Eastham (pp. 154–95), Wellfleet and Truro (pp. 196–201). Yentsch *et al.* (1967) provide a comprehensive bibliography of scientific work on the region.

Chapter 14

Seasonality: an agricultural construct

Joanne Bowen

It is argued that faunal analysis in historical archaeology must draw upon a thorough familiarity with the primary document record in order to develop models of seasonality that, rather than being drawn from prehistory, are based upon the agricultural cycles and market networks characteristic of historical cultures. In this study, account books and other documents are used to reconstruct the exchange networks for meat products within the late eighteenth-century rural agricultural community of Suffield, Connecticut. The findings challenge the prevalent view of New England farming communities and their ties to external markets as well as many of the interpretations made by archaeologists about the significance of faunal remains excavated from historical sites.

As the most frequently occurring evidence of past subsistence systems, faunal remains have played a crucial role in archaeological research in determining the unconscious and deliberate subsistence strategies of mankind (Lyman 1982, 331; Monks 1981, 177–85; Kohl 1981, 101). While the connection is perhaps not obvious at first glance, through attention to regional food procurement systems the study of settlement patterns has increased interest in studying subsistence.

Faunal analysis has provided the crucial data for determining seasonality, that is, determining the time of year at which various animal and plant resources were most abundant. By identifying seasonal patterning in the relative proportions of animals, in the presence or absence of certain animals, and seasonal characteristics like the annual growth rings in fish earbones and scales, we have come to understand much about prehistoric cultures, their environmental adaptation, and their cyclical movements as they 'harvested' seasonally abundant resources.

While seasonality studies have become commonplace in prehistory, efforts in historical archaeology have been minimal. For various reasons, archaeologists have failed to deal with seasonality as a significant factor in historical subsistence systems. A major factor is that seasonality has traditionally been determined on the basis of wild animal and plant remains recovered from archaeological sites. With historical sites there have been very few data to work with. Analysis of the faunal remains from New England historical sites has shown that wild food sources were rarely as important as domestic sources in the colonial diet. Even on frontier sites, people relied almost entirely on domestic foods. With this lack of data on historical seasonal patterns, faunal analysis in historical archaeology has focused on other problems, such as determining socio-economic status differences, butchering practices, dietary patterns, and to a much lesser extent, animal husbandry and marketing (Lyman 1982; Jolley 1983; Reitz and Honerkamp 1983).

Possibly an even more important reason is that the theoretical framework for seasonality lies conceptually within the prehistoric settlement pattern model, a model of a nomadic, non-sedentary society's adaptation to its environment, where the relatively small groups moved with the seasons to harvest the changing abundant resources. Interpreting the importance of seasonal patterns among sedentary peoples has been a problem for historical archaeologists.

With this non-sedentary model being of such little value in explaining seasonal patterns, and with the reliance on wildlife to demonstrate seasonality, we have made very few attempts at studying seasonality. What efforts do exist are based solely on wildlife, but they clearly miss the importance of the environment and its seasonal cycles in a sedentary, agriculturally based society. With our modern methods of food preservation, we seem to have forgotten our relatively recent past, where seasonal factors had a crucial role in the availability, preservation, and consumption of food. The early American society was basically an agrarian one, one that dealt with the environment, climate, and natural resources through its culture, technology, and agriculture.

Without any viable theoretical framework, we have been left on our own to sift through our knowledge of more complex societies and our past. Looking closely at the assumptions in the faunal analyses from historical sites, it becomes obvious that they are remarkably similar to our own commonly held beliefs about the early American's means of subsistence and the effects of environmental constraints on agricultural life. Moreover, faunal analysts working with historical sites have often been ignorant of historical problems and documentary resources. Instead of conducting a systematic search of primary resources, many have relied on their cultural assumptions of what our past culture was like, supplemented with secondary sources, and projections of their own ethnocentric views onto past subsistence systems. Sadly, the rich data available in primary documentary sources have been mostly ignored. As a result the interpretation of subsistence and dietary patterns in historical North America has done little more than to support myths about our past.

The origin of these beliefs is subject to debate. One current notion is that in the late nineteenth century, authors wrote nostalgically about their past and their country's past. Some wrote about their childhood and some about stories related by their parents and grandparents. Over their lifetimes the Industrial Revolution had changed much of the substance of their lives. They looked back to a similar, but simpler, less complex version of their life. Underlying this view of the past were certain assumptions of the modern individual, responsible ultimately to himself. Farms were portrayed as independent entities and farmers were responsible for the family's food supply.

To describe such idealistic past images was, as the historian Carl Becker wrote, to build our conceptions of history partly out of our present needs and purposes, prepossessions, and prejudices, all of which enter into the process of knowing (Becker 1969, 188–9). A certain amount of self-reflection, a certain self-critical attitude towards our work, our models, and our data, can help us to distinguish between different ideas, beliefs, and those we ourselves may be imposing upon what we are studying.

One of the most persistent images of our past is of the independent, self-sufficient farmer. One of the most explicit statements was by Percy Bidwell, who wrote in 1916 about the colonial New England farmer:

> He and his family must have constituted very nearly an economic microcosm, a self-sufficient household economy, supplying their wants almost entirely by their own labor, except for occasional neighborly cooperation, and relying hardly at all on the exchange of products or services with outside communities.   (Bidwell 1916, 355)

In Bidwell's mind the farm and the farmer's source of food were synonymous.

The concept of self-sufficiency has three basic assumptions. The first assumes that a relatively equal wealth distribution existed in New England towns. Few were wealthy, few were very poor, and almost everyone could own land. Farmers, thus, could be self-sufficient, raising by themselves almost all of what they needed to subsist on. The second assumption holds that no class of agricultural laborers existed: thus, farm labor was scarce and costly. Farmers had to rely on their families for labor so they had no choice but to be independent. The third assumption rests on economic interpretations concerning trade and its effect on farming in the colonial period. Some assumed the market for farm products, except in a few places, was either on a very small scale, or very distant from the farmer. Incentives to raise more than his family needed to subsist, therefore, did not exist, and hence comes the term 'subsistence farmer' (Loehr 1952; Clark 1972; Lemon 1972).

The self-sufficiency model has been steadily criticized by historians, who have attacked that assumption of the lack of markets and incentive to produce surplus agricultural products.[1] Within the past decade, a few have begun to research rural exchange networks and to suggest self-sufficiency on a community – not individual – basis. But their work with agriculture and subsistence has only begun. Dietary and agricultural historians, as well as the archaeological community, have yet to benefit from that approach (Henretta 1978; Merrill 1977; Clark 1979; Gross 1976). Although dietary and agricultural historians have not paid much attention to seasonality, its effect on the availability of meat or consumption patterns, seasonality has formed an integral part of their notions concerning self-sufficiency and subsistence. Within seasonal constraints, a self-sufficient farmer had to raise enough animals and preserve the meat to somehow make the supply last the year for his own family, even if the diet was a monotonous one of salt pork supplemented by beef. Knowing that refrigeration did not exist until well into the nineteenth century, those historians assumed fresh meat was obtainable only during the slaughtering season and that the seasonal cycle existed only within the independent self-sufficient farm (Cummings 1940; Root and de Rochemont 1976; Russell 1976; Bidwell and Falconer 1925; Anderson 1971).

A study of the New Englander's agricultural cycle and agrarian economics, however, has revealed a very different

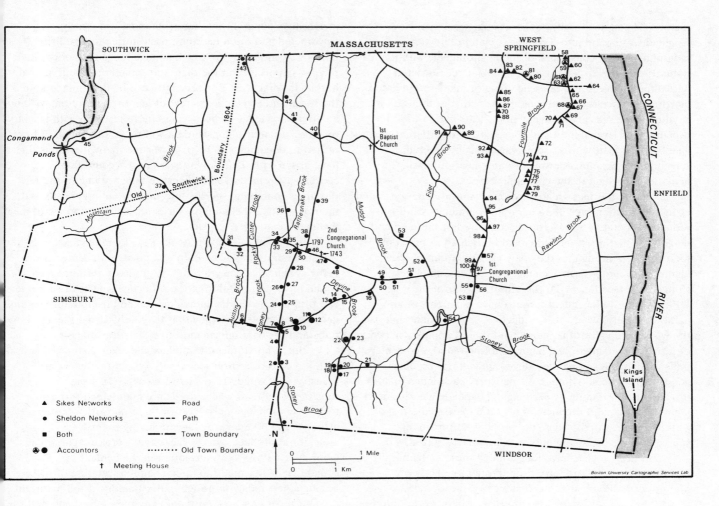

Fig. 14.1. Suffield, Connecticut: Sheldon and Sikes family networks, c. 1760–1800
Heads of Household and Documented Dates of Residence.

1. Benejah Owen ?–181?
2. Hezekiah Lewis, Sr. 1773–1805
3. Rufus Sheldon and Widow Rachel ?1767–1795
4. Aaron Lyon ?1781–1785
5. John Southwell 1750–1776
   Eleazer Rice 1780–1810
6. Phinehas Sheldon ?1743–1807
7. Ebenezer Phelps, Sr. 1782–1805
   Ebenezer Phelps, Jr. 1805–1808
8. Jonathan Sheldon II 1734–1761
   Jonathan Sheldon III 1761–1800
   Jonathan Sheldon IV ?–?1800
   Arastus Sheldon 1800–1835
9. Elijah Sheldon, Sr. 1737–1785
10. Martin Sheldon 1785–1848
11. Daniel Sheldon 1737–1795
    Jacob Sheldon 1780–1796
    ?Timothy Smith 1796–1802
12. Jonathan Sheldon I 1723–1769
    Gershom Sheldon 1769–91
    Ebenezer Sheldon 1791–1800
13. John Southwell 1777–1781
14. Medad Pomeroy 1767–1782
15. Cephas Harmon 1799–1810
16. Enoch Smith, Jr. 1808–1816
17. Oliver Granger 1766–1817
18. Widow Lucy Lacey 1772–1810
    Lizzardus Lacy 1795–?1809
    Jasper Lacy 1795–?1809
19. Joseph Kent Jr. ?1784–1824
20. John Hatheway ?1761–?1810
21. ?Thomas Huxley 1786–?1789
22. ?Enoch Smith 1771–1786
    Thomas Huxley 1786–1788
    Gustavus Austin 1788–1829
23. Caleb Austin 1754–1787
24. Hezekeiah Ingreham ?1800–1808
25. William Middleton 1766–1795
    Eliphalet Case 1792–1795
    Enos Ingreham 1795–1808
    ?Daniel Gillet 1810–1823
    Ebenezer Southwell 1810–1823

26. Josiah Coy 1797–1799
27. Elijah Sheldon Jr. 1761–1810
28. Ebenezer Wyman 1797–1817
29. Rev. John Graham 1753–1796
    ?Daniel Graham ?–1798
30. Daniel Hill 1789
    Eliphalet Case 1791–1793
    Ebenezer Wyman 1791–1795
    William Midleton ?
31. Israel Harmon 1792–?1831
32. Simeon Spencer 1781–1815
33. Jeremiah Ingreham Sr. & Jr. ?–1809
34. ? ditto
35. Thaddeus Taylor 1781–1841
36. Benjamin Denslow ?1782–1794
    ?Timothy Smith ?1796–1802
    Josiah Coy 1801–1815
37. Silas Phelps 1807–?1816
38. John Norton 1792–1813
39. Joseph Austin 1792–1804
40. Asa Warner 1795–1822
41. Samuel Warner ?1781–1792
42. Asher King Jr. ?–1800
43. ?Elijah Rising ?1788–?1794
44. Abner Bellamy 1772–1778
45. Anne Copley 1778–?1809
46. Dan Sheldon ?1799–1802
47. Amos Granger ?1773–?1806
48. Daniel Gillet 1787–1833
49. Phineas Harmon ?1764–1802
50. ?Asa Remington 1786–1800
51. ?Asa Remington 1783–1806
52. Joseph Harmon 1778–?1788
    Oliver Sheldon 1787–1821
53. Timothy Phelps 1790–1798
54. Gahazi Granger 1795–?1813
55. Oliver Phelps 1788–?1801
56. Seth Austin 1761–1806
57. Dr David Wilcocks 1777–?1787

NOTE: Road and homesite locations researched by Joanne Bowen. Resources: Suffield's Land, Probate, Tax, and Genealogical records; *Suffield Land History* by Delphina H. Clark; Lester Smith; and Robert Borg.

picture. The agriculturally based society of colonial New England was bound into a complex relationship with its environment; the constraints of the environment, with its natural resources of land, water, and climate, restricted agricultural choices and the scheduling of many food-related activities. Agricultural and subsistence activities followed the rhythm of the seasons, weaving an intricate cycle of food procurement, availability, and consumption of different meats. The farmers dealt with seasonal variations by carefully scheduling their animal husbandry and meat-processing activities according to the changing seasons.

Culture has its own adaptive mechanisms. The social and economic relationships of an agrarian community can focus around cooperative work groups (composed of kinsmen and neighbors) that assist the individual household in providing food supplies throughout the year. Using a group of late eighteenth-century farm account books from Suffield, Connecticut (see fig. 14.1), this study has shown the self-sufficient, independent farm to have been part of an agrarian society, where the productive, self-sufficient unit was the work group – not the individual farm. A complex network of farmers, craftsmen, and laborers formed fluid, ego-centered units exchanging among themselves agricultural products, goods and services. Through his network, each individual provided for his family by exchanging, depending on his needs, labor, services, and products of his farm or specialized skill. Through these work groups, the problem of providing a subsistence for the community as a whole was solved.

Anthropologists have long studied these agriculturally based communities and have produced a large body of literature on the social and economic organization of agriculture and subsistence. Conrad Arensberg wrote on these 'countrymen at work' within an Irish village, where the smaller of the farms were subsistence farms whose main goal was to provide for their families. The family and farm animals consumed nearly all that was raised. For labor they relied upon the united efforts of their family. But, while an individual's first duties were to his immediate family, his duty also extended into the countryside. The give and take of 'reciprocal aides', the cooperative exchange of any number of goods, labor, and services, was woven deeply into the countryman's traditional reciprocities of sentiment and duty and his obligations of kinship (Arensberg 1937, 49–75). Brush continued this theme:

> In spite of the village's overall self-sufficiency in labor, certain households experience a shortage of labor, while others have a surplus of labor relative to their amount of land. There are mechanisms within the village economic system to adjust this imbalance . . . The nuclear household, the principal economic unit is the scene of pervasive reciprocal relationships.. (Brush 1977, 104–5)

This research project was developed through an interest in interpreting social and economic patterns from faunal remains excavated from many sites in New England. From their analysis, data on animal husbandry and the relative importance of animals have been accumulated, but it has become increasingly apparent that interpretations are poorly constructed and often based on prehistoric models. From these bones we can determine which animals were consumed, their relative importance in the diet, and something about animal husbandry practices. But very little can be determined about the social and economic context of meat consumption. Without a better knowledge of history and more research with primary records, our archaeological data will remain nebulous. I have turned to documents to help answer the many questions that have arisen from faunal analyses. Farm account books were chosen as a primary source because they are one of the few resources containing specific information on individuals and their use of livestock, animal husbandry, and exchange of meat within a community.

Increasingly, account books kept by individuals in New England during the eighteenth and nineteenth centuries are being systematically analyzed. As a primary resource, they contain a wealth of information on many aspects of rural life. But they are also highly individualized and troublesome in their detail. So complex are they that they defy casual use and only reluctantly release information to systematic analysis.

But, while difficult to understand, they also provide us with a record of a rural society, its agricultural economy, industry, and trade. They record an agrarian society's subsistence system, where needs are maintained through reciprocal exchange networks. In these networks, farmers, artisans, and boarders exchanged among themselves agricultural produce, goods, labor, and services. Hired day labor appears too, but more often in the context of commercially oriented farming. The interpretation of these accounts demands a thorough understanding of the nature of account records: who kept them, why they were kept, and the economic system of which they were a part.

If one extracts data from account books without first examining this rural society one can easily arrive at false conclusions. But if studied from the perspective of the functioning farm unit, the analysis of individuals and their transactions can lead to the reconstruction of the household and its productive labor, a system composed of household members, laborers, kinsmen, and friends (Rossi 1980, 261). More important, this analysis can lead to the reconstruction of the subsistence system, a system of the production and distribution of food and materials within an agrarian society.

Suffield, a town located in the Connecticut River Valley, was selected for study because of its extensive collection of almost 200 eighteenth- and nineteenth-century account books. Of those, nearly 100 were either farm or farm-related accounts. To determine the genealogical relationships of those who kept the account books and where they lived, land records, maps, and other resources were analyzed. From this information, a sample of accounts of individuals who lived in close proximity to one another was selected (see fig. 14.1).

From this analysis several clusters of extended families emerged. Two groups, each of which had accounts spanning four and five generations within their families, were chosen.

One, the Sikes family group, lived in the east side of town alongside the Connecticut River, and the other family group, the Sheldons, lived inland in what is now West Suffield.

This sample was still far too large, so the time period was narrowed down to 1765–1800, the earliest period with a sizable number of accounts. In this final group were eight volumes that had been kept by twelve individuals. The total number of individuals in this sample was over 800 – still too large a sample. Further reductions were made by eliminating those individuals who had no meat or animal-related entries. With this final cut, the number of individuals dropped to a more manageable number – approximately 430.

In order to establish social and economic relationships for all these individuals, a wide range of sources was analyzed. A work by a local resident, Delphina Hammer Clark, on Suffield's families and land history, formed the central part of the analysis. Over a period of many years, she researched land records, wills, probates, tax lists, and maps to reconstruct Suffield's 'Land History'. As best she could, she determined who owned land and where they lived. The analysis of individuals who kept these accounts and those with whom they interacted has revealed for Suffield networks composed of farmers, laborers, craftsmen, physicians, and some widows. As has been pointed out for many agrarian societies, there existed in Suffield a certain inequality.

The individuals listed in the 1780 Tax Valuation for Suffield were ranked. When this information was combined with account book data and other sources, a general view of the community has become possible. This analysis is not yet complete, but tentatively three groups have been identified.[2] The lower group has approximately 30% of the taxed heads of households. They all had little or no taxable wealth; many were taxed only one poll tax, and none owned a house. Some had either one cow or one horse, and only a few had an acre or two of land. Among those individuals were sons who had yet to receive their inheritance, but there were also a substantial number of relative newcomers to town. This number seems to be as much as half of the individuals in the lowest percentile groups. Many of these relative newcomers had few or no known kin connections, some rented, boarded with farmers, or owned a house for a brief period. None were what one might call self-sufficient. These individuals were mostly day laborers who exchanged general farm labor, like mowing or butchering, in return for their basic subsistence needs – the use of oxen, boarding of their horse or cow, grains, vegetables, and animal products like meat, cheese, wool, and butter.

The middle group made up the bulk of the households. Almost all owned a house, some land, possibly a pig, a horse, and one to three cows. Many individuals in this group tended to be what one might call 'small farmers'. Others had specialized skills such as blacksmithing, shoemaking, or a profession like medicine. The small farmers tended to exchange a wide range of services and goods, but were far less reliant on others than the laborer for their subsistence needs. It is not yet clear how self-sufficient these individuals were. Those with a specialized skill would often exchange a product or service for foods.

The upper group had only approximately twenty individuals (5%), who each owned one or more houses, had substantial amounts of land (average 180 acres), three to four horses, two pigs, eight cows, and two to three oxen. Between these farmers, exchanges were more equilateral, with only occasional exchanges of food products. It is also this group that tended to keep the account books, and if I have interpreted them correctly, they were also the ones engaged in commercial enterprises like raising beef cattle or owning a sawmill.

Using meat entries from these accounts and data from the networks, discrepancies have been found between the account book data and the self-sufficiency dietary model. The account books revealed a much greater variety of meats than either agricultural or dietary historians have expected, and they show that some type of fresh meat was available all year. What can be concluded from these data is that the colonial New Englander dealt with seasonal variations by carefully scheduling his animal husbandry and meat processing activities according to the changing seasons. Within this rural, agrarian community, the sharing of these meats enabled individuals to solve the problem of disposing of an onslaught of fresh meat that would otherwise quickly spoil and provide meat to many that might not otherwise have had it.

Farm account books are well suited to this type of study. As a record of day-to-day farm activities, they provide detailed information with which to reconstruct seasonal patterns. Dates at which exchanges were made were frequently recorded, and the farmer almost always recorded the type of meat and its weight. For this analysis the data from all the accounts were collated. Assuming that, despite variations that might appear in these individual records, essential environmental constraints would affect everyone regardless of their unique position in the community, these entries could be used to determine seasonal patterns in meat availability. This position was strengthened when the data for each account were compared. Differing proportions of meat appeared in different accounts, but the season in which these different meats appeared remained remarkably constant. Thus, the data from the total sample of account books were combined for this particular study.

When entries with questionable dates were eliminated from the sample and the rest tabulated according to the date they were recorded, rather striking seasonal patterns are revealed – patterns that show the seasonal cycle of animal husbandry, slaughtering, and preservation determined the seasonal availability of different meats (fig. 14.2). By scheduling activities according to climatic variables, principles of animal husbandry, and meat preservation, the community was able to provide through their networks salted meat, as well as a variety of fresh meats during the season in which they could be most advantageously 'harvested'.

14.1 Seasonality
The seasonal cycle revealed by these meat exchanges is consistent with a mixed form of agriculture and its principles of

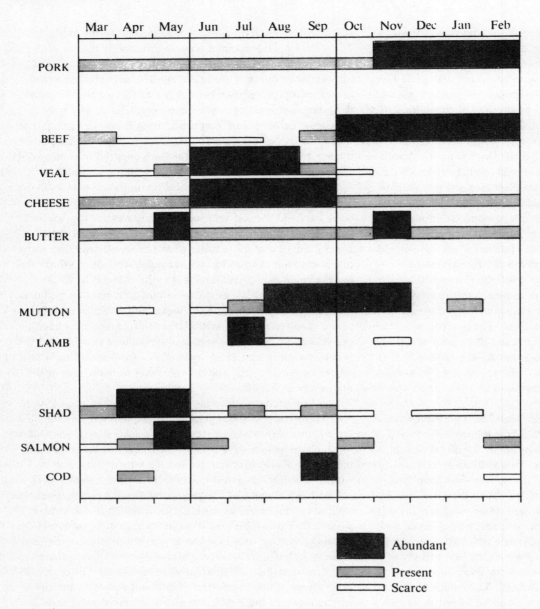

Fig. 14.2. Seasonal importance of meat and dairy products. Suffield, Connecticut, 1765–1800

animal husbandry. An analysis of the meat entries revealed three seasons. The fall/winter season went from October to February, the spring season from March to May, and the summer season from June to September (fig. 14.3).

14.1.1 Fall/winter

During fall and winter months, animal husbandry and meat processing were affected by the harvest of the summer's produce. When field crops had been harvested and stored, the 'harvesting' of meat began. In the eighteenth century, the meadows and the hay cut from them were coarse and less nutritious than what we have today. The meadows were fine for cattle during summer, but when plant growth ceased by late summer, they stopped producing milk and rapidly lost weight (Dabney 1796, 53). For individuals needing to winter livestock

but who lacked enough winter fodder, there were several options. Other farms having sufficient acreage could provide hay, or they could 'board' livestock for those individuals. For the older livestock to be culled from the herd, it was time to be briefly fattened on grass, hay, corn, turnips, or potatoes, then slaughtered as soon as weather would permit. The Suffield accounts show that October and November was the usual time of slaughter. The cold weather was necessary for the butchering of cattle and hogs because the carcass had to chill thoroughly before it could be salted. If the carcass did not cool all the way into the bone, microbial growth would spoil the muscle fiber (Lawrie 1979, 201–3).

With the harvest of the summer crops came the time to fatten pigs (Dabney 1796, 60; Newbury Agricultural Society 1815, 265; Dunstable Agricultural Society 1816–17, 49; Danvers

Agricultural Society 1815, 343; Barnum 1836, 20; Eliot 1934, 21). The pigs were allowed to clear stubble from the fields and were fed mast, potatoes, Indian corn, or other grains. But to feed them for much longer would be a waste. In 1796 John Dabney claimed that 'He who fats a hog in the winter must be a loser' because the feed went more for the animal to maintain his weight than to add to it (Dabney 1796, 30). The farm accounts clearly show this cycle – the dates for slaughtering pigs and cattle ran from September/October through February, and meat entries for pork and beef show tremendous increases during this same period. With such large amounts on hand, other types of meat made up a small proportion of the meat sources. Mutton, lamb, cheese, and butter all produced only small amounts in relation to pork and beef.

14.1.2 Spring

The spring season shows a period of relative scarcity in terms of fresh meat. Agriculturally very little was happening to provide any major meat source. Older animals had been slaughtered in the fall and winter, and others were just giving birth to their offspring. Just after the spring thaw, it would have been difficult to keep meat fresh, and before the spring, calves and lambs would be ready for slaughter. The only major source of fresh meat of any quantity came from the river. Located alongside the Connecticut River, Suffield had active fishing companies from at least the mid-eighteenth century. Salmon and shad, which began to run in March and April and peaked in May, provided a source of fresh meat that could also have been salted for use in other times of the year. The relative weights for this meat source could not be figured because of the way in which it was recorded. But evidence points to it being much more than a minimal amount.

At this time of year, Suffield residents had to rely more on their store of salt pork than at any other time. Swine provided a meat source throughout the year, with fresh meat during the slaughtering season and a preserved source the rest of the year. Year-round, pork was exchanged in a relatively constant amount, except during the fall and winter butchering season when large amounts were exchanged. Undoubtedly, much pork was salted in the winter to provide a supply of meat for the spring months.

14.1.3 Summer

The third season was in the summer. From June to September, the harvest of animal products kept quick pace with the agricultural activities. This was the dairying season; cows had given birth beginning with the first growth of grass. By June they were producing quantities of milk. With its short life span, milk had to be either consumed almost immediately, sold to nearby urban markets, or preserved. Until the mid-nineteenth century, there was very little demand from nearby urban areas, so almost all milk seems to have been made into butter and cheese. Although preserved and thus available to a certain extent all year, the production season for butter and cheese is evidenced by the larger amounts made from April and May until around October.

Another product of the dairying season was veal. Calves born in the early spring and meant to become veal were weaned almost immediately, fed skim milk, meal, and water, and left to graze on the new grass. Generally, they were allowed to mature for one month, but often for as long as two to three months. Beginning in May and continuing through the summer, the spring calves were slaughtered. By June, veal appears in increasing amounts, then stops rather abruptly in September when the pastures could no longer sustain livestock. Thus, veal provided a source of fresh meat in the hot summer months, a time when there was little other fresh meat to be had.

The only important meat not clearly falling into any one season was mutton. The entries are scattered over many months in relatively small amounts, but generally they fall between August and November. Although this pattern does not coincide with the three delineated seasons, the months fall within the cycle of sheep husbandry. In comparison to cattle, sheep required relatively little care. Given adequate pasturage, they could survive throughout the year without supplemental feeding. But the seasonal growth cycles of the pastures determined how the sheep were cared for. The summer pasturage produced fat ewes and fat lambs, and by July they were considered ready for market (Dabney 1796, 51). By the end of August, however, the pastures, including ones with English grasses as well as the 'wild trash', ceased to grow. According to Jared Eliot, this was the best time to take the sheep off the fields, a time when the sheep could be put into harvested fields to scavenge the cornstalks and other remains (Eliot 1934, 19; Trow-Smith 1959, 38). This was also the best time to slaughter those ewes past their prime.

While sheep did not provide a substantial part of the meat diet, the small flocks provided wool essential for bedding and coarse clothing, and mutton as an additional meat. Mutton entries from the accounts show that given seasonal patterns of sheep husbandry, an additional form of fresh meat becomes available at the end of the agricultural year and before the fall butchering season, a time when most of the calves and lambs had already been slaughtered and only small amounts of cured pork remained from the past year.

Chickens, geese, pigeons, and eggs are all listed in the accounts throughout the year, but only sporadically and in very small quantities. The interpretation of this pattern remains problematical for several reasons. The farm accounts are records kept by the male head of household, but traditionally these animals have been within the farm wife's domain. Thus, a distinct possibility exists that many of the exchanges of fowl were among women. On the other hand, the analysis of faunal remains from any number of historical sites has consistently shown that fowl was *never* present in any significant quantity. What *is* clear, however, is that fowl were available year-round, and that even if the quantity was small, they provided a year-round source of fresh meat.

Seasonality and the availability of different meats, as seen

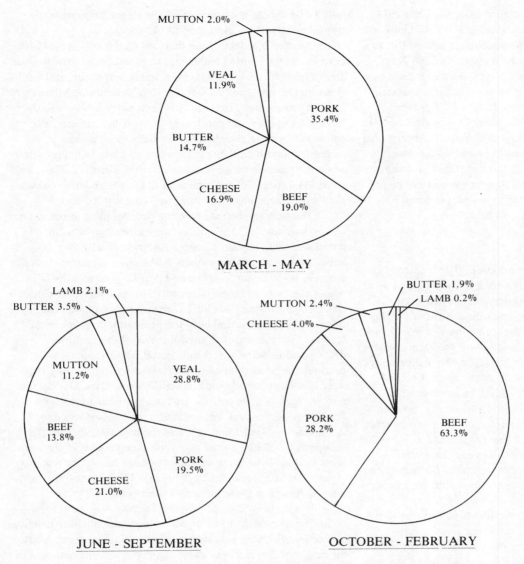

Fig. 14.3. Seasonal importance of meat and dairy products, Suffield, Connecticut, 1765–1800

in the Suffield accounts, reveals a seasonal cycle of meat exchanges strikingly different from that described by dietary and agricultural historians. While the butchering seasons for pig and cattle agreed with what they have written, the variety of meat and the seasons in which they occurred are quite different. The most remarkable difference is an effort to have fresh meat throughout the year. Chickens and geese provided small amounts of fresh meat but beef, mutton, and veal provided substantial amounts at certain times of the year. Preservation, apparently, was not as extensive a problem as presumed, because the fresh meats could be shared among kinsmen and neighbors.

Pork provided a year-round staple. The pork entries occurred year-round in a relatively constant amount, except during the butchering season when large amounts were exchanged. Swine provided a constant meat source, fresh

during the slaughtering season and preserved the rest of the year.

Unlike pork, beef was available only seasonally. The amounts are generally quite a bit larger and they occur only during the cold butchering months, except for small and infrequent amounts. They begin in September, increase to substantial amounts from October to February, then drop off. From the seasonal pattern, it appears that beef was more frequently left fresh than preserved.

Dietary historians have claimed that the overriding factor in preserving meat was the fat content – because salt tended to dry out and toughen meat. Pork, which had the highest fat content, was said to preserve and taste better. Cummings wrote:

Unlike that of the other meats, its flavor actually improves as a result of the preservative process. Tasty smoked hams and bacon could be hung, and other parts of the carcass immersed in brine until needed. This salty meat was relished by the farmers ... Undoubtedly a reliable store of preserved pork was preferable to a serving of fresh meat which might be tainted.

(Cummings 1940)

The historical claim that the only meat that preserved well was pork is not correct, at least from a technical point of view. All the major meats *are* preservable, and early receipt books show receipts for curing beef, mutton, and even veal (e.g. Child 1833; Several Ladies 1897). The basic curing process of salt, saltpeter, and sugar will work for beef, mutton, lamb, and veal as well as pork, but each has different characteristics and responds to the preservation process with varying degrees of success. Which types of meat, and which particular cuts were generally salted or kept fresh, depended upon the water/fat content, type of fat, texture, and tenderness of the muscle fiber.

A criterion even more important than the preserving quality of meat is the *keeping* quality of fresh meat. The type of fat is a crucial factor in determining how long meat will stay fresh. Unsaturated fats are softer, oilier, and tend to oxidize, turning the fat rancid rather quickly. Saturated fats, on the other hand, are harder and less likely to turn rancid. Pork has a greater percentage of unsaturated fats and thus keeps the *poorest* of all (Price and Schweigert 1971, 408). Beef and mutton, which both have more saturated fats, have twice the freezer life of pork. Freezer records today show that beef will keep thirty days at approximately thirty degrees, but pork and lamb one to two weeks and veal less than this (Frazier 1967, 257).

When salting meat, the water content is a variable at least as important as the fat content, because the success of salting depended on withdrawing water from the meat. Generally speaking, the amount of water can vary by species, age of the animal, and anatomical part. Calves and lambs are so young that they have a very low fat and high water content. The meat from these animals was never cured successfully for long periods. Those cuts of meat and those animals with a higher fat content were salted, because the more fat, the less water had to be absorbed from the muscle fiber. Pork, which generally has more fat than either mutton or beef, was more regularly salted than either mutton or beef.

Equally important, some meats actually benefit from being kept fresh as long as possible. When allowed to age, beef, which was far tougher and leaner than the beef we know today, improved in flavor and tenderness. In the cold season it could be kept fresh in an outbuilding, where it would remain frozen solid until spring (Fessenden 1820, 128; Boss 1903, 27–8). Where continued dry cold prevailed during the cold months, it could also be kept by packing it in snow, According to one nineteenth-century source, the meat would neither freeze nor grow dry and would keep perfectly through the cold months (Webster 1856, 196). Thus, it should not seem surprising that pork was the meat most often salted and the one year-round staple. Beef was kept fresh if at all possible.

We have seen climatic constraints, agricultural practices, and meat preserving techniques to have had an important effect on when different meat sources could be best harvested. It may well be, however, that the socio-economic organization within a rural community also influenced the seasons of availability. We have seen that all meats could have been preserved, at least for short periods, but many were not. And we can observe that the larger animals, the pig and cow, were dealt with differently from the smaller ones, the fowl, calves, lambs, and sheep. The cow and pig were always butchered in cold weather, and the smaller ones in the warmer non-butchering season. Thus the slaughtering of the larger animals, which produced more meat than could be easily consumed or even preserved with short-term methods in the warmer months, had to be harvested in the colder months.

If all this follows, then one can almost say that the reason animals were slaughtered and meat either cured or consumed fresh in certain times of the year was because of the size of the animal, not because of personal preferences for type of meat. Seasonal patterns of availability thus may very well be intricately tied in with a society's means of distribution of food resources; in this case, the rural exchange networks. The smaller animals could be easily disposed of among a household and its networks of neighbors and relatives during the summer. The accounts, in fact, frequently recorded the exchange of a quarter of mutton, lamb, and veal. On the other hand, the pig and cow produced such substantial amounts of meat that if slaughtered in the summer, the quantities of meat might well have strained the distribution networks, even with the use of short-term curing methods. A different means of distributing meat within a community, such as a market system with a large consumer population, could easily consume large amounts of meat. Seasonal patterns of availability could have been very different for this system. Beef and pork, for example, may have been more readily available in the summer.

The use of account books to study agrarian lifeways can provide provocative ideas and details about rural life seldom found elsewhere. Unfortunately, results from their analysis may not be as factual as they are provocative. Account books are not complete records, and the cultural rules underlying the recording system have not been determined. So complex are these accounts that there has been a tendency to either avoid them, analyze only a portion of the volumes, or to work with very small samples.

Given the fragmentary nature of the accounts and incompleteness of the data, what, then, is believable about the analysis of exchange networks and subsistence within Suffield? What about seasonality? Seasonal constraints on the availability of meat in this farming community seem compelling, first because the pattern remained consistent in all the account books and second because climatic and biological factors influencing meat and animal behavior are so strong. What does not seem so compelling is the relative importance of meat within the changing season, because that can result from fragmentary data as well as from numerous human factors.

Knowledge of the highly fragmented nature of the accounts ought to – at best – make us suspicious of quantitative data. The quantification of account entries can reveal patterns previously unrecognized, but they can also be very misleading because of a strong tendency to believe these figures to be fact. One should, therefore, attempt to get at the underlying social and economic processes of what, why, and how accounts were kept.

When all the individuals with meat and animal related entries were isolated, one important fact became clear. Without a single exception, the transactions involving meat and any animal husbandry related activity were with individuals who lived within a very close geographical proximity to each other. While these same individuals no doubt traded at least some agricultural products on the market, they did not record them in their farm accounts. The geographical limits of the social and economic relationships between kinsmen and neighbors at least in part demonstrate the fact that subsistence – both the production and distribution of meat – was a community event.

In prehistoric archaeology, seasonal patterns have been defined on the basis of wild animals having clear-cut seasonal markers. One example is migratory birds, present only at certain times of the year. While productive for prehistoric studies in that it has provided the information needed to study the seasonal occupation of sites, this approach is limiting for historical archaeology.

A shift of research orientation is needed. The reliance on wildlife to determine seasonality patterns for historical sites denies the real importance of environmental factors in the lives of the early Americans. Domestic animals were their major meat source, and, until well into the nineteenth century, the successful production and preservation of their food was dependent upon how they adapted to their environment. Seasonal factors *did* have a major impact on subsistence and the availability of types of meat.

This study also has some important implications for some basic analytical methods used in faunal analysis. Zooarchaeologists analyzing faunal remains from historical sites have based their interpretations primarily on the relative importance of identified species. These relative proportions have been explained as being the result of factors such as cultural preferences, socio-economic differences, or a market economy. We can now see that the relative importance of different kinds of animals fluctuates with the agricultural seasons.

This seasonal variability, delineated on the basis of documentary sources alone, can be used to examine archaeological assumptions and interpretations of faunal remains, as well as specific archaeological contexts where seasonal variability could have had a discernible influence on the relative importance of animals. One of the major contributions this type of study can make is to force us to question old assumptions, generate new ideas, refine analytical methods, and ultimately produce far more accurate interpretations of subsistence within agrarian communities.

One context is the cellar holes found in many rural farmsites in New England. An example is the Mott Farm in Portsmouth, Rhode Island, where a cellar was interpreted as having been filled in a relatively short period of time (Bowen 1975a, b). The analysis of the faunal remains showed a high percentage of pig foot bones as well as the entire pelvis of a cow. They were interpreted in terms of agricultural economics, but it now seems that a seasonal perspective should be brought to bear on the earlier interpretation.

In defining the social and economic context of the Mott Farmstead within Portsmouth, the farmstead was seen as potentially being a part of an extended family network, but there was not any real effort to define the social and economic organization of reciprocal interaction. In the end, I relied on my sense of the independent farmer to interpret the faunal remains. They were viewed as being the remains of animals that had been born, raised, worked, and ultimately consumed on the same site. A different conclusion now seems only too obvious.[3]

Notes

1. The self-sufficiency model has seen a steady barrage of criticism by historians. Beginning in the early 1950s, historians have attacked the assumption that self-sufficiency was caused by a lack of markets and incentive to produce surplus agricultural products (Clark 1972; Henretta 1978; Loehr 1952; Merrill 1977; Russell 1976; Gross 1976). Within the past decade, a few have begun to explore the fabric of New England society by examining the socio-economic stratification and kinship, as well as social and economic interaction within these colonial New England towns. Results demonstrate that colonial society was stratified, that families did not exist in isolation of one another, that the economy was based on a barter system of exchange, and that many families could not produce enough for substantial surpluses, let alone supply their own needs. But, while historians have come to view New England society in terms of a rural agrarian barter economy, their work with agriculture and subsistence is still in the formative stages. As Henretta (1978, 3) has said, 'The history of the agricultural population of pre-industrial America remains to be written.'

2. The analysis of seasonality and availability of meat and animal products is an important aspect of a doctoral thesis on an historic ethnoarchaeological study of diet and the relative importance of meat in Suffield, Connecticut, during the late eighteenth century. The thesis is based on the notion that diet and the relative importance of meat are affected by a multitude of cultural, social, economic, and environmental variables, each of which affects the relative importance of meat in the diet in varying ways.

3. I want to thank the many who have helped me with this project. Research was in part funded by an NEH internship at Old Sturbridge Village, and by the American Indian Archaeological Institute. Many libraries and historical societies in Massachusetts and Connecticut generously allowed me to use their manuscript and account book collections. In particular the Connecticut Historical Society, Connecticut State Library, Kent Memorial Library, and Suffield Town Hall were more than generous with their time and information. A number of friends and colleagues provided both professional and personal assistance and support: the Old Sturbridge Village research staff, Caroline Sloat who

introduced me to account books, the Kent Memorial Library's staff, Anne and Bob Borg, Collette Moore, Christine Hoffner, Richard Rush, and Peter Schmidt who provided critical advice as I worked on the data and drafts of this paper. Finally, I am indebted to Delphina Hammer Clark, who spent many years meticulously researching Suffield's families, architecture, and land history. Without her wealth of information, analysis of the exchange networks could never have been accomplished.

Part IV

Consumerism, status, gender and ethnicity

Chapter 15

Classification and economic scaling of nineteenth-century ceramics

George L. Miller

Archaeological classification of ceramics is an outgrowth of the study of material from seventeenth- and eighteenth-century sites and as such reflects the classification system in use during those centuries. By the nineteenth century the range of wares available was greatly reduced because of the success of the English ceramic industry that displaced many fine ware types such as white salt-glazed stoneware and tin-glazed earthenware. The major type available in the nineteenth century was English white earthenware which included creamware, pearlware, whiteware, and the stone chinas. By the nineteenth century classification of these wares by potters, merchants, and people who used them was by how they were decorated (e.g., painted, edged, dipped, printed, etc.) rather than the ware types as defined by archaeologists. Using a classification based on decoration will achieve two things: an ability to integrate archaeological data with historical data, and establishment of a more consistent classification system than is now possible using ware types.

The second part of this paper generates a set of index values from price lists, bills of lading, and account books that can be used to study the expenditures made on cups, plates, and bowls from archaeological assemblages from the first half of the nineteenth century. Expenditure patterns from five sites are discussed.

15.1 Introduction

Ceramic classification by historical archaeologists has developed through a synthesis of ceramic history and knowledge of the common ceramic types recovered from excavations. Prior to the mid-1960s, most historical archaeology projects involved seventeenth- and eighteenth-century sites such as Jamestown, Williamsburg, Fort Michilimackinac, and

Louisbourg. The study of ceramics from these sites established a typology based on ware types: that is, a breakdown of a classification system that separates ceramics into porcelain, stoneware, and earthenware. Each of these broad categories is subdivided into wares. Porcelain for example is subdivided into hard paste, soft paste, bone china, and often by country of origin. Stoneware and earthenware are broken into types based on observable differences in glaze, decoration, and paste, e.g., tin-glazed earthenware, lead-glazed redware, white salt-glazed stoneware, combed slipware, German salt-glazed stoneware, creamware, Rockingham ware, pearlware, lustreware, and many others.

Classification of seventeenth- and eighteenth century wares does not suggest great difficulties because of major recognizable differences between them. In addition to ease of classification, most of them can be identified as to country of origin, which facilitates the study of trade relationships. The terminology used for archaeological assemblages follows that used by the potters, merchants, and the people who bought the ceramics, thus facilitating synthesis of archaeological and historical information. In the nineteenth century, however, things changed.

In the second half of the eighteenth century, a revolution took place in the English ceramic industry. This period saw the introduction of transfer printing, calcinated flint, liquid glazes, Cornish clays, calcinated bone, canals for transporting raw materials and finished products into and out of the potteries, steam power for working clay and pottery, tariffs against Chinese porcelain, favorable trade treaties with the Continent, and astute marketing of creamware that culminated in English domination of the world ceramic tableware trade by the 1790s.

Marketing of creamware wreaked havoc in the pottery industries of England and the Continent. Tin-glazed ware, white salt-glazed stoneware, and to some extent even oriental porcelain were displaced from the market. The pervasiveness of English tableware is well illustrated by the following comment by B. Faujas de Saint-Font in the account of his travels to England, Scotland, and the Hebrides that was published in 1797:

> Its excellent workmanship, its solidity, the advantage which it possesses of sustaining the action of fire, its fine glaze, impenetrable to acids, the beauty and convenience of its form, and the cheapness of its price, have given rise to a commerce so active and so universal that in traveling from Paris to Petersburg, from Amsterdam to the furthest part of Sweden, and from Dunkirk to the extremity of the south of France, one is served at every inn with English ware. Spain, Portugal, and Italy are supplied, and vessels are loaded with it for the East and West Indies and the continent of America.
>
> (as quoted by Hayden 1952, 135–6)

England's conquest of the world tableware market was through the vehicle of creamware. This ware is an eighteenth-century product, and in that context it functions like any other ware, i.e., it is easy to identify through the characteristics of its glaze and paste. Out of creamware evolved pearlware in the 1780s. Later stone china, ironstone, and whiteware were developed. These emerged out of creamware and pearlware and are not nearly as identifiable by differences of glaze and paste.

Table, tea, and toilet ware assemblages from the nineteenth century consist almost entirely of creamware, pearlware, whiteware, stone china, and porcelain along with some fairly rare types such as basalt and lustre-glazed redware. Differences between creamware, pearlware, whiteware, and stone china are minor when compared to the differences between ware types in the seventeenth and eighteenth centuries.

When archaeological interests advanced to include nineteenth-century sites, it was quite natural to expand the ware type classification system as an evolution of the eighteenth-century types such as creamware and pearlware. By the nineteenth century, however, ceramics were being described by the type of decoration they received, and ware types became less important. Ware types used by archaeologists for classification of nineteenth-century assemblages often depend on such things as a slight amount of blueing in the glaze, absence of blueing in the glaze, a slight cream-like color to the paste, and density or compactness of the ware. These differences in the nineteenth century are the result of an evolution of one type out of another such as whiteware out of pearlware. Whiteware does not have a date of introduction, but it is known that by the 1820s it was developing from pearlware. If an assemblage of ceramics from the first half of the

nineteenth century is placed before six archaeologists and they are asked for counts of creamware, pearlware, whiteware, and stone china wares, the results will probably be six different enumerations. The question of how much blueing the glaze has to have before it is pearlware or which sherds have the density to be classified as stone china all hinge on personal opinions. Attempts have been made to define pearlware using the Munsel Color Book (Loftstrom 1976, 6); there is no way, however, of knowing if the archaeological definition of pearlware is the same as that of nineteenth-century potters and merchants.

Archaeological reports dealing with the first half of the nineteenth century leave the reader with the impression that pearlware is one of the major products of that period. When examining nineteenth-century documents such as price fixing lists, account books, bills of lading, and newspaper advertisements, however, the term rarely occurs. Simeon Shaw's *The History of the Staffordshire Potters* (1829) and *Chemistry of . . . Compounds used in the Manufacture of Porcelain, Glass and Pottery* (1837) do not mention pearlware except as an unglazed white body developed by Chetham and Woolley that was similar to jasper and basalt (Shaw 1829, 225). Ivor Noël Hume has shown that the term 'chinaglazed' was used for pearlware in the late eighteenth century, but even this term seems to be rather limited in its occurrences (Noël Hume 1969a). The term 'PEARLWARE' as part of the potter's mark was used by two firms, one being Chetham and Woolley (1796–1810), which used it for its unglazed white stoneware discussed above. The other firm was Skinner and Walker, which was in business during the 1870s (Godden 1964, 580). At least ten other potters used the word 'PEARL' as part of ceramic marks in such combination as 'PEARL STONE CHINA', 'PEARL WHITE', 'PEARL CHINA', and 'PEARL IRONSTONE'. Most of these firms began operating in the 1830s and 1840s, and they were producing whitewares, often with a slight blue tint to the ceramic body rather than the glaze (Godden 1964). Archaeologists have defined pearlware as though it was something static; an article titled 'Pearlware' by Mellany Delhom, however, presents a sequence of eight recipes for pearlware from the Wedgwood factory dating from 1815 to 1846 (Delhom 1977, 62–3). Two Wedgwood plates marked 'PEARL' in the author's collection would fall under our classification of whiteware. One of these pieces has a date code for 1861. (Blue tinted wares from the 1850s through the 1860s are discussed in Miller 1980, appendix A.) Documents examined for this article suggest that pearlware or 'Pearl White Ware' existed throughout most of the nineteenth century, but its characteristics were continually evolving.

Creamware also lasts out the century. From the 1820s on, however, it is rarely found decorated, and the variety of forms in which it was available became limited to such things as large kitchen bowls, chamber pots, and bed pans. In almost all nineteenth-century price lists and potters' and merchants' bills, it is referred to as 'CC ware' and is almost never decorated. In short, the ware types archaeologists are attempting to use to classify their collections are elusive as to their definitions in the nineteenth century.

What does the present classification system for the nineteenth-century ceramics by ware types give us?

1   Chronology? Yes, in a rough sort of way.
2   Country of origin? It is not a question usually asked because almost all fine wares with the exception of porcelains in nineteenth-century sites are English.
3   Ease of classification? Definitely not.
4   Consistency in classification? Definitely not.
5   An ability to integrate data with historical documents? Definitely not.
6   Information on social status? Nothing seems to indicate that the ware type is related to status with the exception of porcelain.

Social status of any commodity is related to how much the objects cost. Prices for pottery were determined by how they were decorated. Fortunately, the Staffordshire potters had a series of price fixing agreements in the eighteenth and nineteenth centuries, and some of them have survived. Price fixing lists are available for 1770, 1783, 1795, 1796, 1814, 1833, and 1846. These price lists provide cost information for the various sizes of vessels according to how they are decorated. They reveal the classification system used by the potters for their products.

These price categories, based on decoration, were well established by the 1790s. Many of these types were used throughout the nineteenth century. Terms like pearlware, whiteware, stone china, and ironstone rarely appear in the price lists and account books. Creamware is the only ware type appearing in the lists, and it appears as 'CC' for cream color. On every list so far examined, CC was used for undecorated vessels, and it was the cheapest type available. All other types are defined by the process used to decorate the object.

Four groups based on decoration become evident from examining these lists. A breakdown of the groups is as follows.

First or lowest level: Undecorated – almost always referred to as CC, but in the second half of the nineteenth century, the terms 'Common' and 'white earthenware' or 'Earthenware' sometimes are used. Undecorated vessels after the 1820s tend to be chamber pots, plates, bowls, and forms related to kitchen use. Plain white ironstone is also called stone china, and white granite became popular in the 1850s and is an exception to the above. It was higher priced than CC vessels.

Second level: Minimal decoration by minimally skilled operatives. Types in this group include shell edge, sponge decorated, banded, mocha, and 'common cable' (finger trailed slip). In all of these types, there is a fairly wide range in the decoration on one vessel compared to another of the same size and form. For example, two mocha bowls are never exactly alike. Shell edge plates are another good example: the color can be applied by a worker of low skill level because all that is involved is a series of short brush strokes along the rim. Later, in the 1840s and 1850s shell edge vessels just have the color applied parallel to the rim, and they depend on the molding to

lend an effect to the edge. The second level encompasses the cheapest ceramics available with decoration.

Third level: This level is made up of painted wares with motifs such as flowers, leaves, stylized Chinese landscapes to geometric patterns. With this group the painters needed to have enough skill to duplicate patterns so that sets of matched pieces could be assembled. Painting at this simple level produced wares that were priced between the second level and transfer printed wares. While painted decoration on utilitarian tea, table, and toilet wares was relatively inexpensive, there is another group of painted wares of much higher quality done by very skilled artist-craftsmen that would rank among the most expensive ware available. Most of the painted wares from North American sites, however, bear simple stylized motifs that required minimal artistic skill and were almost always cheaper than transfer printed vessels. Exceptions to this may be cases where the transfer print is used as an outline for the application of colors. Unfortunately, none of the price lists consulted have provided price information on objects that are decorated by printing in combination with painting.

Fourth level: Transfer printing represents one of the great English innovations in decorated ceramics. By the 1790s underglazed transfer printing was becoming a common way of decorating ceramics in the Staffordshire potteries, as indicated by the price fixing lists of 1795 and 1796 (Mountford 1975: 10–11). With transfer printing it was possible to have intricately decorated and exactly matching pieces at a cost far below similar hand painted pieces. In the 1790s, transfer printed vessels were three to five times more expensive than undecorated CC vessels, but the price differential of printed and CC vessels decreased to between one and a half to two times the cost of CC by the mid-nineteenth century.

Early in the nineteenth century, willow pattern was designated as the cheapest transfer printed pattern available, and, as such, it was given its own column in the price fixing lists. None of the price lists examined indicate any price differential based on the color of the transfer print. At least until the 1850s, however, flow printed patterns were higher priced than regular transfer printed patterns. Most North American archaeological assemblages dating to the first half of the nineteenth century have few wares that exceed transfer printed wares in terms of cost status. The major exception to this is porcelain, for which little has been found in the way of prices. As transfer printed wares became cheaper compared to CC wares, their consumption greatly increased. This is particularly observable on sites dating after the War of 1812.

The above four categories are especially valid for the first half of the nineteenth centuries and account for most of the table, kitchen, and toilet wares recovered from North American sites dating to this period. Porcelain is the major exception to this; its relationship to the Staffordshire earthenwares will be worked out when more price information has been collected.

Beginning in the mid-1850s, a major change took place in ceramic prices and tastes. Until that point, undecorated wares were the cheapest type available. By the mid-1850s price lists and bills began listing large quantities of undecorated white ironstone or white granite. Prices for this new type are often equal to prices for transfer printed wares, and the latter appear to have been replaced by undecorated ironstone. From the mid-nineteenth century, there appears to be a weaker relationship between final cost of the vessels and their decoration. An analysis of the movement of undecorated ironstone into a position of status comparable to transfer printed wares would provide an interesting insight into ceramic marketing at mid-century.

Those who are familiar with ceramics from the first half of the nineteenth century will realize that the type discussed above encompass a large proportion of the ceramics recovered from excavations of that period. The major type missing from the above discussion is porcelain. It too can be segregated into decorative categories. Porcelain rarely occurs undecorated, however, and the author has never seen porcelain decorated at what is labeled level two, i.e., shell edge, sponged, mocha, banded, or common cable. It would appear that persons decorating porcelain had more skill than was needed for level two decoration.

15.2 Ceramic prices

Little research has been done on ceramic prices. This is probably because of the paucity of documents, complexity of the subject, and the relatively small contribution ceramics made to the overall economy. A variety of documents from different levels in the ceramic marketing structure contain ceramic prices and descriptions. Potters' wholesale prices for example, can be recovered from bills, statements, and price lists sent by potters. They are also available from price fixing lists published by potters' associations. Some of the larger potters such as Josiah Wedgwood and John Davenport also maintained retail outlets in London, which means there were potters' retail and wholesale prices (Lockett 1972, 10). The amount of pottery sold directly to the consumer by the potters through their own retail outlets appears to be quite small. Most ceramics were purchased wholesale by two types of middlemen. One was the wholesale jobber who resold the wares at a jobber's wholesale price, and the other was the merchant who resold the ceramics at a retail price to the ultimate user. The number of middlemen can vary from one (potter to user) to many. Each establishment along the chain of sales added their profit to the ultimate cost of the wares to the consumers. From this discussion it can be seen that there are three basic groups of businessmen dealing with ceramics: potters, jobbers, and retail merchants, all of whom could have wholesale and retail prices. Two additional sources of ceramic prices are probate inventories, and accounts of sales, which for the most part deal with second-hand goods. Second-hand prices, however, will not be dealt with in this study.

Besides the mercantile structure, ceramic prices are affected by transportation costs, tariffs, changes in technology, inflation, deflation, and currency fluctuations. Further complications to the study of ceramic prices derive from the

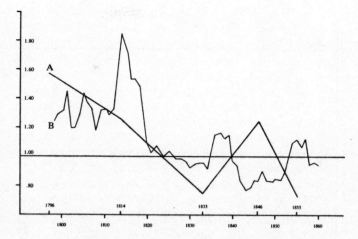

Fig. 15.1. Comparison of ceramic prices and other commodities prices. A = Ceramic prices using the average costs for 1833 and 1846 as a base. Prices derived from 48 vessels (one-third CC, edged, and printed) for the years 1796, 1814, 1833, 1846, and 1855. B = *The New York all commodities Index of Wholesale Prices* using the base period 1824–1842 (Cole 1969, 153–6).

nature of the product. Ceramics range from being a basic necessity to a high status luxury good. These divergent roles are covered by a wide range of forms, types of decorations, and sizes of vessels, and all of these variables affect prices. Such a range of complexities, combined with the relatively minor role ceramics play in the overall economic picture, probably accounts for why price studies such as Tooke and Newmarch's classic six-volume work, *A History of Prices . . . from 1792 to 1856* (1928), do not deal with ceramics.

The study of ceramic prices can be approached from several directions. One would be to attempt the study of prices from one geographic location, such as a port like Montreal or New York. Success of such a study would depend upon the quantity and quality of records that have survived. Research so far indicates that few records are available. A detailed study of ceramic prices and descriptions from a city of importation could provide knowledge of the range of types, forms, and sizes being imported, and cost information that would have application for the immediate surrounding area. Unfortunately, it is not possible to have ceramic price studies for all of the communities where they will be useful. Even if the records were extant, the cost of such a large project would be immense.

A second approach would be to work with potters' wholesale prices; this makes a great deal of sense because of the dominant role played by the Staffordshire potteries. These records tend to be easy to identify, and they usually contain a high level of descriptive information, but documents containing potters' wholesale prices are not common. The potters' price fixing lists of 1796, 1814, 1833, and 1846 along with the 1855 price list from the Fife Pottery in Scotland are detailed and provide an excellent starting point for studying ceramics prices. From these lists, prices for CC, edged, and transfer printed platters, plates, muffin dishes, soup tureens, and sauce boats

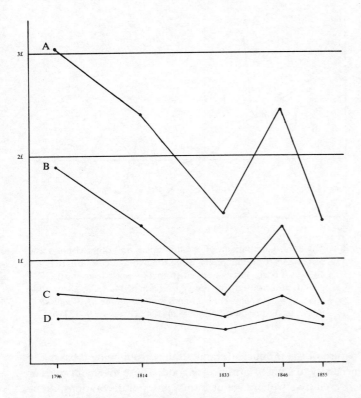

Fig. 15.2. Cumulative prices for 16 vessels for the years 1796, 1814, 1846 and 1855. A = cumulative totals of lines B, C & D. B = prices for the cheapest type of transfer printed vessels, usually willow ware. C = prices for the same vessels in edged (shell edge). D = prices for the same vessels in CC.

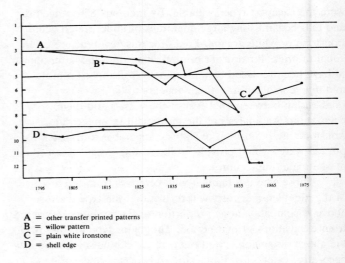

A = other transfer printed patterns
B = willow pattern
C = plain white ironstone
D = shell edge

Fig. 15.3. The number of 8-inch plates available in shell edge, willow pattern, other transfer printed patterns, and undecorated ironstone for cost of 12 CC plates of the same size.

have been abstracted. Using the cost of sixteen different shapes and sizes of vessels in CC, edged, and transfer printed styles, a ceramic price index was generated and plotted against the *New York all Commodities Index of Wholesale Prices for 1798 to 1860* (fig. 15.1). Even though there are only five data points for the ceramic prices, it is still possible to get an impression of the relationship of the cost of ceramics in comparison to the cost of other commodities. It appears that ceramic prices were falling somewhat faster than the other commodities. This picture may change as more price information is collected and such things as porcelain and tea ware are worked into the cumulative price data.

In addition to allowing for a comparison of the relationship between ceramic prices and the range of variation among the costs of CC, edged, and transfer printed vessels, figure 15.2 illustrates the cumulative prices for each of the three groups (CC, edged, and transfer printed) used in figure 15.1. It is clear that most of the price decline took place in decorated wares. This graph also illustrates the great stability of the prices for the CC vessels. From 1796 to 1855 transfer printed vessels dropped almost 70% in wholesale price while shell edge vessels only fell about 37%. CC prices, however, fell only about 19% over the same sixty-year period. The five price lists used to generate figures 15.1 and 15.2 clearly illustrate the productivity

of studying potters' wholesale prices. This approach is limited, however, because of the scarcity of price lists.

A third approach to ceramic prices is to study the changing cost relationships between the various decorative types. Potters' wholesale prices from the 1790s through the 1850s indicate exceptional stability in the prices of undecorated CC ware. This stability makes CC vessel prices a convenient scale for observing changing cost ratios among the various decorative types. For example, figure 15.3 illustrates the number of eight-inch plates available in shell edge, undecorated ironstone, willow pattern, and other transfer printed patterns that one could purchase for the cost of one dozen CC plates of the same size from 1796 to 1874.

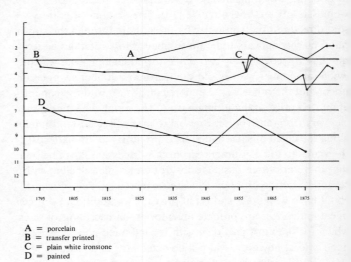

A = porcelain
B = transfer printed
C = plain white ironstone
D = painted

Fig. 15.4. Number of London size handled cups and saucers in painted, printed, undecorated ironstone, and porcelain available for the cost of 12 CC cups and saucers of the same size

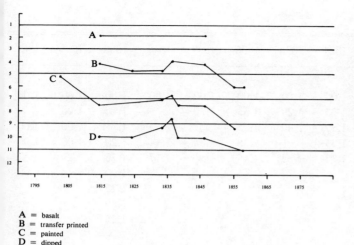

A = basalt
B = transfer printed
C = painted
D = dipped

Fig. 15.5. The number of size 12 bowls available in dipped, painted, printed, and basalt for the cost of 12 CC bowls of the same size

Documents used to generate this graph include potters' and wholesale merchants' prices.

Two things are clear from examining figure 15.3. One is that the prices of the decorative types were declining through time towards the price of CC plates. The second point is that the price of one decorative type does not drop below the price of another decorative type, although they may meet as in the case of shell edge plates and CC plates. This suggests that even though the relationships between the types are changing, the classification of them seems to hold.

Figure 15.4 graphically represents the number of painted, printed, and undecorated ironstone and porcelain cups and saucers that could have been purchased for the cost of a dozen CC cups and saucers. With cups and saucers there appears to be less of a decline towards the price of CC ware. Here again, the types do not cross price lines except for undecorated ironstone. When white ironstone became popular in the 1850s, it came into market at a status level comparable to transfer printed wares.

Figure 15.5 presents the same information for bowls. It again shows prices declining towards CC ware with a maintenance of the decorative classes over time. All three of these figures illustrate the usefulness of CC ware in observing status changes over time. Documents used to create these graphs included Staffordshire potters' wholesale prices, English merchants' wholesale prices, and North American merchants' wholesale prices. By studying price relationships rather than actual cost, the number of usable documents are greatly increased.

The above discussion has demonstrated the usefulness of CC wares as a vehicle for filtering out price differences related to factors discussed earlier. The stability of CC prices provides an excellent scale to measure changes in other decorative types and suggests that prices decline over time towards the cheapest

type available. The ability of the cheapest type to decline in price was limited to its margin above production cost. Because the cheapest type probably already enjoyed economy of scale in production, the only way for its price to decrease was through declines in material cost or improvements in technology. Such changes of course would affect all types. Josiah Wedgwood made an astute observation on the price cycle of ceramics when he began his 1759 notebook of experiments. He summarized the declining of prices for white salt-glazed stoneware as follows:

> White stoneware was the principal article of our manufacture; but this had been made a long time, and the prices were now reduced so low that the potter could not afford to bestow much expense upon it . . .
>
> The article next in consequence to stoneware was an imitation of tortoise-shell, but as no improvement had been made in this branch for several years, the consumer had grown tired of it; and although the price had been lowered from time to time in order to increase the sales, the expedient did not answer, and something new was wanted to give a little spirit to the business.
>
> (Mankowitz 1953, 27)

Increasing demands by lowering prices appears to be a one way process in which consumption is increased, status declines and, when the market is saturated, the demand falls. This cycle can be repeated until the selling price bottoms out at the point where it can no longer be lowered because of production costs. If demand continues to fall beyond this point, then production stops and the consumer is left with the choice of the next more expensive or the next cheaper types. With CC ware, the next lower level was tinware.

Shell edge plates provide an excellent example of this process. By the 1850s, the price for shell edge plates was close to the price of CC plates. Three bills from the Fahnestock Papers from 1858, 1861, and 1862 list the price for blue edge plates as equal to the price for CC plates. Archaeological assemblages and ceramic bills after the 1860s rarely contain shell edge plates. The demand did not exist at the price the potters had to have for production, so it was greatly reduced.

For the archaeologist, or any other scholar studying material culture, the ability to scale assemblages in socio-economic terms is very important. Until now archaeologists have ranked assemblages from sites in relative terms such as the purchase pattern, presence of matched sets, presence of expensive forms such as tureens, and the decorative type present, e.g., sites with transfer printed ware were ranked higher than sites with shell edge wares (Miller 1974a, 1974b; Teller 1968; Stone 1970).

Ranking without an interval-value scale limits the ability to do socio-economic analysis of collections. For example, it is easy to say that an assemblage with a matching set of tea ware represents a higher status than one that lacks it. If one site has a matching set of transfer printed tea ware and another has a matching set of transfer printed table ware, however, the ability to rank begins to break down. Even when assemblages can be

Table 15.1 *CC index values for plates, twifflers, and muffins*

	inch	1787	1796	1802	1814	1824	1833	1836	1839	1846	1855	1858	1861
CC all sizes		1.00	1.00	1.00	1.00	1.00	1.00	1.00	1.00	1.00	1.00	1.00	1.00
Edged	10		1.33	1.37	1.33	1.33	1.29	1.33	1.20		1.20	1.00	
	8		1.29	1.23	1.29	1.29	1.40	1.25		1.13	1.25	1.00	1.00
	7		1.33		1.33	1.33		1.38	1.33	1.14	1.20	1.00	1.00
	6		1.40		1.40	1.33	1.33	1.45		1.17	1.25		
Sponge	10										1.20		
	8										1.25		
	7										1.20		
	6										1.25		
Underglazed	10					1.67							
lined	8					1.71							
	7					1.67							
	6					1.70							
Painted	8	1.67											
	6							2.18					
Ironstone	10											1.69	1.69
	8											1.80	2.00
	7											1.78	2.00
	6												2.00
Willow	10				2.67		1.93	2.50			1.60		
	8				3.00	2.86	2.10	2.44			1.50		
	7				3.00			2.77			1.50		
	6				3.00		2.00	2.73			1.50		
Other	10		4.33		3.33	3.22	2.57	3.00	2.20		1.60		
Transfer	8		3.86	3.43	3.43	3.21	3.00	2.81	2.45	2.63	1.50		
printed	7		4.00	3.50	3.50	2.92			2.44	2.57	1.50		
	6		4.20	3.60	3.60	2.50	2.93	3.00		2.50	1.50		
Flow	10										2.40		
	8										2.50		
	7										2.40		
	6										2.25		
Porcelain	10												
'enameled'	8												
	7												
	6							4.80					

ranked as to status, it is not possible to know how close or far apart two assemblages are from each other. Time adds another dimension to the problem. For example, does an assemblage from 1790 with a matched set of shell edge plates rank above an assemblage from 1855 with a matched set of willow plates? It is easy to see the significance of developing an interval scale of value.

Potters' wholesale prices indicate a high degree of stability in the prices of CC ware. Figures 15.3, 15.4, and 15.5 illustrate the usefulness of CC ware in observing changes in the cost of decorative types. Given this evidence, a series of index values has been generated for plates, cups, and bowls using the price of CC vessels (tables 15.1–15.3).

Generation of CC index values is quite simple. Because plain CC vessels are the cheapest refined earthenware available in the nineteenth century they are given a value of one. Index values are generated by dividing the cost of a CC vessel into the cost of other types for which the index value is wanted. In generating the CC index numbers, the following guidelines were used. Foremost was that each document used was treated as an assemblage. To put it another way, prices from one document were not used against prices in another document. For a document to be usable, it had to have CC wares and size information in addition to the decorative types for which the index values were being calculated. Controlling these factors means that the only variable being observed is decoration. In

Table 15.2 *CC index values for tea cups and saucers*

Type	1770	1795	1796	1802	1814	1824	1846	1856	1857	1858	1860	1871	1874	1875	1881
CC															
NG			1.00			1.00		1.00	1.00	1.00	1.00	1.00	1.00	1.00	1.00
NH	1.00	1.00	1.00		1.00		1.00					1.00	1.00		
HD		2.09	1.86		1.67		1.55								
Sponge															
NG												1.17			
NH															
HD															
White glazed															
NG															
NH					1.33										
HD					2.00										
Painted															
NG				1.60		1.44		1.60							
NH	1.33		1.80		1.50		1.23							1.17	
HD			2.60		2.17		1.77								
Ironstone or white granite undecorated															
NG															3.33
NH								3.60	3.00	4.00	4.00	2.50	2.77	2.00	
HD										5.00	5.00		3.23	2.75	
Printed															
NG						3.00				4.20	4.00				
NH		4.09	3.40		3.00		2.45		3.00						
HD		5.18	4.20		3.67		3.00		4.00						
Porcelain undescribed															
NG						4.00									6.00
NH															
HD															
Porcelain plain white															
NG															
NH									5.83						
Porcelain lustre															
NG														4.00	
NH															
HD															

HD = with handle; NH = without handle; NG = not mentioned

other words, the cost of a seven-inch shell edge plate has to be divided by the cost of a seven-inch CC plate from the same bill, or the cost of a London-size transfer printed cup has to be divided by the cost of a London-size CC cup. In this way the variables are controlled. The resulting index numbers have a great deal of consistency. For example, consider the CC index values for ten-inch shell edge plates worked out from potters' and jobbers' wholesale prices in England and North America (table 15.4).

The consistency of the CC index value regardless of the type and origin of the document suggests something about marketing practices. If the standard practice was for jobbers and retailers to base their prices on a percentage increase of the potters' wholesale prices, then the ratios between the cost of CC and the other decorative types would be intact through the various levels of the mercantile system. Using an index value system based on CC wares greatly increases the number of documents that can be used together to create an overview of

Table 15.3 *CC index values for bowls*

	1802	1814	1824	1833	1836	1838	1846	1855	1858
CC	1.00	1.00	1.00	1.00	1.00	1.00	1.00	1.00	1.00
Dipped		1.20	1.20	1.29	1.40	1.20	1.20		1.10
Sponged								1.10	
White glazed		1.60							
Painted	2.33	1.60	1.67	1.71	1.80	1.60	1.60	1.30	
Printed		2.80	2.50	2.57	3.00		2.80	2.00	2.00
Flow								2.40	
White granite or ironstone									2.00
Basalt		6.00					6.00		

Table 15.4 *CC index values for ten-inch shell edge plates*

Date	CC index value	Document type	Origin of price list
1796	1.33	Potter's price list	Staffordshire
1802	1.37	Jobber's bill	Montreal
1814	1.33	Potter's price list	Staffordshire
1824	1.33	Jobber's account book	Philadelphia
1833	1.29	Potter's price list	Staffordshire
1836	1.33	Potter's bill	Staffordshire
1838	1.33	Potter's bill	Staffordshire
1839	1.20	Potter's bill	Staffordshire
1855	1.20	Potter's price list	Scotland
1858	1.00	Jobber's bill	Philadelphia

Table 15.5 *CC index value for plates from the Franklin Glass Works site*

Type	CC index value	times	No. recovered	Value
CC	1.00	×	5	= 5.00
Edged	1.29	×	24	= 30.96
Willow	2.86	×	1	= 2.86
Other printed	3.21	×	3	= 9.63
Totals			33 plates	48.45

Average value 48.45 = 1.47
$$\frac{48.45}{33} = 1.47$$

the changing relationships of the various types of ceramics available throughout the nineteenth century. If the right documents can be found, it will even be possible to relate tin and glassware to ceramic index values. Catalogs from Sears and Roebuck, Montgomery Ward, and Eatons will be useful for this in the very late nineteenth century.

15.3 CC index numbers and archaeological assemblages

Using CC index values is quite simple. Once the minimal vessel count has been completed, the plates, cups, and bowls should be grouped by decorative type. Then a year is selected from tables 15.1–15.3. If the site has a long occupation, then it might be best to break the assemblages into time units and use more than one scale because the index values change through time. Next, the index values are multiplied by the number of vessels recovered of each type. For example, consider the plates from the factory area of the Franklin Glass Works of Portage County, Ohio. This site was occupied from 1824 to c.1832 (Miller 1974b). The CC scale used for this collection is for the year 1824: that is, as close as the present set of scales can come to period of occupation. The index values used are for eight-inch plates (table 15.5). The average expenditure on plates for this collection is about one and a half times greater than the cost of plain CC plates. Average CC index values were also worked out for cups, bowls, and for the same vessel forms from the assemblage of a house area on the site (table 15.6). From the above index values, it can be seen how this system will allow the economic scaling of assemblages and scaling within assemblages.

For example, consider the difference in expenditure levels between cups, plates, and bowls. Figure 15.6 is a graphical representation of the average CC index values for cups, plates, and bowls for six ceramic assemblages from four sites. In four of the six assemblages, the average expenditure above the cost of CC ware is the highest for cups. The cumulative average for cups is 18% higher than plates and 31% higher than bowls. This suggests that tea ware functioned more in a role of status display than plates or bowls. The low average value of bowls in the CC index scale may be related to their dual functions, i.e., less expensive kitchen ware bowls being averaged with more expensive table ware bowls. From these six assemblages, it is easy to see the usefulness of the CC index numbers in dealing with archaeological assemblages. They would also be useful in dealing with probate inventories that contain descriptions of the decorative types. A comparison of scaling of second-hand prices to one constructed from CC index

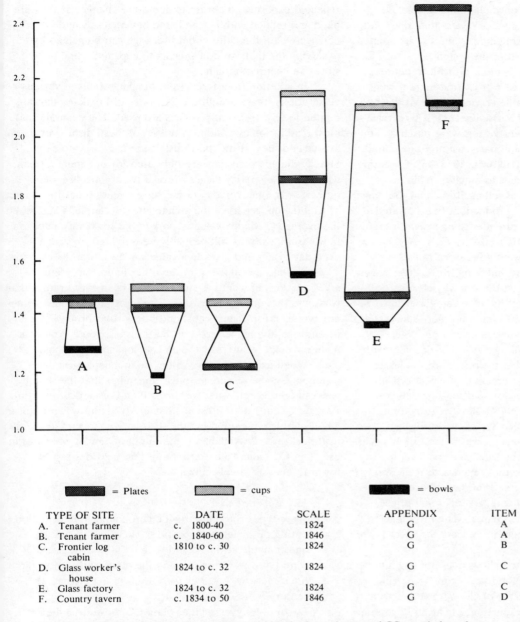

	= Plates		= cups		= bowls

TYPE OF SITE	DATE	SCALE	APPENDIX	ITEM
A. Tenant farmer	c. 1800-40	1824	G	A
B. Tenant farmer	c. 1840-60	1846	G	A
C. Frontier log cabin	1810 to c. 30	1824	G	B
D. Glass worker's house	1824 to c. 32	1824	G	C
E. Glass factory	1824 to c. 32	1824	G	C
F. Country tavern	c. 1834 to 50	1846	G	D

Fig. 15.6. The average value of cups, plates, and bowls above the cost of CC vessels from four sites. Plates plus cups plus bowls equal 100%

numbers would be interesting and could provide information on whether used goods maintained the relative value positions between decorative types or whether they declined in value in a disproportionate pattern. Having an interval value scale for ceramics is going to increase our ability to perform socio-economic analysis of archaeological collections.

15.4 Availability value range

When considering an interval value scale, it is quite natural to wonder what the ends of the scale look like and how great the distance is between the bottom and top. For refined earthenware, plain undecorated CC is the cheapest, and, as

Table 15.6 *CC index values for plates, cups, and bowls from the factory and home areas of the Franklin Glass Works site*

	Factory collection	Home collection
Plates	1.47	1.86
Cups	2.11	2.15
Bowls	1.37	1.54

such, it is the measuring device for the scale. Redware and yellow ware bowls (and possibly mugs), however, probably have an index value of less than one. Plain and enamelled tinware vessels also should have a value of less than one, and when documents are found allowing index values to be created for these types, they will be added to the system.

The upper end of the scale is more difficult to define. Some idea of how far above the cost of CC the market went is provided by the commissioned table service Josiah Wedgwood made for Catherine the Great of Russia in 1775. This service cost about £3,500. If the equivalent vessels were purchased in undecorated creamware, they would have cost fifty-one pounds, eight shillings, and four pence (Mankowitz 1953, 46). Catherine the Great's set cost sixty-eight times as much as plain creamware. Commissioned services tell us little about the range of what was available as standard production, but a printed price list by Ridgeway from 1813 provides some insight into this question. It is titled 'SCALE FOR CHINA, TEA, AND BREAKFAST SETS' and lists twenty-one price ranges for a number of vessel forms (Ridgeway and Sons 1813). Prices given and use of the term 'China' suggest that the vessels are porcelain. Unfortunately, none of the price categories have decorative type descriptions, or information other than vessel form. Twelve cups and saucers range in price from nine shillings to four pounds three shillings. Another problem with this list is that it is not clear whether the prices are wholesale or retail. In the 1814 price fixing agreement of the Staffordshire potters, a dozen CC cups and saucers sold for eighteen pence. If the 1813 Ridgeway list represents wholesale prices for porcelain, then it would appear that the cheapest English porcelain set of twelve cups and saucers was at least six times as expensive as the equivalent CC cups and saucers. The upper end of the scale indicates that the most expensive Ridgeway cups and saucers were fifty-three times more expensive than plain CC ones. If the Ridgeway list represents retail prices, then the differences would not be so great. The fifty-three to one difference, however, does seem to indicate the great range that was available in tea and table ware.

The range of values suggested above does not begin to be reflected in the six assemblages plotted on figure 15.6. The highest average value above the cost of CC ware comes from the Walker Tavern in Cambridge Junction, Michigan (Grosscup and Miller 1968). None of the average values for this site exceed two and one-half times the value of CC, and these are typical assemblages for nineteenth-century sites in North America.

In considering the low average CC index value from archaeological assemblages, it is necessary to keep in mind the process of deposition. Excavated collections usually represent an accumulation of what was broken or discarded. For table ware there are differential breakage rates and potential for discard to be taken into consideration. For example, tin cups or silver mugs will outlast ceramic or glass mugs, and even when they are beyond use, the silver would not be discarded. Different ceramic forms also have differential breakage rates. Cups, for example, are more subject to breaking than saucers because of the amount of handling they receive and their

repeated exposure to abrupt temperature changes as they are filled and refilled with hot and cold beverages. Some perspective on this differential breakage can be gained by observing the high ratio of saucers to cups in second-hand stores and church bazaars.

In addition to differences in breakage rates in various vessel forms, there are differential rates of breakage that are related to how frequently vessels are used. The example that most readily comes to mind is the set of 'best' dishes versus the everyday dishes. If the 'best' dishes are only used to serve Sunday dinner, then they are only used for one meal a week, whereas the everyday dishes average twenty meals a week. In other words, the everyday dishes have twenty times the chance of winding up as part of the archaeological sample. Thus, when the average CC index value is worked out for plates, cups, and bowls from a site, it will probably be weighted towards the everyday dishes and provide a value somewhat on the low side.

Probate inventories, on the other hand, represent accumulations of what has survived and been saved rather than what was broken and discarded. Therefore, if CC index values are averaged for plates, cups, and bowls from probate inventories, the higher ratio of 'best' dishes would provide a higher average value than the archaeological assemblage.

When using CC index values on archaeological assemblages, the researcher must remember that the sample generally represents what was broken and discarded over time. Probate inventories represent what survived and was present in a household at one point in time. It is very important to use the historical records available to round out a view of what was in use. The CC index values are a tool that provides a start towards analysis of collections.

15.5 Conclusions

1. Ware types can only provide chronological information during the nineteenth century. Their identification is questionable at times, and there is little evidence that ware types were used during the nineteenth century in the same way that they were used in the eighteenth century.

2. Decorative types such as plain CC, edged, painted, dipped, and printed were the major classification used during the nineteenth century. Classification based on the decorative types has several advantages.

(a) Integration of historical and archaeological data;

(b) Consistency of identification; and

(c) Classification will reflect economic classes.

3. During the nineteenth century ceramic prices appear to have declined somewhat faster than general commodity prices.

4. Prices of undecorated CC vessels were fairly stable during the nineteenth century, providing an excellent scale against which to measure changes in the value of other decorative types.

5. Using the price of CC vessels, index values have been created from a variety of documents such as bills of

lading, price lists, price fixing lists, account books, and invoice statements.

6. These index numbers can be used to calculate the average cost above CC vessels for plates, cups, and bowls from archaeological sites and inventories, allowing sites to be scaled in terms of their expenditure on ceramics.[1]

Note

1. This paper is an outgrowth of a research project on shell edge decorated wares that was started when I was an employee of the St Mary's City Commission, St Mary's City, Maryland. I would like to thank the Commission for allowing me to take copies of my notes on shell edge and ceramic prices with me when I took my position at Parks Canada, during which time this article was written. I would also like to thank Parks Canada for allowing me to continue my research on shell edge decorated wares and for providing research trips to the Henry Francis du Pont Winterthur Museum, Winterthur, Delaware, and to the Smithsonian Institution, Washington, D.C., to examine ceramic price lists, bills of lading, and account books held by these institutions. I would particularly like to thank Arlene Palmer who brought several important sources to my attention in the Joseph Downs Manuscript Collection in the Winterthur Museum Library. Susan Myers is to be thanked for arranging my use of the Warshaw Collection of Business Americana in the Smithsonian Institution. Lorene Mayo of the Warshaw Collection was helpful in locating price lists and having them copied for my use. My research trip to the Warshaw Collection would not have been nearly so productive without her direction to documents that I would have missed in my search of the collection. Information on price fixing lists from England was provided by Arnold Mountford of the City Museum and Art Gallery of Stoke-on-Trent, and additional price information was provided by V. Tyrrell of the City Central Library of Stoke-on-Trent. I would like to thank Steve Demeter of Commonwealth Associates for providing some prices on American White Granite ware. Last but not least I would like to thank my colleagues at Parks Canada for their helpful suggestions, comments, and encouragement. In particular I would like to thank Lynne Sussman, Dorothy Griffiths, and Louise Lepine.

Chapter 16

**For gentlemen of capacity and leisure:
the archaeology of colonial newspapers**

Stephen A. Mrozowski

This chapter addresses the use of colonial newspapers in historical archaeology. Emphasis is placed upon their use for both analytical and interpretive purposes. Ceramic advertisements are shown to have demonstrated value for refining dating techniques. These same ads are used to examine changes in the marketing of ceramics. The remainder of the chapter deals with the issue of womens' roles in colonial society and how newspapers can contribute to archaeologists' attempts to investigate the emic parameters of such an issue. Attention is given to a 1733 anecdote that describes a husband's concern over his wife's growing consumerism. This anecdote is used as a point of departure for a discussion of the archaeological investigation of changes in women's status during the eighteenth century. It is also argued that the relationship between women's status and material culture can be further explored for use in studies of other complex societies.

16.1 Introduction

When James Franklin began publishing the *Rhode Island Gazette* in 1732 he sought 'Gentlemen of Capacity and Leisure' who wished to 'communicate their thoughts' in his newspaper (*Rhode Island Gazette* 1732). Throughout much of the eighteenth century, colonial newspapers like Franklin's acted as outlets for commentary and opinion on a variety of political, economic, and social issues. In Boston, for example, newspapers became the chief voice of elites and non-elites during the period leading up to the American Revolution (see Nash 1979). As vehicles for the expression of opinion, these early newspapers represent a unique form of documentary source. Newspapers also contained some of the earliest examples of advertisements. Merchants and shopkeepers made frequent use of newspapers to advertise their merchandise. Because they were part of a growing system of communication between commercial centers in the colonies and in Europe, newspapers can provide the archaeologist with a rare glimpse into the world of international exchange. At the same time, more traditional concerns, such as dating techniques like those developed by South (1972, 1977) can be refined through the use of newspaper ads. Even such time-honored topics as seasonality can be examined through the use of these documents (e.g., Potter 1984, 37–50).

The purpose of this chapter is to demonstrate some of the ways in which newspapers can aid the historical archaeologist. Part of the discussion will focus on using ceramic advertisements to refine our dating techniques and to examine shifting marketing priorities. Another point will concern the value of opinions and anecdotes appearing in these early newspapers as potential sources of emically sensitive data. It will be argued that these data can help us in redefining problem domains for the discipline by contributing to the development of cultural contexts for interpreting the archaeological record. A single case study will be presented that suggests we need to rethink our perceptions of gender in terms of the archaeological record in general and of the role of women in structuring the record in particular.

16.2 Advertisements

The primary source of income for most if not all newspapers during the eighteenth century was paid advertisements. Merchants and shopkeepers who wished to expand their markets could place advertisements in a variety of newspapers. Besides the written descriptions of items that these ads contained, there is also evidence of marketing practices designed to target particular sectors of the population (e.g., Miller 1984, 1–5). In some instances terms of exchange are also mentioned in the ads. Advertisements for ceramics were among the more common to be found in newspapers during the eighteenth and early nineteenth centuries. The appendix (p. 190) contains a series of ceramic ads from Newport and Providence, Rhode Island, newspapers covering the period 1762 to 1835. These advertisements form the basis of the discussion of ceramic availability and exchange that follows.

One of the basic concerns archaeologists have is artifact dating. In historical archaeology, dating techniques such as that devised by South (1972, 1977) rely primarily upon the use of median dates of ceramic manufacture. Such dates can be further refined by consulting ceramic advertisements that contain information on the availability of specific wares in a given market. For example, 'Queensware' is first mentioned in three separate ads placed in the *Providence Gazette* in 1771. Cream-colored ware, as it was later called, was last noted in an 1834 ad. There are other examples of how ceramic ads can help refine our temporal controls. The year 1771 is the median date used by South (1977, 212) for 'deeper yellow creamware' in calculating his mean ceramic date. If the three advertisements placed in 1771 accurately represent the year when 'Queensware' was first made available to the Providence market, then the dates proposed by South may be too early for use in the area. The same is probably true for the 1798 median date South suggests for 'lighter yellow creamware' (ibid.). This lighter, cream-colored ware was available after 1830, as evidenced by the ad noted above. South (1977, 210–13) notes that the dates he offers for use in his formula are based upon current data, and thereby he implies that they are subject to refinement. Blue- and green-edged pearlwares and whitewares are noted twice in ads placed in 1797 and 1823. Blue-printed wares are quite prominent in ads of the early nineteenth century, although beginning in 1831 the appearance of 'black, blue, brown, green, red, and purple printed goods' signaled the spread of the popular transfer-printed wares of the mid-nineteenth century. Ads provide the archaeologist with periods of availability that are community- or area-specific dating guides. While not necessarily a substitute for mean manufacturing dates, these dates are more sensitive to local market availability.

In addition to their use for dating purposes, ceramic advertisements furnish a body of data concerning assemblage composition that complements the archaeological record. Charles LaSalle's 1797 ad in the *Newport Mercury* will serve to illustrate this point. In his ad, LaSalle noted that he had for sale:

Tureens in the imitation of a roast turkey, dishes with covers, green, blue and brown edge and cream color also, with pans and covers in the imitation of pies and tarts.

The mention of brown edging on wares is of interest in terms of their availability because of the low incidence of the ware in archaeological assemblages from the region. Its counterparts, both blue- and green-edged vessels, are quite common in site assemblages throughout New England (e.g., Deetz 1973; Faulkner, Peters, Sell and Dethlefsen 1978; Moran, Zimmer and Yentsch 1982; Roussel 1984, 73–84). Ornately designed tureens and pans such as those described by LaSalle are also rare occurrences in archaeological assemblages. 'Enameled stoneware' noted in Nathaniel Balch's announcement in a 1764 *Providence Gazette* represents still another example of a ware that is found infrequently in archaeological contexts.

What appears as a dissonance between the documents and the archaeology may be more a question of preference or cost as opposed to the availability of the wares to which the ads testify. Deetz (personal communication) has noted the presence of red- and yellow-edged pearlware plates on archaeological sites in the western United States. Their apparent unpopularity hindered their sale on the East Coast, so they were sent to a frontier market. Brown-edged ware may have shared this unpopularity during its initial introduction. In the case of enameled stoneware, the extra cost expected from hand painting may have been a factor in the rarity of the ware in mid- to late eighteenth-century household assemblages. In both examples, newspaper advertisements confirm the availability of such wares, thereby providing a set of controls that can aid in formulating alternative hypotheses. Without such controls, the mere lack of availability would be an explanation for their infrequency in the archaeological record, one that would require a great deal of fieldwork to refute.

During the eighteenth century the Newport and Providence newspapers were geared essentially for the town market. Country traders in the rural districts would look to the ads in these papers in order to determine what was available at wholesale prices. Beginning in the late eighteenth century, the urban focus of the newspapers was altered somewhat to account for a growing country trade. Providence merchants, in particular, saw this opportunity, and by shifting their efforts in the direction of the rural districts, were able to eclipse Newport as Rhode Island's chief commercial center (Withey 1984, 91–108). Newport, which had been the mercantile hub throughout Rhode Island's colonial history, relied heavily upon the West Indian and coastal trade. After the devastation of the British occupation during the American Revolution, Newport merchants were hard pressed for the capital necessary to rebuild their commercial fleet. Providence merchants were likewise engaged in the coastal trade, but also grasped the initiative in supplying rural Rhode Island, eastern Connecticut, and southeastern Massachusetts.

The shift in economic focus by Providence merchants may be why the *Providence Gazette* was joined by two new newspapers, the *Providence Journal* and the *Town and Country*

Advertiser, in the waning years of the eighteenth century. Among the ceramic advertisements in the papers (see Appendix) are examples targeted specifically for 'country subscribers'. These ads are different than those aimed at the urban market in that, contrary to the allure of fashion, superior quality and elegance, merchants sought to attract rural customers by stressing durability and low cost. As early as 1801, Benjamin Thurber informed 'country subscribers' that 'wood and grain will be accepted as payment'. With the spread of rural industry in the nineteenth century and the migration to rural districts that accompanied it (cf. Henretta 1973), Providence dealers began advertising to 'country merchants' and 'agents of manufacturing companies' (*Providence Gazette* 1831). A slant toward the country market remains evident at least until 1835, the date of the last paper used in this study. Poetry was even employed as a marketing device, as this 1833 M. G. and D. Cady Jr ad in the *Providence Gazette* illustrates:

> Drop in and see, my country friend,
> goods are cheap, you may depend.

16.3 Summary

It seems clear that by the early nineteenth century newspaper advertisements were being targeted for a variety of markets. Wholesalers and retailers involved in the country trade represent one of the groups identified in the ceramic ads. A second market was the agents of manufacturing companies who were interested in purchasing goods that could be made available to their employees on credit through the company store. One additional group that the ads indicate as a marketing priority is women. Charles LaSalle, for example, solicited women customers in his 1797 ad in the *Newport Mercury* that read: 'Those ladies who call at this store will be pleased of the newest fashion.' It is possible that the express use of terms such as 'fashionable' in advertisements were attempts to appeal to women. This interpretation is based upon the belief that women played a pivotal role in household decisions concerning the purchase of domestic goods. Nash (1979, 132), for example, notes that 'women were the principal marketgoers in the eighteenth century.' There is also evidence to suggest that in the minds of some a desire for fashionable goods fell squarely within the female domain. In support of this thesis the following anecdote that appeared in the Rhode Island Gazette on 25 January 1733 is presented. It was written by someone who described himself as a 'tradesman'. While we must be cautious in interpreting such documents, I believe it is possible to gain some perspective on the emic realities of the period in question.

16.4 Emic perspectives

The tradesman's difficulties began with his marriage. Prior to meeting his spouse, her father was often heard saying that if he liked the man his daughter married, he would give her £200 on the day of her wedding. Unfortunately, our honest tradesman was apparently not to his father-in-law's liking because 'not a farthing' was forthcoming. Still, the couple was

not, as the tradesman noted in 'so poor a condition as the couple described in the Scotch Song who had neither pot nor pan but four bare legs together.' He possessed 'a house tolerably furnished for an ordinary man'. After suggesting that his wife's father was an 'old Carmudgeon' never intending to part with the £200, the tradesman follows:

> I soon saw that with Care and Industry we might live tolerably easy and in credit with our Neighbors: But my Wife had a strong Inclination to be a '*Gentlewoman*'. (emphasis mine)[1]

To illustrate his discovery, the tradesman described the consequences occasioned by the breaking of his 'old fashioned looking glass':

> Since we could not be without a Glass in the Room, My Dear says she 'we may as well buy a larger fashionable one that Mr. Sucha one has to sell, it will cost but little more than a common Glass, and will be much handsomer and more creditable.'

Soon after the looking glass was purchased, the tradesman's wife pointed out that the table in the room was 'by no means suitable for such a glass.' The new table was followed by the purchase of new 'very handsome' chairs prompting the tradesman to lament,

> And thus by Degrees I found all my old furniture stowed up into the Garret; and everything below altered for the better.

With these acquisitions made, the tradesman was hopeful that this rampant display of consumerism was ended. He noted 'Had we stop'd here we might have done well enough.' Unfortunately this was not to be the case, he continues:

> My wife being entertained with Tea by the good Women she visited, we could do no less than the like when they visited us, and so we got a Tea Table with its Appurtenances of China and Silver.

Following the purchase of the tea table, the approach taken by the tradesman's wife changed, or so he suggests:

> Then my spouse overworked herself washing the house, so that we could do no longer without a maid.

By displaying an inability to have dinner on time, the wife was able to convince her husband that a clock was the next necessity. Finally the tradesman bemoaned:

> And lastly, to my Grief, she was frequently troubled with some Ailment or other, and nothing did her so much Good as Riding and [apparently quoting his wife] 'these Hackney Horses were such wretched ugly Creatures' that I bought a very fine pacing Mare which cost £20. And hereabouts Affairs have stood for some months past.

The propensity for consumption on the part of the tradesman's wife was, as he states: 'Utterly inconsistent with my Circumstances.' His solution to the dilemma reveals a set of curious structural oppositions that resulted from a male/female dichotomy concerning common choices that may have been prevalent among other urban households. Upon his wife's traveling to see a relation, the tradesman embraced the opportunity 'to make some alterations.' These changes are telling, to say the least:

I have turn'd away the Maid, Bag and Bagage, we have (except my Boy) none but ourselves. I have sold the Pacing Mare, and bought a good Milchick Cow, with £3 of the money. I have disposed of the Tea Table, and put a Spinning Wheel in its Place, which me thinks looks very pretty: Nine empty Canisters I have stuffted with Flax; and with some of the Money of the Tea Furniture, I have bought a set of Knitting Needles, for to tell you the truth, which I would have to go no farther I begin to want stockings. The Statley Clock I have transformed into an Hour Glass, by which I gained a good round sum; and one of the Pieces of the old looking Glass, squared and framed, supplies the Place of the Great One; which it may possibly remain for years. In Short, the Face of things is quite changed; and I am mightily pleased when I look at my Hour Glass, what an Ornament it is to the Room. I have paid my Debts, and find Money in my Pocket.

He concluded with a friendly note to his wife, whom he hoped upon reading the article would be forewarned of what had transpired.

Portrayed in this anecdote is a male's view of the domestic domain. It is a world in conflict, a world caught between a desire for gentility and the realities of its cost. In the image presented by the tradesman the problem is personified by his wife, whose consumerism is at odds with the couples' position in society. The domestic world is presented as a dichotomy between women of labor and women of leisure, symbolically represented as a series of structural oppositions: a Spinning Wheel vs. a Tea Table; a Milch cow vs. a Pacing Mare; a Maid vs. 'My Boy'. In each instance the tradesman depicts his problem in material terms. While admittedly a biased viewpoint, this anecdote can still provide us with useful insights. The dichotomy drawn by the tradesman between himself and his wife in the anecdote suggests that the material world was structured according to gender. Just how pervasive this view was in the early eighteenth century is a difficult question to answer with the limited data currently at hand. It does seem, however, that merchants and shopkeepers were aware of the gender line; their ads testify to a concern for attracting women to the market place.

Perhaps what is most intriguing about this anecdote is its image of a material world structured by gender. The conflict does not involve the actual expenditure of funds as much as what will be purchased. Milch cows and pacing mares both cost money. The problem concerns whether the woman will play a productive role and devote her time to home industry or concern herself instead with home entertainment. The fact that the tradesman's 'boy' is considered, by him, appropriate, but not the maid, reveals the contradiction in portraying the woman as being the root of the problem. Obviously, caution must be taken in placing too much weight on the interpretive value of such a biased document. Yet, even if it was intended largely as a humorous anecdote over which many a sympathetic male might have a good chuckle, the role of humor in expressing underlying tensions within society cannot be overlooked (cf. Thomas 1977, 77).

There are, however, certain questions that both the anecdote treated at length above and the advertisements discussed earlier raise concerning women and their role in structuring the archaeological record. This question holds particular significance for historical archaeologists who employ the documentary record in their research. As the 1733 anecdote reveals, the written record can be biased in favor of the white Anglo-Saxon males primarily responsible for its production. Before pursuing this question, I would like to present a brief summary of other studies that have focused some attention on women's roles in society. In so doing, I hope to demonstrate that it is impossible to ignore women as a research priority.

According to Anderson (1971) women played a prominent role in the foodways system of seventeenth-century yeoman households. In his discussion of 'domestic geography' (1971, 28–31) he notes that the yeoman homelot was divided into two areas: the 'toft' that included the house and yard, and the 'croft' made up of the orchard and enclosed pasture. The toft, as Anderson (1971, 29) points out, was the domain of women:

Food procurement on the toft – the yard in particular – was the responsibility of the housewife and her servants. She held domestic dominion over the yard with its garden, livestock pens and dairy barns.

Deetz (1977, 52–3) suggests that this yeoman foodways tradition was transported to the New World by the early settlers of Plymouth Colony. The tradition is represented archaeologically by the utilitarian red earthenwares used in dairying. Brown (1973, 41–74) was able to confirm the prevalence of a wide variety of redware forms in the probate records of seventeenth-century Plymouth, Massachusetts, and Essex, England. In seventeenth-century England, dairying was commonly the responsibility of women (Anderson 1971, 119). Whether this aspect of the tradition was transported to the New World is not addressed by either Deetz or Brown. It may be that in the colonial situation a rigid adherence to a gender-delineated division of labor was not possible. Given the importance of dairy products to yeoman households in both England (Anderson 1971, 118–38) and New England (Deetz 1977, 53), questions concerning the status of women in households of this period emerge as a significant – but often ignored – research priority. One need only glance at South's artifact group used to characterize his Carolina and Brunswick Artifact Patterns (1977, 83–139) to recognize that in most cases the 'Kitchen' group alone usually represents close to 60% of all the material recovered. If these materials are reflective of women's activities, then we need to rethink our research strategies.

In order to address questions such as the status of women, we need to determine the material signatures of differential status between men and women. Hodder's (1982,

83–4) ethnoarchaeological research in Kenya indicates that 'In the Baringo area, the overt male/female dichotomy is exceptionally marked and the status of women is especially low.' This low status is expressed in material culture by a level of conformity among women that is not found among the men. Hodder suggests that this conformity in women's material culture is the result 'not only of the male demand for submission, but also of the general sympathy and mutual support among women' (1982, 83). Such interpretations must be tempered, as Hodder notes, by the knowledge that the level of male/female conflict is linked to the nature of the economic relationships within each society (ibid.). These male/female relationships are therefore not static and are subject to change depending upon the type of social or economic system that characterizes the society during the period of study.

Goody's comparative study (1976) of the transition from hoe to plough agriculture also points to a link between economic and social formations. While Goody draws primarily upon anthropological studies conducted in Africa and Asia over the past century, he also attempts to employ historical studies in order to develop a broad evolutionary perspective. In particular, Goody (1976, 8–22) posits a causal relationship between changes in the mode of agricultural production and changes in the way property is transmitted. Women both as property and as the heirs to property again play a prominent role in Goody's thesis. Ember (1983, 285–304) suggests a similar relationship between the mode of agricultural production and the roles of women. She argues that a shift toward more intensified forms of agriculture results in greater domestic labor for women in these societies (1983, 299). One of Ember's more interesting observations is that the increase in domestic labor not only removes women from the public, male-dominated sphere, but also results in a rise in fertility.

Social historians have dealt with the issue of women's status within the context of changes brought about by industrialization and modernization (e.g., Branca 1975, 129–153; Shammas 1980, 3–24; Cott 1978). Cott (1978, 63–100) has dealt extensively with the 'rise of domesticity' whereby the home became the center of 'virtue and sociability' by shedding its links to the cold, competitive world outside. One reason for this was the changing nature of labor under industrialization that saw the factory slowly replace the home as the center of production.

> The canon of domesticity encouraged people to assimilate such change by linking it to a specific set of sex roles . . . the home contrasted to the restless and competitive world . . . The spirit of business and public life thus appeared to diverge from that of the home chiefly because the two spheres were the separate domains of the two sexes.

Shammas (1980, 3–24) has also addressed the issue of 'heightened household sociability' vis-à-vis the status of women. She argues that because the household was becoming the arena for 'non-market social interaction', more money was spent on enhancing the domestic environment. Drawing upon a variety of documentary sources, Shammas indicates that middle-class household expenditures increasingly went for items ranging from bedding and furniture to dinnerware and musical instruments.

What makes Shammas' discussion so provocative is the similarity between what she describes and what Deetz (1977) has recognized archaeologically. Deetz found that on New England archaeological sites occupied after 1760 there was a marked increase in the number of chamber pots and plates, the latter as part of matched sets of dinnerware. His explanation for this increase is

> a new accommodation between the individual and his material culture . . . a one-to-one match, with each person probably having his own plate and chamber pot. This would certainly be an expression of a newly emerging world view characterized by order, control, and balance.
> (1977, 136)

Deetz feels that the source of this new world view was Renaissance thought that spread to England and then to America during the eighteenth century. He feels that this ideology is also evident in mortuary art and in Georgian architecture (Deetz 1977, 64–177; cf. Glassie 1972a, 268–79; Glassie 1975). If such an ideology existed in eighteenth-century New England, it appeared first in the cities, according to Deetz (1973, 30–2). That the material patterns Deetz (1973, 1977) observed were seen first in New England cities appears to be confirmed by archaeological investigations conducted in urban areas (e.g., Faulkner et al. 1978; Moran, Zimmer and Yentsch 1982; Mrozowski 1984a, 31–49). Whether, however, these patterns are indicative of a new world view depend on whether ceramics in trash pits are viewed as a direct reflection of ideology rather than as material expressions of changes in household structure and modes of production. Neither Deetz nor Glassie addresses the question of gender in this emerging world view. But if, however, the individualism Deetz (1977, 59–61) feels is evident in the material record is interpreted as conformity in material culture, then Hodder's observations (1982, 83) concerning conformity may apply in this case as well. A desire for conformity seems evident in the 1733 anecdote. According to the tradesman, his wife could do no less than reciprocate for having been invited to take tea with the 'good women' (see Roth 1961). Does this indicate a low status for these women, as Hodder's (1982, 82–3) interpretation suggests it does among the groups he investigated?

A complete answer to this question may be beyond the scope of this chapter, although some speculations can be offered. Hodder (1982, 83) notes the non-static nature of status, particularly regarding women. As suggested previously, the status of women is likely tied to the economic system. Saffioti, for example, asserts that within capitalist societies there exist 'distinctive cultural patterns which regulate the participation of female labor' (1974, 60). These cultural patterns emphasize women's unique role in the reproduction of labor power. Larguia goes a step further in advocating that these cultural patterns are used coercively by elites to mask the process whereby

Gradually men monopolized the work that produced visible, exchangeable products. Through this process, in the development of a class society, the family took shape as a legal and productive unit by means of which the men, the ruling classes appropriated the surplus labor of women. (1974, 284–5)

The conflict portrayed in the 1733 anecdote centers on the issue of women's labor. Therefore it is possible that the sentiment expressed in the anecdote is meant to counter or mask the process determined by Larguia above. The only problem with this interpretation is that, like most of the literature that deals with the relationship between industrialization and the status of women, Larguia's study assumes that pre-industrial societies were also pre-capitalist. This assumption is now being questioned by students of colonial British American history as part of an overall rejection of the 'traditional/modern' dichotomy long a tenet of social analysis (e.g., Greene and Pole 1984, 11; Lemon 1984, 100–11; Henretta 1984, 279–85). Industrialization may have accelerated earlier changes, but cultural transformations like that described by Larguia (1974, 281–95) and Saffioti (1974, 59–93) were probably not isolated to nineteenth-century, industrial-capitalist societies. It may just be that the real issue is not so much industrialization as urbanization. While some women may have continued their productive activities in the urbanized communities of Britain (e.g., Davidson 1983, 204–5) and the colonies, the image of a 'Gentlewoman' illustrated in the 1733 anecdote suggests that some may have begun to leave them behind. It may be that the ideology described by Deetz and Glassie had as one of its components a new status for women. Determining the spatial, temporal, and social parameters of such a transformation would be a research question worth pursuing.

If such a transformation began first in the urban centers among the elite and those so aspiring, then one might anticipate a gradual spread over time to the middle and possibly lower strata of colonial society. Warner's 1962 study of Boston's suburban development in the late nineteenth century and Strasser's 1982 investigation into the spread of household technology during the same period indicate a change in women's roles among the middle class by this time. Warner in fact suggests that a reliance upon a single, male-derived income was a true characteristic of middle-class, suburban households in Boston during the second half of the nineteenth century (1962, 8–9). Recent ethnoarchaeological research in Boston (e.g., Mrozowski 1984b, 13–36) also indicates that the ways in which ceramics and rooms are classified and used in contemporary households reflect patterns that originated among the urban elite during the eighteenth and nineteenth centuries. Therefore, it is just possible that the archaeological record is among the most sensitive barometers of social change. The material culture deposited in the refuse pits of both urban and rural houselots of the post-Revolutionary era in North America may contain crucial information concerning the shift in women's roles from members of the productive unit to consumers of the products of men's labor.

16.5 Conclusion

In this chapter I have sought to demonstrate how documents can help archaeologists refine both their analytical and interpretive skills. Beyond their subsidiary role, however, documents possess great value for investigating how and what information is passing through a cultural system. In colonial America the flow of information concerning prices, events, and opinions was greatly facilitated by vehicles like newspapers. The importance of controlling the transmission of information cannot be overstated. Merchants and shopkeepers in colonial America, for example, could manipulate the market, influence trade and affect decision-making at the household level concerning the expenditure of capital. Those who controlled the flow of information were therefore able to wield power and influence. Lemon suggests that in colonial America 'social status depended in large measure on controlling information much the same way it does in today's society' (1984, 114).

Most if not all newspapers were published in urban centers during the eighteenth and nineteenth centuries. This is also significant, because cities appear to have always served as centers for the exchange of goods and information whether it be medieval or post-medieval Europe or the earliest states of the Middle East (e.g., Wright 1969; Wright and Johnson 1975, 267–89; Johnson 1978, 87–112). This means that urban dwellers and in particular the elites normally have access to information not afforded to those residing in the hinterlands. Newspapers provided those living in colonial American cities an additional forum for expressing their views. For 'Gentleman of Capacity and Leisure' it was an opportunity to convey their thoughts on the order of things. It seems part of this view may have included a certain role for women. However, this is a question that remains unanswered, especially in terms of timing and causality. Urbanization has been suggested as one possible variable in the equation. It is still unclear what women themselves were thinking. The documentary record dominated by men provides only *their* perceptions of women. And as the 1733 anecdote suggests, males of different classes may not have shared the same values.

Archaeology in the traditional sense is well suited for investigating material relations. Documents can provide that essential link between material culture, its use, and the attitudes held in common about it. They may also allow us insights into the emic perspective of the participants in cultural systems we wish to understand. If, for example, we want to examine the relationship between material culture and the status of women, then the documentary record cannot be ignored. To do so is to deny ourselves a rich resource well suited for the pursuit of archaeological research.

Note

1. A term used to connote 'a woman of good birth or breeding' dating back at least to the thirteenth century (*Oxford English*

Dictionary 1979, 1132). A collection of poems by New England's Puritan poetess, Anne Bradstreet, published posthumously in 1678, referred to her as a 'Gentlewoman from New England' (Hensley 1967).

Appendix
Ceramic advertisements 1762–1835

Date	Seller	Ware types
1763 Providence Gazette	Joseph and William Russel	Boxes of glass, boxes of pipes, delft and glassware, a variety of the newest fashioned stoneware
,,	James Morton	Fine burnt china
1764 Providence Gazette	Joseph Olney	An assortment of hardware, tea kettles, teapots, pipes, and Liverpool ware
,,	Nathaniel Balch	A neat and beautiful assortment of enameled stoneware, wine and cider glasses, oil and vinegar cruets, and 9, 15, and 18 inch pipes by the box, gross, or dozen
1766 Providence Gazette	Benjamin and Edward Thurber's Shops	Quart pots, plates, quart basons, porringers and basons, black tin teapots, fine delft punch bowls of all sizes, and an assortment of teacups and saucers
,,	Samuel Nightingale	An assortment of brown and white stoneware and delft punch bowls
1771 Providence Gazette	Tillinghast and Holroyd	A fine assortment of queensware, very cheap
,,	E. Bridgham, Boston	At the Staffordshire and Liverpool Warehouse on King Street, Boston. An elegant assortment of china, glass, and stoneware, directly from the manufacturers in Staffordshire and Liverpool
,,	Charles Rhodes	Hard and queensware
,,	John Jenkins	Best queensware, next in quality to china Earthenware
1783 Providence Gazette and Country Journal	Thurber and Chandler	Pewter, platters, basins, quart pots, china teacups and saucers, cream-colored teacups saucers, decanters, tumblers, and wine glasses
1785 Newport Mercury	Emanual Cofe	Pewter dishes and plates, teacups, saucers, teapots and bowls, glass and stoneware
1797 Newport Mercury	John Baker	A general assortment of glassware, Liverpool crockery ware, consisting of best printed enameled, penciled and common
,,	Charles LaSalle	Tureens in imitation of a roast turkey, dishes with covers, green, blue, and brown edge, and cream color also, with pans and covers in the imitation of pies and tarts. Very elegant teapots. Those ladies who call at this store will be pleased of the newest fashion
1799 Providence Journal and Town & Country Advertiser	John Young	Handsome china cups and saucers, a number of complete sets for tea, and other china
,,	Benjamin Thurber	China, Liverpool and Delftware
1800 Newport Mercury	Earl T. Whitehouse	Per ship Ann and Hope, from Canton, China on tea sets
1801 Providence Journal and Town & Country Advertiser	Benjamin Thurber	To country subscribers wood and grain will be accepted as payment
,,	Ben Hoppin & Sons Auction	20 crates of well-assorted Liverpool ware, in such lots as shall suit the purchaser
,,	Bowers and Bucklin	'Jappan'd Ware' Item for cash only
,,	,,	50 boxes china, containing each one tea sett
1809 Providence Gazette	John B. Chace	Jars for preserves, china, large Connecticut stoneware butter pots, especially convenient for this season [July]
1812 Providence Gazette	Phillip Peck	Per ship President Adams, via Boston, from Canton. A very great variety of china ware, consisting of enameled and blue and white china cups and saucers; enameled and blue and white coffee bowls, by the chest or at retail – likewise, some very rich burnished tea and coffee setts, 67 pieces each; small tea setts of china from 43 to 48 pieces each; china dining ware per sett, or less quantity

1815 Providence Gazette	Taylor & Talbot	Canton china, consisting of dining sets, tea and coffee sets and large blue and white plates
1823 Providence Gazette	Dunham, Edgar & Co. Auctioneers	Earthenware at auction, seven hundred and forty eight crates and hogsheads containing a complete assortment of cream colored, mocho and fancy enameled, painted, blue and green edged and blue painted ware of handsome patterns
1825 Providence Gazette	Lowell Adams	Crockery and Chinaware. Imported particularly for this market from one of the best manufactories of Staffordshire consisting of BP dining sets, of superior quality and patterns; BP tea and coffee sets; broad gold band china teas and coffees in setts or by the dozen. China sugars, creams, slop-bowls, cake and dessert plates to match, luster pitchers, tea pots, sugars and creams of an excellent quality and new patterns. Edge and cream-colored ware of all kinds
,,	,,	Have just received, of their own importation, an invoice of superior crock- ery ware, per ship Paragon, of Boston, consisting of BLUE PRINTED, Edge and Cream-Colored Ware – the patterns were selected particularly for this market. The above being the third one we have received from Staffordshire since January last, makes our assortment very exclusive, all of which we offer at wholesale and retail at the lowest prices
1830 Providence Gazette	Edward Carlisle	Gold band china – 2 cases gold band china teas and saucers, with plates to match. Also china tea setts, a variety for sale
1831 Providence Gazette	Moses Potter and Co.	New Goods ... 32 crates and hogsheads of black, blue, brown, green, red and purple printed goods, comprising elegant dining setts, tea and coffee do; toilet ware, bowls, jugs, etc. to match, of the newest style

1833 Providence Gazette	M. G. & D. Cady, Jr	Where can be found a general assortment of crockery, glass and china- ware, of the newest patterns, and at such prices as cannot fail ... 'Drop in and see, my country friend, goods are cheap, you may depend.'
1834 Providence Gazette	Carlile and Foster	Importers and wholesalers and retail dealers in china, glass, and crockeryware keep constantly on hand an extensive assortment, consisting of printed dinner and tea setts, all colors and patterns English china tea setts, a great variety of patterns. French porcelain burnished gold band and line and gold edged. Coffee tea cups and saucers and plates. Printed dishes, all sizes, colors and patterns. Edged dishes, all sizes; cream-colored dishes do. Printed plates, all colors and sizes. do do do do do do Printed edged, and cc soup tureens, sauce, vegetable dishes, sauce boats, fruit baskets. Printed tea setts, all patterns and colors. Printed coffee and tea cups and saucers, all colors and patterns. Enameled coffee and tea cups and saucers. Printed, enameled and cream colored pitchers, all sizes. Nappies, bakers, bowls, ewers, basins and all other articles in earthen and chinaware
1835 Providence Gazette	Carlile, Foster & Co.	Earthen, china and glass- ware – (for) country dealers and others

Chapter 17

What happened to the Silent Majority? Research strategies for studying dominant group material culture in late nineteenth-century California

Mary Praetzellis, Adrian Praetzellis and Marley R. Brown III

The recent surge of interest in questions concerning ethnicity in historical archaeology has produced, for the most part, inconclusive results. It is suggested that archaeologists must first obtain a knowledge of the consumer behavior of middle-class Americans before they attempt to interpret variations in archaeological assemblages that may represent ethnic affiliation or socio-economic differences. Catalogs of expositions such as World's Fairs and advertisements in local newspapers are proposed as ideal sources for research into product availability, pricing, and popularity.

Although American archaeologists have been excavating cities, or portions of them, for well over a century in many parts of the world, it is only recently that they have recognized the potential of urban archaeology in their own backyard. If interest in the archaeology of the city in the United States grew rather slowly, it has now achieved almost celebrity status, as witnessed by the steadily increasing public attention directed to this area of research (e.g., Abramson 1982). This current visibility of urban archaeology is the product of many factors, not the least of which is the increasingly effective implementation of federal laws pertaining to the preservation of significant historical and archaeological resources. Historical archaeologists are now confronted with the problem of evaluating the research potential of a broad range of nineteenth-century urban sites and features. In response to this challenge, a number of studies in nineteenth-century urban archaeology have been produced in the last three years. The most promising of these, such as the Alexandria Archaeological Research Center's projects in Alexandria, Virginia, have adopted research strategies that stress the basic problem of social and economic differentiation along class and ethnic or minority lines as it developed within the urban context during the nineteenth century (Cressey 1980). Thus, these projects have emphasized the need to retrieve archaeological samples of households whose members were of different cultural backgrounds and who represented different economic and social levels within urban communities.

17.1 Archaeology and ethnicity

Like historical archaeologists working in other contexts, urban archaeologists have singled out the archaeological remains of certain groups for study, namely Afro-Americans, Overseas Chinese, Native Americans, and other minorities (fig. 17.1). The rationale for this selectivity is that these people, along with the transient poor, are either not represented in the conventional historical record or are presented in an extremely biased light. In placing emphasis on ethnic and minority sites to the exclusion of sites representing other groups, historical archaeologists, particularly those interested in the second half of the nineteenth century, are in danger of ignoring a very important body of data. As was recently observed in the study of the Golden Eagle site, a mid-nineteenth-century hotel in Sacramento:

Fig. 17.1. Chinese brown-glazed stoneware food storage vessel from excavations in Sacramento, California. This type is one of several common and highly distinctive Overseas Chinese ceramic forms, (Photo by Nelson Thompson)

Archaeologists have devoted altogether too much attention to the problem of archaeological evidence of ethnic differences at the expense of identifying the dominant cultural tradition of nineteenth-century America, as it may or may not be expressed in the archaeological record and the material environment in general.   (Praetzellis et al. 1980, 11)
The importance of this observation is simply that archaeological remains from households of this period will provide partial evidence of consumer behavior, that is, the participation of different social groups in the local expression of a national economic system.

If indeed the growth of cities during the nineteenth century was accompanied by increasing spatial segregation of population along social and economic lines, there were, at the same time, assimilative pressures, or 'homogenizing processes' acting upon these communities (Hardesty 1980, 16–18) that resulted in the reduction of observable behavioral and material manifestations of their distinctions. In other words, even though competition or conflict may have intensified class differences during this period of urban growth and increased the social distance separating ethnic groups, the material expression of these differences may not be easily detectable except in extreme cases – clearly, historical archaeologists have

thus far met with only limited success in identifying distinctive material attributes of ethnicity (e.g., Kelly and Kelly 1980).

Depending on the availability and cost of different categories of manufactured goods, patterns of acquisition and disposal at the household level may, indeed, be related to factors of ethnicity and class; the latter, however, cannot be demonstrated until the assimilative pressures contained in consumer production and marketing practices have been adequately considered. To define some of these assimilative pressures it is necessary to examine the consumer tastes of the middle class who made up a significant portion of the urban residential population during this period. The importance of the middle class lies in the fact that the preferences and purchasing power of its members strongly influenced the production and marketing of mass-produced manufactured goods in the second half of the nineteenth-century.

Assuming that the major variables affecting urban residential segregation are usually observable in the material by-products of consumer behavior, and to the extent that residential patterns can be reconstructed from census data, tax records, city directories, and other sources, it should be possible to examine, archaeologically, specific propositions regarding consumer behavior and resulting material correlates. Such factors as social rank, economic status, household composition, occupation, and ethnic or minority status, are most often identified as the primary variables affecting the course of residential differentiation. Control over several other factors will be required before these differences can be precisely defined. These factors include the availability and cost of manufactured goods and patterns of their acquisition, preferably at the household level. More important is the definition of standards of consumer taste against which to measure divergence in consumer patterns. This chapter is an attempt to initiate such an analytical process, with specific reference to the West Coast of the United States.

17.2 Class, ethnicity, and consumer behavior

There is an extensive literature on consumer behavior within the management field (e.g., Engel, Kollat, and Blackwell 1968; Kassarjian and Robertson 1968; Engel 1968; Nicosia and Wind 1977). These works draw on various social sciences to construct models detailing the influences upon consumer choices at the individual and household level. For example, Hansen (1972, 438–61) summarizes twenty-eight consumer behavior models dealing with such variables as the quality, utility, and media exposure of the product and the income, self-image, age, personality, and social class of the consumer. Each variable is defined by characteristics that are believed to influence consumer behavior. In this literature, an individual's social class is often measured by combinations of factors including their occupation, income, place of residence, and education. While this conception of class might be inappropriate for many social science research problems, it has value in the study of consumerism. The dynamics of the relationship between these variables as causal influences on consumer choices of individuals has yet to be resolved. Specifically, the relative importance of class and ethnicity, respectively, on purchasing decisions is an important issue to present-day advertisers, who face a market where class and ethnic affiliation cross-cut each other. In mid-nineteenth-century America, as now, class status was not necessarily a function of ethnicity.

The consumer analysts use individuals or households as their unit of study; their goal is the prediction of consumer behavior. The preliminary analysis presented here is based on the recognition that this literature on consumer behavior should be fully exploited by those historical archaeologists who would use urban domestic sites of the second half of the nineteenth century to investigate the economic and social processes affecting the course of urbanization during this period. Although examples are drawn mainly from California, it is suggested that similar strategies should be employed elsewhere in the country to provide a sound basis for measuring divergence from middle-class ideals and practices on the part of urban populations whose residential pattern and purchasing behavior may reflect the complex dynamic of ethnic and class identification.

Regarding the broader context of consumerism as it emerged during the nineteenth century, the art historian Quentin Bell has written that 'the mechanics of dress are dependent upon the class structure of the society in which they operate' (1976, 117). Thus, changing class structure will produce changing fashions. The 'mainspring of fashion' in Western society, the emulative process whereby members of one class imitate those of another and thereby force the former to exploit new fashions, is possible only in a society in which more than one class can afford the luxury of 'sumptuous dress' and where the relationship between these classes is not static. According to Bell (1976, 115):

> Emulation occurs where status can be challenged, where social groups become strong enough to challenge the traditional patterns of society, in fact in those places where a strong middle class emerges to compete with the aristocracy, and at a later stage, a strong proletariat emerges to compete with the middle class.

Bell confines his discussion of fashion mainly to clothing, an all too perishable object of material culture to be of much concern to archaeologists. The prodigiously successful marketing techniques of the potter Josiah Wedgwood, however, demonstrate that emulation in fashion was not restricted to dress. Wedgwood's success in creating a world-wide demand for his ceramics came partly from his 'capture of the world of fashion' (McKendrick 1960, 412). His position as Queen's Potter enabled Wedgwood to call his cream-colored earthenware 'Queensware', an incredible boon to its quick and complete success. Wedgwood first gained favor with the European nobility and through this was assured a wider appeal, to quote this great entrepreneur:

> The Great People have had these Vases in their Palaces long enough for them to be seen and admired by the Middling Class of People, which class we know are vastly I had almost said, infinitely superior in number to the great, and though a *great price* was, I believe, at first necessary to make the vases esteemed Ornament for Palaces, the reason no longer exists. Their character is established, and the middling People will probably by quantitys of them at a reduced price.
> (Wedgwood Museum Manuscript E. 18392–25. JW to TB, 23 August 1772 in McKendrick 1960, 428; emphasis in the original)

Wedgwood lowered his prices and opened a great new market. He produced a wide variety of goods from ornamental vases to tableware, inkpots, and buttons, but his useful ware, as opposed to the ornamental, consistently made up the greater percentage of his sales (McKendrick 1960, 433). The emulation of Wedgwood's noble patrons by his 'middling' customers was certainly a factor in the successful campaign that enabled Wedgwood to sell at a higher price, pieces that his competitors could not unload at any price (McKendrick 1960, 432).

Significantly, this pattern can be recognized in the study of archaeological materials. Webster's (1972) study of marketing systems of the Attic potters suggests that in the consumer society of Classical Greece rapid change in the subjects depicted on Attic pots reflects a sophisticated

UNITED STATES CENTENNIAL EXHIBITION—1776-1876 CERTIFICATE OF CAPITAL STOCK ISSUED BY THE CENTENNIAL BOARD OF FINANCE

Fig. 17.2. The themes of the Centennial Exhibition – industriousness, technological progress, and international commerce and cooperation – are well expressed in this stock certificate. (Illustration from Norton 1877, 30)

awareness of the potters' market. Trends were set by the Greek aristocracy who commissioned matched sets for their fashionable symposia (Webster 1972, 78, 298).

In emulating the tastes of the ruling class, the middle class can also be seen as the translator of these values to the working classes, whose ranks were filled, in part, by ethnic minorities. The middle class serves as a source of inspiration and emulation for the fashions and pretenses of their social inferiors. It is clear that assimilation of the tastes of the middle class by members of ethnic minorities in the lower class was in many ways a prerequisite to the latter's social acceptance, economic success, and upward mobility. The following example illustrates how acceptance of the tastes of the dominant group led to the acceptance of a member of an unpopular ethnic minority. During the Anti-Chinese Movement of 1886, inspired in part by the alleged murder of a Sonoma County, California, couple by their Chinese cook, local residents organized to drive all of the Chinese out of town. In one local community, however, a Chinese person was allowed to stay; he was, in fact, a very popular fellow. The *Santa Rosa Democrat* (20 February 1886) described him as follows:

> Guerneville's only celestial still remains, Jim Mahoney, so called, and chances are he will continue to stay. Jim's a stayer, so the boys say, . . . Jim is fond of a quiet game of poker and two-fingered glass of whiskey. The boys all like him, he spends his money and enjoys the pleasures obtained thereby the same as other people. Jim avows the intention of cutting his cue off, purchasing a silk hat and going to an American school, and if he makes good his promise, he will be an American citizen and a Guernevillian.

It is interesting that the rationale for Jim's popularity is the exact opposite of those given for the unpopularity of the Chinese in general. The local presence of one Chinese clearly

Fig. 17.3. The international character of the Centennial Exhibition was enhanced by the use of native craftsmen to build the displays of their respective nations. How these Japanese workers' studies would have been affected by smoking opium was known only to the illustrator. (Illustration from Norton 1877, 41)

represented less of a threat than a community of hundreds; nevertheless, it was Jim's display of 'American tastes' that singled him out as a 'stayer'. Jim Mahoney, the atypical Chinese, was, at the last *Democrat* report (24 April 1886), learning to write a fine business hand and strutting about in a plug hat.

17.3 World's Fairs as translators of fashion

The Industrial Revolution, the rise of the middle class, and the Western phenomenon of changing fashion, are interrelated. According to one theory, the newfound respectability of certain kinds of labor and the rise of the wealthy manufacturers changed the rules applicable to sumptuous masculine attire – men no longer needed to appear useless to be fashionable:

> not only the brocade of the nobleman . . . was gone, but also the peasant's smock, the carpenter's hat, and all

other regional and traditional clothes of mankind; for the discrete armies of black-coated businessmen have gone to the ends of the earth. The fashion was born in England along with the Industrial Revolution; wherever the capitalist system has been established the London fashion has gone with it. (Bell 1976, 141)

The World's Fair or International Exposition was another institution spawned by the British middle class. Industrial Exhibitions on a national or state level had been quite common since 1798 when the first was held in Paris. It was not, however, until 1849 that Prince Albert called for an exhibition whose scope and benefits would be world-wide. Queen Victoria and Prince Albert, unfashionable and unpopular in the view of English high society, were the darlings of the middle class. A contemporary biographer describes Victoria as

> the embodiment, the living apex of a new era in the generations of mankind. The last vestige of the

Fig. 17.4. Although commerce and the products of modern technology were emphasized in the Centennial Exhibition, the display of 'traditional customs' – such as smoking hashish – could only lead to better understanding between nations. (Illustration from Norton 1877, 202)

eighteenth century had disappeared; cynicism and subtlety were shrivelled into powder; and duty, industry, morality, and domesticity triumphed over them. Even the very chairs and tables had assumed, with a singular responsiveness, the forms of prim solidarity. The Victorian Age was in full swing. Only one thing more was needed: material expression must be given to the new ideals and the new forces so that they might stand revealed, in visible glory, before the eyes of an astonished world. It was for Albert to supply this want. He mused, and was inspired: the Great Exhibition came into his head.

(Strachey 1921, 195–6)

The Crystal Palace Exhibition, held in 1851, was a

resounding success (Art Journal 1851) and was followed by similar events in major cities of Europe and the Americas: New York 1853 (Greeley 1853; Silliman and Goodrich 1854); London 1862 (Art Journal 1862) and 1871 (Beckwith 1872); Philadelphia 1876 (Secretary of the British Commission 1876a and 1876b; Norton 1877; Smith 1875; Lippincott 1876; U.S. Centennial Commission 1876; McCabe 1876); and Paris 1878 (Art Journal 1878).

Foremost among the stated goals of these exhibitions was the advancement of 'those arts which increase the comforts and heighten the delights of life, the spread of amicable relations among rival countries, and above all, the elevation of labor to its proper dignity' (Greeley 1853, viii). The shareholders'

Fig. 17.5. Visitors to the Centennial Exhibition were invited to learn all about Kingsford's Oswego Starch, one of the first nationally distributed, name-brand consumer products. (Illustration from Norton 1877, 115)

certificate (fig. 17.2; Norton 1877, 30) from the U.S. Centennial Exhibition illustrates many of these values. The organizers also believed that one result of bringing together products from many different nations would be modification in 'many essential national peculiarities, even if it does not end in the assimilation to a common standard of excellence in the arts, both fine and industrial, of all progressive races' (Smith 1875, 505). We will never know the influence of the Centennial Exhibition on the Japanese workmen pictured in figure 17.3 (Norton 1877, 41); however, the Turkish bazaar shown in figure 17.4 and the Chinese exhibit (Norton 1877, 108, 202) were very popular and probably influenced the tastes and future consumer behavior of at least some of the nearly ten million exhibition visitors. Although this was not a published objective, the Centennial Exhibition engendered a sense of pride in American arts and industry, and inspired a 'Buy America' campaign. It displayed the material correlates of American middle-class domesticity for review by groups as yet unassimilated and thus served as a model for such groups.

The development of trade was another goal of these 'World's Fairs', and they certainly provided ample opportunity for advertisement on the part of both nations and individual businesses. The fairs supplied a backdrop for displays of everything from fine art to such mundane items as starch (fig. 17.5; Norton 1877, 115) and baking powder (Norton 1877, 224). Admission was cheap – fifty cents at the Philadelphia Centennial – encouraging the attendance of such as these country folk lost in wonder (fig. 17.6; Norton 1877, 54). This need not, however, discourage visits by the elite who could still maintain social distance through hiring rolling chairs with attendants for seventy-five cents an hour (fig. 17.7; Norton 1877, 84).

The International Exhibitions encapsulate this dominant role of the middle class in the realm of material goods. As catalogs of who was selling what, and when, these events are also of value to students of material culture. Prize-winning ceramic forms from the 1851 Great Exhibition have been found on archaeological sites in old Sacramento (Praetzellis and Praetzellis 1979, 43; Praetzellis 1980, fig. 7.14; see fig. 17.8). In fact, in this instance T. J. and J. Mayer designed a special mark for their award-winning pieces (fig. 17.9). The Mayers further advertised their success in another mark which was used on a

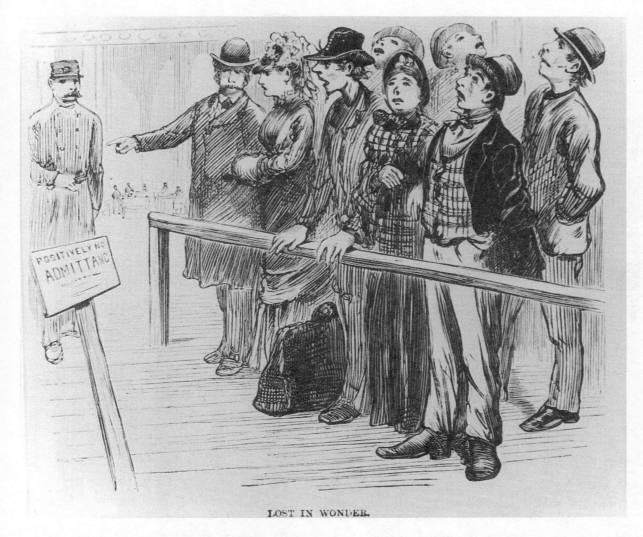

LOST IN WONDER.

Fig. 17.6. The splendor and enormity of the Centennial Exhibition was entirely beyond the experience of many visitors. Numerous tales of the achievements of modern science must have been brought back to the country towns and villages of America. (Illustration from Norton 1877, 54)

number of molded designs registered in 1851. Whether potters commonly used these exhibitions as direct avenues for advertising remains to be seen, but it appears likely. Regardless, in ceramics at least, exhibitors sent not only their most technically innovative and artistically inspired pieces but also their plain, practical, everyday wares. In 1876, Staffordshire potters showed 'fluted' shapes in white ironstone; these are common artifacts from archaeological sites of that period.

17.4 Documenting the middle class

The records of the International Exhibitions are but one documentary source that can be used to reconstruct the tastes of the dominant group. Fashion magazines, etiquette books, contemporary photographs, art, and literature all contain information on consumer ideals. Moving from the international to the local scene, newspapers, particularly advertisements,

provide an extremely valuable source of information on the local expressions of consumer trends. Advertisements give a more explicit indication of the local cost and availability of various classes of consumer goods. The specific details, and thus the interpretive value of ads, vary depending on the newspapers and goods researched. For instance, the latest fashion in shoes, parasols, gentlemen's hats, and cast iron stoves are well illustrated in 1880s issues of the *Santa Rosa Democrat*, while ceramics are advertised simply as 'Queensware', or 'willow ware'. Even advertisements comprised merely of lists give an idea of the possible range of variability within the community. An 1859 Sacramento ceramic advertisement listing 'Gilt dinner sets, Gilt tea sets, Gilt and figures sets, Plain white sets', indicates the possibility for conspicuous consumption and for the material expressions of status differences within the community.

During the middle to late nineteenth century, few

Fig. 17.7. While some mingling between the social classes was unavoidable at the cosmopolitan Centennial Exhibition, the hire of a rolling chair and attendant could protect the dignity of sensitive visitors. (Illustration from Norton 1877, 84)

manufacturers advertised their products on a national level. Local merchants assumed the responsibility for marketing both foreign and parochial goods. Certain brands of patent medicine, bitters, and, at a later date, sewing machines and baking powder, may be exceptions to this in that they were marketed nationally by their manufacturers. Thus newspaper ads often supply the place of origin of their goods, whether it be ice from Sitka, Alaska, apples from Chile, butter from New York, or blackberries from Smith's garden. From this information a partial reconstruction of trade networks is possible. Likewise, public transport – stage, ship, and train lines – advertised their schedules, routes, and fares. The feasibility of travel by public transit examined in combination with non-local advertisements should indicate a community's degree of isolation or involvement in larger interaction spheres.

The various modes of acquisition within an area can also be partially reconstructed from newspapers. Did one general store supply everyone, or were ads directed to those who wanted goods that were the 'cheapest', the 'most fashionable', or the 'most affordable'? The possibility for purchases at auctions and second-hand stores, or for the repair of damaged items, can also be determined in part from the advertisement section.

Aside from detailing some of the possibilities for the local expression of fashion in the national sense, or the material remains of ethnic identity, newspapers give an indication of the

Fig. 17.8. This T. J. & J. Mayer jug won a prize in the 1851 Crystal Palace Exhibition. (Illustration from Jewitt 1883, 453)

social maintenance of ethnic consciousness. This can be followed in the activities of various ethnic social and religious organizations, as, for instance, the German Social Club, or the African Methodist Episcopal Church. The presence of reverse borrowing, that is, the adoption by the middle class of items associated with ethnic minorities, may also be more visible locally than nationally. Finally, a common resource contained in nineteenth-century newspapers, the Weekly Commodities Price List, can be used to gauge the economic climate of the local community.

As a picture forms of the consumer ideals of the middle class and their possibilities for expression on the local level, these can be compared with material remains of households of the same period. It may also be possible to measure the effectiveness of different marketing techniques. The history of American marketing has been called one of the 'dark continents' of the discipline (Shapiro and Doody 1968, 1). Mercantile advertising during the mid-nineteenth century was a simple affair, with merchants stressing availability rather than the characteristics of their goods. 'Standard' brands had not come into use and advertisers had little idea of the potential of appealing to latent desires of consumers. During the 1850s and 1860s use of the 'one price system' was very rare. Merchants did not advertise prices and charged in relation to a number of factors, including the customer's credit and ability to bargain (Atherton 1968, 316–20). Changes in marketing techniques and

patterns of acquisition reconstructed from newspaper advertisements might be connected with changes in trash disposal behavior. For example, does the creation of consumer wants lead to increased consumer waste, in the form of discarded functional but unfashionable items?

17.5 Archaeology and the comparative study of consumer behavior

Historical archaeologists working in urban areas, particularly in those cities involved in urban renewal projects, have a unique opportunity for the comparative study of consumer behavior by households of various ethnic and economic compositions. Urban site-formation processes are such that transitional deposits will be formed at varying intervals through time. Features of the built environment that are most immediately affected by intervals of transition, especially those initiated by a centralized authority, include the following: well, privy, trash pit, cistern, and drain or sump. Each of these features corresponds to an essential activity or service in the supply and maintenance of urban sites, both residential and commercial. When an event such as the passage

Fig. 17.9. Maker's mark designed by T. J. & J. Mayer for one of their prize-winning ceramic forms.

Fig. 17. 10. Part of Sacramento's Chinatown in 1855. During the city's transitional phase the 'flimsey shanties of the Chinese' were interspersed with official buildings and the dwellings of the well-to-do. (Illustration from Barber and Baker 1855, 15)

of a regulation regarding new sewer or water line construction, or sanitation practices, renders any or all of these features obsolete, they share the common characteristic of being 'holes in need of filling'.

For instance, many deposits in Sacramento date to the 1860s, when a city ordinance required property owners to raise the streets in an endeavor to prevent flooding (fig. 17.10). Transitions such as these can produce an extremely valuable body of archaeological data for the synchronic and comparative study of urban populations, because it is at these points that a large number of individual households and commercial establishments contribute to the archaeological record. Particularly at the household level, conscious decisions are made regarding the relative value of particular objects, as evidenced by the large quantity of undamaged objects that are thrown away. The results of such 'housecleaning' have been observed on both rural and urban sites, and in these deposits may be glimpsed aspects of consumer behavior and economic status. At the very least, the study of such disposal episodes offers some insight into changing consumer taste and the timing of obsolescence for certain kinds of material items at different levels of society. It may even be possible to relate this kind of housecleaning to the degree of upward mobility characterizing particular households, given a representative sample of deposits reflecting the same transitional episode in different neighborhoods.

This chapter has attempted to make a case for the importance of the middle class in the nineteenth century. Before it will be possible to formulate specific and testable propositions regarding the archaeological expressions of ethnicity and social class, it will be necessary to confront the problem of the middle class and its consumer tastes. Although not necessarily the creators of fashion, the middle class played a leading role as its generators. During this period its members largely controlled the production, distribution, and marketing of mass-produced consumer goods. They also comprised an important segment of the buying public, and served as a source of emulation for the aspiring members of the lower classes. The documentary record supplies us with many of the variables that marketing analysts recognize and employ in their studies of consumer behavior. The archaeological record of the nineteenth century supplies us with some of the material correlates of decision-making on the part of consumers.

Of course, both records are incomplete. Eventually, however, documentary and archaeological investigations of the kind that have been proposed in this chapter should begin to shed light on the question of the relationship between certain socio-economic variables and consumer behavior, as well as on the influence of the development of modern marketing techniques on the material expressions of these variables.[1]

Note

1. An early version of this paper was presented at the Society for Historical Archaeology annual meetings in New Orleans, Louisiana, January, 1981. The authors would like to express their sincere thanks to Dr Mildred Dickemann, Department of Anthropology, Sonoma State University, for her valuable critique of the earlier draft.

REFERENCES CITED

Abramson, H. S. 1982. Digging up the secrets of our cities. *Historic Preservation* May/June 1982: 32–7.

Aker, R. and Von der Porten, E. 1979. *Discovering Portus Albionis: Francis Drake's California Harbor*. Palo Alto, Drake Navigators' Guild.

Allen, J. 1730. Account book. Dukes County Historical Society Collections. Edgartown, Massachusetts.

Anderson, F. 1979. The experience of provincial military service in eighteenth-century North America: the Crown Point expedition of 1756 as a test case. Unpublished paper. Cambridge, Massachusetts, Department of History, Harvard University.

Anderson, J. 1971. A solid sufficiency: an ethnography of yeoman foodways in Stuart England. Ph.D. dissertation, University of Pennsylvania, Philadelphia, Pennsylvania. Ann Arbor, Michigan, University Microfilms International.

Anderson, J. and Deetz, J. 1972. The ethnogastronomy of Thanksgiving. *Saturday Review of Science* November 25, 1972.

Andrews, C. M. 1938. *The Colonial Period of American History, vol. IV: England's Commercial and Colonial Policy*. New Haven, Connecticut, Yale University Press.

Anonymous 1770. *The Compleat Appraiser*, 4th edn. London.

1802. A description of Mashpee, in the county of Barnstable. September 16th, 1802. *Collections of the Massachusetts Historical Society* 2s 3 (1): 1–12.

1977. *Early American Orderly Books, 1748–1817*. Woodbridge, Connecticut, Research Publication.

Archives of Maryland 1887. *Archives of Maryland*. Judicial and Testamentary Business of the Provincial Court, 1637–1650 (vol. 4). Edited by William Hand Browne. Baltimore, Maryland Historical Society.

Arensburg, C. 1937. *The Irish Countryman*. 1968 reprint. Garden City, New York, The Natural History Press.

Armytage, F. 1953. *The Free Port System in the British West Indies: A Study in Commercial Policy, 1766–1822*. New York, Longmans, Green, and Company.

Arnold, J. N. 1895. *Vital Records of Rhode Island, 1636–1850. Vol. 3, Friends and Ministers*. Providence, Rhode Island, Narragansett Publishing Company.

Arnold, S. G. 1859. *History of the State of Rhode Island*. New York, D. Appleton and Company.

Art Journal 1851. *Art Journal Illustrated Catalogue. The Industry of All Nations, 1851*. London, G. Virtue.

1862. *Art Journal Illustrated Catalogue of the International Exhibition, 1862*. London, J. S. Virtue.

1878. *The Illustrated Catalogue of the Paris International Exhibition*. London, Virtue and Company.

Atherton, L. 1968. Early retail advertising, in S. Shapiro and A. Doody, eds., *Readings in the History of American Marketing: Settlement to Civil War*. Homewood, Illinois, Richard D. Irwin.

Atton, H. and Holland, H. H. 1908. *The King's Customs*. London, John Murray.

Austin, J. O. 1969. *Genealogical Dictionary of Rhode Island*. Reprint of 1887 edn. Baltimore, Maryland, Genealogical Publishing Company.

Avery, C. S. 1978. The Vincent House: The Project. *Dukes County Intelligencer* 20 (1): 5–6.

Babits, L. E. 1981. Military documents and archaeological sites: methodological contributions to historical archaeology. Unpublished Ph.D. dissertation. Department of Anthropology, Brown University, Providence, Rhode Island.

Badger, Rev. S. 1835. Historical and characteristic traits of the American Indians in general, and those of the Natick in particular; in a letter from the Reverend Stephen Badger, of Natick, to Corresponding Secretary. *Collections of the Massachusetts Historical Society* 1s 5: 32–45.

Bailey, A. H. 1975. Glimpses of life on the old Todd Farm. North Smithfield Heritage Association *Newsletter*.

Bailyn, B. 1971. Politics and social structure in Virginia, in S. N. Katz, ed., *Colonial America: Essays in Politics and Social Development*. Boston, Little, Brown and Company.

Baker, A. and Butlin, R. A., eds. 1973. *Studies of Field Systems in the British Isles*. Cambridge, Cambridge University Press.

Baker, M. K. 1978. The Vincent House: The Family. *Dukes County Intelligencer* 20 (1): 61–4.

Baker, V. G. 1977. Historical archaeology at Black Lucy's Garden, Andover, Massachusetts: ceramics from the site of a nineteenth-century Afro-American. *Papers of the Robert S. Peabody Foundation*, vol. 8. Andover, Massachusetts, Robert S. Peabody Foundation for Archaeology.

1979. A comment on contract archaeology of New England sites. *Man in the Northeast* 18: 59–62.

Banks, C. E. 1911. *The History of Martha's Vineyard*. 3 vols. Boston, George Dean.

Barber and Baker (publishers) 1855. *Sacramento Illustrated*. Sacramento, Barber and Baker.

Barber, E. A. 1907. *Saltglazed Stoneware: Germany, Flanders, England and the United States*. New York, Doubleday, Page and Company.

Barck, O. T. and Lefler H. T. 1958. *Colonial America*. New York, Macmillan Company.

Barker, A. J. 1976. *Redcoats*. London, Gordon and Cremonesi.

Barnstaple County, *Probate Records*, Barnstaple County Courthouse, Truro, Massachusetts.

Barnum, H. L. 1836. *The Farmer's Own Book or Family Receipts for the Husbandman and Housewife being a Compilation of the Very Best Receipts on Agriculture, Gardening, and Cooking with Rules for Keeping Farmer's Accounts*. Boston, Charles, J. Hendee.

Bartovics, A. F. 1975. An historical experiment in anthropological settlement. *The Conference on Historic Site Archaeology Papers* 10: 156–64.

Bayles, R. M. 1891. *History of Providence County, Rhode Island*. 2 vols. Providence, Rhode Island.

Beaudry, M. C. 1978a. Worth its weight in iron: categories of material culture in early Virginia probate inventories. *Quarterly Bulletin of the Archaeological Society of Virginia* 33 (1): 19–26.

1978b. A preliminary study of ceramics in York County, Virginia, Inventories, 1730–1750: The Tea Service. *The Conference on Historic Site Archaeology Papers 1977* 12: 201–10.

1979. Analysis of 'semi-literate' texts. Paper delivered to the Society for Historical Archaeology, January, 1979.

1980. 'Or what else you please to call it': folk semantic domains in early Virginia probate inventories. Ph.D. dissertation, Brown University. Ann Arbor, Michigan, University Microfilms International.

Becker, C. 1969. What are historical facts?, in R. H. Nash, ed., *Ideas of History*, vol. 2. New York, E. P. Dutton & Co., Inc.

Beckwith, A. 1872. *International Exhibition, London, 1871. Pottery. Observations on the Materials and Manufacture of Terra Cotta, Stone-ware, Fire Brick, Porcelain, Earthen-ware, Brick, Majolica, and Encaustic Tiles, with Remarks on the Products Exhibited*. New York, D. Van Nostrand.

Bell, Q. 1976. *On Human Finery*. New York, Schocken Books.

Benes, P., ed. 1980. *New England Prospect: Maps, Place Names, and the Historical Landscape*, Dublin Seminar for New England Folklife, *Annual Proceedings*. Boston, Boston University Scholarly Press.

1981. *New England Prospect: A Loan Exhibition of Maps at the Currier Gallery of Art*. Boston, Boston University Scholarly Press.

Benton, J. 1905. *Early Census-Making in Massachusetts*. Boston.

Beston, H. 1928. *The Outermost House*. 1951 edn. New York, Ballentine.

Bidwell, P. W. 1916. Rural economy in New England at the beginning of the nineteenth century. *Transactions of the Connecticut Academy of the Arts and Sciences* 20: 241–399.

Bidwell, P. W. and Falconer, J. I. 1925. *History of Agriculture in the Northern United States, 1620–1860*. Washington, D.C. [Bowen cites 1941 reprint: New York, Peter Smith].

Bigelow, B. M. 1930. The commerce of Rhode Island with the West Indies before the American Revolution. Unpublished Ph.D. dissertation, Brown University, Providence, Rhode Island.

Biglow, W. 1830. *History of the Town of Natick, Massachusetts, from the days of the Apostle Eliot, MDCL, to the Present Time*. Boston, March, Capen, and Lyon.

Binford, L. R. 1962. Archaeology as anthropology. *American Antiquity* 28: 217–25.

1964. A consideration of archaeological research design, in M. P. Leone, ed., *Contemporary Archaeology*. Carbondale, Illinois, Southern Illinois University Press.

1967. Smudge pits and hide smoking: the role of analogy in archaeological reasoning. *American Antiquity* 32 (1): 1–12.

1968. Archaeological perspectives, in S. R. Binford and L. R. Binford, eds., *New Perspectives in Archaeology*. Chicago, Aldine Publishing Company.

1972. Model building-paradigms, and the current state of Paleolithic research, in L. R. Binford, ed., *An Archaeological Perspective*. New York, Seminar Press.

1979. Organization and formation processes: looking at curated technologies. *Journal of Anthropological Research* 37: 195–208.

Black, J. D. 1950. *The Rural Economy of New England*. Cambridge, Massachusetts, Harvard University Press.

Blades, B. S. 1977. Doctor Williams' privy: cultural behavior as reflected in artifact deposition at the Dr. Thomas Williams House, Deerfield, Massachusetts, in P. Benes, ed., *New England Historical Archaeology*. Boston, Boston University Scholarly Press.

Blalock, H. M., Jr 1960. *Social Statistics*. New York, McGraw-Hill.

Bond, D. F., ed., 1965. *The Spectator* nos. 252, 299, 336, 499, 563. Oxford, The Clarendon Press.

Borchelt, J. 1981. *Alley Life in Washington*. Chicago, University of Chicago Press.

Boss, A. 1903. *Meat on the Farm: Butchering, Curing and Keeping*. Farmer's Bulletin No. 183. Washington, D.C., U.S. Department of Agriculture, Government Printing Office.

Boston, City of, Engineering Department. 1903. *List of Maps of Boston Published between 1600 and 1903*. Boston, Municipal Printing Office.

Bowen, J. V. 1975a. The Mott Farm: zooarchaeology and colonial New England foodways. Unpublished Master's thesis, Department of Anthropology, Brown University, Providence, Rhode Island.

1975b. Probate inventories: an evaluation from the perspective of zooarchaeology and agricultural history at Mott Farm. *Historical Archaeology* 9: 11–25.

1978. The use of account books in archaeology. Paper presented to the Society for Historical Archaeology, San Antonio, Texas.

Bragdon, K. J. 1977. Functional groupings of material objects revealed by analysis of probate inventories and artifact assemblages. Unpublished Master's thesis, Department of Anthropology, Brown University, Providence, Rhode Island.

1979. Probate Records as a source for Algonquian ethnohistory. *Papers of the Tenth Algonquian Conference*. Ottawa, Carleton University.

1981. 'Another tongue brought in': ethnohistorical study of native writings in Massachusetts. Ph.D. dissertation, Brown University. Ann Arbor, Michigan, University Microfilms International.

1983. Native Christianity in eighteenth-century Massachusetts: ritual as cultural reaffirmation. Paper delivered at the Laurier Conference on Ethnohistory and Ethnology, Wilfred Launer University. May 1983.

Branca, P. 1975. New perspectives on women's work: a comparative typology. *The Journal of Social History* 11 (2): 129–53.

Brasser, T. J. C. 1971. The coastal Algonkians: people of the first frontiers, in E. B. Leacock and N. O. Lurie, eds., *North American Indians in Historical Perspective*. New York, Random House.

1975. *A Basketful of Culture Change*. Ottawa, Canadian Ethnology Service.

Braudel, F. 1984. *The Perspective of the World: Civilization and Capitalism 15th–18th Centuries*. New York, Harper and Row.

Brew, J. O. 1946. Archaeology of Alkali Ridge: southeastern Utah. *Papers of the Peabody Museum of American Archaeology and Ethnology* 21. Cambridge, Massachusetts, Harvard University.

Bridenbaugh, C. 1938. *Cities in the Wilderness*. London, Oxford University Press.

1955. *Cities in Revolt: Urban Life in America, 1743–1776*. New York, Alfred A. Knopf.

1967. *Vexed and Troubled Englishmen 1590–1642*. New York, Oxford University Press.

1974. *Fat Mutton and Liberty of Conscience*. Providence, Rhode Island, Brown University Press.

Brigham, W. 1836. *The Compact with the Charter and Laws of the Colony of New Plymouth*. Volume A. Boston, Sutton and Wentworth.

Brown, M. R. III 1973. Ceramics from Plymouth: the documentary record, in I. M. G. Quimby, ed., *Ceramics in America*. Charlottesville, University Press of Virginia.

1975. The behavioral context of probate inventories: an example from Plymouth Colony. Paper delivered to the Society for Historical Archaeology, January, 1975.

1977. A survey of historical archaeology in New England, in P. Benes, ed., *New England Historical Archaeology*. Boston, Boston University Scholarly Press.

Brush, S. B. 1977. *Mountain, Field, and Family: The Economy and Human Ecology of an Andean Valley*. Philadelphia, University of Pennsylvania Press.

Burns, R. 1763. Ecclesiastical Law. Volume 2.

Calvert, E. 1965. *Hancock's Resolution*. Annapolis, Maryland, Historic Annapolis, Inc.

Camp, H. B. 1975. *Archaeological Excavations at Pemaquid, Maine 1965–1974*. Augusta, Maine, Maine State Museum.

Carr, L. G. 1973. The St Mary's town land community: ceramics from the John Hicks Site, 1723–1743, in I. M. G. Quimby, ed., *Ceramics in America*. Charlottesville, University Press of Virginia.

1974. 'The Metropolis of Maryland': a comment on town development along the tobacco coast. *Maryland Historical Magazine* 69 (2): 139–45.

Carr, L. G. and Jordan, D. W. 1974. *Maryland's Revolution of Government: 1689–1692*. Ithaca, New York, Cornell University Press.

Carr, L. G. and Menard, R. R. 1979. Servants and freedmen in early colonial Maryland, in T. W. Tate and D. L. Ammerman, eds., *The Chesapeake in the Seventeenth Century: Essays on Anglo-American Society and Politics*. New York, W. W. Norton and Company.

Carr, L. G. and Walsh, L. 1976. How colonial tobacco planters lived: consumption patterns in St Mary's County, Maryland,

1658–1777. Paper delivered to the Southern Historical Association, 1976.

1977. The planter's wife: the experience of white women in seventeenth-century Maryland. *William and Mary Quarterly* 3s 34: 542–71.

Carson, B. G. 1970. Illustrations and extracts from the text of Randle Holme's *The Academy of Armory*. Unpublished manuscript. Plymouth, Massachusetts, Plimoth Plantation.

Carson, B. G. and Carson, C. 1976. Styles and standards of living in southern Maryland, 1670–1752. Paper delivered to the Southern Historical Association.

Carson, C. 1978. Doing history with material culture, in I. M. G. Quimby, ed., *Material Culture and the Study of American Life*. New York, W. W. Norton and Company.

Carson, C. and Walsh, L. S. 1981. The material life of the early American housewife. Paper presented at a Conference on Women in Early America, Williamsburg, Virginia, November, 1981.

Carson, C., Barka, N. F., Kelso, W. M., Stone, G. W. and Upton, D. 1981. Impermanent architecture in the southern colonies. *Winterthur Portfolio* 16 (2/3): 135–96.

Carson, E. 1972. *The Ancient and Rightful Custom: A History of the English Customs Service*. Hamden, Connecticut, Archon.

Cassels, R. 1972. Locational analysis of prehistoric settlement in New Zealand. *Mankind* 8: 212–22.

Ceci, L. 1980. Maize cultivation in coastal New York: the archaeological agronomical, and documentary evidence. *North American Archaeologist* 1 (1): 45–74.

1982. Method and theory in coastal New York archaeology: paradigms of settlement pattern. *North American Archaeologist* 3: 5–36.

Celoria, F. S. C. and Kelly, J. H. 1973. A post medieval pottery site with a kiln base found off Albion Square, Hanley, Stoke-on-Trent, Staffordshire, England SJ 885 474. *City of Stoke-on-Trent Museum Archaeology Society Report* 4.

Cescinsky, H. 1929. *English Furniture*. Grand Rapids, Michigan, The Dean-Hicks Company.

Chace, P. G. 1969. Ceramics in Plymouth Colony, Massachusetts, analyses of the 1631–1675 estate inventories. Unpublished Master's thesis, Oneonta, New York State University College.

1972. Ceramics in Plymouth Colony, an analysis of estate inventories, 1631–1675. *Occasional Papers in Old Colony Studies* 3: 1–12.

Chalklin, C. W. 1974. *The Provincial Towns of Georgian England: A Study of the Building Process, 1740–1820*. London, Edward Arnold.

Chamberlain, B. B. 1964. *These Fragile Outposts – A Geological Look at Cape Cod, Martha's Vineyard, and Nantucket*. Garden City, New York, Natural History Press.

Chapin, H. M. 1926. *Rhode Island Privateers in King George's War 1739–1748*. Providence, Rhode Island, E. E. Johnson.

1928. *Privateering in King George's War 1738–1748*. Providence, Rhode Island, E. E. Johnson.

Charleston, R. J. 1969. Porcelain as room decoration in eighteenth-century England. *Antiques* 96 (6): 894–9.

Chatterton, E. K. 1912. *King's Cutters and Smugglers 1700–1855*. Philadelphia, J. P. Lippencott Company.

Chaudhuri, K. N. 1978. *The Trading World of Asia and the English East India Company*. Cambridge, Cambridge University Press.

Cheney, J. F., Laden, G., and Seasholes, N. S. 1983. Phase II archaeological site examination: Weston farmstead and Nichols Blacksmith shop, Windsor, Massachusetts. Cambridge, Massachusetts, Institute for Conservation Archaeology, Peabody Museum, Harvard University.

Cheney, J., Seasholes, N. S., Laden, G., Lewis, S. P., Krase, E., Woods, S., and Gordon, E. W. 1983. Archaeological survey of the Third Harbor Tunnel/Central Artery, Boston, Massachusetts, vol. 1: Dewey Square to Causeway Street. Cambridge, Massachusetts, Institute for Conservation Archaeology, Peabody Museum, Harvard University.

Child, L. 1833. *The American Frugal Housewife*. 12th edn. Boston, Carter, Hendee, and Co.

Chyet, S. F. 1970. *Lopez of Newport: Colonial American Merchant Prince*. Detroit, Michigan, Wayne State University Press.

Clark, A. H. 1887a. The blackfish and porpoise fishery, in G. B. Goode, ed., *The Fishes and Fishery Industry of the United States*. Volume 5, part 1. Washington, D.C., United States Fish and Wildlife Commission.

    1887b. The fisheries of Massachusetts, in G. B. Goode, ed., *The Fishes and Fishery Industry of the United States*. Volume 5, part 3. Washington, D.C., United States Fish and Wildlife Commission.

    1887c. The whale fishery, in G. B. Goode, ed., *The Fishes and Fishery Industry of the United States*. Volume 5, part 15. Washington, D.C., United States Fish and Wildlife Commission.

Clark, A. H. 1972. Suggestions for the geographical study of agricultural change in the United States, 1790–1840, in D. P. Kelsey, ed., *Farming in the New Nation: Interpreting American Agriculture 1790–1840*. Agricultural History Society 46 (11).

Clark, C. 1979. Household economy, market exchange, and the rise of capitalism in the Connecticut Valley 1800–1860. *Journal of Social History* 13: 168–89.

Clark, W., ed., 1895–1907. *The State and Colonial Records of North Carolina*. Raleigh, State of North Carolina.

Clough, S. C. 1919. Remarks. *Publications of the Colonial Society of Massachusetts* 21: 251–4.

    1927. Remarks on the compilation of the Book of Possessions. *Publications of the Colonial Society of Massachusetts* 27: 6–21.

Cohn, B. S. 1971. *India: The Social Anthropology of a Civilization*. Englewood Cliffs, New Jersey, Prentice Hall.

Cole, A. 1969. *Wholesale Commodity Prices in the United States 1700–1861*. New York, Johnson Reprint Corp.

Cole, W. 1980. A survey of early nineteenth-century sites in Rockbridge County. Unpublished manuscript. Laboratory of Anthropology, Washington and Lee University, Lexington, Virginia.

Collard, E. 1967. *Nineteenth-Century Pottery and Porcelain in Canada*. Montreal, Canada, McGill University Press.

Collet, J. 1770. A compleat map of North Carolina from an actual survey. Raleigh, North Carolina, Department of Cultural Resources.

Commonwealth of Massachusetts Archives Division, n.d. *Taverns, etc.* Volume 3. Boston, Massachusetts.

Conkey, L. E., Boissevain, E., and Goddard, I. 1978. Indians of southern New England and Long Island: late period, in B. Trigger, ed., *Handbook of North American Indians*. Volume 15. Washington, D.C., United States Government Printing Office.

Corvisier, A. 1979. *Armies and Societies in Europe 1494–1789*. (Translated by A. T. Siddall.) Bloomington, Indiana, Indiana University Press.

Cosans, E. J. 1974. The Franklin Court report. Unpublished manuscript, National Park Service, Independence National Historic Park, Philadelphia, Pennsylvania.

Cott, N. F. 1978. *The Bonds of Womanhood: Woman's Sphere in New England, 1780–1835*. New Haven, Connecticut, Yale University Press.

Cotter, J. L. 1958. Archaeological excavations at Jamestown colonial national historic site, Virginia. *Archaeological Research Series No. 4*. Washington, D.C., National Park Service.

Cressey, P. J. 1980. Sharing the ivory tower. Paper delivered to the Society for American Archaeology.

Crèvecoeur, J. H. St J. de 1782. *Letters from an American Farmer*. New York, Everyman's Library.

Cronon, W. 1983. *Changes in the Land*. New York, Hill and Wang.

Cumming, W. P. 1980. The colonial charting of the Massachusetts coast. *Publications of the Colonial Society of Massachusetts* 52: 67–118.

Cummings, A. L. 1964. *Rural Household Inventories*. Boston, The Society for the Preservation of New England Antiquities.

Cummings, R. O. 1940. *The American and his Food*. Revised edn. Chicago, The University of Chicago Press.

Dabney, J. 1796. *An Address to Farmers*. Newburyport, Massachusetts.

Daniels, B. 1973. Defining economic classes in colonial New Hampshire, 1700–1770. *Historical New Hampshire* 28: 53–62.

Danvers Agricultural Society. 1815. Answers to inquiries addressed to farmers. *Massachusetts Agricultural Repository and Journal* III.

Danvers, F. C. and Foster, W., eds., 1896–1904. *Letters Received by the East India Company from its Servants in the East*. London.

Davidson, C. 1983. *A Woman's Work is Never Done: A History of Housework in the British Isles 1650–1950*. London, Chatto and Windus.

Davidson, J. W., and Lytle, M. H. 1986. *After the Fact: The Art of Historical Detection*. 2nd edn, vol. 1. New York, Alfred A. Knopf.

Davis, R. B., ed., 1963. *William Fitzhugh and His Chesapeake World, 1676–1701*. Chapel Hill, University of North Carolina Press.

Davisson, W. I. 1967a. Essex county price trends: money and markets in seventeenth-century Massachusetts. *Essex Institute Historical Collections* 103: 1–52.

    1967b. Essex county wealth trends: wealth and economic growth in seventeenth-century Massachusetts. *Essex Institute Historical Collections* 103: 291–342.

Dawes, N. H. 1949. Titles as symbols of prestige in seventeenth-century New England. *William and Mary Quarterly* 6 (3): 69–83.

Deetz, J. 1960a. Excavations at the Joseph Howland Site (C5), Rocky Nook, Kingston, Massachusetts, 1959: a preliminary report. Supplement to the *Howland Quarterly* 23: 24.

    1960b. The Howlands at Rocky Nook: an archaeological and historical study. Supplement to the *Howland Quarterly* 24 (4): 1–8.

    1967. *Invitation to Archaeology*. New York, Natural History Press.

    1968. Late man in North America, the archaeology of European Americans, in B. Meggers, ed., *Anthropological Archaeology in the Americas*. Washington, D.C., Anthropological Society of Washington.

    1970. Archaeology as a social science, in M. P. Leone, ed., *Contemporary Archaeology*. Carbondale, Illinois, Southern Illinois University Press.

    1973. Ceramics from Plymouth, 1635–1835: the archaeological evidence, in I. M. G. Quimby, ed., *Ceramics in America*. Charlottesville, University of Virginia Press.

    1977. *In Small Things Forgotten: The Archaeology of Early American Life*. Garden City, New Jersey, Anchor Press.

    1979. Scientific humanism and humanistic science: a plea for paradigmatic pluralism in historical archaeology. Paper delivered to the Society for Historical Archaeology, January, 1979.

Deetz, J. F. and Dethlefsen, E. S. 1967. Death's head, cherub, urn, and willow, in R. L. Schuyler, ed., *Historical Archaeology: A Guide to Substantive and Theoretical Contributions*. Farmingdale, New York, Baywood Press.

Delhom, M. M. 1977. Pearlware, in A. R. Luedders, ed., *Wedgwood: Its Competitors and Imitators 1800–1830*. Ann Arbor, Michigan, Ars Ceramica Ltd.

Demos, J. 1970. *A Little Commonwealth: Family Life in Plymouth Colony*. Oxford, Oxford University Press.
  1982. *Entertaining Satan: Witchcraft and the Culture of Early New England*. New York, Oxford University Press.
Diaz, M. N. 1967. Introduction: economic relations in peasant society, in J. M. Potter, M. N. Diaz and G. M. Foster, eds., *Peasant Society: A Reader*. Boston, Little, Brown, and Company.
Dickey, W. J. 1978. Family and policy in Atlantic England. Unpublished Ph.D. dissertation, University of Chicago, Chicago, Illinois.
Doran, J. E. and Hodson, F. R. 1975. *Mathematics and Computers in Archaeology*. Cambridge, Massachusetts, Harvard University Press.
Douglas, M. 1970. *Witchcraft Confessions and Accusations*. London, Tavistock Publications.
Dow, G. F. 1927. *The Arts and Crafts in New England: 1704–1775: Gleanings from Boston Newspapers*. Topsfield, Massachusetts, The Wayside Press.
Dukes County Historical Society. n.d. Manuscripts, various. Thomas Cooke House, Edgartown, Massachusetts.
Duncan, T. B. 1972. *Atlantic Islands*. Chicago, University of Chicago Press.
Dunn, R. S. 1972. *Sugar and Slaves: The Rise of the Plantation Class in the English West Indies, 1624–1713*. New York, W. W. Norton and Company.
Dunstable Agricultural Society. 1816. Answers to inqueries addressed to farmers. *Massachusetts Agricultural Repository and Journal*, IV.
Dwight, T. 1821. *Travels in New-England and New-York*. Volume III. New Haven, Connecticut. (1969 edn edited by B. M. Solomon) Cambridge, Massachusetts, Belknap Press, Harvard University.

Eastman, C. M. 1975. *Aspects of Language and Culture*. San Francisco, California, Chandler and Sharpe, Inc.
Eckholm, E. and Deetz, J. 1971. Wellfleet Tavern. *Natural History* 80 (7): 49–56.
Eliot, J. 1647. The day-breaking of the Gospel with the Indians. Reprinted in *Old South Leaflets* 6 (143), 1834: 381–404.
  1934. *Essays Upon Field Husbandry in New England and Other Papers 1748–1762*. Ed. by H. J. Carman. New York on Morningside Heights, Columbia University Press.
Ember, C. 1983. The relative decline in women's contribution to agriculture with intensification. *American Anthropologist* 85 (2): 285–304.
Emerson, A. F. 1935. *Naushon Data*. Privately printed.
Emmison, F. G. 1938. *Jacobean Household Inventories*. Bedfordshire Record Society Publications, Number 20.
Engel, J., ed. 1968. *Consumer Behavior: Selected Readings*. Homewood, Illinois, Richard D. Irwin.
Engel, J., Kollat, D., and Blackwell, R. 1968. *Consumer Behavior*. New York, Holt, Rinehart and Winston.
Engs, R. F. 1979. *Freedom's First Generation*. Philadelphia, University of Pennsylvania Press.
Evans, G. N. D. 1969. *Uncommon Obdurate: The Several Public Careers of J. F. W. DesBarres*. Toronto, University of Toronto Press.
Evans, W., comp. 1846. Art and history of the potting business, compiled from the most practical sources, for the especial use of working potters. *The Journal of Ceramic History* 3: 21–43.

Fahnestock Bros. 1855–1863. Bills to Fahnestock Brothers, a general store in Gettysburg, Pennsylvania. Originals owned by George L. Miller.
Fairbank, J. K., et al. 1978. *East Asia: Tradition and Transformation*. Boston, Houghton Mifflin company.
Farjeon, J. 1938. *The Compleat Smuggler*. New York, Bobbs-Merrill.

Faujas de Saint-Fond, B. 1907. *A Journey through England and Scotland to the Hebrides in 1784, by B. Faujas de Saint Fond, revised edition of the English translation, ed., with notes and a memoir of the author, by Archibald Geikie*. Glasgow, H. Hopkins.
Faulkner, A., Peters, K., Sell, D. and Dethlefsen, E. 1978. *Port and Market: Archaeology of the Central Waterfront, Newburyport, Massachusetts*. Atlanta, Georgia, Interagency Services, National Park Service.
Ferguson, G. 1961. *Signs and Symbols in Christian Art*. New York, Oxford University Press.
Ferris, A. M. 1968. Seventeenth-century transitional porcelains: the development of landscape painting. *Oriental Art* 14 (3): 184–93.
Fessenden, T. G. 1820. *The Husbandman and Housewife. A Collection of Valuable Recipes and Directions Relating to Agriculture and Domestic Economy*. Bellows Falls, Bill Blake and Co.
Fewkes, J. 1893. A-wa'-to'bi: an archaeological verification of a Tusayan legend. *American Anthropologist* 6: 363.
Field, E. 1897. *The Colonial Tavern: A Glimpse of New England Town Life in the Seventeenth and Eighteenth Centuries*. Providence, Rhode Island, Preston and Rounds.
Fiester, L. M. 1975. Analysis of the ceramics found at the Vereberg tavern site, Albany County, New York. *Man in the Northeast* 19: 2–16.
Finlayson, R. W. 1972. *Portneuf Pottery and Other Early Wares*. Don Mills, Ontario, Longman Canada Ltd.
Firth, R. 1967. *Tikopia Ritual and Belief*. Boston, Beacon Press.
Fitch, J. M. 1972. The didactic role of historic preservation. *Chronicle* 8 (4): 1–10.
Flannery, K. V. 1967. Archaeological systems theory and early Mesoamerica, in B. G. Meggars, ed., *Anthropological Archaeology in the Americas*. Washington, D.C., The Anthropological Society of Washington.
Flannery, R. 1939. An analysis of coastal Algonquian culture. *Catholic University of America Anthropology Series* No. 7. Washington, D.C., Catholic University of America Press.
Forman, H. C. 1938. *Jamestown and St Mary's: Buried Cities of Romance*.
  1956. *Tidewater Maryland Architecture and Gardens*. New York, Bonanza Books.
  1967. *Old Buildings, Gardens and Furniture in Tidewater Maryland*. Cambridge, Maryland, Tidewater.
Foster, W., ed., 1906–27. *The English Factories in India, 1642–45*. Oxford, Oxford University Press.
Frazier, W. C. 1967. *Food Microbiology*, 2nd edn. New York, McGraw-Hill Book Company.
Freeman, F. 1858. *History of Cape Cod: The Annals of Barnstable County and of Its Several Towns, Including the District of Mashpee in Two Volumes*. Boston. Reprinted 1965 by Parnassus Imprints, Yarmouthport, Massachusetts.
Freeman, J. 1807. Description of Dukes County. *Dukes County Intelligencer* (1971) 12: 4.

Garner, F. H. and Archer, M. 1972. *English Delftware*. London, Faber and Faber.
Garner, Sir H. 1975. *Chinese Export Art in Schloss Ambras*. Second Hills Gold Medal Lecture. London, Oriental Ceramic Society.
Gibson, S. G. 1979. Refuse disposal behavior and concepts of disease etiology c.1620–1900. Paper read to Society for Historical Archaeology Conference, Nashville, Tennessee.
Glassie, H. 1972a. Folk art, in R. Dorson, ed., *Folklore and Folklife: An Introduction*. Chicago, University of Chicago Press.
  1972b. Eighteenth-century cultural process in Delaware Valley folk building. *Winterthur Portfolio* 7: 29–58.
  1975. *Folk Housing in Middle Virginia: A Structural Study of Historic Artifacts*. Knoxville, University of Tennessee Press.

1982. *Passing the Time in Ballymenone*. Philadelphia, University of Pennsylvania Press.

Goddard, I., and Bragdon, K. J., in press. *The Massachusett Texts: An Ethnohistorical and Linguistic Analysis*. American Philosophical Society *Proceedings*.

Godden, G. A. 1964. *Encylopedia of British Pottery and Porcelain Marks*. New York, Bonanza Books.

1979. *Oriental Export Market Porcelain*. London, Grenada Publishing Company.

Godelier, M. 1977. *Perspectives in Marxist Anthropology*. Cambridge, Cambridge University Press.

Goody, J. 1976. *Production and Reproduction: A Comparative Study of the Domestic Domicile*. Cambridge, Cambridge University Press.

Gookin, D. 1806. Historical collections of the Indians in New England. *Collections of the Massachusetts Historical Society* 1s 1: 141–229.

Gordon, E. 1977. *Collecting Chinese Export Porcelain*. New York, Universal Books.

Gould, R. A. 1966. *Archaeology of Pt. St. George Site and Tolowa Prehistory*. Berkeley, University of California Press.

1981. The archaeology of war: wrecks of the Spanish Armada of 1588 and the Battle of Britain, 1940. Paper delivered to the Society for American Archaeology.

Greeley, H., ed. 1853. *Art and Industry as Represented in the Exhibition at the Crystal Palace, New York*. New York, Redfield.

Greenberg, J. 1966. *Language Universals*. Mouton, The Hague.

Greene, J. P. and Pole, J. R. 1984. Reconstructing British-American colonial history: an introduction, in J. P. Greene and J. R. Pole, eds., *Colonial British America: Essays in the New History of the Early Modern Era*. Baltimore, The Johns Hopkins University Press.

Greven, P. J. Jr 1970. *Four Generations: Population, Land, and Family in Colonial Andover, Massachusetts*. Ithaca, New York, Cornell University Press.

Grimm, J. L. 1970. Archaeological investigation of Fort Ligonier: 1960–1965. *Annals of the Carnegie Museum* 42. Pittsburg, Pennsylvania.

Gross, R. A. 1976. *The Minutemen and their World*. New York, Hill and Wang.

Grosscup, G. and Miller, G. L. 1968. Excavations at Walker Tavern, Cambridge State Historical Park. Unpublished manuscript. Michigan Department of Conservation.

Gudeman, S. 1978. *The Demise of a Rural Economy*. London, Routledge and Kegan Paul.

Gumerman, G., ed., 1971. *The Distribution of Prehistoric Population Aggregates*. Prescott, Arizona, Prescott College Press.

Hackwood, F. W. 1909. *Inns, Ales and Drinking Customs of Old England*. London, T. Fisher Unwin.

Haggar, R. and Adams, E. 1977. *Mason Porcelain and Ironstone 1796–1853: Miles Mason and the Mason Manufactories*. London, Faber and Faber.

Hall, C. C. ed. 1967. *Narratives of Early Maryland*. New York, Barnes and Noble.

Hamshere, C. 1972. *The British in the Caribbean*. Cambridge, Massachusetts, Harvard University Press.

Hampshire Gazette 1821. *Hampshire Gazette* (from the Morristown Palladium), June 13, 1821.

Handsman, R. G. 1981. Early capitalism and the center village of Canaan, Connecticut: a study of transformations and separations. *Artifacts* IX (3): 1–22.

Hanna, W. L. 1979. *Lost Harbor: The Controversy over Drake's California Anchorage*. Berkeley, University of California Press.

Hansen, F. 1972. *Consumer Choice Behavior: A Cognitive Theory*. New York, Free Press.

Hardesty, D. 1980. Historic sites archaeology on the Western frontier:

theoretical perspectives and research problems. Paper delivered to the Society for Historical Archaeology.

Harrison, W. 1968. *The Description of England*. Edited by G. Edden. The Folger Shakespeare Library. Ithaca, New York, Cornell University Press.

Hassan, F. A. 1979. Demography and archaeology. *Annual Review of Anthropology* 8: 137–60.

Havinden, M. A. 1965. *Household and Farm Inventories in Oxfordshire, 1550–1590*. London, Her Majesty's Stationery Office.

Hay, J. 1963. *The Great Beach*. New York, Doubleday and Company.

1969. *In Defense of Nature*. Boston, Little, Brown and Company.

Hayden, A. 1952. *Chats on English China*. Revised and edited by C. G. E. Bunt. London, Ernest Benn Ltd.

Hayes, C. F. 1965. *The Orringh Stone Tavern and Three Seneca Sites of the Late Historic Period*. Rochester, New York, Rochester Museum Association.

Hayter, A. J. 1978. *The Army and the Crowd in Mid-Georgian England*. Totowa, New Jersey, Rowman and Littlefield.

Hedges, J. B. 1968. *The Browns of Providence Plantation: The Colonial Years*. Providence, Rhode Island, Brown University Press.

Henretta, J. A. 1973. *The Evolution of American Society, 1700–1815: An Interdisciplinary Analysis*. Lexington, Massachusetts, D. C. Heath and Company

1978. Families and farms: mentalité in pre-industrial America. *The William and Mary Quarterly* 35: 3–32.

1984. Wealth and social structure, in J. P. Greene and J. R. Pole, eds., *British Colonial America: Essays in the New History of the Early Modern Era*. Baltimore, The Johns Hopkins University Press.

Hensley, J. 1967. *The Works of Anne Bradstreet*. Cambridge, Massachusetts, The Belknap Press.

Herman, L. L., Sands, J. O., and Schecter, D. 1973. Ceramics in St Mary's County, Maryland during the 1840s: a socioeconomic study. *The Conference on Historic Site Archaeology Papers* 8: 52–93.

Hill, H. N., and Evans, R. K. 1972. A model for classification and typology, in D. L. Clarke, ed., *Models in Archaeology*. London, Methuen and Company.

Hiss, P. H. 1943. *Netherlands America: The Dutch Territories in the West*. New York, An Essential Book.

Hodder, I. 1982. *Symbols in Action: Ethnoarchaeological Studies of Material Culture*. Cambridge, Cambridge University Press.

1983. *The Present Past*. New York, Pica Press.

Hodge, F. W. 1897. The verification of a tradition. *American Anthropologist* 10: 302.

Hogan, J. R. 1971. The inn: the Rich family association. *Kinfolk* Spring: 3–6.

Holme, R. 1688. *The Academy of Armoury*. Chester, England.

Holme, R. 1905. *The Academy of Armoury, Part 2*. Edited by I. H. Jeayes. London, printed for the Roxburghe Club.

Honey, W. B. 1933. *English Pottery and Porcelain*. London, A. and C. Black Ltd.

Hood, G. 1971. *American Silver: A History of Style*. New York, Praeger.

Hoon, E. E. 1938. *The Organization of the English Customs System (1696–1786)*. New York, D. Appleton Century.

Hoskins, W. G. 1963. *Provincial England*. London, Macmillan and Company Ltd.

Hosmer, C. B. 1978. The broadening view of the historical preservation movement, in Quimby, I. M. G., ed., *Material Culture and the Study of American Life*. New York, W. W. Norton and Company.

Howard, D. S. 1974. *Chinese Armorial Porcelain*. New York, Faber and Faber.

Howard, D. S. and Ayers, J. 1978. *China for the West: Chinese*

Porcelain and Other Decorative Arts for Export Illustrated from the Mottahedeh Collection. Vol. 1. New York, Sotheby, Parke Bernet.

Howland Quarterly. n.d. The biography of Joseph Howland. Volume VII.

Huey, P. R. 1966. Preliminary report on excavations at the Man Full of Trouble Tavern, Feature I. Unpublished manuscript, University of Pennsylvania, Department of American Civilization, Philadelphia, Pennsylvania.

Hussey, A. R., Jr, 1938. Preliminary report on title to land at Rocky Nook, Kingston, Plymouth County, Massachusetts. Unpublished manuscript on file, Plimoth Plantation, Plymouth, Massachusetts.

India Office Library, Factory Records, China and Japan, G/12/1, 'China, 1664, Voyage of the Surat Frigate to Macao'.

India Office Library, *Home Miscellaneous Series*, 9, 12, 14.

Isaac, R. 1974. Evangelical revolt: the nature of the Baptists' challenge to the traditional order in Virginia, 1765–1775. *William and Mary Quarterly* 31 (3): 345–68.

Jameson, J. F., ed., 1923. *Privateering and Piracy in the Colonial Period: Illustrative Documents*. New York, Macmillan Company.

Jenkins, C. W. 1899. *Three Lectures on the Early History of the Town of Falmouth*. Falmouth, Massachusetts, L. F. Clarke.

Jennings, H. A. 1890. *Provincetown, or Odds and Ends from the Tip End*. 1976 facsimile edn, Provincetown, Massachusetts, Peaked Hill Press.

Jensen, M. 1968. *The Founding of a Nation*. New York, Oxford University Press.

Jenyns, S. 1965. *Later Chinese Porcelain: The Ching Dynasty (1644–1912)*. New York, Thomas Yoseloff.

Jernegan, M. W. 1929. *The American Colonies, 1492–1750: A Study of Their Political, Economic and Social Development*. New York, Longmans, Green and Company.

Jewitt, L. 1883. *The Ceramic Art of Great Britain*. New York, R. Worthington. (Reprinted by Ward Lock Reprints, London 1970).

Jochim, M. 1981. *Strategies for Survival: Cultural Behavior in an Ecological Context*. New York, Academic Press.

Johnson, G. A. 1978. Information sources and the development of decision-making organizations, in C. Redman et al., eds., *Social Archaeology*. New York, Academic Press.

Johnson, W. P., ed., 1957. 1771 and 1772 tax lists of Surry County, North Carolina. *The North Carolinian* III (3): 340–4, (4): 396–401.

Johnson, W. P. 1974. Caswell County 1777: tax list. *The North Carolinian* XX (1): 2908–20.

Jolley, R. L. 1983. North American historic sites zooarchaeology. *Historical Archaeology* 17 (2): 64–79.

Jones, A. H. 1970. Wealth estimates for the American middle colonies 1774. *Economic Development and Cultural Change* 18 (4): Part 2.

1972a. Wealth estimates for the New England colonies about 1770. *Journal of Economic History* 32: 98–127.

1972b. Codes used in late colonial wealth study. Unpublished manuscript.

1977. *American Colonial Wealth, Documents and Methods*. 3 vols. New York, Arno Press.

1980a. Estimating wealth of the living from probate sample: a hindsight view. Paper delivered to the Conference on Economic Growth and Social Change in the Early Republic, 1775–1860, Chicago, Illinois.

1980b. *Wealth of a Nation to Be: The American Colonies on the Eve of the Revolution*. New York, Columbia University Press.

1982. American probate inventories: a source to estimate wealth in 1774 in thirteen colonies and three regions, in Van der Woude, A. and Schuurman A., eds., *Probate Inventories*. Papers presented at the Leeuwenborch Conference, Afdeling Agrarische Geschiedenis Bijdragen 23, Landbouwhogeschool, Wageningen.

Kassarjian, H. and Robertson, T., eds. 1968. *Perspectives in Consumer Behavior*. Glenview, Illinois, Scott, Foresman and Company.

Kelly, M. and Kelly, R. 1980. Approaches to ethnic identification in historical archaeology, in Schuyler, R. L., ed., *Archaeological Perspectives on Ethnicity in America*. Farmingdale, New York, Baywood Publishing Company.

Kendall, K. K. 1976. *Caswell County, 1777–1877: Historical Abstracts of Caswell County, North Carolina*. Raleigh, North Carolina, Multiple Image Press.

Kilburn, R. S. 1981. *Transitional Wares and Their Forerunners*. Hong Kong, Oriental Ceramic Society of Hong Kong.

Kinsman, D. M. 1976. Meat preparation and preservation in colonial America. Paper presented at the 29th Reciprocal Meat Conference of the American Meat Science Association, Brigham Young University, Utah, June 20–23, 1976.

Kittredge, H. C. 1930. *Cape Cod: Its People and Their History*. Boston, Houghton Mifflin Company.

1937. *Mooncussers of Cape Cod*. Cambridge, Massachusetts, Riverside Press.

Knollenber, B. 1960. *Origins of the American Revolution: 1759–1766*. New York, The Macmillan Company.

Kohl, P. L. 1981. Materialist approaches in prehistory. *Annual Review of Anthropology* 10: 89–110.

Kulikoff, A. 1975. Tobacco and slaves: population, economy, and society in eighteenth-century Prince George's County, Maryland. Unpublished Ph.D. dissertation, Brandeis University. Ann Arbor, Michigan, University Microfilms International.

Lamb, G. 1881. Old Boston compiled from the Book of Possessions (map). Boston, Boston Public Library.

Land, A. 1976. Economic base and social structure: the northern Chesapeake in the eighteenth century, in T. H. Breen, ed., *Shaping Southern Society*. New York, Oxford University Press.

Larguia, I. 1974. The economic basis of the status of women, in R. Rohrlich-Leavitt, ed., *Women Cross-Culturally: Change and Challenge*. The Hague, Mouton.

Lawrie, R. A. 1979. *Meat Science*, 3d edn. Oxford, Pergamon Press.

Leach, E. 1966. Anthropological aspects of language: animal categories and verbal abuse, in E. H. Lenneberg, ed., *New Directions in the Study of Language*. Cambridge, Massachusetts, MIT Press.

1973. Complementary filiation and bilateral kinship, in J. Goody, ed., *The Character of Kinship*. Cambridge, Cambridge University Press.

Lemon, J. T. 1967. Household consumption in eighteenth-century America and its relationship to production and trade: the situation among farmers in southeastern Pennsylvania. *Agricultural History* 41: 59–70.

1972. *The Best Poor Man's Country*. New York, W. W. Norton and Company.

1984. Spatial order: households in local communities and regions, in J. P. Greene and J. R. Pole, eds., *British Colonial America: Essays in the New History of the Early Modern Era*. Baltimore, The Johns Hopkins University Press.

Lender, M. D. 1980. The social structure of the New Jersey brigade: the Continental Line as an American standing army, in P. Karsen, ed., *The Military in America*. New York, The Free Press.

Leone, M. P. 1978. Archaeology's relationship to the present and the past. Paper delivered to the American Anthropological Association, Los Angeles, California, November, 1978.

1982. Some opinions about recovering mind. *American Antiquity* 47 (4): 742–60.

Lewis, K. E. 1977. A functional study of the Kershaw house site in Camden, South Carolina. The Institute of Archaeology and Anthropology *Notebook* IX: 1–87. Columbia, South Carolina.

1980. Pattern and layout on the South Carolina frontier: an archaeological investigation of settlement function. *North American Archaeologist* 1: 177–200.

Lewis, S. P., Seasholes, N. S., and Laden, G. 1982. Archaeological survey of the Third Harbor Tunnel Crossing: Boston, Massachusetts. Cambridge, Massachusetts, Institute for Conservation Archaeology, Peabody Museum, Harvard University.

Liggett, B. 1978. *Archaeology at New Market Exhibit Catalogue*. Philadelphia, The Atheneum.

Linn, J. W. 1974. *Surry County, North Carolina Will Abstracts*. Salisbury, North Carolina, privately printed.

Lippincott, J. B. & Co. (pub.). 1876. *Visitor's Guide to the Centennial Exhibition at Philadelphia May 10th to November 10th, 1876*. Philadelphia, J. B. Lippincott and Company.

Little, E. 1980. Probate records of Nantucket Indians. *Nantucket Algonquian Studies* 2. Nantucket, Massachusetts, Nantucket Historical Association.

Livermore, S. 1749. Map of Natick, Massachusetts. Massachusetts Archives, Map Collection. 3s 33 (17): 633.

Lockett, T. A. 1972. *Davenport Pottery and Porcelain: 1794–1887*. Rutland, Vermont, Charles E. Tuttle Inc.

Lockridge, K. A. 1968. A communication. *William and Mary Quarterly* 25: 516–17.

1974. *Literacy in Colonial New England*. New York, W. W. Norton and Company.

Loehr, R. C. 1952. Self-sufficiency on the farm. *Agricultural History* 26: 37–41.

Loftstrom, E. U. 1976. A seriation of historic ceramics in the Midwest, 1780–1870. Paper delivered to the Joint Plains–Midwest Anthropological Conference.

Loring, A. P. 1980. 'The Atlantic Neptune.' *Publications of the Colonial Society of Massachusetts* 52: 119–30.

Lowe, A. 1968. *A History of Eastham*, 2nd edn. Eastham, Massachusetts, Eastham Historical Society.

Lyman, R. L. 1982. Archaeofaunas and subsistence studies, in M. B. Schiffer, ed., *Advances in Archaeological Theory and Method*, vol. 5. New York, Academic Press.

Lynch, K. 1972. *What Time is this Place?* Cambridge, Massachusetts, MIT Press.

McCabe, J. 1876. *Illustrated History of the Centennial Exhibition*. Philadelphia, National Publishing Company.

McClennan, W. S. 1912. *Smuggling in the American Colonies at the Outbreak of the Revolution*. New York, Moffat, Ward and Company.

McDaniel, J. and Potter, P. P. 1978. The application of Stanley South's mean ceramic date formula to a Scotch–Irish site in the Shenandoah Valley. *Quarterly Bulletin of the Archaeological Society of Virginia* 38 (1): 1–8.

McKendrick, N. 1960. Josiah Wedgwood: an eighteenth-century entrepreneur in salesmanship and marketing techniques. *Economic History Review* 12 (2): 408–33.

McMahon, S. F. 1980. Provisions laid up for the family: toward a history of diet in New England, 1650–1850. Report no. 7980–14 delivered at a Workshop in Economic History, Harvard University, Cambridge, Massachusetts.

McManamon, F. P. and Childs, S. T. 1981. Historic period settlement and land use on outer Cape Cod. Paper delivered to the Society for Historical Archaeology.

McMullen, A. 1982. Woodsplint basketry of the eastern Algonkian. *Artifacts* X (5): 1–9.

1983. Tribal style in woodsplint basketry: early Paugusset influence. *Artifacts* XI (4): 1–4.

McNulty, R. H. 1971. Common beverage bottles: their production, use and form in the seventeenth- and eighteenth-century Netherlands. *Journal of Glass Studies* 13.

Macy, O. 1835. *The History of Nantucket*, 2nd edn. Mansfield, Massachusetts, Macy and Pratt. Reprinted 1970 by Research Reprints, Inc., New York.

Main, G. L. 1972. Measuring wealth and welfare: explorations in the use of probate records from colonial Maryland and Massachusetts. Unpublished Ph.D. dissertation, Columbia University, New York.

1974. The correction of biases in colonial American probate records. *Historical Methods Newsletter* 8: 10–28.

1975. Probate records as a source for early American history. *William and Mary Quarterly* 32: 89–99.

Main, J. T. 1965. *The Social Structure of Revolutionary America*. Princeton, Princeton University Press.

Mankowitz, W. 1953. *Wedgwood*. London, Spring Books.

Markinson, D. H. 1964. *Barbados: A Study of North American–West Indian Relations 1739–1789*. The Hague, Mouton.

Marten, C. 1970. The Wampanoags in the seventeenth century: an ethnohistorical survey. *Occasional Papers in Old Colony Studies* No. 2. Plymouth, Massachusetts, Plimoth Plantation.

Martha's Vineyard (Dukes County) n.d. Probate Records. Dukes County Registry of Probate, Town Hall, Edgartown, Massachusetts.

Maryland Provincial Records (St Mary's County) n.d. *Testamentary Proceedings* 5 and 6. Annapolis, Maryland, Hall of Records.

Massachusetts, Commonwealth of, General Court 1794. *Resolves of 1794*, Chapter 101, passed June 26, 1794.

Massachusetts, Commonwealth of, General Court 1830. *Resolves of 1829*, Chapter 50, passed March 1, 1830.

Massachusetts Society of Mayflower Descendants, n.d. *The Mayflower Descendant*. Boston.

Massachusetts (Commonwealth of) n.d. Collections of the Massachusetts State Archives. Archives Division, State House, Boston, Massachusetts.

Mastromarino, M. 1984. Cry havoc and let loose the dogs of war: canines and the colonial military experience. Unpublished Master's thesis, The College of William and Mary, Williamsburg, Virginia.

Mathews, A. 1914. The term Pilgrim fathers and early celebrations of Forefathers' Day. *Proceedings of the Colonial Society of Massachusetts* November, 1914: 293–393.

Mathews, A. E. 1976. *Society in Revolutionary North Carolina*. Raleigh, North Carolina, Department of Cultural Resources.

Matthiessen, P. 1959. *Wildlife in America*, 1964 edn. New York, Viking Press.

Medley, M. 1976. *The Chinese Potter*. New York, Charles Scribner's Sons.

Meighan, C. 1960. More on oral tradition. *Journal of the American Folklore Society*. 73: 59.

Menard, R. R. 1974. Economy and society in early colonial Maryland. Unpublished Ph.D. dissertation, University of Iowa.

Menard, R. R., Harris, P. M. G. and Carr, L. G. 1974. Opportunity and inequality: the distribution of wealth on the lower western shore of Maryland, 1638–1705. *Maryland Historical Magazine* 69 (2): 169–84.

Merrill, M. 1977. 'Cash is good to eat': self-sufficiency and exchange in the rural economy of the United States. *Radical History Review* 3: 42–71.

Michael, R. 1973. Ceramics from a nineteenth-century SW

Pennsylvania tavern. *Pennsylvania Archaeologist* 42 (1): 1–13.

Middlesex County n.d. *Probate Records*. Middlesex County Registry of Probate. Middlesex County Court House, Cambridge, Massachusetts.

Miller, G. L. 1974a. A tenant farmer's tableware: nineteenth-century ceramics from Tabb's Purchase. *Maryland Historical Magazine* 69 (2): 197–210.

1974b. History of the Franklin Glass Works, Portage County, Ohio, 1824-ca. 1832. Unpublished manuscript. Cleveland, Ohio, The Western Reserve Society.

1980. Classification and economic scaling of nineteenth-century ceramics. *Historical Archaeology* 14: 1–41.

1984. Marketing ceramics in North America: an introduction. *Winterthur Portfolio* 19 (1): 1–5.

Monks, G. G. 1981. Seasonality studies, in M. B. Schiffer, ed., *Advances in Archaeological Method and Theory*. New York, Academic Press.

Montgomery, C. F. 1973. *A History of American Pewter*. New York, Weathervane Books.

Moran, G. P., Zimmer, E. F. and Yentsch, A. E. 1982. Archaeological investigations at the Narbonne House, Salem Maritime National Historic Site, Massachusetts. *Cultural Resources Management Study* No. 6. Division of Cultural Resources, North Atlantic Regional Office, National Park Service, Boston, Massachusetts.

Morgan, E. S. 1975. *American Slavery, American Freedom: The Ordeal of Colonial Virginia*. New York, W. W. Norton and Company.

Morse, H. B. 1926. *Chronicles of the East India Company Trading to China, 1635–1834*. Oxford, Oxford University Press.

Morton, O. F. 1980. *History of Rockbridge County, Virginia*. Staunton, Virginia, McClure Press.

Morton, R. L. 1960. *Colonial Virginia*. Chapel Hill, University of North Carolina Press.

Mountflorence, L. C. 1781. Account of provisions collected by Lt. Col. Mountflorence for use of the Southern Army under the command of the honorable Mjr. Genl. Greene. *Treasurer and Comptroller Papers, Military Papers*, Box 6, North Carolina Archives. Raleigh, North Carolina.

Mountford, A. R., ed., 1975. Documents related to English ceramics of the 18th and 19th centuries. *Journal of Ceramic History* 8: 3–41.

Mouzon, H. 1771. An accurate map of North and South Carolina. Map collection no. 229. Raleigh, North Carolina, Department of Cultural Resources.

Mowry, W. A. 1878. *The Descendants of Nathaniel Mowry of Rhode Island and a Family History of Richard Mowry of Uxbridge, Massachusetts*. Privately printed.

1909. *A Family History: The Descendants of John Mowry of Rhode Island*. Privately printed.

Mrozowski, S. 1981. Archaeological investigations in Queen Anne Square, Newport, Rhode Island: a study in urban archaeology. Unpublished M.A. thesis, Department of Anthropology, Brown University, Providence, Rhode Island.

1984a. Prospects and perspectives on an archaeology of the household. *Man in the Northeast* 27: 31–49.

1984b. Setting the table for the ethnoarchaeologist, in R. Gould, ed., *Toward an Ethnoarchaeology of Modern America*. Research Papers in Anthropology 14: 13–36, Department of Anthropology, Brown University, Providence, Rhode Island.

Mrozowski, S., Thorbahn, P. and Gibson, S. 1979. The archaeological investigation in Queen Anne's Square, Newport, Rhode Island. Unpublished manuscript. Public Archaeology Laboratory, Brown University, Providence, Rhode Island.

Murphey, M. G. 1973. *Our Knowledge of the Historical Past*. Indianapolis, Indiana, Bobbs-Merrill.

Nantucket County n.d. Probate Records. Nantucket County Registry of Probate. Town Hall, Nantucket, Massachusetts.

Nash, G. B. 1979. *The Urban Crucible: Social Change, Political Consciousness and the Origins of the American Revolution*. Cambridge, Massachusetts, Harvard University Press.

Natick C.R. n.d. First Congregation Church of Natick, Records of Oliver Peabody and Stephen Badger.

Nebiker, W. A. 1976. *The History of North Smithfield*. Somersworth, New Hampshire, New England History Press.

Neiman, F. D. 1980. *The 'Manner House' before Stratford (Discovering the Clifts Plantation)*. Stratford, Virginia, Robert E. Lee Memorial Association.

Netting, R. McC. 1971. *The Ecological Approach in Cultural Study*. A McCalem Module in Anthropology. Philippines, Addison, Wesley Publishing Company, Inc.

Newbury Agricultural Society 1815. Answers to queries addressed to farmers. *Massachusetts Agricultural Repository and Journal*, vol. III.

Newport Historical Society Archives n.d. Newport, Rhode Island.

The Newport Mercury 1785–1800.

Nicosia, F. and Wind, Y., eds. 1977. *Behavioral Models for Market Analysis: Foundations for Marketing Action*. Hinsdale, Illinois, Dryden Press.

Noël Hume, I. 1961. The glass wine bottle in colonial Virginia. *Journal of Glass Studies* 3: 91–118.

1962. Excavations at Rosewell, Gloucester County, Virginia. *United States National Museum Bulletin* 225. Washington, D.C., Smithsonian Institution.

1968. Excavations at Clay Bank in Gloucester County, Virginia. *Contributions from the Museum of History and Technology*. Washington, D.C., Smithsonian Institution.

1969a. *A Guide to Artifacts of Colonial America*. New York, Alfred A. Knopf.

1969b. Pearlware: forgotten milestone of English ceramic history. *Antiques* 95: 390–7.

1969c. *Archaeology and Wetherburn's Tavern*. Williamsburg, Virginia, Colonial Williamsburg Foundation.

1975. *Historical Archaeology*. New York, W. W. Norton and Company.

1976. *Pottery and Porcelain in Colonial Williamsburg's Archaeological Collections*. Williamsburg, Virginia, Colonial Williamsburg Foundation.

1977. Early English delftware from London and Virginia. *Colonial Williamsburg Occasional Papers in Archaeology*. Williamsburg, Virginia, Colonial Williamsburg Foundation.

Norton, F. H., ed. 1877. *Frank Leslie's Historical Register of the U.S. Centennial Exposition 1876*. New York, Frank Leslie's Publishing House.

Olsen, S. 1972. Faunal analysis of remains from Plymouth sites. *Occasional Papers in Old Colony Studies* 3: 13.

Olsen, S., Robadue, D. D., Jr, and Lee, V. 1980. *An Interpretive Atlas of Narragansett Bay*. Coastal Resources Center, *Marine Bulletin* 40. Kingston, University of Rhode Island.

Oriental Ceramic Society of Hong Kong. 1979. *Southeast Asian and Chinese Trade Pottery: An Exhibition Catalogue*. Hong Kong, Oriental Ceramic Society of Hong Kong.

Orwin, C. S. and Orwin, C. S. 1967. *The Open Fields*. Oxford, Oxford University Press

Oswald, A. and Hughes, R. G. 1974. Nottingham and Derbyshire stonewares. English Ceramic Circle *Transactions* 9 (2).

Otis, A. 1888. *Genealogical Notes on Barnstable Families*. Barnstable, Massachusetts, The Patriot Press (edited and revised by C. F. Swift. Reprinted 1979 by Genealogical Publishing Company, Baltimore, Maryland).

Otto, J. S. and Banks, W. B. 1982. The Banks family of Yell County, Arkansas: a 'plain folk' family of the highlands south. *Arkansas Historical Quarterly* 41: 146–67.

Pagan, J. 1982. Dutch maritime and commercial activity in mid-seventeenth-century colonial Virginia. *Virginia Magazine of History and Biography* 90 (4): 485–8.

Panofsky, I. 1962. *Studies in Iconology: Humanist Themes in the Art of the Renaissance*. New York, Harper and Row.

Parry, J. H. and Sherlock, P. M. 1956. *A Short History of the West Indies*. London, Macmillan.

Peacham, H. 1962. *The Complete Gentleman*. Ithaca, New York, Cornell University Press.

Pease, R. L. 1885. Letter to Everett Allen Davis. February 10, 1885. Dukes County Historical Society Collections, Box 125B.

Pendergast, D. M. and Meighan, C. 1959. Folk tradition as historical fact: a Paiute example. *Journal of the American Folklore Society* 72: 128.

Penn, W. A. 1902. *The Soverane Herbe: A History of Tobacco*. London, Grant Richards.

Perley, S. 1891. *Historic Storms of New England*. Salem, Massachusetts, The Salem Publishers and Printing Company.

Pichey, M. 1970. Great Island glass. Unpublished manuscript. Department of Anthropology, Brown University, Providence, Rhode Island.

Pierce, E. 1861. *Colonial Lists 1621–1700*. Boston, A. Williams and Company.

Pike, K. 1954. *Language in Relation to a Unified Theory of the Structure of Human Behavior*. Volume 1. Glendale, Illinois, Summer Institute of Linguistics.

Pinson, A. 1980. The New England rum era: drinking styles and social change in Newport, Rhode Island, 1720–1770. Working Papers on Alcohol and Human Behavior, No. 8. Providence, Rhode Island, Brown University Department of Anthropology.

Plymouth County, *Court and Probate Records*. Plymouth, Massachusetts.

Pope, J. A. 1956. *Chinese Porcelain from the Ardebil Shrine*. Washington, D.C., Freer Gallery of Art, Smithsonian Institution.

Potter, P. 1984. Digging in the Sunday paper: a study of seasonality as reflected in newspaper advertising, in R. Gould, ed., *Toward an Ethnoarchaeology of Modern America* (Research Papers in Anthropology No. 4: 37–50). Providence, Rhode Island, Department of Anthropology, Brown University.

Powell, S. C. 1963. *Puritan Village: The Formation of a New England Town*. Middletown, Connecticut, Wesleyan University Press.

Praetzellis, A. and Praetzellis, M. 1979. Ceramics from old Sacramento. Sacramento, California, California Department of Parks and Recreation.

Praetzellis, M. 1980. Ceramics, in M. Praetzellis, A. Praetzellis, and M. R. Brown III, eds., 1980.

Praetzellis, M., Praetzellis, A. and Brown, M. R. III, eds., 1980. *Historical Archaeology at the Golden Eagle Site*. Rohnert Park, California, Anthropological Studies Center, Sonoma State University.

Pratt, Rev. E. 1844. *A Comprehensive History, Ecclesiastical and Civil of Eastham, Wellfleet and Orleans, County of Barnstable, Massachusetts, from 1644–1844*. Yarmouth, Massachusetts, W. S. Fisher and Company.

Price, C. R. and Price, J. E. 1978. Pioneer settlement and subsistence on the Ozark border: preliminary report on the Widow Harris cabin site project. *The Conference on Historic Site Archaeology Papers* 12: 145–69.

Price, J. F. and Schweigert, B. S. 1971. *The Science of Meat and Meat Products*. 2nd edn. San Francisco, W. H. Freeman and Company.

The Providence Gazette and Country Journal 1783.

The Providence Journal 1783–1801.

Pulsifer, D., ed. 1861. *Records of the Colony of New Plymouth in New England 1620–1680*. Vols. I–VIII. Boston, William White.

Quimby, I. M. G., ed. 1973. *Ceramics in America*. Charlottesville, University Press of Virginia.

Radcliffe-Brown, A. R. 1933. *The Andaman Islanders*, 2nd edn. Cambridge, Cambridge University Press.

Rainbolt, J. C. 1970. The alteration in the relationship between leadership and constituents in Virginia, 1660–1720. *William and Mary Quarterly* 27 (3): 411–34.

Rapaport, A. 1968. Sacred space in primitive and vernacular architecture. *Liturgical Arts* 36 (2): 36–9.

1982. Sacred places, sacred occasions and sacred environments. *Architectural Design* 52 (9–10): 75–82.

Rathje, W. 1979. Modern material culture studies, in M. B. Schiffer, ed., *Advances in Archaeological Method and Theory*, vol. 2. New York, Academic Press.

Rathje, W. and Schiffer, M. B. 1982. *Archaeology*. New York, Harcourt Brace Jovanivich.

Reeser, G. C. 1967. Oral interviews with Mr Earl G. Rich, Wellfleet, Massachusetts, October, 1966, and August, 1967. Ms. on file, National Park Service, North Atlantic Regional Office, Boston, Massachusetts.

Register, A. K. 1973. *State Census of North Carolina 1784–1787*. Baltimore, Genealogical Publishing Company.

Reid, J. D. Jr 1976. Antebellum Southern rental contracts. *Exploration in Economic History* 13: 69–83.

Reitz, E. and Honerkamp, N. 1983. British colonial subsistence strategy on the southeastern coastal plain. *Historical Archaeology* 17 (2): 4–26.

Reps, J. W. 1973. Boston by Bostonians: the printed plans and views of the colonial city by its artists, cartographers, engravers, and publishers. *Publications of the Colonial Society of Massachusetts* 46: 3–56.

1984. *Views and Viewmakers of Urban America: Lithographs of Towns and Cities in the United States and Canada, Notes on the Artists and Publishers, and a Union Catalog of Their Work, 1825–1925*. Columbia, Missouri, University of Missouri Press.

Reynard, E. 1934. *The Narrow Land: Folk Chronicles of Old Cape Cod*. Boston, Houghton Mifflin Company (1962 edn).

Rhode Island Gazette 1783.

Rich, S. 1883. *Truro, Cape Cod: Landmarks and Seamarks*. Boston, D. Lothrop.

Ridgway & Sons, J. 1813. Scale for china tea, and breakfast sets, Job Ridgway & Sons' Manufactory, Cauldon Place, Staffordshire Potteries, commencing January 1st, 1813. Allbut and Gibbs, Hanley, Staffordshire. Hanley, Stoke-on-Trent, Staffordshire County Library.

Riling, J. R. 1966. *Baron von Steuben and His Regulations*. Philadelphia, Ray Riling Arms Books Company.

Roberts, A. W. 1942. *The French West Indies*. Indianapolis, Indiana, Bobbs-Merrill Company.

Robinson, P. A., Nebiker, W. A., and Gustafson, G. P. 1974. Phase I reconnaissance survey, reconstruction of Route 104, Douglas Pike, Route 7 to North Smithfield–Woonsocket line, North Smithfield, Rhode Island. Report prepared for C. E. McGuire, Inc. Providence, Rhode Island, Rhode Island Historic Preservation Commission.

Rochmore, M. 1979. Documentary review of the historical archaeology of the Cape Cod National Seashore. Unpublished report on file at the Division of Cultural Resources, North Atlantic Regional Office, National Park Service, Boston, Massachusetts.

Rockman, D. D. and Rothschild, N. A. 1984. City tavern, country tavern: an analysis of four colonial sites. *Historical Archaeology* 18 (2): 112–21.

Ronda, J. 1981. Generations of faith: the Christian Indians of Martha's Vineyard. *The William and Mary Quarterly* 34 (1): 66–82.

Root, W. and de Rochemont, R. 1976. *Eating in America: A History*. New York: William Morrow and Company.

Rosaldo, R. 1980. *Ilongot Headhunting 1883–1974: A Study in Society and History*. Stanford, California, Stanford University Press.

Ross, E. B. 1980. Patterns of diet and forces of production: an economic and ecological history of the ascendancy of beef in the United States diet, in E. B. Ross, ed., *Beyond the Myths of Culture: Essays in Cultural Materialism*. New York, Academic Press.

Rossi, I. 1980. *People in Culture*. New York, J. F. Belgin Publishers, Inc.

Roth, R. 1961. Tea drinking in 18th-century America: its etiquette and equipage. *United States National Museum Bulletin No. 225 Contributions from the Museum of History and Technology*. Paper 14. Washington, D.C., Smithsonian Institution.

Roth, S. 1965. *Chinese Ceramics Imported by the Swedish East India Company*. Goteburg, Gothenburg Historical Museum.

Rothenberg, W. A. 1981. The market and Massachusetts farmers, 1750–1855. *Journal of Economic History* XLI: 238–314.

Rouse, I. 1972. *Settlement patterns in archaeology*. Warner reprint.

Roussel, D. E. 1984. Hart-Shortridge House, in Museum of Our National Heritage, *Unearthing New England's Past: The Ceramic Evidence*. Lexington, Massachusetts, Scottish Rite Masonic Museum of Our National Heritage.

Ruell, D. 1983. The bird's eye views of New Hampshire: 1875–1899. *Historical New Hampshire* 38 (1): 3–85.

Russell, H. S. 1976. *A Long, Deep Furrow: Three Centuries of Farming in New England*. Hanover, New Hampshire, University Press of New England.

Rutman, D. B. 1967. *Husbandmen of Plymouth*. Boston, Beacon Press.

Sachs, W. S. and Hoogenboom, A. 1965. *The Enterprising Colonials: Society on the Eve of the Revolution*. Chicago, Argonaut.

Saffioti, H. I. B. 1974. Female labor and capitalism in the United States and Brazil, in R. Rohrlich-Leavitt, ed., *Women Cross-Culturally: Change and Challenge*. The Hague, Mouton.

Sahlins, M. 1981. *Historical Metaphors and Mythical Realities*. ASAO Special Publications Number 1. Ann Arbor, University of Michigan Press.

  1985. *History and Anthropology*. New York, Columbia University Press.

Sainsbury, E. B., ed., 1907–38. *A Calendar of the Court Minutes of the East India Company, 1635–1679*. Oxford, Oxford University Press.

Salwen, B. 1978. Indians of southern New England and Long Island: early period, in B. Trigger, ed., *Handbook of North American Indians*. Vol. 15. Washington, D.C., United States Government Printing Office.

Sassoon, C. 1978. Chinese porcelain marks from coastal sites in Kenya: aspects of trade in the Indian Ocean, XIV–XIX Centuries. *British Archaeological Reports* (International Series) 43.

Schiffer, M. B. 1972. Archaeological context and systemic context. *American Antiquity* 37: 156–65.

  1976. *Behavioral Archaeology*. New York, Academic Press.

  1983. Toward the identification of formation processes. *American Antiquity* 48 (4): 675–706.

Schlereth, T. J. 1980. *Artifacts and the American Past*. Nashville, Tennessee, American Association for State and Local History.

Schlesinger, A. M. 1939. *The Colonial Merchants and the American Revolution 1763–1776*. New York, Facsimile Library.

Schmidt, P. 1978. *Historical Archaeology*. New York, Greenwood Press.

Schneider, D. M. 1968. *American Kinship: A Cultural Account*. Englewood Cliffs, New Jersey, Prentice Hall.

Schneider, H. K. 1974. *Economic Man: The Anthropology of Economics*. New York, The Free Press.

Schofield, R. S. 1973. Dimensions of illiteracy, 1750–1850. *Explorations in Economic History* 10 (4): 437–54.

Secretary of the British Commission 1876a. *Philadelphia International Exhibition, 1876. Official Catalogue of the British Section*. London, Her Majesty's Stationery Office.

Secretary of the British Commission 1876b. *The International Exhibition of 1876, Philadelphia. Exhibitors Commercial Guide*. London, Her Majesty's Stationery Office.

Secretary of State n.d. Land entries for Guilford, Caswell, and Surry Counties. *Secretary of State Papers*. North Carolina Archives, Department of State. Raleigh, North Carolina.

Secretary of State n.d. Will indexes for Guilford and Caswell Counties. *Secretary of State Papers*. North Carolina Archives, Department of Cultural Resources. Raleigh, North Carolina.

Sellers, J. R. 1974. The common soldier in the American Revolution. Military history of the American Revolution, *Proceedings of the Sixth Military History Symposium, U.S. Air Force Academy*. Washington, D.C., Library of Congress.

Sellers, J. R., Gewalt, G. W., Smith, P. H., and van Ee, P. M. 1975. *Manuscript Sources in the Library of Congress for Research on the American Revolution*. Washington, D.C., Library of Congress.

Several Ladies 1897. *The Pocumtuc Housewife*. Reprint, Deerfield, Massachusetts, 1905.

Shammas, C. 1980. The domestic environment in early modern England and America. *The Journal of Social History* 14 (1): 3–24.

Shangraw, C. and Von der Porten, E. 1981. *The Drake and Cermeno Expeditions' Chinese Porcelain at Drakes Bay, California, 1579 and 1595*. Santa Rosa, California, Santa Rosa Junior College and Drake Navigators Guild.

Shapiro, S. and Doody, A., eds. 1968. *Readings in the History of American Marketing: Settlement to Civil War*. Homewood, Illinois, Richard D. Irwin.

Shaw, L. C., Seasholes, N. S., and Loring, S. 1983. Phase I intensive archaeological survey of the Route 213 Merrimack River crossing: Lowell, Dracut, and Chelmsford, Massachusetts. Cambridge, Massachusetts, Institute for Conservation Archaeology, Peabody Museum, Harvard University.

Shaw, S. 1829. *History of the Staffordshire Potteries: and the Rise and Progress of the Manufacture of Pottery and Porcelain: With References to Genuine Specimens, and Notices of Eminent Potters*. 1968 reprint. Great Neck, New York, Beatrice C. Weinstock.

  1837. *The Chemistry of the Several Natural and Artificial Heterogeneous Compounds used in the Manufacturing of Porcelain, Glass and Pottery*. 1900 reprint. London, Scott, Greenwood and Company.

Sheridan, R. B. 1974. *Sugar and Slaves*. Baltimore, Johns Hopkins University Press.

Shih, H. 1976. Ming Dynasty wood block prints. Ph.D. dissertation, University of Chicago.

Showman, R. K. 1976. *The Papers of General Nathanael Greene*. Chapel Hill, University of North Carolina Press.

Shurtleff, N. B. 1890. *A Topographical and Historical Description of Boston*, 3rd edn. Boston, City Printers.

  1855. *Records of the Colony of New Plymouth in New England, Court Orders, Volume One, 1633–1640*. Boston, William White.

  1856. *Records of the Colony of New Plymouth in New England. Court Orders: Vol. VI, VIII 1678–1691*. Boston, William White.

  1857. *Records of the Colony of New Plymouth in New England, Misc. Records Vol. IX 1633–1689*. Boston, William White.

Silliman, B. and Goodrich, C. R. 1854. *The World of Science, Art and*

Industry Illustrated from Examples in the New York Exhibition 1853–1854. New York, G. P. Putnam and Company.

Simmons, W. 1979. Conversion from Indian to Puritan. *The New England Quarterly* 52 (2): 197–218.

1986. *The Spirit of the New England Tribes*. Lebanon, New Hampshire, University Press of New England.

Simon, A. L. 1927. *Bottlescrew Days: Wine Drinking in England during the Eighteenth Century*. Boston, Smith, Maynard and Company.

Sisk, G. 1981. Slavery and blacks in Rockbridge County 1790–1900. Unpublished manuscript. Laboratory of Anthropology, Washington and Lee University, Lexington, Virginia.

Slotkin, R. 1973. *Regeneration through Violence: The Mythology of the American Frontier, 1600–1980*. Middletown, Connecticut, Wesleyan University Press.

Smith, C. A. 1976. Analyzing regional social systems, in C. A. Smith, ed., *Regional Analysis*. New York, Academic Press.

Smith, D. S. 1975. Underregistration and bias in probate records: an analysis of data from eighteenth-century Hingham, Massachusetts. *William and Mary Quarterly* 3s 32: 100–12.

Smith, K. and Shay, E. 1936. *Down the Cape*. New York, Dodge Publishing Company.

Smith, W. 1875. *The Masterpieces of the Centennial Exhibition. Vol. II. Industrial Art*. Philadelphia, Gebbie and Barrie.

Smith, W. C. 1913–17. *A History of Chatham, Massachusetts*. Chatham Historical Society. 1971 edn. Yarmouthport, Massachusetts, Parnassus Imprints.

Smolek, M. A. and Clark, W. E. 1982. Spatial patterning of seventeenth-century plantations in the Chesapeake. Paper delivered to the Society for Historical Archaeology.

Smolek, M. A., Pogue, D. and Clark, W. E. 1984. Historical archaeology of the 17th-century Chesapeake: a guide to sources. Jefferson Patterson Park and Museum *Occasional Paper* No. 1. Maryland, Jefferson Patterson Park and Museum.

Snow, E. R. 1943. *Great Storms and Famous Shipwrecks of the New England Coast*. Boston, The Yankee Publishing Company.

South, S. 1972. Evolution and horizon as revealed in ceramic analysis in historical archaeology. *The Conference on Historic Site Archaeology Papers 1971* 6: 71–116.

1974. *Palmetto Parapets: Exploratory Archaeology at Fort Moultrie, South Carolina*. University of South Carolina, Columbia, South Carolina, Institute of Archaeology and Anthropology, *Anthropological Studies* No. 1.

1977. *Method and Theory in Historical Archaeology*. New York, Academic Press.

Spaulding, A. C. 1953. Statistical techniques for the discovery of artifact types. *American Antiquity* 18: 305–13.

Speck, F. 1947. *Eastern Algonkian block-stamp decoration*. Trenton, New Jersey, The Archaeological Society of New Jersey.

Spindler, G. D. 1948. American character as revealed by the military. *Psychiatry* II: 275–81.

Spitulnik, K. 1972. The inn crowd: the American inn, 1730–1830. *Pennsylvania Folklife* 22 (2): 25–41.

Stachiw, M. O. 1978. The Vincent house: archaeology. *Dukes County Intelligencer* 20 (1): 29–60.

Staffordshire Potteries 1814. Staffordshire potteries prices current of earthenware. Tregortha, Burslem, Staffordshire.

Staffordshire Potteries 1833. Staffordshire potteries at a general meeting of manufacturers. Monday, October 21.

Starbuck, D. 1980. *Seventeenth-Century Historical Archaeology in Cambridge, Medford, and Dorcester*. Boston University, Boston, Massachusetts.

Starbuck, M. 1683–1766. Account book. Peter Foulger Museum, Nantucket, Massachusetts.

State Art Collections of Dresden, German Democratic Republic 1978. *The Splendor of Dresden: Five Centuries of Art Collecting*. New York, George Braziller.

Steer, F. W. 1962. Probate inventories. *History* 47: 287–90.

ed., 1950. *Farm and Cottage Inventories of Mix-Essex, 1635–1749*. Essex Record Office Publications No. 8. Chelmsford, England, Essex County Council.

Steere, T. 1881. *History of North Smithfield*. Privately printed.

Stilgoe, J. R. 1982. *Common Landscape of America, 1580–1845*. New Haven, Connecticut, Yale University Press.

Stokinger, W. and Moran, G. P. 1978. A final report of archaeological investigations at Fort Independence 1976–1977. Unpublished manuscript on file, Metropolitan District Commission, Boston.

Stone, G. W. 1970. Ceramics in Suffolk County, Massachusetts, inventories, 1680–1775: a preliminary study with divers comments thereon, and sundry suggestions. *The Conference on Historic Site Archaeology Papers 1968* 3 (Part 2): 73–90.

1974. St John's: archaeological questions and answers. *Maryland Historical Magazine* 69 (2): 146–68.

1977. Artifacts are not enough. *The Conference on Historic Site Archaeology Papers 1976* 11: 43–63.

1982. Society, housing, and architecture in early Maryland: John Lewger's St. Johns. Unpublished Ph.D. dissertation, University of Pennsylvania, Philadelphia, Pennsylvania. Ann Arbor, Michigan, University Microfilms International.

Stone, G. W., Little, J. G., III, and Israel, S. 1973. Ceramics from the John Hicks site, 1723–1743: the material culture, in I. M. G. Quimby, ed., *Ceramics in America*. Charlottesville, University Press of Virginia.

Strachey, L. 1921. *Queen Victoria*. New York, Harcourt, Brace, and Company.

Strahler, A. N. 1966. *A Geologist's View of Cape Cod*. Garden City, New York, Natural History Press.

Strasser, S. 1982. *Never Done: The Ideology and Technology of Household Work, 1850–1930*. New York, Pantheon.

Sturtevant, W. 1975. Two 1761 wigwams at Niantic, Connecticut. *American Antiquity* 40 (4): 437–44.

Suffield, Connecticut 1940–. Suffield land history, by Delphina, Hammer Clark. Ms on file, Kent Memorial Library, Suffield, Connecticut.

Suffolk County, Massachusetts, *Probate Records 1650–1800* (Microfilm: Graphic Microfilm of New England), vol. 27.

Swift, C. F. 1897. *Cape Cod: The Right Arm of Massachusetts*. Yarmouth, Massachusetts, Register Publishing Company.

Syz, H. 1969. Some oriental aspects of European ceramic decoration. *Antiques* 95 (5): 670–81.

Tate, T. W. 1984a. The ecology of early America: a review essay. *American Quarterly*. 36 (4): 587–92.

1984b. The perception and modification of the natural landscape: an interpretation of early American agriculture and forestry. Paper delivered to the Organization of American Historians.

Taylor, W. W. 1967. *A Study of Archaeology*. Carbondale, Illinois, Southern Illinois University Press.

Teller, B. G. 1968. Ceramics in Providence 1750–1800: an inventory survey. *Antiques* 94 (4): 570–7.

Thirsk, J. 1955. The content and sources of English agrarian history after 1500. *Agricultural History Review* 3: 66–79.

1957. *English Peasant Farming: The Agrarian History of Lincolnshire from Tudor to Recent Times*. London, Routledge and Kegan Paul.

ed., 1967. *The Agrarian History of England and Wales*, vol. IV, 1540–1640. Cambridge, Cambridge University Press.

Thomas, I., Jr 1804. *Thomas, Junr's Massachusetts, Connecticut, Rhode Island, New Hampshire and Vermont Almanack*. Worcester, Massachusetts.

Thomas, K. 1971. *Religion and the Decline of Magic*. New York, Scribners.

1977. The place of laughter in Tudor and Stuart England. *The Times Literary Supplement*, pp. 77–81.

1983. *Man and the Natural World*. London, Allen Lane.

Thompson, M. 1979. *Rubbish Theory*. New York, Oxford University Press.

Thorbahn, P. F. 1979. The precolonial ivory trade of East Africa. Unpublished Ph.D. dissertation, University of Massachusetts, Amherst. Ann Arbor, Michigan, University Microfilms International.

1984. Br'er elephant and the briar patch. *Natural History* 93 (4): 70–81.

Thoreau, H. D. 1849–57. *Cape Cod*. Reprinted 1951 by Bramhall House, W. W. Norton, New York (edited by D. C. Lunt).

Tobias, P. M. 1983. The socioeconomic context of Grenadian smuggling. *Journal of Anthropological Research* 39 (3): 383–400.

Todd, G., ed., 1920. *The Todd Family in America or the Descendants of Christopher Todd, 1637–1919*. Compiled by J. E. Todd. Privately printed.

Tooke, T. and Newmarch, W. 1928. *A History of Prices of the State of the Circulation from 1792 to 1856*. 4 vols. Reprint. New York, Adelphi Company.

The Town and Country Advertiser 1783–1801.

Trigger, B. 1980. Archaeology and the image of the American Indian. *American Antiquity* 45: 66–76.

Trow-Smith, R. 1959. *A History of British Livestock Husbandry 1700–1900*. London, Routledge and Kegan Paul.

Tyler, S. A. 1969. *Cognitive Anthropology*. New York, Holt, Rinehart and Winston, Inc.

Underwood, F. H. 1893. *Quabbin: The Story of a Small Town with Outlooks upon Puritan Life*. Boston.

United States Centennial Commission 1876. *International Exhibition 1876. Official Catalogue*. 4 vols, 2nd edn. Philadelphia, John R. Nagle and Company.

United States Fish Commission 1871–2. *Report of the U.S. Commissioner of Fisheries 1871–1872*. Washington, D.C., United States Fish and Wildlife Commission.

Upton, D. 1979. Early vernacular architecture in southeastern Virginia. Ph.D. dissertation, Brown University. Ann Arbor, Michigan, University Microfilms International.

1982. Vernacular domestic architecture in eighteenth century Virginia. *Winterthur Portfolio* 17 (2/3): 95–120.

n.d. Thinking about historic houses. Unpublished manuscript.

van der Pijl-Ketel, C. L., ed. 1982. *The Ceramic Load of the 'Witte Leeuw' (1613)*. Amsterdam, Rijksmuseum.

Vann, R. T. 1974. Literacy in seventeenth-century England: some hearth tax evidence. *Journal of Interdisciplinary History* 5: 287–93.

Vansina, J. 1965. *Oral Tradition*. Chicago, Aldine Publishing Company.

Vaughan, A. T. and Richter, D. K. 1980. Crossing the cultural divide: Indians and New Englanders, 1605–1763. *Proceedings of the American Antiquarian Society* 90(1): 23–100.

Volker, T. 1971. *Porcelain and the Dutch East India Company*. Leiden, E. J. Brill.

Von der Porten, E. 1968. *The Porcelains and Terra Cottas of Drakes Bay*. Point Reyes, California, Drake Navigators' Guild.

1972. Drake and Cermeno in California: sixteenth century Chinese ceramics. *Historical Archaeology* 6: 1–23.

Von der Porten, E. and Peron, R. K. 1973. *Archaeology in the Point Reyes National Seashore, 1973*. Point Reyes, California, Drake Navigators' Guild.

Von Dumreicher, A. 1931. *Trackers and Smugglers in the Deserts of Egypt*. New York, The Dial Press.

Wadbury, G. 1951. *The Great Days of Piracy in the West Indies*. New York, W. W. Norton and Company.

Wagner, H. R., trans. 1924. Report of visit to California in 1595, by S. R. Cermeno. *California Historical Society Quarterly* 3: 00–0.

Wall, R. E. 1965. A new look at Cambridge. *Journal of American History* LII (1): 599–605.

Wallerstein, I. 1974. *The Modern World System: Capitalist Agriculture and the Origins of the European World Economy in the Sixteenth Century*. New York, Academic Press.

Walsh, L. 1979. A culture of 'rude sufficiency': life styles on Maryland's lower western shore between 1658 and 1720. Paper delivered to the Society for Historical Archaeology, January, 1979.

Walsh, L. and Menard, R. R. 1974. Death in the Chesapeake: two life tables for men in early colonial Maryland. *Maryland Historical Magazine* 69 (2): 211–27.

Warner, S. B. 1962. *Streetcar Suburbs*. Cambridge, Massachusetts, Harvard University Press.

Washburn, W. E. 1957. *The Governor and the Rebel: A History of Bacon's Rebellion in Virginia*. Chapel Hill, University of North Carolina Press.

Waterman, T. T. 1946. *The Mansions of Virginia, 1706–1776*. Chapel Hill, University of North Carolina Press.

Waterman, T. T. and Barrows, J. A. 1969. *Domestic Architecture of Tidewater Virginia*. New York, Dover.

Watkins, C. M. 1960. North Devon pottery and its export to America in the seventeenth century. *Contributions from the Museum of History and Technology* 13. Washington, D.C., Smithsonian Institution.

1968. *The Cultural History of Marlborough, Virginia: An Archaeological and Historical Investigation of the Port Town for Stafford County and the Plantation of John Mercer*. Washington, D.C., Smithsonian Institution Press.

1973. Ceramics used in America: comparisons, in I. M. G. Quimby, ed., *Ceramics in America*. Charlottesville, University Press of Virginia.

Watkins, L. W. 1950. *Early New England Potters and Their Wares*. Cambridge, Massachusetts, Harvard University Press.

1966. Early New England pottery. *Sturbridge Village Pamphlet Series* No. 10.

Webb, M. C. 1974. Exchange networks: prehistory. *Annual Review of Anthropology* 3: 357–83.

Webster, Mrs A. L. 1856. *The Improved Housewife or Book of Receipts*. Boston, Phillips, Sampson, and Company.

Webster, T. B. L. 1972. *Potter and Patron in Classical Athens*. London, Metheun.

Westmoreland County, Virginia, n.d. *Deeds, Wills and Patents 1653–1659*. Westmoreland County Courthouse.

Westmoreland County, Virginia. n.d. *Deeds and Wills 1660–1661*. Westmoreland County Courthouse.

Westmoreland County, Virginia n.d. *Deeds, Patents and Accounts 1665–1677*. Westmoreland County Courthouse.

White, J. T. and Lesser, C. H., eds., 1977. *Fighters for Independence*. Chicago, University of Chicago Press.

Whitehill, W. M. 1968. *Boston: A Topographical History*, 2nd edn. Cambridge, Massachusetts, Harvard University Press.

Whitman, L. 1794. A topographical description of Wellfleet. *Collections of the Massachusetts Historical Society* 1s 3: 117–25.

1802. Note on Wellfleet. *Collections of the Massachusetts Historical Society* 1s 8: 196.

Willets, W. and Poh, L. S., eds., 1981. *Nonya Ware and Kitchen Ching. Ceremonial and Domestic Pottery of the Nineteenth and Twentieth Centuries Commonly Found in Malaysia*. South East Asian Ceramic Society, West Malaysian Chapter. New York, Oxford University Press.

Williams, C. A. S. 1976. *Outlines of Chinese Art Motives*. New York, Dover Publications.

Williams, N. 1961. *Contraband Cargoes: Seven Centuries of Smuggling.* Hamden, Connecticut, The Shoe String Press.

Williams, R. 1936. *A Key into the Language of America.* Edited by H. M. Chapin. Providence, Rhode Island, Rhode Island and Providence Plantations Tercentenary Committee, Inc.

Willoughby, C. C. 1935. *Antiquities of the New England Indians.* Cambridge, Massachusetts, Peabody Museum, Harvard University.

Wilmsen, E. 1968. Lithic analysis in paleoanthropology, in M. P. Leone, ed., *Contemporary Archaeology.* Carbondale, Illinois, Southern Illinois University Press.

Wilson, C. 1966. Setting – topography and ecology. Unpublished manuscript, Man Full of Trouble Tavern Report. University of Pennsylvania, Department of American Civilization, Philadelphia, Pennsylvania.

Wilson, C. A. 1974. *Food and Drink in Britain.* New York, Harper and Row.

Winsor, J. 1880. The earliest maps of Massachusetts Bay and Boston Harbor, in J. Winsor, ed., *The Memorial History of Boston,* vol. I. Boston, Ticknor and Company.

1881a. Estates and sites; maps and plans, in J. Winsor, ed., *The Memorial History of Boston,* vol. II. Boston, Ticknor and Company.

1881b. Maps of the Revolutionary period, in J. Winsor, ed., *The Memorial History of Boston,* vol. III. Boston, Ticknor and Company.

Winthrop, A., Hutchinson, E., Flynt, H., Wigglesworth, E. and Appleton, N. 1729. Report of the Commissioners of Indian Affairs and the Corporation of Harvard College on Indians of Natick. *Collections of the Colonial Society of Massachusetts* 16: 575–7.

Withey, L. 1984. *Urban Growth in Colonial Rhode Island: Newport and Providence in the Eighteenth Century.* Albany, State University of New York Press.

Wood, G. S. 1974. The democratization of mind in the American Revolution, in Third Library of Congress Symposium on the American Revolution, *Leadership in the American Revolution.* Washington, D.C., Library of Congress.

Wood, J. 1971. Fitting discrete probability distributions in prehistoric settlement patterns, in G. Gumerman, ed., *The Distribution of Prehistoric Population Aggregates.* Prescott, Arizona, Prescott College Press.

Wright, H. 1983. Insurance mapping and industrial archaeology. *IA: The Journal of the Society for Industrial Archeology* 9 (1): 1–18.

Wright, H. T. 1969. The administration of rural production in an early Mesopotamian town. *Anthropological Paper* No. 38. Ann Arbor, University of Michigan Museum of Anthropology.

1971. Archaeological fieldnotes and report on a survey at Hancock's Resolution. Unpublished manuscript on file. Annapolis, Maryland, Historic Annapolis, Inc.

Wright, H. T. and Johnson, G. 1975. Population, exchange, and early state formation in southwestern Iran. *American Anthropologist* 77 (2): 267–89.

Wright, R. and Baker, N. T. 1980. *Hancock's Resolution. An Historic Structure Report of the Hancock Family Farm, Anne Arundel County, Maryland.* Annapolis, Maryland, Historic Annapolis, Inc.

Wrigley, E. A. 1966. *An Introduction to English Historical Demography.* London, Weidenfeld and Nicholson.

Yellen, J. E. 1977. *Archaeological Approaches to the Present.* New York, Academic Press.

Yentsch, A. E. 1974a. Oral interview with David Forbes about house sites on Naushon Island, Massachusetts, August, 1974.

1974b. Oral interviews with Mrs Anna Hennessey, West Falmouth, Massachusetts, and with Captain Charles Davis, Falmouth, Massachusetts. Transcripts in author's possession.

1975. Understanding seventeenth- and eighteenth-century colonial families – an experiment in historical ethnography. Unpublished Master's thesis, Department of Anthropology, Brown University, Providence, Rhode Island.

1977. Subsistence patterns of eighteenth-century Cape Cod towns: towards the interpretation of probate inventories. Paper delivered to the Northeastern Anthropological Association.

1977. Farming, fishing, trading, and whaling: subsistence patterns revealed by probate inventories for eighteenth-century Cape Cod. Paper delivered to the Society for Historical Archaeology.

1980. Expressions of cultural diversity and social reality in seventeenth-century New England. Unpublished Ph.D. dissertation, Brown University. Ann Arbor, Michigan, University Microfilm International.

1981. Phase II archaeological survey of the reconstruction of Rt. 104, North Smithfield, Rhode Island. Cambridge, Massachusetts, Institute for Conservation Archaeology, Peabody Museum, Harvard University.

1983. Expressions of cultural variation in seventeenth-century Maine and Massachusetts, in A. E. Ward, ed., *Forgotten Places and Things: Archaeological Perspectives on American History* (Contributions to Anthropological Studies No. 3). Albuquerque, New Mexico, Center for Anthropological Studies.

Yentsch, A. E., Carriker, M. R., Parker, R. H. and Zullo, V. A. 1965. *Marine and Estuarine Environments, Organisms and Geology of the Cape Cod Region: An Indexed Bibliography.* Woods Hole, Massachusetts, Marine Biological Laboratory.

Yentsch, A. E. and Stein, J. in prep. Plymouth Colony Probate Documents.

York County, Virginia, Deeds, Orders, Wills 2, 1645–49. York County Courthouse, Yorktown, Virginia.

INDEX